John Pungente SJ
and Monty Williams SJ

Finding God in the Dark II

Taking the Spiritual Exercises of St. Ignatius to the Movies

Foreword by John English SJ

NOVALIS

© 2011 Novalis Publishing Inc.

Cover design: Audrey Wells
Layout: Christiane Lemire, Francine Petitclerc and Audrey Wells
Cover artwork: Sarah Hall (www.sarahhallstudio.com)

Published by Novalis

Publishing Office
10 Lower Spadina Avenue, Suite 400
Toronto, Ontario, Canada
M5V 2Z2

Head Office
4475 Frontenac Street
Montréal, Québec, Canada
H2H 2S2

www.novalis.ca

Library and Archives Canada Cataloguing in Publication

Pungente, John J.
    Finding God in the dark II : taking the spiritual exercises of St.
Ignatius to the movies / John J. Pungente and Monty Williams ; foreword by John English.

Second ed. of: Finding God in the dark.

ISBN 978-2-89646-316-9

1. Ignatius, of Loyola, Saint, 1491-1556. Exercitia spiritualia.
2. Motion pictures--Religious aspects--Christianity. 3. Spiritual exercises.
I. Williams, Monty, 1944- II. Title.

BX2179.L8P85 2011   261.5'7   C2011-902095-5

Printed in Canada.

Scripture quotations are from the Revised Standard Version of the Bible, Oxford: Oxford University Press. Translations of the Spiritual Exercises are from the following works: George E. Ganss SJ, *The Spiritual Exercises of St. Ignatius: A Translation and Commentary* (St. Louis: The Institute of Jesuit Sources, 1992); Louis E. Puhl SJ, *The Spiritual Exercises of St. Ignatius: Based on Studies in the Language of the Autograph* (Chicago: Loyola Press, 1997); other translations by Monty Williams SJ.

We acknowledge the financial support of the Government of Canada through the Canada Book Fund for business development activities.

5 4 3 2 1   15 14 13 12 11

"... the lover gives
and shares
with the beloved what he possesses."

—*St. Ignatius of Loyola* (1491–1556)
The Spiritual Exercises, 1522–1524

In gratitude for the vision of Ignatius continued by the Jesuits in Canada,
we celebrate that time, four hundred years ago, when Jesuits –
Fathers Pierre Biard and Ennemond Masse –
first arrived in Canada at Port Royal, Nova Scotia, on May 22, 1611.

Within that tradition, The Jesuit Communication Project humbly acknowledges its identity
and mission as an apostolate of the Society of Jesus in Canada.

John J. Pungente SJ
Monty Williams SJ

Contents

Preface to the Second Edition

Several years ago when – as part of the work of The Jesuit Communication Project – we decided to write the first edition of *Finding God in the Dark*, it was to address a felt need to make spiritual direction available to those who did not have access to that means of living a more full life. The book was written as an experiment. We did not want to attach moral lessons to popular film, but to use film to get people to access their own spiritual lives and to develop their own ways of communicating with God and of learning how God speaks to them.

We were surprised by the book's success. It won first place in the Spirituality category (paperback) at the 2005 Catholic Press Association Awards for its creativity and insight. It has been used by individuals and groups in many nations around the world, including Australia, Hungary, England, India, Malaysia, Hong Kong, Canada, the United States, and various countries in the Caribbean. The book finds its success in personal, pastoral, and academic settings, and in a large cross-section of ages, from people in their late teens to the retired.

The common assessment was that this book makes spiritual direction accessible in ways that are both profound and personal, and that the book shifted the way people looked at films, adding to their entertainment an unexpected dimension of discernment and media literacy.

The book's success has led people to write us asking us to make films that were released after it was published accessible to the analysis and reflection we used. Since that first edition appeared, our thinking on the dynamics of spiritual literacy and of the Spiritual Exercises of St. Ignatius has become deeper and more nuanced. We wanted those insights to be made available to the public.

The book you now hold contains these new insights as well as analysis and reflection on new films. In fact, it could be considered a new book.

If you have enjoyed and have been helped by *Finding God in the Dark*, we hope that this new edition allows you to continue your journey deeper into the spiritual intimacy that is the gift of God to each and all of us. If you are using this book for the first time, we welcome you as fellow pilgrims along the path to the fullness of life. We hope you find the book entertaining, provocative, illuminating. We hope that in using the book you find your life transformed.

Blessings on your journey,

John J. Pungente SJ
Monty Williams SJ
Easter Sunday, April 24, 2011

Foreword

It is an honour to write the Foreword to this book. That privilege has nothing to do with self-esteem – that prime disorder of human nature noted in the Spiritual Exercises of St. Ignatius. Rather, it has to do with tradition. Tradition is a handing on and a handing over of the gift of the Spirit, a gift that was handed over to the giver by one who came before, and so on back through the ages.

I was given the gift of the Exercises of St. Ignatius when I entered the Society of Jesus in the Upper Canada Province in 1949. Those Exercises have shaped my life. As a Novice Master I gave them to one generation of young Jesuits in the turbulent years of the late 1960s and early 1970s. Since then I have given them to a now large but forgotten number of other Jesuits, religious men and women, and lay people. In giving them I have made them my own. I have prayed them, prayed about them, taught them, written about them and presented them in ways that I have always considered essential for our times.

In the beginning I was convinced that these Exercises were more effective if they were given individually rather than preached to groups, which was the custom that was passed down to me. The individually directed retreat was, to my way of thinking, more personal. It allowed for the adaptation that St. Ignatius encouraged; the retreatant was seen as one of a kind, and discovered in a unique way God's personal love for him or her.

That new way of presenting the Exercises took off and became, for most of the Christian world, the norm for the latter part of the 20th century. But the Spirit was not satisfied with only that. Even though we are individuals and each of us has a unique relationship with God, we are communal beings. We live in community – in communities – and these communities mediate God's presence to us. So the next big question for me was how to give the Exercises in a way that would foster that integral communal dimension of our lives. Creating small communities whose individual and communal lives were shaped by communal discernment became my next project. My creative energies over the last quarter century were spent promoting and fostering Christian life communities rooted in Ignatian spirituality.

In praying and discerning with these communities, the broader dimension of community – the relationship with all of creation, and specifically with the ecological dimension of our human existence – began to impress itself on me. To be human is to realize that we, all of us together, are in a dynamic, fluid relationship with each other and with all of creation. The spiritual implications of this relationship have shaped my life.

These three areas of my work have, thanks be to God, been sown in good soil. They have taken root and have thrived, and I feel that I have handed on the gift of the Spirit – in all of its creative energies – that has been given to me.

But it has grieved me that the gift of the Exercises has been restricted to those who have been fortunate to have good spiritual directors and good spiritual direction. I have always been conscious of the evangelical passion of St. Ignatius. He preached the good news to all he met – the poor, the rich, the learned and the simple – on street corners, in classes, around the dinner table, at the pulpit. My concern has always been finding ways to emulate that high ideal in our contemporary world, with its distrust of religion, its growing secularism, and its equally strong cry for spiritual sustenance in a world overwhelmed by destructive forces.

It is out of this concern that I welcome this present work by my fellow Canadian Jesuits John Pungente and Monty Williams. They belong to the generation after me. Both were my tertians (tertianship is the final intensive year of Jesuit training) and Monty Williams was also my novice from 1967 to 1969. In tertianship and novitiate, Jesuits are in formation. They do the full Exercises and also have classes on them.

Since those days of formation, John has distinguished himself throughout the world in media literacy; Monty has been giving retreats and conferences in spiritual direction as well as writing about it for about 25 years. They both bring to their work a passion for contemporary culture and analysis.

What they have done in this book is remarkable. They have had the insight that cinema today is the form of contemporary church that is attentive to the concerns of a postmodern world, and they have laid out the way church – as a community seeking, embracing, and living out of the creative Spirit of God – functions in the world today.

In this new but obvious paradigm, when you think about it, they find the language of the Exercises today, which presents the way God communicates a merciful love that can heal and transform each of us. Since the Exercises also offer us a mode of discerning how to live most humanely and lovingly in the world, it is no surprise that we find in this book that same Ignatian mode of discernment.

The heart of Ignatian spirituality is the overwhelming, compassionate mercy of God for us and for all of creation: it heals us and invites us to labour with those other creative forces and energies and people throughout history. It creates community that extends beyond the personal to the social, communal, ecological – even, dare I say, cosmic – where life is more valued than death, love overcomes hatred, and alienation is no more. Even though that process will not be completed in our lifetimes, still we acknowledge our common heritage and our common goal.

I have passed on to many what was given to me. I am grateful to John and Monty for accepting what was given to them, and for giving it over – transformed but yet the same – to others. This is the gift of life. I hope that whoever reads this book receives this gift. A blessing on you, and on that journey.

John English SJ
May 2004

Introduction

A Jesuit Dinner Party

This book was first conceived, in typical Jesuit fashion, at a dinner party one night. A group of English-Canadian Jesuits meets several times a year, over drinks and a meal, to discuss the state of Jesuits today and to support each other without falling into that trendy title of a support group. Conversation is frank, funny, and wide-ranging. One night, the conversation got around to the failure of traditional retreat houses to attract the growing population of the spiritually hungry. It was not as if these retreat houses did not have some of the expertise of contemporary spiritual practitioners. They could not be accused of irrelevance. On the contrary, they might be accused of selling out when it came to ways of becoming spiritually literate that have been around for hundreds of years. The question was how to make that form of literacy available today. Then again, retreats are quite expensive, and subsidies from religious orders are no longer a viable option to support institutions with diminishing sources of income. Another concern was the inability to find good spiritual directors. And even if it was possible to contact a spiritual director, many people in today's busy world find it hard to find time to commit to a retreat. The hunger for direction is there: what is absent is a simple, inexpensive way of presenting valid spirituality and grounded spiritual practice in an accessible way to those who, because of constraints of time and economy, as well as a suspicion of the complicit use of spirituality by religious institutions, are unable to understand and develop their spiritual life.

We were two of the Jesuits at that dinner party. John Pungente is a world-famous authority on media literacy; Monty Williams, besides being interested in contemporary culture and critical analysis, is on staff at Regis College, University of Toronto, and worked at Loyola Retreat House in Guelph – a place with an established reputation for solid, creative work on spirituality and, in particular, on the Spiritual Exercises of St. Ignatius of Loyola. Why not, we wondered, combine our two interests? To be sure, work had already been done on religious themes and images in film. Studies are available on the spirituality of such classic and somewhat esoteric European directors as Bergman, Bresson, Olmo, and Kieslowski. As this Introduction will show, film is profoundly spiritual. But what about popular films?

And so, from one dinner party and these two Jesuits comes this book. It uses popular films to engage the reader on a significantly personal and transformative journey through the Spiritual Exercises of St. Ignatius. The Exercises, since their establishment in the first half of the sixteenth century, have formed the spiritual fabric of the Society of Jesus. They have influenced founders of other religious orders, statesmen, artists, writers, educators, philosophers, not a few saints, and countless millions of women and men, all of whom have discovered in them a personal, passionate, and intimate spirituality that transformed their lives and their culture.

Who Is Ignatius?

To understand the Exercises, it is helpful to know something of the man who created them and something about the spirituality of the Jesuit tradition, which has kept alive these Exercises for the last 450 years. Ignatius of Loyola was born of minor Basque aristocracy in about 1492. Like the nobility of his time, he was interested in maintaining his position in the world by promoting himself through honour and glory. He was vain, venal, and charismatically aggressive, obsessed with the secular ideals of courtly love and chivalry. The public image he sought to promote came crashing down at Pamplona, Spain, in 1521, when he was badly wounded and had to return to Loyola for a long period of enforced recuperation. There he distracted himself by reading both the lives of the saints and the worldly romances of chivalric exploits and love. He discovered that both stirred his heart to perform deeds of dramatic action. But he also noticed that the excitement he felt while reflecting on the lives of the saints remained with him, while the pleasure he felt reading the romances soon evaporated, leaving him desolate. He decided to follow the path of the saints rather than seek earthly glory.

Then began a long period of the purification of his desires. In 1522, he found himself in a cave at Manresa, where he spent the next several months in a regime of extreme asceticism, alternating between severe depression, scruples, thoughts of suicide, and amazing mystical experiences. He decided to use his religious experience there – upon which the Spiritual Exercises as we know them today are based – to help others. Indeed, Ignatius used these Exercises to direct others, and in 1540, with some of these people formed the Society of Jesus, the Jesuits. The Jesuits receive their charism from that direct encounter with God that Ignatius discovered is possible for all. For St. Ignatius and in Jesuit spirituality, God is in constant and intimate dialogue with us; we experience this in our daily lives as feelings of union with or disconnection from God. When we reflect on these movements within ourselves, we discover that language of love for each one of us.

The Exercises and Film

The Spiritual Exercises that you are holding in your hands right now, which has been tested for over 400 years, is a way to discover God's unique love for each of us and to learn that language of love in which God speaks to us. We learn this language by looking at our own lives and at the forces that shape them.

These Exercises are divided into what is called Four Weeks. But Ignatius did not expect the person making the Exercises to complete them in a calendar month. They are meant to be adapted, as we have done here, to accommodate your personal situation. Ignatius writes, "It is not meant that each week should necessarily consist of seven or eight days …. It may be necessary … at times to shorten the Week, and at others to lengthen it" (#4). What is crucial is not fitting into a specific time frame, but having enough time to get "the fruit that is proper to the matter assigned" (#4). For Ignatius, the matter assigned in these Exercises is divided into four parts. The first part invites us to discover God's love for each one of us by looking at those areas of our lives where we have not experienced love. That week ends when we experience a personal liberation from the forces that make us see ourselves as unlovable and unloving. The second part channels those liberated energies into a personal relationship with Christ, who manifests the Compassionate Mercy of God. The third part invites us to accompany that love in the face of suffering and death; the fourth part celebrates the triumph of God's love over the forces of destruction and invites us to share in that triumph by working together to transform the world through acts of love.

You need to work through the weeks in order, since one week builds on the next, and within each week, one Exercise builds on the one preceding it. At the beginning of each week, material is given to prepare you to enter the Week; at the end, material is again given to help you see what has happened to you during that Week. At the end of the Four Weeks in this book, a final chapter ties together the whole journey. By that time you will have experienced the complete Spiritual Exercises of St. Ignatius using the contemplative vehicle of film.

Underlying each section is the constant mercy of God. The weeks elaborate on this basic attitude of God towards us. The First Week contains the theme of us as loved sinners. The Exercises here help us get in touch with the fact that God loves us even as we sin, and desires to free us from the entrapment and illusions of sin. Within the material of the First Week is an eight-day retreat on the Beatitudes, which carries us through a process of liberation to joyful service. The theme in the Second Week is one of growing intimacy with Christ as the embodiment of the Father's mercy. The Third Week deals with the passion Christ has for his God, which allows Christ, and us, to endure the passion and destruction common to all humankind without falling into despair. In the Fourth Week we experience the joy of Christ's resurrection and our entry into it, which allows us to become manifestations of God's mercy to all.

Because this book presents the Spiritual Exercises of St. Ignatius of Loyola using the medium of film, it is almost impossible to do the full exercises in 30 days. They can be done over three months, six months, or a year. It is a wonderful way to integrate spiritual growth into your daily life, at home or with others. It presents the significance of the Exercises using contemporary popular film, where watching the film becomes the act of contemplative prayer.

The book is designed for individuals or groups, at home or in retreat, pastoral, academic, or parish settings. Such a broad range of applications is possible because the Exercises of Ignatius focus on the imagination as embodying spirituality. Imagination does not exist in particular contexts. Imagination is the context out of which we live our lives and in which the Incarnation occurs – that is, where God encounters us, communicates with us, and transforms us.

The Stories We Live By

To understand how God brings us to fullness of life, we must start by looking at how we understand our life. Our experiences have shaped the way we live. Of course, how we live is determined by more than our personal experience. It is shaped by our families, our society, the times we live in. That larger experience makes us. In trying to understand ourselves, we create the stories that both reflect our experience and turn our eyes away from it. The stories we live by do not necessarily emerge from the truth of our lives. This truth is that we are loved by God, and are capable of loving as God loves and of accepting love as God's beloved. Often, the stories we hold to be real are distortions of that basic truth.

Held in God's Love

God does not desire that we live out of these misleading representations of ourselves. The path to intimacy starts when we allow God to enter our stories. When this happens we discover that that same God is willing to accept us as we are, but the love we are shown in that acceptance lets us want to reject the lies that prevent us from being fully ourselves. We discover the courage to risk abandoning the false myths that have established our identity, because we know we are always held in God's love. It is only when we realize this that we give ourselves over to that love, which reveals to us how the stories we live in trap us. Ignatius was aware of this point. The First Week of his Exercises offers us ways of being released from those stories that deny us life and the joy of living. These exercises place us in the larger story of God's constant and abiding love for us. In that First Week of the Exercises, we experience the liberating power of the Incarnation coming into our personal lives in an intimate way. That power transforms the false story we have lived out of, and invites us to live another story: the story that allows us to accept ourselves as truly loved, in all our flaws and disorders.

Ignatius realized that the worlds we live in and operate out of are creations of our imagination. He understood that, for us to be changed, and for the worlds we live in to be changed, the way we imagine those worlds needs to change.

We live in imagined worlds as if they were real. This does not mean there is no such thing as reality, but suggests that we appropriate and construct that reality through the imagination, and imagination incarnates itself through stories. We read reality through those stories. We may help in the construction of those stories, but, by and large, we live in those stories and those stories construct us. For example, we live out of the stories of our families and the stories of our cultures, our ethnicities, our spiritualities. We can even say that we live out of the stories of our biologies, and that we are shaped by the narratives that are the forms of our DNA. These stories do not present us with closed myths that fix our identities, though certain ideologies would have us read ourselves in that way.

The Closed Myth

Sin traps us in forms of closure that offer us the illusion of security and allow us to justify ourselves and to demonize what is not ourselves as "other." The closed myth claims to be the most true form of reading reality. As such, it sets and maintains standards, integrity, values, and tradition. It offers security, clarity, and stability. But in effect, it benefits only a select few, and controls the media by appeals to orthodoxy. It maintains itself by violence that coerces or destroys what is different from it. The stranger, the alien, the outsider are all forms of the "other." At times even God – however that mystery is enstoried – is given the qualities of the other, and treated with fear, dread, and suspicion. There is a move to domesticate such a God in theologies, displacing spirituality with rituals and institutionalized religion. Then there is the struggle to control orthodoxy; its politics are maintained by the quality control of systematics, canonicity, and the authority of professionalism. The closed myth manifests itself in fundamentalism of any sort and in the displacement of truth by ideologies. They become the breeding ground of revolution, where one narrative displaces another.

Stories are never closed, but interpretations of stories can be. When we try to impose closure on the stories we live out of – in the form of closed myths – we destroy parts of ourselves and others. We eliminate or distort relationships. We consign ourselves to death. The long process of moving out of closed myths is called conversion. Through conversion, we move from one story to another. It is not an easy process. We move out of it by facing our fears; we abandon the illusions of clarity and the myths of transparency, simplicity, ease, and comfort. We question. We even question the basis of our questioning. We realize how trapped we are in patterns of perception sanctioned by personal habits, society's laws, cultural norms, and the many levels of tradition that inform us about who we are.

The Broken Myth

At this stage we come to the realization that we live not out of a closed myth, but within broken myths. Broken myths claim to be countercultural, but they define and maintain themselves only in relationship to the closed myth they profess to reject. In effect, broken myths are smaller and less stable versions of the closed myth. Like the closed myth, they use violence to replace what they seek to overthrow. The ethos behind the broken myth is either a nostalgia for a fabled past or a fantasy of a utopian future. Broken myths do not offer us a viable way forward.

The Open Myth

This does not mean that we are trapped by our past, however. We can look forward if we live in the context of an open myth. The open myth sees the limitation of the closed and broken myth, but it also is attentive to and seeks the possibilities of life trapped in these. It faces the unknown without trying to control it. Those committed to the open myth risk even their very lives to incarnate their intimacy with God. They give up security, clarity, at times even their liberty, and exclusivity obtained by affiliation to one particular myth, in order to witness to their call of spiritual intimacy. The God they embrace calls them beyond themselves. Their authenticity lies in walking in the darkness, in which they seek God and in which God seeks for them. That incarnate intimacy is prophetic. We are all invited to live out of that relationship with God, which alone leads to the fullness of life.

Here it might be helpful to think of ourselves as lovers defined by how the past has interpreted us.

That interpretation includes closed, broken, and open myths. But we are also defined by our relationship to the beloved. That beloved holding us in love offers us, here and now, the invitation to step away from closed myths, to abandon our self-image as victims caught in broken myths, and to journey into deeper intimacy that ushers us into life. We discover ourselves constantly being transformed by the Creator. We journey, as lovers, into a love that has no end. We live the open myth.

The open myth, though beset by insecurities and the reversals of fortune, human bias, and cultural chaos, faces the darkness, which is the face of the future, as the context of emerging possibilities based on relationship. Those relationships invite, call, seduce, beckon, and impel us forward. We leap into the furnaces of affliction, bearing with us the materials of closed and broken myths to create new worlds. These, in their turn, are subject to the vicissitudes of time: decay, closure, entombment. We are constantly called to be who we truly are by continually moving beyond them when they cease to offer us new life.

The dynamics of the closed, broken, and open myth have been present throughout human history. They have made us who we are today. Our work as we desire a closer intimacy in the Trinity – the community we call God – is first to ask how these myths operate in our world. Our contemporary world is driven by four basic narratives: security, meaning, liberty, and belonging.

The Stories of Our Times

Security

The chaos of our times has challenged us to our core. We have become destabilized by the rapid changes in our world. Ways of communicating have changed; borders have been redrawn and are in flux;

our neighbours speak languages we did not grow up with; we have become suspicious of those in authority, whether secular or ecclesial. One can even regard the officials of law enforcement as just another gang. These are just a few obvious manifestations of our unstable world. In the midst of this, we are driven by our basic and deep desire for security. Closed myths offer us security in these times. They claim that their political, or social, or ecclesial ways of reading reality are the true and divinely approved ones. In our vulnerable state, we are often tempted and seduced into accepting their claims. But we need to be aware of how these closed myths operate. They exclude and demonize those who do not go along with them. They maintain their authority by fear. Their orthodoxy and law are established by a centralized government that uses the politics of coercion to intimidate and suppress. The path of intimacy offered those who reject the security of the closed myth is a rootedness in God. Intimacy is found not in belonging to socially approved groups, maintained by shame and guilt, but in the shameless and liberating embrace of God.

Meaning

Our postmodern age has often been defined by its lack of meaning. Our search for an understanding of what is going on, for clarity and direction is urgent. We find ourselves attracted to leaders who promise us such meaning. They offer an authority that will deal with the crises in our religious, social, and political worlds. Often they claim their authority is from God. Yet their behaviour and their policies do not accord with our own awareness of how God operates. The path of intimacy that allows us to witness to God's compassionate mercy leads us not to clarity and systems of meaning, but rather to mystery. Intimacy creates real relationships. We are asked to live those relationships in the mystery we call God, rather than in the clarity of systems. We are asked to place our first trust in God, rather than in leaders. What such leaders want from us is orthodoxy, not intimacy with God.

To live in mystery does not mean we abandon meaning, institutions, and those socialized forms of interaction that give us access to ourselves and each other. To live in mystery means that we appreciate these ways of being as like fingers pointing to the moon. Institutions give us socially approved ways of living, yet they avoid the deeper question of whether those ways of living are spiritually healthy.

Liberty

Too often we confuse license, liberty, and freedom. License is the social permission to behave in particular ways that can be ethical or unethical. Liberty defines license. Institutions can grant us liberty, but our understanding of liberty is dependent on that institution to which we adhere. The quest for liberty is often seen as the overthrow of oppression and victimization. But what is not understood is that the secular longing for liberty – personal, social, or cultural – creates oppression for some other. The price of the liberty we desire may be the enslavement of some other. We must distinguish very carefully between liberty and freedom. Christ in the Garden of Gethsemane gives up his liberty to maintain his freedom. Freedom is how spiritual intimacy manifests itself in the world. That intimacy declares that the right relationship with God is more human than the social constructions of liberty. It declares that sometimes, to be human, we give up our liberty to be free. When we abandon our freedom and seek liberty, on the other hand, we inflict violence on our world. This is not to say that we do not desire liberty, or that it is not a good thing. But the liberty we desire flows from freedom, not from enslaving others.

14

Belonging

Often we define our freedom by myths of belonging. We demand to be free to worship, to live out social and cultural identities of race, gender, or creed. These identities create boundaries. The other becomes the alien. But before we are defined as racial, or gendered, or members of a religious tradition, we are first human, everyone a creature of God. We are all called to spiritual intimacy. Each call is unique but of equal value. To abandon that call divides us into camps, ghettos, and forms of exclusivity. By accepting our identity as defined by such, we deny or ignore a simple fact. As creatures, we do not define ourselves. God defines us. We are unfinished business. We are open myths; exclusivity of any sort traps us into accepting ourselves as closed myths. When we live this way, we use violence to assert who we are by destroying the other.

Security, meaning, liberty, and exclusivity are the plots of the stories by which we live today. These are not bad things in themselves. But they become harmful when they replace a relationship with God. Then socially defined forms of orthodoxy replace spiritual intimacy. The desire for social acceptance betrays the deeper human desires for a rootedness in God, for a life lived in mystery, for freedom, and for the drive to community where no one and nothing is excluded.

God Enters Our Closed and Broken Myths

Closed or broken myths freeze our growth into humanity. The gift that is God's love for us enters into those myths. It seeks to liberate us into seeing, knowing, and loving ourselves as the Father sees, knows, and loves us. We need to experience the power of that love in our own lives before we can become aware of its presence in the world — not just some 2,000 years ago, but today, here and now. What happened in the Incarnation happens to us when God's love enters into our personal lives and liberates us so that we can live in such a way that others become liberated. We experience the entry of God into our own brokenness as a spiritual intimacy. Our journey with God as those who are freed into love is a deepening of that intimacy. That path of intimacy carries us to the boundaries of being human. It calls us beyond how we imagine ourselves, and it brings us to a creativity that builds up the community of love in which we are all intimately connected. We share a common vision shaped by an incarnate imagination.

Our Imagined Worlds

St. Ignatius had the insight that we all live in imagined worlds, and that our imagination constructs the worlds in which we live using our experiences, our lived contexts, our hopes, our pains, and our joys. In effect, we live in a highly selective world, and this world defines what is possible for us. It also defines how we see ourselves, how we interact with others and the contexts in which we find ourselves.

It is now a postmodern cliché that we are shaped by the media. But humans have always been shaped by the media of their day: the preachers in a predominantly oral culture; the frescos and paintings of religious themes in a visual culture; the spiritual dramas and novels of a literate culture. Each of these media interacted with the imaginations of their times to create a living faith, effect a conversion, or deepen people's relationship with God.

Today, the media that shape us are film and television. Television uses the sensibilities of a culture formed by film. Film proposes to us forms of the world and ethical ways of living in the world it creates. When we watch a film, we are not just being entertained; we are being formed and shaped. We are exposing ourselves to narratives that shape what is possible, and we live out of those possibilities.

Ignatian prayer uses the imagination to present to us our world, and allows us to open ourselves to the dynamic presence of God in the world. For St. Ignatius, God desires to be fully present to us and in us, and the interface between us and God occurs in the imagination during prayer. In this personal and sacred space of encounter, the energies of our lives are integrated with the divine energies of God. It is not that we are doing all the creating, or that God is doing all the creating. The creation of the world we contemplate is done by God and us working together. Later on in this book you will find the ground rules for that mutual co-operation: self-revelation, self-understanding, and communication. How they work becomes clear as you enter into the Exercises. Film is the contemporary way of entering into this mutual self-revelation of us and God; using film merely brings Ignatius' basic insight of the power of the imagination to our present world.

This book presents the basic insight that God's own medium is the Christ, and the Christ incarnates the divine mercy of God in the world. The medium is not only the message and the massage; here it becomes, even more radically, the dynamics of the one doing the Exercises. We become the living word of God in our world. For Ignatius, this is "contemplation in action."

When we enter the process of this book, we enter into the process of incarnating God in the world. We become changed, and in so changing, we become agents of change. We can do this by contemplating the films that guide us through the spiritual path that leads in love, and through love, to love.

Cinema Is Church

Why do we go to the movies? We want to be entertained, to be distracted, to be informed; we have "a thing" for one of the stars; we like the genre; the gang is going; the issues and topics attract us; we are curious. But when we look more closely at our reasons, we see that they are rooted in the basic experiences of being human and that those basic experiences are themselves expressions of the human desire for self-transcendence. The desire to be entertained and distracted comes from the attempt to escape boredom, that entrapment within oneself. To be informed comes from the quest for knowledge and truth. To be a fan of a star is to engage in a form of identification through idealization that ritualizes our own religious longings for self-awareness. Genre movies appeal to basic drives within us. Detective flicks call upon our innate desire for order; horror movies allow us to face the fears of unknown powers that can destroy us; love stories affirm the power of relationships to maintain and foster identity. And if we go to the movies to be with friends, then we see the cinema as a place for celebrating community. Finally, those who go to the cinema because of work are asked, if they are critics, to be creative; if ushers, to be welcoming; if projectionists, to be attentive and responsible. If we fill such roles in some way when we go to the movies, we are exercising, whether consciously or not, a religious sensibility, which engages us in the rituals of self-transcendence.

Cinema is contemporary church. Beyond the postmodern axiom that image is reality — that what we see on the screen is God inasmuch as it creates and defines what is real for us — the cinema has taken on for most of our culture the effects and resources of religious worship. This is not surprising. The earliest forms of drama were religious in nature; reading originated in spirituality; visual representation was, and is (considering censorship), conscribed by the politics of the holy; and the imagination, as Samuel Coleridge defined it and as William Blake has etched on our awareness, is the divine in human form. The films we see, from the most profound to the most banal, all share those manifestations of the divine.

Sacred Space

Picture yourself in a movie theatre. Literally, spiritually, and metaphorically. The architecture of the theatre is ecclesial in nature. It is designed for a religious ceremony so that we can be both individual and yet community. We sit in a sacred space differentiated from our everyday world by its manipulation of space and time. At the movies, it is neither day nor night. The attendant darkness is divorced from time of day or season of the year. It is its own time. What time occurs is determined by what is enacted in front of our eyes. Both the context and what we are there to see are technically designed to engage and focus all our senses in a deliberately selective manner. That engagement is not passive.

A bright light shines through a moving strip of celluloid, projecting onto a screen a series of static images which, in their superimposition, give the illusion of movement. The mind transforms that illusion into a semblance of reality, and the individual takes on the critical task of evaluating the commitment he or she will make in accepting what is imagined as real. Realism is not reality. It is a cultural convention. Thus the audience spontaneously determines the level of allegorical meaning to be attached to what is being presented. Indeed, political censorship often revolves around the question of allegory, where one thing is taken to represent something else. But beyond that issue of interpretation is the broader question of how what is seen to be presented is created: production values, plot, characters, techniques used to depict the conventions of reality acceptable to an audience. The process the industry uses to present a product is the same as the process the audience uses to translate into a product the raw data it is given.

Only then do questions of engagement and alienation occupy the audience. Both the process and the questions are profoundly spiritual in nature. The process is one of creativity; the questions of engagement are about the nature of contemplation and, in uniquely Ignatian terms, about contemplation in action. What we are looking at here is the broader notion of media literacy. Media literacy is expertise in reading and understanding media – which today includes television, cinema, and the Internet – based on the premise that the media are not transparent instruments that transmit objective messages from sender to receiver. Rather, each instrument is shaped by both sender and receiver, and manipulates the data it processes. Thus the evening TV news has been carefully tailored for its audience – including attention span and demographics – according to the ideologies of the networks that broadcast it. The technology of television determines what is shown and how it is shown. Media literacy teaches that what is presented is objectively and immediately real. What is shown, how it is shown, what is received and how it is received are all products of the creative imagination.

Spiritual Literacy

When God communicates with us, the same dynamics of the imagination are employed. Rawly put, media literacy is spiritual literacy; this book contains a series of exercises to make people spiritually literate by developing their media literacy. The medium in question is God's self-communication to us, in what the theology of St. John calls "the Word-made-Flesh," through the workings of the imagination. God is creative; the imagination is creative; and we are creative. In spiritual literacy, these creativities fuse in the act of contemplation.

Illiteracy, on the other hand, has a linear concept of time and a sense of inevitability. The sequence of the celluloid images admits no deviation. Its inevitability leads to a tragic view of life. What is recorded cannot be changed. This is a monolithic reading of film, of narrative, and of life. Film, though it advances, simply does not operate in this way. Flashback, simultaneity, cross-cutting, reversals, overlays, changes in perspective, tempo, lighting, tone – all create a sense of multiplicity that allows for an understanding and imagining of a God who is not caught up by a Greek chronos, by inevitability, and by tragedy, but rather allows for variation, change, the carnavalesque – all that seems to some like chaos. To read the pattern in chaos, to see chaos as part of a bigger pattern, is spiritual literacy. The journey from a monolithic view of life – regarded as natural and then, by extension, divinely ordered – requires exposure to polyvalent forms of difference. The dialogue with "otherness" requires not just a suspension of disbelief in the realism of what is other; it presupposes an ability to be present to the other in a common ground that extends beyond what has been accepted as normal. We begin to discover that we are more than who or what we think we are. That pilgrim journey into the unknown is facilitated by the films we see. We observe and reflect upon the actions and choices of the characters that attract our attention, and on the worlds in which they find themselves. We also reflect upon the way those characters and worlds are presented to us. Out of the encounter with what we contemplate, we fashion our lives and their contexts. Such contemplation is spiritual literacy.

This literacy is not a spectator sport, but a commitment. It is engaged with and defined by what it sees. Even without conscious acknowledgment, that awareness is changed by what it sees. The exposure to different films – with their different plots, techniques, rhythms, forms of narrativity and cultural sensitivities – frees an audience's perspective and imagination. This literacy is an engagement with the world common to those on a spiritual path.

What Is Contemplation?

But how does this work? Watching a film is an act of contemplation. In contemplation, you open yourself to what you contemplate, just as what you contemplate opens itself to you. In that encounter, both are changed. In Ignatian contemplation, you take a scripture passage and enter into the action. There are levels of involvement here as there are in watching a film. You can be a spectator – an enormous involvement because you attribute unity and coherence to what you are watching. A deeper level is possible when you get emotionally involved and become part of the action. Or you can even be so moved that the experience is visceral and transformative. In all of these levels, the creative energies of the imagination engage the whole person, which is different from fantasy or daydreaming, where there is limited or superficial involvement. In contemplative prayer, intentionality is important. We desire to make contact with God; in prayer, God also desires to make contact with us. In that prayer, human creativity meets divine creativity through the imagination. When one uses film as prayer, the same thing happens.

In that act of mutual presence, the viewer experiences a story that explores possibilities within a defined context and embodies values in actions and choices. This occurs in the content of the film and in the way that content has been formulated technically. Editing, camera angle, lighting, sound, even the stock used all contribute to an overall sensation that, though spontaneous, has been mediated by a creative process. A person watching has instinctive reactions to what is being presented, which are experienced as feelings. In watching a film, we are present to a depiction of certain values that reinforce, erode, or challenge our value systems. In contemplation, we are attuned to our imagination; we resonate with or come into conflict with what we value. As a result, we enter a state of either consolation or desolation.

Consolation and Desolation

These Ignatian terms need explanation. In the Spiritual Exercises of St. Ignatius, the terms are used in a nuanced way. Those who delight in selfishness experience consolation when they get the opportunity to live selfishly. But those who are trying to be free from their selfishness experience desolation as they struggle against those habits that give pleasure but are not liberating. The terms are used in this way for people oriented towards their own interests. They are used differently, however, for those people whose orientation is away from selfishness and towards any form of self-transcendence, such as care for others and the betterment of the community. One experiences consolation when one moves to the good and to the greater good, but desolation when one rejects the greater good. Consolation and desolation are not feelings. They are indicators of the direction in which we are pointed based on our underlying attitude. If we are basically selfish, looking at the greater good causes desolation; if we are basically caring, then looking at the greater good causes consolation. In spiritual direction, a good director will first allow us to find out who we are, and then to help us see which direction we are going in, and help us figure out the next step to take on the path.

A Liturgical Act

So when we watch a film, what we feel depends on our basic commitment. The film shows us who we are. This is a profoundly spiritual act, but going to a movie is also a liturgical act. Going to the cinema is public prayer; watching a DVD or a video with friends or alone can be communal or private prayer. That prayer is an encounter with an "otherness" that helps us define ourselves, for we define ourselves through acts of the imagination. Film is a product of that imagination. Today, life is often mistakenly separated from the imagination. Some authorities denigrate imagination and try to restrict what is "real" to what happens. But the contemplative act – whether watching a film or praying – fuses imagination and life. What happens is only one version of what is real, of what is possible. Film explores those possibilities and allows us to explore imaginatively our possibilities in the world. As in prayer, that engagement occurs in a context that is secure enough for us to become vulnerable so that we may engage with imagination. We do not just hand ourselves over to the film to imprint itself upon our awareness, just as we do not simply hand ourselves over to prayer. Both are relationships, and the communication is mediated by our imagination.

For Ignatius, God is not separate from us. A constant dialogue has been going on between God and us all through our lives and all through creation and human history. For God, and for us, creation is not a fixed, self-enclosed entity. What we experience as creation is the ongoing process of God creating. Creation is not complete; for the Christian, creation is open and incomplete and finds its integrity beyond itself in God. Sin, in whatever form it takes, is alienation from God. Sin seeks to find its integrity without God. Transcendence is going beyond self-enclosure, not into nothingness but into dialogue with God that results in an ever-more inclusive relationship with God. Within human history, that dialogue is symbolized in the holy people of the times, then through the Christ and through the gift of his Spirit in each of our lives and in our world.

When we enter into contemplative prayer and find our imaginations enacting the drama of a scriptural passage, is this just a willed projection of our desires and fears? Sometimes it can be that. But in moments of true prayer, we find ourselves carried out of ourselves into places of surprise or to insights that we could not have imagined or created by ourselves. What happens then is that the history, the concerns, and the energies of our lives become the material and the media God uses for self-expression.

But just as there is within each of us that basic desire to be one with God and within God to be one with us, there is within us a selfishness that does not desire self-transcendence. Each of us, without exception, is trapped in encompassing forms of destruction that distort human freedom and seek to frustrate the human desire to love and be creative and to create community. Often, knowingly or unknowingly, we participate in them. Sometimes our institutions — religious, cultural, or juridical — destroy the innocent, the marginalized, or those without power or voice.

In those contexts we are asked to align ourselves with the good, to overcome our selfishness, and to be creative in transforming the world. But before we can do that, we need to understand who we are and what is possible for us. Otherwise we contribute to the patterns of destruction out of ignorance or a self-will that deludes itself that it is working for the good.

Seeing Ourselves

We cannot step out of ourselves or out of the creation to make some sort of objective judgment about the situations in which we find ourselves. What we can do is enter into the dialogue with the One who makes creation. That dialogue occurs in the contemplative mode, and this is where film becomes significant. With film we get the opportunity to see ourselves in two basic ways.

First, in film we are shown representations of life that interact with our horizons of consciousness. We begin with what we know; then there is what we know we do not know; next is what we do not want to know; and beyond that is what we do not know we do not know.

In film, more than in any other medium, we are in touch with that diversity; through that contact we discover that our world extends beyond our immediate concerns and interests.

Second, the films we watch stir up in us the basic opposition of consolation and desolation. These two modes of relationship reveal to us where and how we are situated in our path to self-transcendence when we approach film as a contemplative act. For example, the film *Apocalypse Now* can bring us face to face with the levels of self-deception — personal, political, military, religious, and cultural — endemic in our society. Even the exuberant self-conscious indulgence of the film's production values reveal a fascinated disgust with evil that shows a complicit entrapment with its subject. The film displays a clarity of reality that is both thrilling and sobering. It challenges us to examine the ways in which each of us copes with the chaos of a postmodern world. It shows us the broken myths by which we might try to make sense of or control that world. It brings us to a felt experience of entrapment in that world. How we spontaneously respond to that felt sense reveals to us where we are in regards to that entrapment. There may be the consolation that the truth of the world is revealed, that its lies have been exposed. There may be desolation if one sees the human effort as all that is possible in such a world.

Here it might be helpful to look at one of the reasons St. Ignatius gives for our experience of desolation. He holds that "God wishes to give us a true knowledge and understanding of ourselves so that we may have an intimate perception of the fact that it is not within our power to acquire or attain great devotion, intense love … or any other spiritual consolation" (#322). A film such as *Apocalypse Now* forces us to examine the limitations of trying to transform the world by purely human means.

The risk that God takes with us is to allow us to experience starkly the destructive consequences of the disorder of creation. Our response can be despair if we lose our sense of that larger context in which we live. God is merciful. God knows and loves us better than we know or love ourselves. God knows our basic nature is for union with God, and, in that union, for a life-giving mutual relationship. When we come to the limits of human possibility we discover the compassionate presence of a God who, in and through creation, maintains and supports our basic sense of life without denying us our freedom to try to destroy ourselves. If we can enter into our unredeemed history and face the disorder in our personal lives, the disorder in our family history, those in our societies and cultures, we discover the abiding presence of a divine Mystery whose creativity is to maintain our life and to transform the disorder of history into a new creation. It is in and through creation that creation is transformed. In the mysticism of St. Ignatius, which we share as we do the Spiritual Exercises, God enters creation and we discover God by our full participation in creation.

Participating in Creation

There are levels to this participation. Although we are part of creation, we can live as if we were separate from it, or we can dominate it, or we can live our lives as a purely unspiritual manifestation in creation. But we can go beyond these three levels. We can acknowledge the conflicting forces of good and evil in creation, and enter into the critical task of discerning good from evil and into the creative task of transforming evil into good. To perform these last three works we need to discover how we are individually structured: that is, how God communicates with us and the ways in which we personally need God's help to become truly creative. We also need to know what traps reinforce our narcissism and how to get the help we need to avoid those traps.

This is where film is invaluable. God communicates through our imagination, and in the exercise of our imagination we learn the language and the grammar of that communication. Coleridge says in his *Biographia Literaria* that human imagination incarnates the Divine creativity. Moreover, he would claim that as we perceive from our imaginations – or, as William Blake would put it, "I see through my eye, not with my eye" – the act of perception is essentially creative. Everything that is a human construct is a product of the imagination, and so manifests some trace of the divine creativity. Art raises that level of creative awareness to a self-conscious activity, and film combines the diverse manifestations of human creativity in sound, image, drama, and community in the most flexible and fluid ways to offer the most comprehensive shapings of space and time available to human consciousness. When we watch a film attentively, we participate in a form of contemplation that allows us to experience the imagination fully engaged in creating. We are not accustomed to thinking about it this way, but it is prayer.

There is a sentimental way of thinking about prayer: as an escape from the world or as a way of attaining God's unquestioning acceptance through affirming our own sense of self-identity. In effect, prayer gives us an entry into God's love. That love seeks out the damaged in creation – including us – to repair, console, and transform. Inasmuch as we participate in that love, we too are carried into the pain of the world and past the illusions of ourselves that contribute to the pain of the world. We become present to the source of creativity. By bringing our own creativity into a mutual engagement, we co-operate with God in showing compassionate mercy to the people and situations in our lives.

That engagement manifests itself in the act of contemplation. We contemplate God contemplating us. We can use Scripture or film. In our culture today, the Scriptures of the Old and New Testament are venerated as classic documents that have helped shape our institutions. But they no longer give access to our spiritual myths and identity as they once did. It is not just the secularism of the times that has devalued them, or that the ways they have been used to justify destructive religious perspectives have rendered their import suspect. The easy and present accessibility of multicultural spiritual traditions has relativized their importance. What has replaced them in the postmodern imagination is film.

Film represents the collective cultural unconscious of our time, and offers us a creative product that enters into a self-conscious dialogue with our personal stories and interests. That cultural unconscious as a manifestation of creation – or, rather, of God's ongoing creativity with the productions of human longing and effort – is not a closed myth that we quarry for stories, form, and content, nor is it a broken myth of master narratives that we pillage for pragmatic ends. Rather, it is an open dynamic that holds the repositories of the creative effort, both positive and negative, to be one with God, one that has existed since the birth of time. The energies of that dynamic are not exhausted by human limitation, because it is the presence of the Spirit of God, restless and unquenchable until it transforms all into the creative image of God. Film shows us the spiritual questing of humanity in our time in ways that are symbolic of and appropriate for the postmodern consciousness. We contemplate them, as the icons of our time, because they provide us with the language of our communication with God.

Contemplation and Spirituality

Contemplation is a spiritual exercise. Ignatian contemplation is structured to a particular end, which is to be disposed to receive the grace that we seek in a given prayer period. That grace is a particular response to our deepest desire, an ever-growing intimacy with God. At one time it may be our profound awareness of God's mercy holding us even when we, blinded by our disorders, sinned to find what we thought was love. At another time it may be such a personal bonding with Christ, the human manifestation of God, that we desire fully to be with him as he reveals to the world God's unceasing and compassionate mercy for creation. Or, it may be to follow the path of that divine love through the misery and destructiveness of this world. At the end of the Ignatian Exercises, we pray for the grace to be a part of that joyful labour that transforms our world.

We ask for these graces with the expectation that we will receive them in our prayer. At the end of that prayer, we look back over what we have experienced to see where and how we have received them. Our understanding is that God desires to communicate with us, and that by disposing ourselves to receive that communication, we signal to God our desire to accept this free and loving gift.

There are, as we well know, levels of gift. A gift can be offered and not received; a gift can be received and not accepted; that gift can be accepted but not opened; opened but not used; used but not shared; shared but not celebrated. The journey through the Exercises, using the world of contemporary popular film, carries us through the levels of gift to the place where we become one with the giver, one with what is given, and one with the creation to whom that gift is always offered.

How to Use This Book

This book is a manual. Like all manuals, it will yield limited results if you read it without taking the time to engage in the process it lays out. Yet you can reap some benefits by simply reading a section when the spirit moves you and then reflecting on it. More good will be achieved if you commit to preparing yourself to enter into the process. To that end you will need to set aside some time to read each section and reflect on the questions at the end of that section. This will prepare you to watch the film in question with a certain intention and focus; this controlled disposition results in viewing of the film becoming a contemplative act. There are more questions to reflect on after you have watched the film. Do not

move to the next section until you have exhausted the riches contained in the present section. In Ignatian terms, this is called "repetition." Repetition is not just repeating an exercise, but focusing on the points that were significant in your prayer and reflection. You could think of this as a "zoom in," in which you pray and ponder over important aspects of a general view to reveal important insights and connections in your life. We recommend keeping a journal of the key moments you experience.

In the journal it is helpful to write

- the questions that were the most significant in each exercise and your response to them,

- what took place in prayer (the significant consolations and desolations), and

- the grace asked for; how it was received and how it was given.

How to Prepare to Watch

Each section in this book is an exercise in prayer. Just as you prepare for physical exercise, you dispose yourself for prayer. Find a time and a space where you can pray without being disturbed. Start by being intentional about what you want. This is called asking for the grace; each section presents the grace to be prayed for. Asking for a grace focuses your awareness. Then ask for the Spirit to help you receive the grace. Read the text slowly and reflectively, pausing where you feel moved. At the end of the reading, return to those points that moved you and allow them to be the entry into prayer. At the end of that prayer, go through the questions that follow the text, paying special attention to those questions that stir up something in you. Record in your journal what moved you in the prayer and the reflections.

All of this disposes you to the contemplative act of watching the film. The films we suggest are not intended to provide moral examples of the insights of the prayer; rather, they manifest those energies — both positive and negative — that you will experience as you enter into those meditations and contemplations set out by Ignatius in the Exercises. You enter the film as a contemplative act: you are to notice its effect on you — what it evokes in terms of consolation and desolation, the significant movements of the spirits within you.

You will not have time to do a whole section of reflection and film at one sitting. It is better to proceed at a slower pace, and watch the film only after you have absorbed the material for reflection. This disposition will allow you to encounter the full power of the film as a contemplative moment.

After Watching

After watching the film, it will be helpful to have a conversation with the Father, or with Jesus, or with a significant spiritual figure in your life about what occurred in the prayer period. You might wish to discuss something that moved you, or something that came up during the prayer, such as a memory, an association or a question. St. Ignatius, following Christ, addresses God as "Father." God, of course, is neither masculine nor feminine, but has qualities of a Father, a Mother, and much more than we can ever imagine. We are aware of the bias today of calling God "Father," but also of the intimate personal relationship that Christ has with the Mystery he calls Father; Ignatius had a similar relationship to this identification of God. It was on a pilgrimage to Rome that Ignatius had a vision at La Sorta where he beheld the Father telling the Son about Christ," I want you to put this man under your standard." For these reasons this book has used "Father" to maintain that relationship between that identification of God and the person doing the Exercises. If another term is more appropriate for you, feel free to use it.

Journalling this prayer helps you focus on the significant moments in the experience and on why they are significant. For the Ignatian method of discernment, it is important to pay attention to the times where you were moved either to consolation or desolation. (Consolation refers to those times when you are encouraged or feel alive and connected to God, to others and to yourself. Desolation is the opposite; it describes times when you are feeling apathetic, disinterested in what is good and life-giving, trapped and despairing.) For St. Ignatius, such moments reveal something significant about ourselves: through them God speaks to us, and so we need to return to them to discover what is being said. They reveal whether we are turned to God or away from God.

Discernment

Discernment is not that simple, however. When we are turned away from God, we might get feelings of pleasure from doing what is wrong. That is not consolation. Moreover, even if we are on the right path and are doing what is pleasing to God, we can still be given a false consolation: what we think and feel may be good, but it leads us away from the true good. We only know that it is a false consolation when we see the effects and discover that entering into that "good" feeling leads us to disturbed and ego-centred states. When you note in your journal your consolations and desolations, you also need to note where they lead you.

Consolations and desolations reveal to us, like bearings on a compass, where to go and how to behave if we truly are seeking to know God. If on our path to God we experience desolations, we know that we are encountering forces that seek to block our progress. It helps to examine what might be causing that disturbance. Does it come from an inappropriate attitude or understanding of our relationship to ourselves, to others, or to God? Bringing that blockage to consciousness allows us to bring it to prayer. Then God's mercy can deal with whatever is hindering us from loving freely and joyfully. It might be a hurt in our past or an undeveloped aspect of ourselves that has become so much a part of our personality that we are unconscious of it, but that influences the way we see and feel and behave.

Consolations also help carry us closer to God. Ignatius defines consolation as being so inflamed with the love of God that we love in an ordered manner and so "can love no creature on the face of the earth for its own sake, but only in the Creator of them all" (#316). That love can move us to tears for our sins, and to sorrow for the sufferings of any member of the Body of Christ. It is present when we relish things properly, when we grow in faith, hope, and love and are attracted to all that leads to God filling our soul with peace. Consolation is not just feeling good. Sorrow and pain can also be signs of consolation. What is significant, for our spiritual awareness, is what the feelings mean and whether they orient us to seeking God.

So the first step in discernment is being able to identify the feeling. The second step is to become aware of what those feelings mean. As you gain more experience, you will find it easier to identify these more quickly. The third stage in discernment is seeing in which direction the state that manifests itself in a particular feeling is tending. This discernment is extremely personal. These are your feelings and no one else's. They indicate your particular language with God and God's own language with you. You might think of your feelings in prayer as the language lovers use with each other.

Journalling these states of consolation and desolation, together with what aroused them, allows you to come to a better understanding of yourself and of how you operate in the world. God's communication with you is always about how to live your life in a way that is more focused and more rooted in love. Journalling also allows you to see the patterns in your life; you will soon discover that the consolations, like desolations, are interconnected. They reveal to us our redeemed history and God's care for us even in those times when we might have felt far from God, or not even particularly concerned with spiritual things. Bringing this to our awareness enables us to appropriate more deeply God's constant mercy for us and communication with us.

The First Week: The Mercy of God

Ignatius' missionary thrust is to make all become aware that God loves us, and that God always and at every moment communicates with us. Ignatius even devised an examination of consciousness whereby at the end of every day we reflect on where we found consolation and desolation. He asks us to be grateful for moments of consolation and to reflect on moments of desolation to see why they happened and how we can prevent them. Ignatius believes that God wants us to be happy, and that God works in the world to bring us to our true self and to our true happiness.

To achieve that happiness we sometimes find ourselves having to make important decisions. The Exercises give us a process through which to make correct discernments. The Exercises are not techniques for discovering God's will, however. Rather, they dispose us to a true relationship with God and offer us a language by which God communicates with us. We can love someone and talk meaningfully with them but still make bad decisions. This is an existen-

25

tial truth. But that love and communication limit the possibility of making bad decisions. The Exercises make us prone to making good and life-giving decisions through the personal language of consolation and desolation.

The Second Week: Walking with God

Ignatius places decision-making in the Second Week of the Exercises, because people first need to experience radically that God loves them even though they have been and remain sinners. The First Week establishes a foundational openness to God; unless that happens, the decisions you make will be skewered by blindness to your true identity and to your true relationships with others and with God. By the end of the First Week, you will have come to an overwhelming sense of God's mercy in all aspects of your life – personal, communal, social, and cultural – as well as a deep sense of how disorder on all levels of your existence corrupts your true awareness of your life. The liberation experienced in the First Week is a liberation to love, be loving, and accept love. It is felt as a deep desire to live that love out in the world.

But how are we to do this? The Second Week of the Exercises introduces us to God's way of operating in the world as manifest in the presence and actions of Jesus Christ.

In that Second Week we are invited to journey with Christ and to pray for the grace of such an intimate knowledge of him that we desire only to love and to follow him. In the contemplations of that Week we can bring the decision we wish to make to the prayer and to discussions we have with God following the prayer. We check to see if, in those moments of dialogue, we are filled with consolation or desolation as we ponder our decision. Consolation means that we have made the right decision; desola-

tion tells us that we are on the wrong track. But even in the contemplations themselves we can learn something useful. If we find God distant or uninvolved with us in those contemplations, we know something is wrong. Or if in those contemplations we find that we are acting in ways not consonant with Jesus' own activity, then we know we are on the wrong path. The liberated energies of our life are embodied in the decision we are trying to make; these shape the way we relate to the Christ as he journeys through his own earthly life. If those energies are consonant with the energies of the Christ, then we have consolation and the felt assurance that we are one with the Christ on mission. If there is dissonance, we experience desolation and the signs of a bad decision.

The Third Week: A Passionate Lover

In the decision-making process, that consonance and dissonance continue throughout the remainder of the Weeks of the Exercises. If we are making the right decision, we find that we can journey in union with Christ through his passion and death and resurrection. We suffer and are sad with Christ suffering. Indeed, at times we might even feel nothing, that same nothing we feel during the last days of someone we love, when the emotion that dominates our life is too deep even for feeling. With the wrong decision, we find ourselves distant from the suffering, or we want to stop the suffering, or we are distracted from the main event by our own preoccupations, imposing our own attitudes and perspectives on the drama we are contemplating.

We are not to be masochistic or sadistic here. We do not delight in suffering for its own sake, nor do we take on that suffering to show just how good and holy we are. Christ did not choose his suffering. He chose, as always, the Father and his path to the Father. The disorders of the world and of evil resisted his manifestation of the Father as Compassionate Mercy by imposing a suffering designed to break his relationship or to eliminate him altogether. Similarly, the suffering we experience in the Third Week is one of identification with someone whom we love and follow, and with whom we now have the same path, the same spirit and the same passion.

The Fourth Week: A Transforming Life

That passion for the Father leads us to the Fourth Week. In this week we experience Christ's resurrection from the dead. The Christ does not raise himself from the dead; the Father manifests his love for him and reaches into the ultimate power of sin – death – and brings Christ, not back to life, but to a new level of creation, uncorrupted by evil: resurrection. Ignatius invites us at this point in our spiritual journey "to ask for the grace to be glad and rejoice intensely because of the great joy and the glory of Christ our Lord" (#221). We are not asked to experience joy because of what we have done, but rather to share Christ's joy and glory in his return to the Father. This is crucial for our discernment process, because here we can see if our decision has united us with the Christ. If it has, then we can experience the pure gift of Christ's joy; if it hasn't, then we will not.

The awareness of consolation and desolation can attune us more closely to the creative presence of God in our world and can give us a personal language for listening to God. For Ignatius, God is never silent in the world, but manifests in every one of us, no matter who or what or where we are. Ignatius would go even further and say that God uses everything to communicate with us. This book uses film because it is contemporary contemplation, and in contemplation one enters into communion with God. But this communication is not restricted exclusively to periods of prayer.

Ignatius, in the manual called the Spiritual Exercises, introduces the exercises themselves in the context of a daily examination of consciousness. In this examination he asks us to look at our day prayerfully at the end of each day and see where we were consoled and where we experienced desolation. Even in the ordinariness of daily life, God speaks. Ignatius suggests that we give praise for where, in the ordinary, we were consoled, and that we examine the moments of desolation to see what God is telling us. Ignatius' emphasis on the ordinary is echoed in the films we have chosen. We could have chosen art films or foreign films with a certain aesthetic sensibility, but instead we chose films that are available at the major commercial cinemas, at video and DVD rental stores throughout the country, and as online downloads.

The Key Concepts of Media Literacy

Reading these popular films using the techniques of spiritual literacy given in this chapter is not just a professional, academic, or religious task. Such reading is based on the techniques of media literacy that we absorb by reflecting on what we see in the media culture we live in today. The following eight key concepts provide a theoretical base for all media literacy, and give a common language and framework for media discussion.

1. *All media are constructions.* This is arguably the most important concept. Media do not simply reflect external reality. Rather, they present carefully crafted constructions that reflect many decisions and are the result of many determining factors. Media literacy works towards deconstructing these constructions (i.e., taking them apart to show how they are made). Our imaginative projects and our perceptions occur in the same way; the spiritual discipline of contemplation and reflection frees a person from being trapped by forces that determine what we see and imagine and how we spontaneously evaluate those seemingly natural acts.

2. *The media construct aspects of reality.* The media are responsible for the majority of the observations and experiences we use to build our personal understandings of the world and how it works. Much of our view of reality is based on pre-constructed media messages with built-in attitudes, interpretations, and conclusions. Thus the media, to a great extent, give us our sense of reality. In fact, the media also give us our sense of spirituality, but it is the dynamic nature of spirituality to refuse to be constrained by such constructions, just as it is the very nature of God to refuse to be constrained by creation.

3. *Audiences negotiate meaning in media.* If the media provide us with much of the material we use to build our picture of reality, each of us finds or "negotiates" meaning according to individual factors: personal needs and anxieties, the pleasures or troubles of the day, racial and sexual attitudes, family and cultural background, moral standpoint, and so on. Spiritual literacy examines the dynamics of that mediation in the light of our own consolations and desolations, which reveal in an intimate manner our relationship with the mystery we call God.

4. *Media messages have commercial implications.* Media literacy aims to encourage awareness of how the media are influenced by commercial considerations, and how these impinge on content, technique, and distribution. Most media production is a business, and so must make a profit. Questions of ownership and control are central: a relatively small number of individuals control what we watch, read, and hear in the media. This may seem Marxist, in that it suggests the economic basis for all media messages and for all cultural artifacts. Marxism is useful in unveiling the mystification of motives by using a hermeneutic of suspicion. But Marxism contains the drive to self-transcendence that underpins all human activity, including Marxist analysis itself. Spiritual literacy focuses on that basic drive to self-transcendence and on its satisfaction in the free gift of love by a creative and compassionate God.

5. *Media messages contain ideological and value messages.* All media products are advertising, in some sense, values and ways of life. The mainstream media convey, explicitly or implicitly, ideological messages about such issues as the nature of the good life and the virtue of consumerism, the role of women, the acceptance of authority, and unquestioning patriotism. Our perceptions and imagination are shaped by these values. We can never be value free, and we can never escape the ideologies that can underpin those values. But we do not have to be imprisoned by those ideologies and values if we experience them as always inadequate manifestations of our true nature, which is to be in conscious union with the divine. Spiritual literacy builds on media literacy, for while media literacy can examine from a certain point of view the messages that are the media, it cannot examine itself. Spiritual literacy allows that examination and promotes the freedom that such an examination raises.

6. *Media messages contain social and political implications.* The media have great influence in politics and in forming social change. For example, television can greatly influence the election of a national leader on the basis of image. The media involve us in concerns such as civil rights, famines in Africa, and HIV/AIDS. They give us an intimate sense of certain national and global concerns so that we can imagine we have become Marshall McLuhan's global village. We should be hesitant about such a quick generalization, however. We all know that what we are being given is not all there is; we also know that we are unable to assimilate even that much. Similarly, we know that the media that is our imagination and our perception is also limited. Who we are is a mystery, and the implications of our actions in the world we live in are beyond our control. Inasmuch as our presence in the world is also media, we embody and represent social and political values. We are not just receptors of media messages, we are transmitters. Consider the enormous significance of designer labels and ideo-grams attached to our clothes, our food, our living styles. We embody mystery, but within the operative freedoms of our culture. How we choose to appropri-ate that freedom and manifest it in our lives becomes a matter of spiritual literacy. How others read that is media literacy.

7. *Form and content are closely related in media message.* As McLuhan noted, each medium has its own gram-mar and codifies reality in its own way. Different media will report the same event but create different impressions and messages. When we contemplate a gospel passage, our personality and the energies that compose our life shape the way that passage and encounter with Christ come alive. Even the represen-tation of Christ is shaped by those energies. But it would be a serious mistake to think that such con-templations are just projections from our own per-sonality. The contemplations are also the product of God's activity within the very intimacy of our psyche. In fact, God uses those images and energies to create a media message appropriate to our personal path. The form and content of what we experience in a contemplation reveals the unique communication and language that God has with us. The ability to read that communication is spiritual literacy.

8. *Each medium has a unique aesthetic form.* Just as we notice the pleasing rhythms of certain pieces of poetry or prose, so we ought to be able to enjoy the pleasing forms and effects of the different media. You will notice in prayer that, if it goes well, you have a sense of time passing without notice. If it does not go well, time drags; you are distracted, bored, irritable, or wishing you could do something else. Personal prayer has an aesthetic in what is represented, in its modes of representation, in its narrative flow and editing. When we pay attention to our contempla-tions, we must look not only at the insight we think is given, but at all the factors that compose that con-templation.

Clearly, contemplation is like film; film, viewed as a spiritual discipline, and contemplation are identi-cal. Media literacy, at the level of spirituality, becomes the reflection tool for what occurs in our prayer. This book suggests using film, not to reinforce the particu-lar insights of the Spiritual Exercises, but as manifes-tations of the Exercises themselves. It sees media lit-eracy as spiritual literacy: film as contemplation, and cinema as making available to a mass audience con-temporary forms of prayer that discuss relevant issues and the quest for transcendence.

You can see, then, how what appears to be "just" a film becomes an instrument for a dialogue with God. The consolations and desolations we experi-ence in that context alert us to the ways we are ori-ented, or not oriented, to God. Using a journal to note the different movements of the spirits within us, and the contexts in which those spirits are moved, sharpens our skills at learning our personal language with God. This makes us more flexible in walking through the currents of our world with freedom and integrity and a certain joy this world cannot give.

We invite you now to that freedom and that joy.

An Outline to Follow in Using This Book

Below we give an outline of the process we describe in this chapter. It will provide a handy guide until you become familiar with the structure of the prayer.

1. Make sure you have enough time for the exercise.

2. Find a quiet space and ask for the Spirit to help you make a good prayer.

3. Ask for the specific grace that is suggested in the introductory reflection.

4. Read the reflection slowly and carefully. Dwell on those sections, one at a time, that have moved you the most, either to a sense of well-being or to a sense of discomfort.

5. Invite God to enter into your prayerful journey through those sections.

6. Discuss with God what emerges in that journey and in those deliberations.

7. Use the questions provided at the end of the reflection to appropriate your experience or to enter further into prayer.

8. Journal the significant moments of this prayer experience.

When you feel you have appropriated the reflection, you are ready to watch the film.

A. Make sure you have enough time to watch the whole film at one sitting.

B. Make sure that you will not be disturbed or distracted.

C. Ask for the same grace as suggested in the introductory reflection.

D. Watch the film.

E. Examine yourself: Where in the film were you especially moved?

F. Use the questions given for each film to appropriate better that contemplative experience.

Note 1. Each of the three sections of reflections that follow the movie contains a number of questions for reflection. You do not need to deal with all of these questions. Read the questions and respond to those that move you – in terms of attraction or repulsion.

Note 2. The questions are not intended to deal with every aspect of the film. There is simply not enough space to do so. For example, a number of the movies are adaptations of short stories or novels. We have chosen not to deal with the issues of expectations about the story and/or the characters in such films.

G. Have a discussion with God about what moved you in the film and your reflections on the film.

H. Write in your journal what has been significant in this prayer period and reflection. It is helpful every so often to review your journal entries to see if you can discern a pattern or path.

I. At the end of every Week of the Exercises, reread carefully the journal entries for that Week. Try to summarize the overall movement of that Week. At the end of the Four Weeks, take time to reread all your journal entries. Summarize what has been given to you in your experience of journeying through the Exercises of St. Ignatius in this way.

John Pungente SJ and Monty Williams SJ

Theme
We are God's Beloved Trapped by Sin

Scripture verse

But now thus says the Lord,
He who created you, O Jacob,
He who formed you, O Israel:
Fear not, for I have redeemed you;
I have called you by name, you are mine.
When you pass through the waters I will be with you;
And through rivers, they will not overwhelm you;
When you walk through fire you shall not be burned,
And the flame shall not consume you.
For I am the Lord your God, .
The Holy One of Israel, your Saviour. (Isaiah 43:1-3)

From the Spiritual Exercises

I shall also thank God for this, that up to this very moment He has shown himself so loving and merciful to me.
(Sp. Ex. #71)

Grace to be prayed for

Lord, teach me to be generous
teach me to serve you as you deserve
to give and not to count the cost
to fight and not to heed the wounds
to toil and not to seek for rest
to labour and not to seek reward
save that of knowing I do your most Holy Will.
(prayer of St. Ignatius of Loyola)

Most of us live in the world unreflectively. We read our lives with a set of preconditioned stories from our upbringing and culture that define who we are and what we should want. We are even conditioned how to think. At best, we are concerned only with our own interests and projects. These reveal to us and to others our sense of ourselves. The only time we question that sense of self is when something disturbs our carefully controlled universe: the death of someone significant, the loss of a job, bad news from the doctor ... even misplacing our car keys or losing a night's sleep. When those things happen, we struggle to return to our previous state of comfort. But when that cocoon of comfort is no longer available, we are driven to forms of accommodation and adjustment. Sometimes those substitutes work; sometimes they do not.

A spiritual journey often begins when we can find no substitute for what we have lost. It was the illness that confined Ignatius to his sickbed that prompted his journey to a spiritual life. Two centuries before Ignatius, in 1204, a serious illness was the beginning of another saint's journey to becoming Francis of Assisi. Illness, pain, loss, poverty, lack of social success, and deprivations are things the secular world does not value. But their presence – and they are present in each of our lives – reveals to us that neither we nor the world are in control. This leads us to ask the simple question that starts every spiritual journey: "Given this very human situation, how can I be happy?" Often we try what the world offers. For many, the pursuit of those things is distracting enough to keep them engaged for some time. But their achievement is no substitute for what we truly desire, because at the root of our being we *are* desire. Nothing less than the fullness of life can satisfy that desire. Even when good things happen to us, affirming our sense of self-entitlement, we accept them as gift rather than as privilege. The blindness of illusion lets us confuse the two. This illusion prompts the observation that "Those whom the gods wish to destroy they give gifts to." We tend to equate ourselves with those gifts, living as if we were our gifts. We lose our integrity as creatures radically dependent on others and on God. When bad things happen to us, we discover what beggars we truly are. We cry out for help. And whatever is given to us then is given as gift. Bad things force us to question ourselves — who we are, what we can do, what we must do. Most of us react against such self-examination in the normal circumstances of our lives. Yet only when we do so do we discover the path to spiritual intimacy and towards the fullness of life.

Ignatius, in the First Week of his Spiritual Exercises, sets up a program that allows us to conduct such radical self-examination. Its aim is not to destroy us, but rather to help us abandon the false self-images we have of ourselves and the false stories we maintain about ourselves. At the same time, it permits us to see, understand, and experience the deeper truth of ourselves: that we are always and everywhere loved by God, who seeks us out as a lover searches for a lost beloved. That lover will not rest until the beloved knows at a profound level the personal and intimate love that constantly creates, supports, and transforms him or her.

The encounter between the beloved and the lover, between ourselves and God, occurs in the context of examining not only our personal history, but also our social and cultural history — indeed, all human history — within the cosmic history of creation. Considering ourselves in this vast context helps diminish the value we place upon our ego, which is a tiny, fragile thing in the vast tides of human and cosmic history.

Creation of the earth began fifteen billion years ago in a burst of creativity that produced galaxies, stars, solar systems, and the blue planet we call Earth. The forces and energies that shape this ongoing process of creation also feature significantly in our own moments of self-consciousness. The divine love that expresses itself in creativity from the beginning of time also expresses itself in every act of human creativity. The stories we live by, the imagined worlds we live in, have their source in that divine creativity. Unfortunately, some choose to live out of those stories as ends in themselves rather than as continuing expressions of the beloved's relationship to the lover. They value the story more than the relationship. They commit the basic act of idolatry by constraining the creativity of divine love to a particular expression of it. Stories never encompass the fullness of reality. At best, they point beyond themselves to aspects of that reality. They are doors through which we encounter God and God encounters us.

This is not to belittle story. We cannot live without story. It is within stories that we find ourselves and find a sense of ourselves.

Most of the elements of what makes up my story existed before I was born. For example, one of the stories we live out of is our heritage. We are shaped not only by our parents' genes, and our parents by those of their parents back to the dawn of humanity, but also by the historical forces surrounding us and them. Those forces are in turn subject to the environmental and ecological dimensions that mitigate against, or promote, our well-being. All of those forces are caught up in the cosmic tides of a creation that has not yet reached its fulfillment. That fulfillment is to be found only in the mystery we call God. In brief, we come from God and we return to God, and the path we walk in spiritual intimacy is a gift of God. But we are not God.

So who are we? The answer lies before and beyond ourselves. Maybe it is even the wrong question to ask. Maybe a better question to ask is this: What do we think or believe or understand of ourselves? Closely tied into that question are three others: What makes us think of ourselves this way? How does this perception shape the way we see and relate to ourselves, to others, and to that mystery we call God? And how does that perception change?

St. Ignatius knew that when we admit that God desires us passionately, and when we open ourselves to that passionate desire as the desire we truly desire, we change. We fall in love. The world changes, unimagined possibilities open, and we become focused and creative in our daily lives.

The First Week of the Spiritual Exercises invites us to walk this path of love.

Questions for Reflection to Prepare for the First Week

1. Who are you?

2. Why do you say you are this person?

3. Where does this self-understanding come from?

4. Are you content with this self-understanding?

5. What do you think is missing?

6. How do you experience that missing self?

7. How did your family shape that self-understanding? Your relationships with your parents? With your siblings? With the other members of your family? With your spouse or partner?

8. How is your self-image shaped by the culture(s) you grew up in and the one(s) you live in now? List the ways in which you are shaped by your social background, class, ethnicity, economic status, gender, sexuality, the part of the world you come from or now live in.

9. How does the environment shape your self-awareness? Which season resonates most with you? Are you a day person or a night person? Why do you say this?

10. What is your image of God? Of religion? Of spirituality? How do your relationships reveal to you who you are?

11. What questions haunt your life? How do you deal with them? How do they deal with you?

12. In what ways is your life in your control?

13. In what ways is your life beyond your control?

14. What do you really desire?

15. How does that desire manifest itself in your life?

16. What happens when you sit in prayer with your desire?

The Movie
INCEPTION

Director: Christopher Nolan (2010 – 148 mins.)
Starring: Leonardo DiCaprio, Joseph Gordon-Levitt, Ellen Page, Tom Hardy

1. Synopsis

Dom Cobb steals valuable secrets from deep within the subconscious during the dream state, when the mind is most vulnerable. This ability has made him a coveted player in this new world of corporate espionage, but it has also turned him into a fugitive and cost him everything he has ever loved.

Now he is being given a shot at redemption. To get his life back, he must do the impossible: not to steal an idea but to plant one. Only Cobb could have predicted the enemy that knows every move they are about to make.

2. About the Movie

1. "If movies are shared dreams, then Christopher Nolan is surely one of Hollywood's most inventive dreamers, given the evidence of his commandingly clever *Inception*. Applying a vivid sense of procedural detail to a fiendishly intricate yarn set in the labyrinth of the subconscious, the writer-director has devised a heist thriller for surrealists, a Jungian's 'Rififi,' that challenges viewers to sift through multiple layers of (un)reality." (Justin Chang, *Variety*, July 5, 2010)

Simply put, this film is, in some ways, a con-game film, only the action takes place entirely within the characters' minds while they dream.

Do you agree with this view or is there another entire layer to the film that tells us that this is much more than a simple heist thriller? What scenes can you refer to that helped you form your opinion?

2. "Like the films of his idols Kubrick, Ridley Scott, and Michael Mann, Nolan's work is typically known for its emotional cool. But Nolan admits that *Inception* reflects an evolution of philosophy. 'As a filmmaker starting out, there was a resistance to emotion, because you so often see the insincere version of it in movies,' he says. 'Yet over time, and during the Batman movies in particular, I was forced to reexamine my own process of watching a film. What I realized is that what I respond to most is emotion – which is what audiences respond to the most as well.'" (Jeff Jensen and Adam B. Vary, "*Inception*: Dream a Little Dream," *Entertainment Weekly*, July 30, 2010)

Nolan's statement to the contrary, critics of this film have said that the film lacks any real emotional element. Do you agree with the critics or do you find real emotion in this film? Why? Why not?

3. "Viewers will have to work to keep up with all the shifting perspectives and layers of deceit.

Inception is like the coolest, toughest final exam – or like the dream of one, in which you're suddenly in class and you realize you didn't prepare for the big test. This is a movie that you'll wish you had crammed for." (Richard Corliss, *Time*, July 14, 2010)

How does having to "work" while watching a film increase the enjoyment of a film? Or do you prefer not to be challenged in that way, to just let the film entertain you?

4. "Beware the critic who claims the ability to analyze *Inception* authoritatively after one viewing. As engrossing and logic-resistant as the state of dreaming it seeks to replicate, Christopher Nolan's audacious new creation demands further study to fully absorb the multiple, simultaneous stories Nolan finagles into one narrative experience. First time around, the movie – part sci-fi fantasy, part gun-toting heist pic, part mindfreak, all filmmaker brio – is dazzling and buzzy. It's a rolling explosion of images as hypnotizing and sharply angled as any in a drawing by M.C. Escher or a state-of-the-biz videogame; the backwards splicing of Nolan's own *Memento* looks rudimentary by comparison. Only repeated exposure can clarify for each spectator not only what's going on, but also whether the emotional payoff deepens enough to warrant the arbitrary complexity of the game." (Lisa Schwarzbaum, *Entertainment Weekly*, July 20, 2010)

Do you think that the film needs to be viewed a second time to better understand what is happening and if – as Schwarzbaum says – "the emotional payoff deepens enough to warrant the arbitrary complexity of the game"? Why? Why not? Did you, in fact, find a second viewing of the film was a help to you in your understanding of what the director was hoping to accomplish? How well did he succeed?

5. "If *Inception* is a metaphysical puzzle, it's also a metaphorical one: It's hard not to draw connections between Cobb's dream-weaving and Nolan's filmmaking – an activity devoted to constructing a simulacrum of reality, intended to seduce us, mess with our heads and leave a lasting impression. Mission accomplished." (Justin Chang, *Variety*, July 5, 2010)

How might this film be an elaborate metaphor for our digital age of immersive, interactive entertainments, for moviemaking and for movie-going?

6. Before *Inception* opened in theatres, the film critics – who had been given private screenings – were very divided about the film – some hated it, some declared it a masterpiece – and angry defences of each position were offered. Then an amazing thing happened. The movie opened. "For the most part the conversation had shifted away from the criticism of criticism toward other, more relevant matters. What did the last shot mean? Is Cobb still in a dream at the end? Whose dream is it? What's going on? What is odd about these questions, which shrewdly invite a second viewing, is that they seem to come at the end of the argument about *Inception* rather than at the beginning. Film culture on the Internet does not only speed up the story of a movie's absorption into the cultural bloodstream but also reverses the sequence. Maybe my memory is fuzzy, or maybe I'm dreaming, but I think it used to be that 'masterpiece' was the last word, the end of the discussion, rather than the starting

point." (A.O. Scott, *The New York Times*, July 21, 2010)

Does not all of this really put us back to where we should have started in looking at this film? What is the movie all about? What does it mean? What do the various symbols stand for? What are the important plot points? And, perhaps, even one all-important question – what did the final shot mean?

3. The Relationship of the Movie to the Theme of the Exercise

1. Possibly more than even he knows, Cobb is trying to find out who he really is. He is plunged into a voyage of inward discovery much like the one St. Ignatius plans for those involved in the First Week of the Exercises. Does he succeed in this search for meaning?

2. What drives Cobb in this search? What is he really trying to attain?

3. We all live in and out of our dreams – we create our own reality. Why could you say that Cobb's has gone so far down that he creates his own reality as he lives it?

4. What is reality? Who defines it? Would you say that our deep needs create what we see? How does the tension between belief and truth surface in the film?

5. What does Cobb think of himself? Of his wife? Of his children? Does his love for them make possible an understanding of the ending of the movie in a way that is positive for Cobb no matter what happens to the spinning top?

4. The Relationship of the Movie to One's Self in the Exercise

It is the level of subjective response – when the film leaves the screen and enters into your experience – that matters most. The search for the meaning of this film involves, as St. Ignatius tells us, a turning inward.

1. What of Cobb do you see in your own life? How do you respond to that?

2. Cobb is driven – called – to find out how to be with his children. He is changed by that call. How are you changed by your response to God's call?

3. Christopher Nolan made a film about the various levels of consciousness we all have. He wanted that film to inspire wonder, awe, and terror. What does it inspire in you? Why?

(1) Cosmic Disorder

This contemplation asks us to consider how we find ourselves surrounded by the forces of destruction that have been there even before human history began, but it is not God's desire that we remain so trapped.

Then I saw a new heaven and a new earth; for the first heaven and the first earth passed away, and the sea was no more. And I saw the holy city, a new Jerusalem, coming down out of heaven from God, prepared as a bride adorned for her husband; and I heard a loud voice from the throne saying, "Behold, the dwelling of God is with mortals. He will dwell with them and they shall be his people, and God himself will be with them; he will wipe away every tear from their eyes, and death shall be no more, neither shall there be mourning nor crying nor pain no more, for the former things have passed away.

(Revelation 21:1-4)

We should apply memory to the sin of the angels, that is recalling they were created in the state of grace, that they did not want to make use of the freedom God gave them to reverence and obey their Creator and God, and so falling into pride, were changed from grace to hatred of God, and cast out of heaven into hell. (Sp. Ex. #50)

To ask for a sense of how I, and all humanity, am implicated in a disorder larger than ourselves and how I, consciously, or unconsciously, participate in and contribute to that disorder.

St. Irenaeus affirms that creation is not sinful by nature but rather is distorted by sin. Everything God creates is good. That goodness comes because it is connected to God. Only in that relationship with God does creation find itself fulfilled. It is the nature of evil to try to separate creation from God. It does this by suggesting that creation can find its meaning within itself, or within the relationships it tries to establish within itself away from God. At times it may suggest that even God is just another aspect of creation. Evil is whatever denies the mutual intimacy and desire God and creation have for each other. This mutual desire does not make one of these desires absorb the other, so that all becomes God or all becomes creation. Rather, such love lets God be God and lets creation be creation. That mutual love allows the integrity of God and of creation to be maintained.

Mutual love is not possessive. It does not seek to control. Mutual love gives the other the freedom to be, in all of the mysteriousness of what that might mean. In the freedom of loving it, God gives creation the choice of a free response in love. Creation is not compelled to love God in return for being created and loved. That would be servitude.

Creation can discover that, in loving God freely, passionately, and intimately, it comes to a fulfillment that it can never find within itself. Within that freedom, which is God's gift to creation, lies creation's freedom not to love or respond to God. It can choose instead to love the goodness it finds in itself. It may be seduced by that lesser love because of the power of self-determination this offers. When this happens, creation separates itself from God. The passionate and intimate relationship of love is broken on one side. Creation becomes sick and distorted. It experiences itself as fragmented, because it is incomplete within itself. In its separated desire for completeness, it closes in on itself. God is no longer an intimate, the lover to delight in and to delight. God becomes the alien Other. Creation becomes fearful of the Other's approaches, because in creation's present state of selfishness, such overtures of love by God wooing back the lost beloved are seen as threatening and disempowering. Creation becomes frightened by the feelings of vulnerability the invitation to love creates.

That is why it is often only in times of vulnerability – such as sickness, the death of a loved one, the loss of a job, or the change from familiar surroundings – that we experience our creaturehood and the awareness of how much of our life is out of our control. Then we go seeking God – often, at the beginning, with the wrong motives of wanting a return to the familiar. Instead, that search carries us past the illusions of a secure and self-sustained life into the mystery of a passionate relationship with God.

The Spiritual Exercises of St. Ignatius carry us on that path to such spiritual intimacy.

Ignatius sees all of creation intrinsically finding its meaning and fulfillment in responding lovingly and freely to God, who creates in love, with love, and by love. This love makes all free, and in that freedom all have the choice of how to find meaning and fulfillment. The mystery of evil is that we can choose not to love, or not to respond to love. We can set ourselves up as knowing better than God how to be or how to manifest our identity.

In Ignatius's mythology, certain cosmic powers, called angels, were the most radical level of created spirituality to misuse free choice. It is hard to imagine that extremely spiritual beings could opt to be evil, yet even in the human realm we know of very spiritually gifted people who become cult leaders or religious fanatics, or who abuse their gifts for selfish or misconceived ends. The truth is that the closer we are to God spiritually, the greater the freedom we have, and the more available are opportunities of turning away from God. That is why the saints who are closest to God often describe themselves as the greatest sinners. Their sensitivity to freedom is so great that they see how they can turn away from God even in the smallest things. Some angels, in their freedom, behaved in such a way. Their disorder contaminated all of creation, all of our human history, and even our very selves. As we pray for an understanding of this cosmic disorder, we pray to begin to recognize how we are complicit, knowingly and unknowingly. We pray for the grace to experience how we are trapped by sin and evil, and how they affect our relationship with God, and even how we understand God.

Ignatius does not try to understand the mystery of evil and sin. For him, these are existential realities. He knows that it is possible to turn away from love. It is possible to become destructive because of that turning away. Sin entered creation because of that one act, and it is unimaginable to hold in one's awareness the damage that that one act has created. When we are asked to meditate on that one single act and on its consequences, we find ourselves in a state of confusion and horror. This state of confusion is the grace Ignatius asks us to pray for as we allow ourselves to become aware of the depths of that absurdity of the angels and of the implications for every single created being.

Ignatius does not ask us to enter into this meditation to depress us, or to titillate us with some Gothic darkness that excites our fantasies and casts us in the role of victims. Indeed, we are warned against those ways of maintaining our egos. Rather, Ignatius asks us to enter into that dimension of the reality of our lives so we will realize that, in spite of our own vulnerability, we have not been overwhelmed, subjugated, and destroyed by such powers. How is this possible? It's simple: God chooses in a loving freedom to protect and maintain us without taking away from us whatever freedom we still have under these circumstances.

Second, Ignatius wants us to realize that, just as that single act of the dark angels created a world of destruction, any one of our many destructive acts also creates and contributes to that unleashing of chaos and suffering. He asks us to enter into that profound feeling of shame for our own rejection of love, for times when our acts that lack mercy or compassion create a domino effect of pain, hurt, and alienation beyond our control. Each selfish act opens a Pandora's box of evils. And yet, we discover that we are still loved by God and by those who align themselves to goodness.

We must become aware of that love that sustains and forgives and re-creates us, but we can do so only when we realize how strong is the opposition to our living good and creative lives.

What usually happens at the beginning of our spiritual journey now is denial of the dreadful and profound facts of evil and sin and the ways each of us is contaminated and implicated. We are not unaware of evil, destruction, or loss. This awareness is usually what starts our journey. But we are unaware of just how contaminated we are by what we seek to remove ourselves from. This can be as simple as a refusal to believe that what Ignatius proposes we examine prayerfully – the reality of cosmic disorder – is true. Or our awareness can be a little more nuanced, and we can consider this reality from a detached point of view. We can say to ourselves, "Yes, I suppose it is true – if you believe in that sort of thing – but it really has nothing to do with me." We can even go further and think about the mystery of evil as an intellectual problem, considering why the angels did what they did, why God permits evil, and how evil and God can co-exist. Then we substitute theological inquiry for prayer. We may enter into these meditations emotionally and feel overwhelmed by what is presented. Often at this level, incidents from our own past – whether we were the aggressor or the victim – emerge. Then we are trapped once again in sin.

In all of these responses, the ego struggles to maintain itself as the centre of its universe. But Ignatius wants us to realize that in the midst of being dreadfully implicated in cosmic spiritual disorder, we are held by a compassionate God who cherishes us even as we act out of our blindness and disorder. Here the prayer is, as always, an encounter with God, who holds us intimately and compassionately as we struggle to come to terms with our place in an ancient and ever-present realm of cosmic disorder operating even today in all the dimensions of our lives, from the sub-atomic to the galactic. Every aspect of creation is involved and implicated. In that prayer, as we begin to face the awful reality of our situation, we see that this evil has not destroyed the cosmos, and has not annihilated us. We are still here. And we are here at this moment held in prayer – held by a God who passionately enters through the corridors of time and history, through all the dimensions of space, to come to us in this moment holding us, as the lover holding a wounded and bewildered beloved. The wonder of it! Our prayer is to stay in this moment and to accept what unfolds.

Questions for Prayer and Reflection

1. How do you feel when you watch the daily news? How does that feeling contribute to the disorder you see around you? How are you made to feel that what you see is all of reality, or the most significant parts of it?

2. As you contemplate the above reflection, what aspects move you the most? Why? What do they trigger in you?

3. In what ways do you see yourself as a victim of the larger forces around you? How do you respond to that sense of victimhood and entrapment?

4. Within that larger context of disorder, in what ways do you feel truly empowered? Where does that sense of empowerment come from? How does it sustain you?

5. What questions about the nature of God as good or compassionate does the reality of evil raise in your life?

6. In your spiritual life, how do you reconcile a good God with the suffering of the powerless and the innocent?

7. How do you think evil operates? How does it operate in you and on you? What are your areas of vulnerability where you are most susceptible to evil?

8. How are you protected and defended from having that evil destroy you?

9. In your daily life and your life as a whole, how are the forces of life and creativity at work in you and around you?

10. How are you conscious of these forces? What response do you offer to them?

The Movie
BABEL

Director: Alejandro González Iñárritu (2006 – 143 mins.)
Starring: Brad Pitt, Kate Blanchett, Peter Wright, Harriet Walter

1. Synopsis

We are presented with four interlocking stories that interweave the unfortunate circumstances of a Moroccan, an American, a Mexican and a Japanese family all somehow connected by a single gun.

In Morocco, a troubled American couple are trying to resolve their differences. A Moroccan herder buys a rifle for his sons to keep the jackals away from his herd. A girl is struggling to cope with modern life in Tokyo, Japan. Meanwhile, the American couple's Mexican nanny brings their two children with her to her son's wedding in Mexico, but meets up with trouble on the trip back.

2. About the Movie

1. At its core, *Babel* is about the difficulty of human communication, and even though stories unfold in four different countries and in five languages (English, Arabic, Spanish, Japanese, and Sign), language is far from the principal obstacle. This film is more concerned with cultural assumptions and biases that tend to obscure reality, and with how our perceived differences keep us from connecting to each other. Would you agree with this statement? Why? Why not?

2. If you were asked to recommend this movie, would you recommend it because of its ability to cope with issues of global importance while also presenting characters whose individual struggles are no less compelling? Why or why not?

3. "The way the story resolutions are distributed among the various characters may disturb some discerning viewers in their racial/ethnic makeup, and there could be carping in some quarters about a degree of exoticism, despite the fact that Gonzalez Inarritu has gone to great lengths to properly portray all the locations, present everyone in an untouristy way (including the tourists) and cast non-pros recruited locally in many roles, very effectively so." (Todd McCarthy, *Variety*, May 23, 2006) How successful do you think the director and writer were in presenting a "real" view of the various cultures?

4. What sequences or images touched you the most in the film? Why do you think that happened?

5. "Surely, something must hold this world – or, at any rate, this film's vision of the world – together. Whether anything does is the question most likely to fuel the cafe-table arguments *Babel* will surely provoke. The individual scenes are sometimes so powerful, and put together with such care and conviction, that you might leave the

theater feeling dazed, even traumatized. *Babel* is certainly an experience. But is it a meaningful experience?" (A.O. Scott, *The New York Times*, October 27, 2006) This same critic sums up his feeling about the film by writing, "It's a folly, and also, perversely, a wonder." How does this match up with your own opinion of the film?

3. The Relationship of the Movie to the Theme of the Exercise

1. "People today are cut off from each other by race, language, culture, and tradition. Although the mass media and the Internet claim to be uniting us, the separations are more egregious now than ever before. Ideas about who belongs in our communities, coupled with prejudice against outsiders, strangers, and foreigners, make us feel ill-at-ease wherever we are. We cluster in small units of family and community while eschewing religious allegiance to the human family. We emphasize differences rather than celebrate commonalities. The Babel of the Bible is nothing compared to the many forms of Babel in our time. Babel exists wherever people are at each other's throats or stuck in situations that bring out their fear, anger, hatred, or violent behavior." (from www.discerningthetimes.com).

   How does the film reflect what could be seen as a contemporary version of the cosmic disorder that the Exercise mentions?

2. In the film little things trigger off a whole range of consequences that no one in the film could have imagined. What happens when we consider that the little choices we make for the good or for evil have effects beyond our imagining?

3. Love is celebrated in all the world's religions as the most powerful and poignant emotion. How does this film give you access to the many shades of love? Consider how the film shows what happens when love is ignored, squandered, or annihilated by anger, fear, hatred, and violence.

4. The Relationship of the Movie to One's Self in the Exercise

1. What questions does the film raise about the spiritual disorder within your life?

2. What questions does the film raise about the ways in which you handle that spiritual disorder in your life?

3. What do you have to do to change your world for the better? What would that "better" be? How do you know that it is "better"?

4. Can we imagine a power in this world that is greater and more patient and loving than the forces of deception and destruction which seek to diminish or destroy us? What happens when we imagine this? How does it change the way we live?

(2) The Disorder of Adam and Eve/ The Sin of Humanity

This contemplation asks us to see in our own lives the human history
which has produced me as riddled with disorder yet we are not personally destroyed.

God said, "Let us make mortals in our image, after our likeness ...." So God created mortals in his own image, in the image of God he created them; male and female he created them. And God blessed them .... Now the serpent was more subtle than any other wild creature that the Lord God had made.   (Genesis 1:26-31; 3:1)

Recall to memory how on account of [the sin of Adam and Eve] they did penance for so long a time, and the great corruption which came upon the human race that caused so many to be lost in hell.   (Sp. Ex. #51)

To experience how I am trapped in the fallen human condition and how I contribute to it and from this to experience shame and confusion.

There was a time when the concept of original sin did not need any explanation. It proposes that we are born in destructive contexts, and that patterns, habits, tendencies, and dispositions to destructiveness are inbred in us. We know about inherited traits. In our biologies, we have dispositions to certain diseases. We find in ourselves behaviour patterns, such as anger or melancholy, that are part of our family line; or we discover that, like everyone else, we were born into a dysfunctional family. We can reflect on how our family's way of behaving has shaped how we behave. We might even consider the patterns of disorder in our culture that we accept as part of our national character. One may suggest that, in certain cultures, the exaltation of individualism at the expense of the common good is destructive to healthy community. Yet we simultaneously pride ourselves on that rugged individualism. These are all manifestations of original sin.

Original sin is not an abstract theological concept. It describes an existential reality that touches everyone. We are implicated in sin even before we are born. The families we are born into, our parents, the very genes we inherit — all are tainted with a disorder that, in different ways and forms, work against our original goodness. Original sin indicates the very human fact that, because we are all interconnected, the destructiveness of one person affects the lives of all. The destructiveness in the cosmic powers affects the rest of creation. The effects of the destructiveness in historical events generations ago, even centuries ago, are felt even today. Current international and cultural conflicts have their beginnings centuries in the past. We are born into those destructive situations. They affect us. They threaten our vulnerability and we withdraw into self-protective modes of behaviour that stop us from living fully. This, too, is a manifestation of original sin.

43

The term "original sin" came from St. Augustine, who used it to counter the Pelagian heresy that free will alone was sufficient to live a full Christian life and obtain full salvation. This heresy suggests that we do not need the constant help of God to achieve fullness of life. But we know that even having a free will cannot make us free, because the context in which we exercise our freedom is dynamically corrupted and distorting. This reality is as old as humankind. The Genesis story exposes that truth. In the Genesis story, Adam and Eve were tempted and fell when God was absent. Even in Paradise, Adam's and Eve's freedom could not sustain the way of their continual relationship with God.

Ignatius asks us to pray the Genesis myth of our first parents to allow us to see that we are situated in a corrupted universe in which human history is further corrupted. That prayer shows us how we are implicated in the web of evil.

In the protected context of the mythical garden of Eden, humans are created by God. But because of the malice of the sin of the fallen angels, that context is already threatened; it is insecure and unstable. Nevertheless, it is the place where humans still communicate intimately and unselfconsciously with God. Against the simplicity of that relationship comes the temptation of the evil one. It raises doubts in us about God's love for us. It queries the limitations of our creaturehood by suggesting the possibility of an unlimited liberty and creativity. It does not point out the costs and implications of trying to live out of that suggested possibility. It leaves unsaid its rationale — malice — for broaching the subject. Instead, it stirs up the desire for an impossible good to be attained by human effort alone, the performance of one sinful act.

That one sinful act has harmful consequences for the sinners themselves: it damages their relationships with each other and forces them self-consciously to isolate themselves from God. When their broken trust is brought to their attention, they defend themselves by rationalizing it and by blaming others, but they still suffer the consequences of their actions. While the sinners hide from God, God seeks them out and confronts them with the reality of their choices.

Once again Ignatius asks us to reflect prayerfully on this. He asks us to consider how temptation causes mistrust of God, offers an illusory way for immediate gratification, and incites the ego to seek an equality with God. Sin offers the illusion that creatures may take on the role of Creator. We no longer allow God to be God, because we desire to be more than just human. We desire to be like what we imagine God to be – not loving and creative, but omniscient and omnipotent. We desire to displace God and become the centre of the universe. Through this sin of pride, we separate from God and are thrust into a heightened and alienating self-consciousness, now burdened with the humanly impossible task of redeeming ourselves. Out of this presumption comes our restless striving and our despair.

The object of this meditation is to become vividly aware of the human cost of choice, especially such choice that is made without taking into account its implications and consequences. Every human act is significant for all of creation. The enormity of this notion is overwhelming. What are we to do? What is the right thing to do? How do we judge what is right? We find ourselves confused in the face of such implacable questions. It stretches the ego beyond its boundaries and defenses, which normally prevent it from thinking of such things. This meditation works against the ego's illusion of believing that it knows best how to behave, and so does not need God, or that it knows better than God how things should operate. The ego's self-maintained superiority collapses, because it realizes that it does not know all that is going on. When the ego's defenses are broached in this way, there arises in the self a sense of confusion and shame.

Confusion occurs when the tidy systems we live by are discovered to be inadequate; shame arises when we are compelled to enter into the taboo areas of our psyche to discover that we operate very much as Adam and Eve did.

Of importance in this meditation is our growing discovery of the constructions of our ego. We see that we are shaped by our parents — by their genetic makeup, their attitudes and values, their experiences in the world, and their own parents' struggles in raising them. In an almost infinite regress, we discover that our identity has been shaped by the prison of DNA, of family histories, of social and economic class, of cultural and ethnic background, of an intricate weave of multi-layered histories in which we find that our self-identity is not as unfettered as we thought. We discover that our way of relating to ourselves, to others, and even to God has been determined in ways that are closed and broken. As Ignatius puts it, it is "to see in imagination ... my whole composite being as an exile here on earth" (#47). If these reflections now produce a growing sense of entrapment, we are bringing to light the real situation of our lives, devoid of the illusions that seduce us. This may be painful. We can endure that pain only when we realize that we are held by God even as we break out of the cocooned comfort of our deceptions. While we might think and feel we are far from God, God is not at all far from us. Indeed, that loving God is closer than we are to ourselves — that God has been holding us, and saving us from destruction, even when we were blind, even as we sinned.

Questions for Prayer and Reflection

1. How do you see yourself as trapped?

2. What do you do to escape these traps?

3. In what ways can you not escape these traps?

4. How does that make you feel?

5. How can you live with the notion of "no escape"?

6. In what ways do those traps define who you are?

7. In what ways do those traps define how you relate to others?

8. In what ways do your image of religion and of God entrap you?

9. How do you feel when someone says to you in your traps, "God loves you"? Does it feel real? Does the true knowledge of God's love not only come from a real sense of being freed? Have you ever experienced that sense of being freed? That sense of constantly being freed?

10. What does being free feel like for you? How do you experience being free? How does it manifest in your daily life?

The Movie
PARADISE NOW

Director: Hany Abu-Assad (2005 – 90 mins.)
Starring: Lubna Azabal, Kais Nashif

1. Synopsis

Two close friends, Palestinians Said and Khaled, are recruited by Jamal to carry out a suicide mission in Tel Aviv. They are made to look like Israeli settlers on their way to a wedding, then strapped with explosives. On the way to their deadly mission, their operation is compromised and Said goes missing. Khaled goes to find his friend and complete their mission if they can.

Note: If at all possible, watch the subtitled version. Much of an actor's art lies in the use of voice to express emotion, mood, and character. Dubbed movies can never have the full impact of the original.

2. About the Movie

1. In what ways does the film show how people are trapped in personal, family, and cultural stories that are destructive?

2. "Given the explosive political climate in the Middle East, humanizing suicide bombers in a movie risks offending some viewers in the same way that humanizing Hitler does. Demons make more convenient villains than complicated people with their complicated motives. Especially after 9/11, it is easier for some in the United States to imagine a suicide bomber as a 21st-century Manchurian Candidate – a soulless, robotic shell of a person programmed to wreak destruction – than it is to picture a flesh-and-blood human being doing the damage." (Stephen Holden, *The New York Times*, October 20, 2005) How does the film portray Said and Khaled so that they are never less than fully human characters?

3. The film must carry off two tricky balancing acts. One is to give the story a political context without bogging it down in essayistic debate and laborious historical background. The other is to maintain a balanced political perspective given the one-sided views of these all-too-human terrorists. How successfully is this done?

4. Suha, the woman Said meets at his work place, confronts the two men. She articulates the arguments against suicide bombing by speaking not only to the grief of surviving loved ones but also to the political fallout from suicide bombing: the tragic pattern of revenge begetting revenge that will further oppress Palestinians. How does this make her the film's moral and emotional grounding wire?

5. Media literacy tells us that who we are plays an important role in how we look at any media text. What pre-dispositions did you bring to the

watching of this film? How were those pre-dispositions reinforced and/or undercut?

3. The Relationship of the Movie to the Theme of the Exercise

1. It is far too easy to come away from this film thinking that none of this applies to us. After all the notion that we might become a suicide bomber seems totally unrealistic. Yet there are forces that can lead you to make choices in your life without being aware of their implications and complications. What might some of those forces be that can so lead people in the wrong way?

2. It could be said that the film reveals the ways in which our self-identity is shaped by forces larger than ourselves and outside of ourselves. How do various characters in the film respond to those forces? What are the choices possible? What are the implications of each of those?

4. The Relationship of the Movie to One's Self in the Exercise

1. What forces do you see outside of yourself that try to shape your self-identity?

2. Do you feel trapped by these forces and feel that you have no control over what you do? Consider the forces that are at work on Said and Khaled.

3. How do you respond to those forces?

4. These forces can carefully entrap you – piece by piece and step by step – until you find yourself able to justify just about anything. How does this apply to your own situation?

47

(3) The Sin of One

Have mercy on me, O God,
According to your steadfast love;
According to your abundant mercy
Blot out my transgressions.
Wash me thoroughly from my iniquity,
And cleanse me from my sin!
For I know my transgressions,
And my sin is ever before me.
Against you, you only have I sinned,
And done what is evil in your sight.   (Psalm 51:1-4)

Imagine Christ Our Lord present before you upon the cross and begin to speak with him asking how it is that though he is the Creator, He has stooped to become human, and to pass from eternal life to death here in time, that thus he might die for my sins.   (Sp. Ex. #53)

This conversation is made by speaking exactly as one friend speaks to another, or as a servant speaks to a master, now asking for a favour, now blaming himself for some misdeed, now making known his affairs to him, and seeking advice in them.   (Sp. Ex. #54)

To be open to what Christ offers me.

Here Ignatius asks us to consider the personal destructiveness of one deadly sin. In the scriptures, the most common understandings of sin are (1) the intentional rejection of the known will of God, (2) rebellion against God and God's love, and (3) guilt, as the way sin twists and distorts a person's integrity. The example of David's manipulations for Bathsheba (2 Samuel 11:2-28) reveals these three aspects. In committing adultery, David rebelled against God's commandment, placed greater value in his lust than in God's love, and sacrificed his conscience by his abuse of power in taking what he desired. In none of this is God essentially harmed. Those harmed are the sinner, those connected to the sinner, and, ultimately, humanity and all of creation.

The New Testament deepens and transforms these themes, because it depicts a more intimate relationship between us and God, who becomes human to be with us. He becomes mortally vulnerable to the ravages of sin. The blind malice of evil, as manifested by Judas's betrayal, by the conspiracy of the Jewish priesthood in Jerusalem to silence Jesus, and by the Roman bureaucracy in maintaining a status quo, results in the death of Jesus – whose sole mission was to reveal the depth of his Father's love for a creation turned against God.

Ignatius asks us to consider how one radical sin can destroy a person spiritually, just as a single foolish or impassioned or negligent act can destroy a person physically. A tainted needle, a moment of blind anger, an unbuckled seatbelt, and a life is lost. Ignatius asks us further to consider just how many such acts have actually killed real people, and how many times we have committed such acts or worse without having been destroyed.

The point is not to drive us to a position of hyper-attention, as if we can be in total control of all aspects of every situation all the time. That would just submit us further to the tyranny of the ego trying to maintain control. Rather, the point is to admit and feel and experience *not* being in control – that sense of confusion, of vertigo almost – which results when we see that the illusions we build our lives on are without substance. We experience that profound sense of shame as we realize the many times and the many ways we have tried to maintain control at the cost of losing our integrity and our soul. As Jesus asks, "What does it profit us to gain the whole world and to suffer the loss of our own soul?"

The goal of the prayer is our experiencing the amazing and unacknowledged mercy of God as we realize that we have not destroyed ourselves, but have been rescued time and again from self-destruction or from the destruction of others. Often we are not even aware that we are so protected and helped. This does not deny that we have been wounded or have wounded others. But we have not been destroyed, and we have been given the time and the opportunity to return to God. This holds true not only for those who have wounded us, but also for those whom we have wounded. At this place in the Exercises, we can simply rest in the wonder of such a love and allow that love to encounter our intransigence. Our unredeemed selves experience this encounter as shame and confusion; our redeemed selves know a growing sense of wonder and gratitude. Let us aban-don ourselves to that all-encompassing embrace of God. Let us allow ourselves to be loved shamelessly and passionately. What we might feel as shame and confusion is simply transformation into love at those levels of our being that are beyond our control. What we experience as awe and wonder is our coming home to a right relationship with God.

Questions for Prayer and Reflection

1. Do you experience God as forgiving?

2. Do you experience God as creatively building new life out of the ruins of your life?

3. And building a new life out of the ruins of those whose lives you have ruined?

4. Can you bring to mind the situations and moments when you have been destructive? Self-destructive?

5. Why were you not destroyed?

6. How did your destructiveness affect you? How did it affect others? What were the consequences?

7. How do you live with those consequences?

8. Can you allow God to enter into those areas? How does it feel when you let that happen?

The Movie
THE READER

Director: Stephen Daldry (2008 – 124 mins.)
Starring: Ralph Fiennes, Jeanette Hain, David Kross, Kate Winslet

1. Synopsis

The year is 1958. The place is Germany. Michael Berg, a teenager, becomes ill and is helped home by a stranger twice his age whose name is Hanna. After he recovers from scarlet fever, the two begin a passionate but secretive affair. Michael finds out that Hanna loves being read to; their physical relationship grows deeper. When Hanna disappears one day, Michael is heartbroken.

He meets her again in 1966, at the Nazi war crimes trial of six female former S.S. concentration camp guards, including Hanna. He realizes that he has information that could save Hanna from a prison sentence, but knows that she does not want to disclose this information. Michael is torn between his differing views of justice.

2. About the Movie

1. The film is a story about truth and reconciliation. Specifically, the film appears to be about the Holocaust and the generation of Germans who came of age after that catastrophe. How does one generation come to terms with the crimes of another? What do you think the film is really all about?

2. Based on the novel by Bernhard Schlink, the film touches on issues that are monumental – crime, guilt, complicity, conscience. How well are these subjects integrated into the relationship between the woman and the man? How important is it that this couple is the film's subject and that their interaction is its source of drama? What happens when that interaction no longer is there? What prevents the rest of the film from becoming just an intellectual exercise, without suspense or revelation?

3. "In 1995, when the book was first published, the rave reviews for its courage in going there at all were followed by angry letters to the editor accusing Schlink of making a victim out of a former concentration-camp guard. Humanizing someone isn't the same as apologizing for them – the horror of Hitler was precisely that he was human, which implicates us all – but having read the book twice, I can't make up my mind on that one. Which is rather the point, for Schlink's subject is the bewilderment and moral uncertainty of a German generation whose parents maintained a stubborn silence about what they knew and did – or didn't know and didn't do – in the war." (Ella Taylor, *The Village Voice*, December 10, 2008) In what ways does the film version put across these points?

4. Not every critic liked the film. In *The New York Times* (December 10, 2008), Manohla Dargis wrote: " Although the commercial imperatives that drive a movie like this one are understandable – the novel was a best seller – you have to wonder who, exactly, wants or perhaps needs to see another movie about the Holocaust that embalms its horrors with artfully spilled tears and asks us to pity a death-camp guard. You could argue that the film isn't really about the Holocaust, but about the generation that grew up in its shadow, which is what the book insists. But the film is neither about the Holocaust nor about those Germans who grappled with its legacy: it's about making the audience feel good about a historical catastrophe that grows fainter with each new tasteful interpolation." How much are you in agreement with this critic?

3. The Relationship of the Movie to the Theme of the Exercise

1. Here are a list of the "themes" found in the novel that the film is based on:
   The capacity (never the duty) of the victim alone to grant forgiveness.
   The uncertainty of reconciliation.
   The contamination of guilt that comes from loving or merely tolerating the guilty.

   How does the film version portray these themes? How do these themes relate to this Exercise?

2. It could be said that we see this film from Michael's point of view. Do we find ourselves not only drawn to him, but somehow becoming part of him, getting into his head? How does this help us to experience his doubts and anxieties?

3. There might be no doubt that Hanna has committed a serious crime – a serious sin – but could the same be said for Michael? What would his sin be? As Ignatius asks, how many times have you committed such acts? Why then are you not destroyed?

4. The Relationship of the Movie to One's Self in the Exercise

1. We can see in the film just how there is often something seductive about sin that comes from our desires. Yet by giving in to them – as is evident in the movie – we hurt ourselves and others. How is this evident in your own life?

2. Do the anxiety and doubt that Michael feels lead him to sin? How often have you let doubts and anxieties control your life?

3. Does Michael appear to have sacrificed his own conscience by not revealing Hanna's secret thus starting a series of events that ends tragically? What have you been willing to sacrifice in your own sinfulness?

2nd Exercise
Repetition

Create a clean heart in me, O God,
And put a new and right spirit within me.
Cast me not away from your presence,
And take not your holy Spirit from me.
Restore to me the joy of your salvation,
And uphold me with a willing spirit. (Psalm 51:10-12)

I shall reflect upon my self and ask:
"What have I done for Christ?"
"What am I doing for Christ?"
"What ought I to do for Christ?" (Sp. Ex. #53)

To experience my whole being as an exile here on earth
(Sp. Ex. #47) and being offered the path home to the
fullness of life.

Carrying Our Past

Most of us live our lives focused on our immediate needs and problems. If we think beyond these, it is usually in terms of our immediate relationships. We figure, pragmatically, that the past is the past and cannot be changed, and so much of the future is beyond our control that it is no use worrying about it. We see ourselves as tiny, insignificant people caught in a world too large and complex and powerful for us. We consider such a perspective mature; it certainly helps us avoid lots of anxiety and insecurity.

But such an approach to life is not real, not true. It carries with it the barely hidden burdens of repression, blindness, and despair. During moments of quiet reflection, or during a sudden interruption of our daily habits, we are forced to reconsider who we are and what we are doing. These are the cracks that let in the light.

Our lives are shaped by our past. Often we carry that past around with us, as if we were houses haunted by ghosts that refuse to leave. These are the traumatic moments that have stunted our healthy growth and made us cautious, closed off, insecure, pained, and wounded. Unless those moments are brought to light and transformed by love, they fester and pervert us. They can even kill us spiritually. They are the sorts of things that make us think we must look after ourselves. No one else will.

This brokenness renders us immobile in the larger sphere of world action. It is also the nature of the world to create passive citizens who maintain the status quo. We do this by denying our responsibility towards creation. That responsibility goes beyond social justice and ecological wholeness. It goes beyond understanding our evolving creation on a purely natural level. We are not asked to be involved in the social and political and cultural dimensions of our world; we *are* involved. We must become aware of our involvement: that each of us matters, and that any one of us can be an instrument for change – for good or for evil. If we understand that, then we can examine how we, personally, have been involved and complicit with the human world.

Living with Disorder

We also have relationships with the natural world through the ways our innate urges for territory, dominance, survival, food, sex, transcendence, and bonding are caught up in moral systems and behaviours that aim either towards good or away from it. Spiritualizing the natural merely creates ideologies of Romanticism. Rather than finding God through nature, we try to find God in nature. The natural, which includes spiritual forces, finds its fulfillment in the divine. To live in the natural as simply natural is ultimately frustrating and subversive.

Yet often we unconsciously do just this. Most of us would like to believe that, as civilized persons, we have achieved some form of transcendence of the natural. We see then that we are not purely natural – though we are still creatures. That is good. When that transcendence is short-circuited, we fall into more civilized forms of disorder. Then the natural is subjected to other forms of ideology. It is treated as distinct from us and becomes a thing to be used and manipulated. We enter the world of privilege. Technology seeks to dominate or reconfigure the natural. Cosmetics abort the aging process; commercial forms of energy pollute the environment.

We cannot escape this disorder that is woven into the very fabric of our lives. Our personal disorder is part of and contributes towards social disorder, which in turn is part of and contributes to cultural disorder. Cultural disorder is a part of and contributes to the disorder of the human race. The human race is contextualized in the natural and the cosmic. We are all part of creation. We act on it and it acts on us. But we can only find out how this operates if God, who is beyond creation, shows us. This second exercise directs us to ask for and to seek such a revelation.

We usually receive this understanding when we enter into all the dimensions of our lives. This inner journey of self-discovery leads to an outer journey, where we find our place in the universe and in God's love. We must learn these things from our own lives. No one else can teach us. Let us try to enter these places now.

In this prayer period, we explore where we are in our relationships with others, with creation, and with God. We ask for the grace to see how we affect others and are affected by them. At the end of the prayer period, have a conversation with Christ, as the Word through whom the Father creates the universe, about whatever arises from the prayer or your concerns.

Questions for Prayer and Reflection

1. How was this prayer different from the previous three prayer periods?

2. Did anything come together for you in this prayer period – in terms of insight or emotion or your relationship with God?

3. What was the most consoling moment in this prayer? What did it mean for you?

4. What was the most desolate moment in this prayer period? What does that mean for you?

5. What is happening to the ways in which you understand yourself?

6. What is happening to the ways you understand the relationships and moments in those relationships that have come up in your prayer?

7. How do you experience the world in this prayer?

8. Is there any healing you would like to see happen to you now? In your own life? In relationships that have shaped you? In the way you deal with the world and the world deals with you?

The Movie
NO COUNTRY FOR OLD MEN

Director: Ethan Coen, Joel Coen (2007 – 122 mins.)
Starring: Tommy Lee Jones, Javier Bardem, Josh Brolin, Woody Harrelson

1. Synopsis

In 1980 rural Texas, Llewelyn Moss discovers the remains of several drug runners who have killed each other in deal that went wrong. Instead of reporting the discovery to the police, he keeps the $2-million he finds.

A psychopathic killer, Anton Chigurh, murders nearly everyone in his path as he pursues his quarry and the money. Meanwhile, Sheriff Ed Tom Bell tries to face the enormity of the crimes he is working to prevent.

Note: Rated R for strong graphic violence and some language.

2. About the Movie

1. "*No Country for Old Men* offers an embarrassment of riches. Jones, Bardem and Brolin all give award-caliber performances. Roger Deakins again proves himself a poet of light and shadow as director of photography. Carter Burwell's insinuating score finds a way to nail every nuance without underlining a single one of them. Props are also due editor Roderick Jaynes, who no one's ever seen, since he's a pseudonym both Coen brothers hide behind." (Peter Travers, *Rolling Stone*, November 1, 2007) Filmmaking is a cooperative venture. How have the people Travers lists contributed to the success of the film? What about the directors? What role do they play? Are they – as one critic wrote – "the breath of cinematic life and this is their stirring success?" (Lisa Schwarzbaum, *Entertainment Weekly*, November 16, 2007)

2. "Chigurh is less a person than a conceit: an angel of death, stalking the landscape like a plague …. The movie charts no moral shift in Chigurh, or indeed in the men around him; all of them are set in stone from the beginning (Sheriff Bell appears to be made from stone), and we gradually realize that "No Country for Old Men" is not telling a tale – the plot remains open-ended – but reinforcing the legend of a place, like a poem adding to an oral tradition. Texas is presented as a state of being, where good and evil circle doggedly around each other." (Anthony Lane, *The New Yorker*, November 12, 2007) If Chigurh is a meant to be "an angel of death," what do the other characters stand for?

3. In another interview, Javier Bardem, who plays the psychopath Anton Chigurh, said, "This is a story of people trying to use violence to resolve things and realizing it only destroys things. One reason I said I want to do this movie is when they

say 'no country for old men.' I see no 'world' for old men – old men in the sense of values and ethics. That is an important message in a culture of guns." (*Maclean's*, November 19, 2007) Why would Bardem see this as an important message in today's world?

4. "No guts, no glory. That's my standard for giving pride of place to the year's best movies. I'm not looking for formal perfection, just the passion and exhilaration of personal filmmaking that walks the high wire and dares to fall on its ass. For me, no 2007 film experience had more creative juice than *No Country for Old Men*, a transfixing meditation on good and evil." (Peter Travers, *Rolling Stone*, December 27, 2007 – January 10, 2008) What do you think caused Travers to react as he does to this film? The story? The acting? The directing? What does a film have to do to reach the top of your own "best of the year" list?

3. The Relationship of the Movie to the Theme of the Exercise

1. " The movie is a literate meditation on America's bloodlust for the easy fix … Good and evil are tackled with a rigorous fix on the complexity involved. Recent movies about Iraq have pushed hard to show the growing dehumanization infecting our world. *No Country* doesn't have to preach or wave a flag – it carries in its bones the virus of what we've become. The Coens squeeze us without mercy in a vise of tension and suspense, but only to force us to look into an abyss of our own making." (Peter Travers, *Rolling Stone*, November 1, 2007)

The Exercise tells us that cultural disorder is part of and contributes to the disorder of the human race. How is this shown to be true in this film? In these characters?

2. In this Exercise we learn that a sudden interruption in our daily habits helps us to see beyond our immediate relationship. How is this true of Moss and the decision he makes when he finds the money?

3. How do the pasts that Moss, Chigurh, and Bell carry with them impact on the journey they each make in the film? Do they learn anything about themselves – or do they remain as they were? Is there any sign that – as the Exercise says – there are cracks that let light into their lives?

4. The Relationship of the Movie to One's Self in the Exercise

1. Are there any points in the movie where people share secrets with each other? What things in your life to you keep to yourself that you ought to share?

2. God gives each of us gifts – whether it be to be a lawman like Bell or a hunter like Moss. Do they use these gifts? What is the moment in your life when you become aware – perhaps because someone tells you – that you are hiding the gifts that God gave you and that this will leave you wounded?

Destruction

Out of the depths I cry to you, O Lord!
Lord, hear my voice!
Let your ears be attentive
To the voice of my supplications!
If you, O Lord, should mark iniquities,
Lord, who could stand?
But there is forgiveness with you.   (Psalm 130:1-4)

I will conclude with a colloquy, extolling the mercy of God, our Lord, pouring out my thoughts to Him, and giving thanks to Him that up to this very moment He has granted me life.   (Sp. Ex. #61)

This is to ask for what I desire. Here it will be to ask for a growing and intense sorrow and tears for my sins, emerging from a love of God rather than from self-pity.

The third exercise asks to us to examine thoroughly the ways we have been actively or passively involved in, or have contributed to, the destructiveness of sin. Ignatius asks us now to pray for "a growing and intense sorrow and tears for my sins" (#55:2). The thrust of this exercise is to break down the defenses of the ego so that it becomes aware of its limitations and defects in contrast to the goodness, mercy, wisdom, and life-giving creativity and generosity of God. We realize here that we are not God; we are not the centre and the meaning of the universe. God, the centre and meaning, cares for our true selves, and sustains, maintains, and cherishes them. This exercise focuses on the mercy of God as realized by our new and growing understanding of our sinful nature. It aims at developing from our side the relationship with God that we have neglected or displaced.

People falling in love usually share their deepest secrets with the other, almost to test if the beloved could bear to love them in their darkness. In this exercise, we are encouraged to share those secrets: not to debase ourselves but to confirm to ourselves that we are loved to the core of our being, and that we can be held even as we admit those moments when we were unloving, unlovable, and unloved.

Because this exercise is difficult, breaking it up into separate parts is helpful. We will use the path through the Beatitudes in Matthew's gospel to discover our poverty of spirit and God's overwhelming love for us in this state. We will look at the ways we destructively compensate for that poverty of spirit. To experience God's love, we are called to enter into those tragic dimensions of our lives. When we do this prayerfully and patiently, we discover the transforming power of God's love. The Beatitudes, which embody the Christian vision, are a powerful way of opening ourselves to conversion. Most of us live out of our hurts. Praying the Beatitudes transforms those hurts into encounters with God's compassionate mercy. This journey will carry us to experience passionately a love that embraces us into the fullness of life. It is the essence of the First Week of the Exercises. The personal dimensions we encounter here embody the very brokenness of our lives and God's invitation to hold them up to the power of resurrection.

In Matthew's gospel, Jesus Christ is presented as the new Moses leading his people out of slavery through the desert into the promised land. Praying the Beatitudes carries us from the bondage of whatever stops us from being free, with its illusions about freedom, to a life that rejoices in a personal intimacy with God.

To enter the Beatitudes and be carried by them, we must spend time with the first one. This allows us to experience both the degree to which our lives are beyond our control as well as how much we are held and cherished by God. The unfinished business that arises in our prayer from each beatitude carries us in an intensely personal way to the next one. This path leads to an ever-deeper awareness of the presence of God in our lives. Allow enough time to enter into the dynamics of each beatitude. Each is a blessing that reveals its depths only in patience and prayerful reflection. The love that surrounds us will reveal what we need to know and do. This first beatitude describes the human condition and God's gift to us as we truly are.

1. Blessed are the poor in spirit; theirs is the kingdom of God.

Followers of Jesus follow the path of Christ. We realize that our lives are handed over to the mystery we call God, not in some abstract way, but here and now, concretely: not only with who we are, but who we are with, and in the situations within ourselves, within our immediate communities, our families and friends, and within the manifestations of the Church today. To realize this is to realize our poverty.

We have little control over these areas of our lives. Often we prefer to hide from this poverty and from the fact that we are truly broken people. We are broken intellectually, physically, emotionally, spiritu-

ally, communally. Today we are asked to take time to acknowledge the brokenness in our lives – the brokenness that is our life. We put aside, gently but firmly, the illusions we have of being whole, and stop pretending that we are God. Truly we are the emptiness that only God can fill.

Before we can be filled, we must admit our poverty. When we do this, we open ourselves to the path that leads to the kingdom of God. Instead of viewing our poverty as a horror and a burden, we may see it as a door that we need to walk through. We need to be led and carried by our poverty to the wounded places where we are raw, vulnerable, naked. There we contact our own poverty, other people's poverty, and the poverty of the world. Poverty allows us to discover community, which is the kingdom of God in our midst.

Poverty of spirit is the radical awareness of our nothingness and of our dependence on Divine Providence for health, approval, image, identity, friendship, and even life itself. To enter into poverty of spirit is to enter the realm where we are stripped of illusions – even the illusions of our illusions. Poverty of spirit sentences us to death, beyond the awareness of our mortality. When we live out of that poverty, the unexpected happens. We see every moment as a gift, a luxury. Every moment is one of pure wonder. Such poverty cuts a lot of nonsense out of our lives. Because we cannot compromise that poverty, we do not need to defend ourselves or sacrifice ourselves to maintain false images. We can be simple and tolerant in our suffering and the suffering of others.

The discipline of poverty is to remain empty. In that emptiness comes the presence of God as God in the surprising forms of Divine Providence. There the scandal of the cross is transformed into the awe of the resurrection. To live in that emptiness is to change our self-image and our expectations of others. It changes the way we imagine the world. We become so open that the energies of God can flow through us into the world.

Poverty of spirit is liberation from illusion; it is the ground of detachment. Here we can simply and shamelessly be passionate with God, and God is simply and shamelessly passionate with us, even in our bodies. Right here and right now.

Questions for Prayer and Reflection

1. What are your gifts? How do you use them? How are you trapped by them?

2. What are your poverties? How do you hide from them? What happens to you when you enter into those areas?

3. What are the areas in which you do not believe in yourself? What are the areas in which you do not believe in others, or in God?

4. Where do you feel threatened? Where does your body tell you that you are threatened?

5. How are you threatened by God? by your family and friends? by your community? by yourself? by your prayer? How do you experience that threat in your body? (that feeling is the first embrace of God – the fear of God is the beginning of wisdom)

6. What are the areas of vulnerability in your life?

7. What are the areas that can humiliate you?

8. What are the areas in which you are humbled?

9. Poverty takes only what is needed from this world, nothing more. Can you distinguish between what you want and what you need? To know what that is requires discipline, spirit, and wisdom. Can you pray for that grace – generally, and in specific instances?

10. With what aspects of your own poverty of spirit do you feel called to spend some more time? How will you do that? Can you sit in the presence of God and allow God to encounter your own poverty of spirit? What happens when you do that?

Scripture passages for prayer

Matthew 5:3
Psalm 136:34
Isaiah 41:17-20; 55:1—56:9
Luke 1:5-38
Phillipians 2:1-11
Revelation 3:14-22

When we enter our poverty of spirit, we discover that there are aspects of our lives that trap us and stop us from living joyfully, simply, and compassionately. We need to be liberated from these. The second beatitude offers us the next step in that liberation.

2. Blessed are those who mourn, for they shall be comforted.

To mourn is to acknowledge death and the call to a life beyond death. Mourning is the movement to resurrection, where we are saved, not by anything we have done or can do – not even by our hope – but by the generosity of God. In mourning, we let go of our dead into the shaping spirit of the One who forms us all. Mourning is our responsibility to the dead. In mourning them, we are present to them and allow God to reach through us to touch them. Mourning reminds us that we, living and dead, are still being created. That process of creation is a constant transformation. When we hold onto the dead, or allow the dead to hold onto us, we stop that work of transformation and creation. We reject God's gift of creativity in our lives and in our world.

To mourn, then, we must first acknowledge the presence and effect of the dead in our lives. To only remember the dead as they were is to create a tomb; it equates this life with all that they are. But that is not all they are. They are now embraced by a love that transforms them as they accept it. If we fail to believe this, and so often we do, then we fear to mourn, and we hold on to a rotting corpse. We seek ways to pretend that what is dead is alive. The only way this is possible is to become dead ourselves. We become trapped by a past that gives no life. So imprisoned, we deny life to ourselves and to those around us. By pretending that the dead are alive, we repress death and enter into a false freedom where the dead possess us unconsciously because we have not released them into the power of resurrection. Then they shape the path we walk. Our fear of abandonment, our desire for the security we once knew, is a form of despair that, in reality, death is the end. We can be so blinded that we cannot see the corruption and the stink we carry. Yet it manifests itself in our cynicism, our despair, our rigidity, our self-righteousness. Then we do not bring life to others, but rather take it away. The basis of this is fear. Such a fear denies that God is stronger than death and more compassionate and life-giving than we are.

We must first look at the ways we are trapped by fear. This can only be done in the context of a love that holds us securely. Our prayer at this time offers us that love. Then, we can become conscious of the ways the dead influence our perceptions, our ways of thinking and acting. We can fight against this awareness or we can welcome it. In so doing, we begin to realize how our traditions – personal, family, cultural, religious – affect us. Tradition is the handing on of life and of spirit. Some aspects of our tradition free us; other aspects do not. We are asked always to choose life and to hand on life. We are asked to hand over to resurrection what traps us in death. Then we will see death as part of life, rather than living life as part of death. When we acknowledge the presence of the dead and their effect on our lives, we become aware of the work we must do in our desire for liberation. We note that we ourselves cannot transform death into life. Resurrection is always a gift from God. But we can dispose ourselves for resurrection by accepting the love that raised Christ from the dead. That love did not resuscitate the dead Christ, but transformed the dead Christ into a new creation. This same love does not bring our dead back to life, but transforms our dead into a new life. Our work is to bring the dead to that transforming love.

We offer the dead our mutual path to the resurrection, where the fullness of life is possible only when all of creation comes together as one in joy and in the shared gratitude of being redeemed into a common life. For to mourn is to enter into community; the comfort offered to those who mourn is the growing realization that the very act of mourning is also the act in which resurrection happens. Mourning creates joy. Mourning transforms grief into hope. In grieving we become aware of loss and of the fragility of the "world" in which we live and find our meaning. We admit our inability to maintain that world. And in grieving, we live with the fragments of that world and with the empty spaces between those fragments that nothing can fill. Grief kills. Mourning brings life. When we mourn we bring all our grief to God. There we abide in the lived consolation of being companions together in this dreadful adventure, and wait in prayer for the tombs to open and the new life we call resurrection to occur.

Questions for Prayer and Reflection

1. What are the dead of your life? What are the things you despair over, believe are unchangeable in your life, in the life of families, in the larger communities? How do these things relate to your poverty of spirit?

2. What are the dangers you encounter in your mourning? For example, how do you distinguish between mourning and being critical? Can you distinguish between "coming back from the dead" and "resurrection"?

3. How does your grieving alienate you from others? What happens when your identity becomes fixated in grief or nostalgia?

4. Who, or what, have you found personally helpful in your process of mourning?

5. Do you have any instances of resurrection in your life? How were you surprised? How have you shared the resurrection you have received?

6. What things, places, works, and/or people in your life would you like to experience resurrection? What ways have you tried, or do you try, to promote resurrection to these? Here is another way of asking that question: How do you comfort others?

7. What is the difference between solitude and loneliness?

8. Can you experience solitude without being lonely? How is this possible?

9. What illusions has your personal encounter with death removed from your life? What illusions has that encounter provoked?

10. Heidegger says we are beings thrown towards death. How do you live in this radical contingency that questions every aspect of your life?

11. Our relationship with Christ does not allow us to evade death. We must all die. How do you experience that relationship with Christ in the face of death? How do you experience your relationship with the Father in the face of death?

Scripture passages for prayer

John 11:1-45
Luke 7:11-17
Matthew 9:1-7
Matthew 17:1-13
Luke 4:14-30
Luke 23:50—24:11
John 20:11-18

When we mourn, we discover a certain liberation. This manifests itself in a loss of fear, a certain flexibilty in our attitudes, the ability to delight in what is given as gift without clinging to it. But we also discover those elements in our lives that refuse to let us be free. They do violence to us, and we are tempted to do violence back to them in our struggle to be free. Because we are not always conscious of them, they also incite us to be violent in our relationships with other people. The third beatitude addresses this issue of violence, because, as Christ has pointed out, "The kingdom of heaven is overtaken by violence; the violent bear it away" (Matthew 11:12). Violence destroys the community love seeks to create.

3. Blessed are the gentle; they shall inherit the earth.

We are all vulnerable. If we were to meditate on our vulnerability, we would discover in ourselves opposing tensions as we live out of our vulnerability. Such vulnerability can breed fear when we internalize the forces that threaten us. Fear creates alienation when we understand the "other" to be inimical to our well-being, and alienation manifests itself in violence as we try to defend that space in which we find our identity. Then "the kingdom of heaven is taken by violence and the violent destroy it" (Matthew 11:12).

But there is another approach to being vulnerable. Vulnerability opens us to the dimensions of Divine Providence in our lives when we realize, in examining our very histories, that we are not destroyed, but instead are saved in spite of ourselves. The awareness of our lives being held in God's care moves us to gratitude, especially when we grasp how easily we can be destroyed. This spirit of gratitude manifests itself in the gentleness with which we deal with ourselves, others, and the world. We do not have to be violent to maintain ourselves. God's power comes "to save all the meek of the earth" (Psalm 76:10).

To be gentle is, first of all, to face not only our vulnerability, but also the horror, the abject nakedness, and the blind misery that masquerade as the powers of this world, without becoming paralyzed or trapped by fear – our own or others'. To be gentle calls us to be attentive (as opposed to blind) to the forces that comprise our world; to be discerning, insightful, political, and flexible in dealing with these forces; and to be responsible – rather than reactive – for the transformation of the oppressor and the oppressed. To be gentle calls us to dance in the flames, and in the ashes, and in the hard places of this life. The witness of this gentleness lies neither in our devotion to an ideology of social justice nor in withdrawal from the arenas of social effect. It lies in the manifest joy of knowing with our own body the presence of the powers of good that are holding, protecting, affirming, and guiding us along the path that is salvation.

This joy allows us to see, in the cracks and the terrors of this world, the promise of paradise. It invites us to co-operate with the powers of good by being present, humbly and gratefully, at precisely those places, so that through our simple presence, the mystery we call God can enter the world.

Questions for Prayer and Reflection

1. What are the areas of violence in your life [individually, communally]?

2. In what ways does your lifestyle create violence to your integrity, to your family, to the larger community?

3. How do you feed your violence, communicate your violence – in your silence, apathy, speech, narcissism, and in the practice of your daily life?

4. What difficulties do you have in reconciling your notions of gentleness with your idea of what it means to inherit the earth?

5. What possibilities of transformation open up when you do not assert your self-righteousness?

6. What comes to you when you pray for the grace to be gentle?

7. How can you affirm others in being a person for/with others in the context of your limited resources?

8. Moses was called "the meekest of men" (Numbers 12:3). How does this give you some indication of what meekness is? Can meekness then be seen as a disposability to the will of God, as opposed to pride, which makes you the centre of meaning and creation?

9. How is gentleness different from apathy, conformity, weakness, powerlessness, cowardice, passivity, victimhood?

10. How do the meek attract the heart and open it? What in you cries out to be opened now?

Scripture passages for prayer

Matthew 27:15-23
Matthew 11:25-30
Matthew 7:7-12
Isaiah 29:13-21
Isaiah 61:1-4
Psalms 37; 75; 131; 138

It is always shocking to discover the violence that is in us, and the violence that is around us. In fact, we have become so accustomed to violence that we might consider it a normal part of living, and characteristic of being human. But when we discover how much of our lives are caught up in violence from which there seems to be no escape, we feel helpless and overwhelmed. We cry out for a different reality. We cry out for conversion. Those who hunger and thirst for such a transformed world, and who place themselves on the path to such a life, enter into the work of the fourth beatitude.

4. Blessed are those who hunger and thirst for justice; they shall be satisfied.

The practice of freedom lies in the midst of evil, not beyond it. If our choices enslave anyone, we are not free. The freedom that liberates is generated through God's saving activity and our abiding intimacy in that relationship, which God's constant creativity establishes and maintains here and now, even in the midst of suffering caused by the aggressions of narcissism. God's love for us sets us free. When we are rooted in that love, we may strive for the justice that liberates all. True justice comes only from justification. As we accept that everyone is loved – even when we sin – we approach what it means to be justified. Otherwise, our understanding of justice remains fallen, defined in terms of recompense, and of contract and social norms. Then our commitment to justice on whatever level – personal, communal, social, or cultural – is maintained within the boundaries of self-knowledge and self-interest. This is the position of the Pharisees and the Zealots. It is the position of those who destroy others, and even themselves, to maintain what they think is right.

Such a position denies the depths of what it means to be human. First, it denies the pervasiveness of sin in our lives, so that we are blind to our blindness. Second, below the manifestations of that sin, it denies the constant hunger we *are* for God. Moreover, it manipulates people's hunger for God into accepting cult and ritual through guilt and repression. But we are not saved by the word of the law, whether religious or secular. We are saved only by the Giver of the spirit that finds some inadequate expression in the law. Our hunger is not satisfied by the law, but in a relationship with the living Word under whose Cross we find our life. To hunger and thirst for salvation is to commit to that life, not only for ourselves, but for all. It is to experience the agony of the passion as we struggle with all of our energies so that the fullness of life may be tangibly present to all in the sacrament of daily life.

On the Cross, Christ is at his most creative. In this act, he overcomes those powers that, in their blindness, self-service, and malice, attempt to prevent life from being given to all who desire it. When we hunger and thirst for God, we hunger and thirst for a set of relationships for everyone in which the only criterion is mutual love. In John, Jesus prays to the Father for his companions, "that they may be one even as we are one, I in them and thou in me, that they may become perfectly one" (17:22-23).

The justice we embody is the witness of the justification we experience. How we treat ourselves and others manifests not only what we love, but *how* we love. That love is where we put our lives. Ignatius says that "love ought to manifest itself in deeds rather than in words"; he continues, "the lover gives and shares with the beloved what he possesses" (#230:1, 231:2). When we hunger and thirst for justice we live our poverty in a way that allows the mercy of God to be manifest through us. We experience that desire even in our bodies, for our bodies are how we are in this world. We incarnate our desire with our bodies. Our desire is for the community of love that includes all without exception. That desire is met and embraced by God's desire to create that community of love. That passion the Father has for the world makes us also his living words in the circumstances in which we find (and lose) ourselves.

We desire to be saved, because we cannot save ourselves. When we follow the path of that desire, we allow God to come to us, and through us, into the world. The joy and gratitude we experience when that happens embolden us to continue God's mission in the world, because we discover we are all one.

Questions for Prayer and Reflection

1. Can you accept that you are loved? What stops you from accepting this?

2. What areas in your life are silenced, not believed, oppressed, marginalized, colonized? How are they to be loved into life?

3. What are you passionate about?

4. What is the connection between the way you see social justice and the way you experience God?

5. How do you inflict alienation on others? Do others experience you as an open door to the mystery we call God?

6. In what ways do you need to be more joyful?

7. What subverts your creativity into anger or apathy?

8. What excites your creativity? What affirms your creativity in the present situation? In what ways can you commit yourself to your creativity?

9. What happens when you allow yourself to be passionate for God, and allow God to be passionate with you?

10. What happens when you ask for this in prayer?

Scripture passages for prayer

Psalm 130
Matthew 5:20-28
Luke 18:1-14
Romans 8:1-39
Romans 12:9-21
Exodus 3:1-18

When we experience the gift of being loved, we start to see how destructive violence is. We realize that love loved us even when we were unloving, even when we were violent in our inability to love. This is the experience of mercy. It renders us merciful to those we encounter who have not yet experienced this gift. We give what we have received. In that giving, we enter deeper into the kingdom by making it more available to all.

5. Blessed are the merciful, for they shall obtain mercy.

Mercy is absurd. It is neither prudent nor politic. It has no aims, expects no rewards, and is not self-congratulatory. It strives to love its enemies, expecting nothing in return. In this it imitates God, who is "kind to the ungrateful and the selfish" (Luke 6:36). The merciful are always aware that God is good to us even as we sin, and so they come to realize that God's justice is his mercy, his constancy of help, and his patience, which manifests itself in the gift of time. That mercy is not pity, which sees the suffering of the other and is only interiorly moved by it. Human mercy, like divine mercy, goes out of itself to transform the suffering of the sinner. Human mercy flows as an act of gratitude at having experienced divine mercy. That gratitude covenants God and man. That spirit of gratitude does not abet sin, but strives to bring those trapped in sin to the truth of their lives – the acceptance of the fact that they are loved, and that, in the circumstances of their lives, they can be loving.

The merciful are not judgmental. They know what it is to be trapped, what it is to be freed from those traps, and how easily, but for the constant support of God, they may be trapped again. Their personal history makes them attentive to the broken ones of the world, whether rich or poor, powerful or weak, shamed or shameless. It gives them the lived experience from which they can distinguish between "want" and "need," and allows them to respond to the need in people's lives. They realize the interconnectedness of all life, and the desire of all to be rooted in that interconnectedness. They realize that everything concerns them and evokes their compassion.

Yet we cannot do everything; the attempt to do everything denies us mercy. We can do only what we have been gifted to do. Our gifts are at the service of those we meet on our daily path. We are to be as open doors through which the world's needs meet God. In every encounter, that need is manifest, because no one is fully saved until all are fully saved. The preferential option for the poor recognizes the poverty in everyone and addresses it as Jesus did in his gospel life, scandalizing the self-righteous, who were blind to their own needs, and thus blind to the needs of others (Matthew 25:34-40).

We can never be as merciful as we would wish, but we can be merciful as we are, with the little we have. In sharing that poverty, we discover what it means to be human. For the hard heart that cannot be hurt cannot love, either. To be merciful is to take the risk that one will be taken advantage of and be made a fool. Indeed, this is often the case if we are concerned with self. But if we give what we have been given, this is never the case. It is easy to abuse God's gifts. Human history is the history of such abuse. Yet God does not stop giving; our history is also one of salvation. Mercy is rooted in the absurdity of love – of being loved and of being offered the opportunity to love. It is expressed as gratitude for that felt knowledge.

Questions for Prayer and Reflection

1. Have you ever received mercy? Have you ever offered mercy? What was the experience like – then, and now as you reflect on it?

2. What are you truly grateful for? What do you accept as your right? What is the difference? What do you reject out of that sense of your rights?

3. What gifts can you offer others now?

4. What gifts can you offer your community? What do you do if your gifts are not accepted by the community?

5. How do you deal with rejection?

6. What can you risk to create community? What do you risk to create community?

7. Have you ever been trapped? How did you become free of that trap?

8. How do you direct your energies towards the life given you, rather than in building your defences against that inevitable last breath?

9. What are the things that stop you from being merciful? Is it the fear of being used, of seeming weak; is it simple blindness; is it your preoccupation with your own needs?

10. How does your understanding of righteousness in your daily life stop you from being merciful?

11. How do we distinguish between mercy and pity? Why is mercy the expression of our common, naked vulnerability?

12. At this moment, where do you need mercy? Can you ask for it? At this moment, where can you show mercy? Can you give it? Is it to yourself?

13. What moves you as you stay with this prayer?

Scripture passages for prayer

Psalms 22 and 23; 86; 88 and 118
Luke 6:27-38
Luke 18:9-14

John 8:2-11
Luke 23:32-46

We are never fully converted, and will never be until every aspect of creation is fully united to God, because every aspect of creation, including ourselves, is interconnected. But we are on our way, and along our way, through our acts of mercy, we offer to all the gift of living in God. When we live this way we are turned towards God. Then we desire God and we desire to find God in all things and all persons, and in all the circumstances of our lives. To live this way is to be pure of heart. Jesus, in the sixth beatitude, assures us that as we live our lives this way, as we walk this path, we shall embrace God, our beloved.

6. Blessed are the pure in heart, for they shall see God.

Our deepest desire is from God. Our deepest desire seeks God in all things. That desire directs our spiritual path. In the course of living our lives, we discover that we are shaped by many desires, and we seek discernment: which desires lead to the building up of the kingdom of God and which do not? The manifestations of our deepest desire move us to be companions of Christ. Those other desires are energies, or patterns of energy, that have somehow become detached from our deepest desire and lead a separate existence. They can be identified by that separation. Consolation occurs when our desires harmonize with the energies of the Spirit; joy occurs when our energies harmonize with those of those around us; happiness occurs when those energies surrounding us harmonize with ours; pleasure occurs when those energies submit to us. The range between consolation to desolation is from community to narcissism.

To be pure in heart is to be on the path to integration where all the energies of our life — spiritual, social, communal, personal, emotional, intellectual, sexual — are woven together by our deepest desire. That deepest desire carries us beyond our present sense of self into truer and more intimate modes of being with others. The focus of that path is on relationship rather than ritual, on prophecy rather than professionalism. The integrity of the weave of those energies makes no distinction between private and public, between self and other. To be pure in heart is to realize the unity of all that exists and to value all that exists. This unity includes the energies that comprise the self, and this unity manifests singleness of purpose. As we move on the path of purity of heart, we discover a singleness of purpose that makes us flexible to the Spirit. That union of spirit — the passion for community — carries us to those places where displaced and separated energies come to light. Then we endure the exorcisms of encountering a love that reweaves those straying energies into a simpler and more integrated life

The trials of living this way embody the struggle between narcissism and community. As we walk the path and struggle for that more total integration, we discover that nothing human is foreign to us. Such self-awareness makes us humble; in that humility, we become more and more disposed to the dance of the energies, more open to the darkness in which God dwells, where we see first not with the eyes, but with the heart.

What the heart sees is that everything that exists is holy. To be pure in heart is to enter into the struggle of creation, in which everything is involved. It is to realize that call to holiness in all the circumstances of life. Evil is fragmented holiness; the task of the pure in heart is the careful gathering up of those fragments into unity — the unknotting of the tangled energies that hold us in the bondage of compulsion and oppression. The pure of heart, by the simple act of being present, heal the afflicted, bind up the brokenhearted, give sight to the blind, set free the enslaved, and announce to the world the presence of God among us, so that they can freely enter into the play and the delight of the life where God dwells.

Questions for Prayer and Reflection

1. What are the current divisions in your personal life? in the life of your community?

2. How do those divisions affect you? What are you concretely doing about them?

3. What are the difficulties you encounter as you strive to witness to the integrity of God?

4. Can you discern between passion and compulsion? Between indifference and apathy? Between pilgrimage and forced marches?

5. Where are the freedoms in your life? How do those freedoms come together? What aspects of your life are in pilgrimage (as opposed to bondage and its forced marches)? Where do you celebrate? How? With whom?

6. What is the witness of your life? Who witnesses God to you?

7. Purity of heart only opens the doors of perception. Purity of heart does not create what is perceived. What is given to the pure of heart is a gift. It sees what has always been there waiting to be celebrated. What has been given to you in your own vision quest?

8. Have you ever had an experience that you considered a personal revelation? How has it shaped your life?

9. Can you talk about the stages of your spiritual journey that led to an encounter with the divine?

10. Can you talk about the stages of your spiritual journey following that encounter with the divine?

Scripture passages for prayer

Genesis 22:1-19
Psalm 116
Romans 8:1-39
Matthew 4:1-11
Mark 5:1-20
Revelation 19:9-11

As the pure of heart walk towards God, they gather up the broken, the disaffected, the alienated, and the fearful, along with the rich, the powerful, the gifted, the lucky, in an open community of common affection, mutual sharing, and respect. It is the work of the peacemaker to help create and maintain such communities. They are the kingdom of God on earth.

7. Blessed are the peacemakers; they shall be called the children of God.

Hatred destroys not only the other but also us. In maintaining hate we sacrifice ourselves to the lie that the enemy deserves to die. This war, breeding more war, "is only a cowardly escape from the problems of peace" (Thomas Mann). The only way to overcome an enemy is to make the enemy a friend. The problem of peace is *how* to make an enemy a friend. To make peace is to move beyond apathy or tolerance. To make peace is to create community. Community is created when we live in such a way that the energies of all are allowed positive expression. It is a question of imagination. Because we live in imagined worlds, what we imagine as real defines how we relate with others. When we indulge ourselves to imagine the world, instead of allowing ourselves to live as God imagines us, we follow the path of fantasy. In his poem "The Stare's Nest by My Window," Yeats observed of those fighting against each other in Ireland's civil war,

We had fed the heart on fantasies,
The heart's grown brutal from the fare ....

Before we can create community, we need to ask what fantasies shape our lives, and, further, what forces in our lives maintain those fantasies. If we see only through the filter of our hurts – rather than the call to creativity that gives us our vision – we project onto those we hate what has hurt us and what we deny in our own lives. We know these fantasies exist because they trap us and we experience feelings of hate.

We become peacemakers only as we make peace with ourselves, only as we acknowledge the hurt in our life, through a healing of memories and sensibilities within the vision that gives our life meaning. That vision emerges when we accept that we are all held in the compassionate mercy of God, and that no one is outside of that mercy. This meaning becomes real in our lives, not in terms of satisfaction, but through the modes of consolation. In consolation we are redefined, not according to fantasy, but through an immediate openness to God. That state "without any previous cause" moves us beyond our boundaries to a new awareness of reality in which what we consider impossible is possible. In this openness, the enemy can become the friend. This openness does not manipulate the other into becoming a friend. The other is always free to choose. Even self-sacrificing love – radical openness – does not make the other free. But it is the most we can do. We can love our enemy without indulging our enemy's destructiveness, and hope for the best. This is our calling as human beings. We love each other, or we die.

Christ, the peacemaker, comes to show us how to reconcile ourselves to God, to each other, to ourselves, and to all the forces of creation. Reconciling the estranged is Christ's mission. He does it by showing that we all have a common source, the Father, and that we are all one in that same Father. We, Christ's companions, inherit that same mission from God, according to today's beatitude. Community can be built only if persons share a common vision in which everyone maintains a common good. That common good is manifested differently according to different gifts, but underlying these differences is the same spirit and a common vocation. The dynamics of integration required to be a person of peace are also necessary to be a community. Prayer, dialogue, openness, intimacy, and celebration create life. The path of the peacemaker leads to the broken and hard places of our own life, community, and world. It takes up the Standard and Cross of Christ, our brother. We stand in those places, simply and humbly, as open doors, in our poverty of spirit. As open doors, we allow the mercy of God to enter the world, and allow the pain of the world to pass through us to be held by that transforming love of God.

Scripture passages for prayer

John 14:15—15:17
Galatians 5:13—6:2
Ephisians 2:8-22, 4:1-16
Romans 5:1-11
Daniel 10:15-19
Isaiah 11:1-11

Questions for Prayer and Reflection

1. Who is your community – the ones you share your life with? Why do you think so? How did you come to those relationships?

2. How do you find your community? Does it support your integrity? Are you inspired by the community, the society, the culture you live in?

3. What ideals of community life do you hold that alienate you from the people you live with?

4. Do you know the estranged parts of your life? Do you know the integrated parts of your life? Do you live out of alienation or integration with yourself, with your community? How do you realize, individually and collectively, your call to be a peacemaker where you find yourself now?

5. Who is not your community? Why do you say that? How do you treat those others?

6. What boundaries do you impose upon the way you imagine yourself? Are those boundaries open or closed?

7. How do you experience yourself, and others, as mystery? With whom are you intimate?

8. How are you intimate with yourself – in terms of self-awareness, self-knowledge, being comfortable with yourself, loving yourself into transcendence?

9. How are you intimate with others?

10. How are you intimate with God, so that God can be fully present through you in the world?

11. What difficulties do you have with intimacy? What stops you from trusting? What concrete elements stop you from risking – moving beyond trust into the darkness? What forms of fear, of

established positions, of power, of disillusionment possess you?

12. Where do you find life? Where do you give life? Where do you take life?

13. To whom, and with whom, and for whom do you feel responsible even with your very life?

14. Can you distinguish between peace-lovers, peacekeepers, and peacemakers? Where do you find yourself as members of a common humanity? of a common culture? of a common church? as an individual?

15. What do you do to bring about the kingdom of God in your daily life?

16. How is this beatitude a manifestation of the gospel reality of the passion of Christ?

17. How does your prayer on this beatitude reveal to you your own divided heart, the ways in which you are invited to do good, and the ways in which you succumb to evil?

18. In your conversations with God at the end of your prayer, what manifested itself to you?

Scripture passages for prayer

John 17:6-26
1 John 1:5—2:17
1 Corinthians 12:1-14
Genesis 22:1-14
Genesis 32:24-31
Song of Songs 3:1-5; 8:6-7
Revelation 21:1-8
John 14:15—15:17
Galatians 5:13—6:2
Ephesians 2:8-22, 4:1-16
Romans 5:1-11
Daniel 10:15-19
Isaiah 11:1-11

To be a peacemaker is to enter the dark and dangerous places of life where there is conflict, violence, separation, and distrust, and to allow ourselves to be an instrument of God's mercy there. It is to be a prophet. The hope and life offered by peace run counter to the powers of evil that seek destruction and despair. These turn against the peacemaker in violence. Because evil is not creative, the pattern of its destructiveness is the same throughout the ages. The lives of prophets witness their intimacy with a power greater than evil. They have found this intimacy by walking the path of the Beatitudes. They have found a love they offer to the world.

8. Blessed are those who are persecuted for righteousness' sake.

When our hearts are filled with longing for the kingdom, that longing shapes everything we do. We hold values different from the world's, trust what the world neither sees nor believes in, and then, because we are judged as "other," we become the objects of derision or fear or hatred. A Hasidic tale tells of a house where there was a wedding festival. The musicians sat in a corner and played their instruments, the guests danced to the music and were merry, and the house was filled with joy. But a deaf man passed outside of the house; he looked in through the window and saw the people whirling about the room, leaping, and waving their arms. "See how they fling themselves about!" he cried. "It is a house filled with madmen!" For he could not hear the music to which they danced.

To be possessed of the desire only for God is to be judged crazy or eccentric, as was Francis of Assisi when he stripped naked in the public square of his father's town. It is to be accounted dangerous by the moral guardians of society, as when the Inquisition imprisoned Ignatius of Loyola, who asserted that God could be found in this world. This hunger for God makes us fools for Christ's sake, and lets us share in the passion the Father has for his Son and in the passion the Son has for the Father. That passion to say yes to life, to make the leap of faith in every moment of life, and to return to the marketplace bearing gifts is the Spirit.

The path of the Beatitudes always returns us filled with the Spirit to a world needing to be transformed. We leave that world because it does not satisfy our needs; in that journey, we discover the dead we carry with us and experience the humility of the powerless who have been saved. The zeal our transformation engenders is tempered into a mercy that makes us one with God in compassion for the world. Living compassionately in this world, we manifest the prophetic presence as living words of God, companions of Jesus. In each stage of the path, there are trials to be endured. Each stage brings a death and a resurrection. Then, like Paul, "We rejoice in our hope of sharing the glory of God. More than that we rejoice in our suffering, knowing that suffering produces endurance and endurance produces character, and character produces hope, and hope does not disappoint us, because God's love has been poured into our hearts through the Holy Spirit that has been given to us" (Romans 5:3-5).

Through the Beatitudes, our devotion becomes the sacrifice making the world holy, and unites us in the embrace of God. In living that embrace, we live not for ourselves or through ourselves. When we fully commit ourselves to life, the lives we lead are Revelation for others. Then, Christ lives in us and through us.

You are the salt of the earth; but if salt has lost its taste, how shall it be restored? It is no longer good for anything except to be thrown out and trodden under foot. You are the light of the world. A city set on a hill cannot be hid. Nor does anyone light a lamp and put it under a bushel, but on a stand, and it gives light to all in the house. Let your light shine before all, that they may see your good works and give glory to your Father who is in heaven.

(Matthew 5:13-16)

Our desire is that all may have life and have it to the fullest. In that desire for fullness of life, every death is embraced so that it becomes the door to a deeper and fuller life. This life is a gift always offered to everyone.

Questions for Prayer and Reflection

1. How are you to live here and now?

2. What do you need to live that life?

3. Which beatitude gives you the greatest consolation? Which beatitude challenges you the most? What does this tell you about your path and about your shadow?

4. How do the people you admire live the Beatitudes? How do you live the Beatitudes?

5. What is the concrete relationship between the Beatitudes and your daily life, the way you see yourself and others, the ways you share life and make decisions?

6. Where are you now?

7. What work needs to be done to continue your experience of being loved into life by God?

Scripture passages for prayer

Psalm 42 and 24
John 21
John 1:13-23

Luke 21:1-4
Acts 2:1-28
Mark 3:13-35

Oscar Wilde, in his essay "The Soul of Man Under Socialism," says, "A map of the world that does not include Utopia is not worth even glancing at, for it leaves out the one country at which Humanity is always landing."

Every true map of the world contains utopia. We set off looking for it, and when we arrive, we find that that it is not what we desire. And so we set off again. We are driven by desire. Do we know what we desire? How do we satisfy our desire?

Do we think that the kingdom of God is just a utopia? If we cannot satisfy our desire, can we allow God to do so? How can we do that?

Questions about the Beatitudes

1. Journeying through the Beatitudes carries us out of one story into another. We move from one set of desires to another. What are the elements of the old story (call it Act I) that you experience in your life?

2. What do you imagine the new story to be like?

3. Why do you not know the new story as yet?

4. What happens when you project (call it Act II) the dynamics of the old story onto the new story?

5. What has to be given to you to start the new story?

6. What elements of that new story have already been given to you? What do you desire now, having gone through the Beatitudes?

7. What desires you?

Question about The Path Through the Beatitudes

The eight Beatitudes are listed below, along with some statements you've been given about them.

A. *The poor in spirit:*

"We are broken intellectually, emotionally, spiritually, communally."

"Poverty of spirit is liberation from illusion."

B. *Those who mourn:*

"Acknowledge the presence of the dead in our lives."

"Become conscious of the ways the dead influence our thinking and acting."

"To mourn is to enter into community."

C. *The gentle:*

"Face our own vulnerability and also the powers of this world without becoming paralyzed or trapped by fear – our own or others.'"

"To be gentle calls us to be attentive and to be responsible for the transformation of the oppressor and the oppressed."

D. *Those who hunger and thirst for justice:*

"Commit to life, not only for ourselves, but for all."

"How we treat ourselves and others manifests not only what we love, but how we love."

E. *The merciful:*

"Mercy strives to love its enemies, expecting nothing in return."

"To be merciful is to take the risk that we will be taken advantage of."

F. *The pure in heart:*

"Our deepest desire is from God and moves us to be companions of Christ."

"The pure of heart, by the simple act of being present, heal the afflicted."

G. *The peacemakers:*

"To make peace is to create community."

"The path of the peacemaker leads to the broken and hard places of our own life, community and world."

H. *The persecuted:*

"When our hearts are filled with longing for the kingdom, that longing shapes everything we do. We hold values different from the world's."

"That passion to say yes to life and to return to the marketplace bearing gifts is the Spirit."

The Path

When we enter our poverty of spirit prayerfully, we move towards liberation. In that movement we discover the traps that stop us from experiencing gratitude at being embraced by God. So we pray to be liberated from those traps, the deaths that take away our joy. As we pray to mourn, we discover more freedom. That freedom allows us to admit that there are still areas in our life where the dead have taken over and we are possessed by violence. We pray to have that violence transformed into creativity, and discover the creativity that seeks conversion of heart. When we discover our lack of conversion in so many areas, we cry out to God for mercy. Knowing what it is to be a sinner, we judge no one else. In fact, we then work to bring ourselves and all to that simple path where we acknowledge that not only we, but all, are loved and lovable. This purity of heart makes us peacemakers, makes us willing to enter into the struggle for a world where all can live their identities as "the beloved." Such a struggle is not without its sufferings, but we accept those sufferings in union with Christ and with all who do good, because that creativity is the expression of our identity. It witnesses to the meaning of our lives. It allows us to restore, and re-story, the world as imagined by God.

The path through the Beatitudes makes us co-creators of the community that extends through all time and all space, and incorporates everyone and everything. Here all are loved and can share love freely and simply and joyfully. To walk this path is to open and live the gift of intimacy with a God who desires us.

The Movie
MAGNOLIA

Director: Paul Thomas Anderson (1999 – 188 mins.)
Starring: Jason Robards, Julianne Moore, Tom Cruise, William H. Macy, Philip Seymour Hoffman

1. Synopsis

On one random day in the San Fernando Valley, a dying father, a young wife, a male caregiver, a famous lost son, a police officer in love, a boy genius, an ex-boy genius, a game show host, and an estranged daughter will each become part of a dazzling multiplicity of plots, but one story.

Through a collusion of coincidence, chance, human action, shared media, past history, and divine intervention, they will weave and warp through each other's lives on a day that builds to an unforgettable climax. Some will seek forgiveness, others escape. Some will mend frayed bonds, others will be exposed.

2. About the Movie

1. "This imposing tapestry about the mysterious workings of fate and coincidence and the need for interconnection and love interweaves the story of a dozen characters as they embark on a moral odyssey during one intense day." (Emanuel Levy, *Variety*, December 13-19, 1999)

The soundtrack music plays an important role in developing this tapestry, becoming almost another character. What do the opening song and the images that go with it tell you about each of the characters?

2. Each character has a parallel or an opposite. For example, child genius Stanley is juxtaposed with Donnie Smith. Here is a list of the major characters. Which do you think is the parallel or the opposite of each?

Earl Partridge (Jason Robards) – dying of cancer.

Linda Partidge (Julianne Moore) – falling in love with a man she married for money.

Frank Mackey (Tom Cruise) – self-styled television guru who has to face his dying father.

Stanley Spector (Jeremy Blackman)– a child genius turned quiz show star who needs his father's love.

Rick Spector (Michael Bowen) – a failed actor who lives off his son's brilliance.

Donnie Smith (William H. Macy) – 1960s quiz show star who dreams of love.

Jimmy Gator (Philip Baker Hall) – quiz show host and icon of family values whose illness causes him to reveal a painful secret.

Rose Gator (Melinda Dillon) – Jimmy's wife who had to face the consequences of her husband's confession.

Claudia Wilson Gator (Melora Walters) – living on cocaine and wanting to tell the truth to someone.

Officer Jim Kurring (John C. Reilly) – a bumbling LAPD officer whose faith gives him hope.

Phil Parma (Philip Seymour Hoffman) – a home-care nurse, Phil is a caregiver who struggles to maintain his professionalism.

3. There are two sequences that viewers refer to with a degree of puzzlement:

1) The Frog Scene: Throughout the movie, signs appear that refer specifically to the plague of frogs described in Exodus 8:2. Here the ferocious and surreal rain of frogs is a device that serves to bring lonely characters together.

2) In a type of climax, just before each character acts for the last time, they all – one by one (including two who are comatose) – join in singing "Wise Up," with songwriter Aimee Mann. The director thought that such a moment flowed naturally from all that had gone before, and that many people –when they are lonely or sad – sing along with a song on the radio.

Which of these two scenes was the more difficult for you to accept? Why do you think the director uses such devices? Do they convey his theme successfully?

4. "Anderson does not know that he was making a movie about the absence of grace. He sets the stage for two ministers of grace – a melancholy Christian policeman and a compassionate male nurse – and a spectacular act of God." (Steve Lansingh, *Christianity Today*, July 24, 1999)

Forgiveness is at the heart of *Magnolia* – but it is a forgiveness that gives life. LAPD Officer Jim Kurring is the embodiment of this – the Common Man if you want. At the end of the film he states, "Sometimes people need a little help, sometimes people need to be forgiven, and sometimes people need to go to jail. The hard part is to forgive." We as Christians are expected to extend forgiveness to ourselves and to all.

a. How effective are the two "ministers of grace" – one explicitly religious, one implicitly – in their role?

b. What tasks do they set themselves?

c. Of which Beatitudes are they examples?

d. Not knowing anything about the background of the director (who was 28 when he made this movie), why do you think there seems to be such a good match between the Beatitudes and the characters of the film?

3. The Relationship of the Movie to the Theme of the Exercise

1. You have been told: "In this third exercise we are encouraged to share those secrets not so as to debase ourselves but actually to confirm to ourselves that we are loved to the core of our being, and that we can be held even as we admit those moments when we were unloving, unlovable, and unloved at that time."

Describe the scene in the film that best demonstrates this point. How do I do this in my own life and in the lives of those with whom I come in contact?

2. The eight Beatitudes – the keys to the second Exercise – are listed below together with some statements you've been given about them. Which characters are either examples of the particular Beatitude or are still caught in the sin that prevents them from reaching a particular Beatitude?

A. *The poor in spirit:*

"We are broken intellectually, emotionally, spiritually, communally."

"Poverty of spirit is liberation from illusion."

B. *The gentle:*

"Face one's own vulnerability and also the powers of this world, without freezing or being trapped by fear – our own or others."

"To be gentle calls one to be attentive and to be responsible for the transformation of the oppressor and the oppressed."

C. *Those who mourn:*

"Acknowledge the presence of the dead in our lives."

"Become conscious of the ways the dead influence our thinking and acting."

"To mourn is to enter into community."

D. *Those who hunger and thirst for justice:*

"Commit ourselves to life not only for ourselves but for all."

"How we treat ourselves and others manifests not only what we love but how we love."

E. *The merciful:*

"Mercy strives to love its enemies, expecting nothing in return."

"To be merciful is to take the risk that one will be taken advantage of."

F. *The pure in heart:*

"Our deepest desire is from God and is to be a companion of Christ."

"The pure of heart by the simple act of being present heal the afflicted."

G. *The peacemakers:*

"To make peace is to create community."

"The path of the peacemaker leads to the broken and hard places of one's own life, community, and world."

H. *The persecuted:*

"When our hearts are so filled with longing for the kingdom, that longing shapes everything we do, and we hold different values from the world."

"That passion to say yes to life that makes us return to the marketplace bearing gifts is the Spirit."

3. One of the songs in the movie says, "It's not going to stop till you wise up./It's not going to stop so why not give up?" Which of the characters "wise up," and which "give up"? Does giving up have to be fatalistic? Can giving up be a conscious, life-affirming recognition of the fact that we don't have everything under control nor do we need to do so?

4. The Relationship of the Movie to One's Self in the Exercise

1. Go back to the exercise above where you looked at the individual Beatitudes and how the characters in the movies related to them. Now, using the same format, look at the ways in which you have undergone experiences similar to those of the characters regarding the Beatitudes, and consider how they have affected your life.

2. Asking for and granting forgiveness in modern life is a very risky business, but *Magnolia* shows us just how beautiful it can be to do this. The path of the Beatitudes returns always to a world to be transformed.

What needs to be sacrificed/transformed in your life – right here, right now – before you can embrace God?

4th Exercise
Repetition

O Lord, you have searched me and known me,
You know when I sit down and when I rise up;
You discern my thoughts from afar.
You search out my path and my lying down,
And are acquainted with all my ways. (Psalm 139:1-3)

This exercise will consist in repeating the previous Exercises. In doing this we should pay attention to and dwell upon those points in which we have experienced greater consolation or desolation or greater spiritual appreciation. (Sp. Ex. #62)

A deep knowledge of my sins and a feeling of abhorrence for them; an understanding of the disorder of my actions, that filled with horror of them, I may amend my life and put it in order; a knowledge of the world, that filled with horror I may put away from me all that is worldly and vain. (Sp. Ex. #62)

The Three Goals of Repetition

Ignatius, as you will soon discover, uses repetitions of previous prayer materials to reinforce a point, or to achieve depth, or even to move the retreatant to a different place by exhausting his or her sense of curiosity. This allows the deeper elements of the prayer exercise to emerge.

This exercise asks you to repeat the most significant points you have discovered in the previous exercises. You need to examine what you have found in yourself, and what you need to do with what you have found. This is not an issue of mere technique. It is one of intimacy. Sin makes us avoid intimacy. There is a way of becoming disciplined so that we can enter into intimacy and maintain it. It is intimacy that transforms us.

The easiest way to do this is to ask what has been the most significant moment in the previous exercises, and to stay with it in prayer. If there were several significant moments, you will need to spend prayer time with each one before moving on.

The second way is to ask what has brought you closer to God (note that this does not necessarily mean what has been pleasant) in each prayer period so far, and what has taken you away from God (e.g., distractions, boredom, agitation, daydreaming, pleasant or otherwise). Going back to those moments brings us to intimacy. In the first instance, we go where the intimacy invites us to deeper intimacy. In the second instance, we return to the place where intimacy needs to happen because that experience has triggered a flight from intimacy.

Let us consider the movement of the Exercises so far. We might think of them as opening up with a wide-angle shot from a camera that slowly zooms in. It opens with cosmic disaster, the sin of the angels. Then there is the middle shot, the sin endemic to the human race. Next is the tightly focused shot, where one human sin is explored. In this exercise, the sin of just one human – you – is exposed. But this foreground shot can be seen only in the light of the background of God's passionate love for all of creation, for all of humanity, and for each of us person-

76

ally. We can become truly aware of this disorder only if we are given a perspective from which to comprehend it. That perspective comes from the growing realization of the love that works to sustain creation and us as we struggle for identity, meaning, and satisfaction. Repetition aims at bringing to our consciousness this dual awareness of our sinfulness and of how we are loved. The gift of love allows us to examine our very selves with increasing close-ups, without collapsing back into that very self that is disordered. Love makes us aware that we are more than just that disordered self. Love makes us desire to shun the habits and patterns of that disordered self and of the disordered world that feeds it. And so this repetition aims for three things.

First Goal

First, it aims to give us a deep experience of our own disorders, seen from the new perspective of intimacy with God. We do not have to re-enact or re-engage in them, but we do feel abhorrence for them. Sin traumatizes us by defining us in an obsessive-compulsive way, and by desensitizing us from the horror of what we have done. We need to re-enter those moments of trauma – this time from the context of being held in God's love – and walk through each trauma with God or Jesus as our companion. The love we now experience will make us aware of the destructive nature of what we have done, and give us a sense of horror at its effects.

Second Goal

Second, this exercise aims to help us understand those disorders – how they arise, what triggers them, how we manifest them. Filled with a horror at them, we might amend our life and allow it to be renovated by God's love. It is one thing to re-experience those moments and patterns of sin from a self-conscious perspective of being loved by God, even as we sinned, and to recall those sins. The deeper level is that of integration. That level seeks to understand the reasons why we sinned, and the patterns underlying our actions.

Third Goal

Third, this exercise aims to give a true knowledge of the nature of the world and how, filled with horror at it, we put away from ourselves all that tends to destructive worldliness. Here we look at the ways of the world that seduce us into sinning, or trap us in sin. At this level, we ask for the grace to find out how that world operates and how we are rendered complicit in its activities.

Breaking the Cycle

These three goals ask us to look at our actual experience, at our inclinations and habits that dispose us to sin, and at the disordered contexts in which we live. We don't do this to save ourselves. We cannot, nor can we save anyone else. What we can do is pray for the grace to have a firm purpose of amendment. We pray to find ourselves so caught up in love that we can resist our inclinations to live out of any lesser desire than the desire for God. That purpose resolves itself in a hatred for what we have done, a desire to discover why we have done it so as to avoid repeating it, and a resolution not to do it again. Even if we have been sinned against, we seek to end that cycle of sin and destruction and to ask God's grace in doing this. We hold it up to be redeemed, and to transform what is destructive into what gives life. We also must understand the nature of the world that drives us to such a condition, and find out how it makes us complicit in its activities. These are the graces we pray for as we consider, at a deeper level, not our sinfulness in itself, but how we can co-operate with the merciful love of God in re-creating the world and the relationships we have damaged. This is the first step in responding lovingly to the love that we have discovered.

Ignatius does something interesting in this exercise of repetition. He encourages us to call upon those forces of love that have rejected the sin of the cosmos and the sins of humanity to intercede for us. In the spirit of humility, we first ask Mary, the Mother of God; then Jesus Christ, the Messiah; and finally, the source of life itself, the Father. Our alignment with the forces of God and the good occurs when we seek their help to obtain the graces we pray for in this exercise.

Questions for Prayer and Reflection

1. What were the significant moments of the previous prayer periods for you?

2. Can you divide these moments into consolations and desolations?

3. What happened in these prayer periods when you prayed over each of those moments?

4. Did you find you were receiving the three graces you asked for?

5. What are the sins of your life? How does sin operate in your life? How does the corruption in the world affect you?

6. What happens when you discuss the answers of these three questions with Mary, with Jesus, and with the Father?

The Movie
THE SOCIAL NETWORK

Director: David Fincher – (2010 – 120 mins.)
Starring: Jesse Eisenberg, Andrew Garfield, Justin Timberlake

1. Synopsis

It is the fall of 2003. Harvard student and computer programming genius Mark Zuckerberg starts working on a new idea that soon becomes a global social network and a revolution in communication. Six years later, Zuckerberg is the youngest billionaire in history, but his triumph results in both personal and legal complications. Drawn from multiple sources, the film moves from Harvard to Palo Alto, capturing the thrilling early days of a culture-changing phenomenon and how this experience divided the young people who started it all.

2. About the Movie

1. "It has the staccato wit of a drawing-room comedy, the fatal flaw of a tragic romance and the buzzy immediacy of a front-page headline, all powered by a kinetic engine typically found in an action flick. And that's just the opening scene, a pre-credit sequence that neatly sets the tone and the theme for everything that follows." (Rick Groen, *The Globe and Mail*, October 1, 2010)

How does this opening scene set the tone for the rest of the film? What is the theme that this opening scene presents? Would it have something to do with the fatal flaw in Zuckerberg's character that we first see in this opening scene?

2. "The conspicuous paradox that *The Social Network* plays with is that the world's most popular social networking Web site was created by a man with excruciatingly, almost pathologically poor, people skills. The benign view of Facebook is that it creates "a community," a sense of intimacy, which is of course one reason it also creeps out some of its critics…. In *The Social Network*, a character lashes out at both Mark and 'the angry' who haunt the Internet, but Mr. Lanier takes the view that it's fear that drives the idolizers of what he calls the 'new strain of gadget fetishism.'" (Manohla Dargis, *The New York Times*, September 23, 2010)

What is your view of the notion that Facebook creates community? How does the film create the paradox that Dargis refers to? What scenes from the film reinforce this notion?

3. "There have been complaints from early screenings that no one is very likable in this movie. You'll get no argument here but that's beside the point. 'Mark Zuckerberg' is thoroughly unlikable but he is an original. Ask yourself: How many truly original characters show up in American movies?" (Kirk Honeycutt, *The Hollywood Reporter*, September 21, 2010)

How would you answer Honeycutt's question? How many "truly original" characters can you name in American films? Why are there so few such characters?

4. "From the first scene to the last, *The Social Network* hints at a psychological shift produced by the Information Age, a new impersonality that affects almost everyone. After all, Facebook, like Zuckerberg, is a paradox: a Web site that celebrates the aura of intimacy while providing the relief of distance, substituting bodiless sharing and the thrills of self-created celebrityhood for close encounters of the first kind." (David Denby, *The New Yorker*, October 4, 2010)

Karl Marx suggested that, in the capitalist age, we began to treat one another as commodities. How does *The Social Network* suggest that we now treat one another as packets of information?

5. "Is *The Social Network* one of the fall season's best big movies? Without question. It's also the subject of one of those feverish social-media marketing campaigns that makes major pop-culture spectacles, sight unseen, carry all kinds of irrelevant Zeitgeisty baggage. I guess the Marxist word for this would be 'reification,' where movies are seen as metaphysical projections of the collective unconscious instead of internally conflicted products that blend art and commerce, while new masterpieces emerge every few weeks (and are then abandoned) and debate is preempted by a Rotten Tomatoes rating. (At this moment, for this movie, still 100 – and I assume I've done nothing to change that.) Still, the question remains: Did Mark Zuckerberg create this world, or just figure out how to cash in on it?" (Andrew O'Hehir, Salon.com, September 23, 2010)

Do you follow either the Marxist view of movies, or the other view that Hehir presents, or some other view entirely different from those two? Does knowing – or not knowing – what Rotten Tomatoes is make any difference to your view?

3. The Relationship of the Movie to the Theme of the Exercise

1. *The Social Network* has as its protagonist a character drawn in a Shakespearean mode, a high-achieving individual who carries within him the seeds of his own destruction. Zuckerman gains the whole world but loses his most meaningful asset because of a fatal flaw on view in the very first scene. How is that flaw – that disorder – revealed in the first scene of the film?

2. We are asked "to have a deep experience of our own disorders." You might say that this Exercise is a series of close-ups; *The Social Network* offers us a close-up look at Mark Zuckerberg. What are the disorders in Zuckerberg's life? Does he see these disorders and does he manage to overcome them?

4. The Relationship of the Movie to One's Self in the Exercise

1. We are asked to "understand these disorders – how they arise, what triggers them." Does Zuckerberg ever come to the point of understanding his disorders? What do you think triggers them in him? Is it as simple as his not being "popular"? What triggers the disorders in your own life?

2. Why did you/did you not create your own Facebook page? What role does Facebook play in your own life? Do you believe that Facebook can bring disorder into your life? How do you deal with this?

5th Exercise
Repetition

"You shall love the Lord your God with all your heart, and with all your soul, and with all your mind. This is the great and first commandment. And the second is like it, You shall love your neighbour as yourself."

(Matthew 22:37-39)

We are created to praise, reverence, and serve God our Lord, and by this means to save our souls. The other things on the face of the earth are created for us to help us attain the end for which we are created."

(Sp. Ex. #23)

To see, know and love ourselves the way God sees, knows and loves us and to see, know and love all others the way God sees, knows, and loves all.

Being Named

Ignatius asks us in this prayer period to repeat the third exercise. This repetition carries us further into self-disclosure. Maybe we need to pray to be disposed for that gift of self-recognition. Such naming does not involve applying a label to ourselves, nor does it mean accepting the labels others apply to us. Rather, self-recognition reaches up from the depths of our being as it encounters a love that has been searching for it since the beginning of time. We need to sit in that profoundly contemplative space and allow that connection to be made. Where this naming happens, it is often beyond words or images. It simply resonates with a felt intimacy. Deeper than the original sin that traps us is the original grace in which we were created. More profound than the social sin that takes away our freedom is the gift of the Spirit, which is not blocked by such disorder. More creative than the power of death that destroys our bodies is the glory of the resurrection which is God's constant gift to us. We come from God and we return to God. The desire that names us is the desire for life. If we sit with our sin in prayer, we discover the life that is our life. Buddhism asks this question: What is your face before you were born? At this level of Christian prayer, we discover the answer. The experience of life is our true nature. That life is experienced as the simple, profound, and all-encompassing relationship we share with God.

We can abandon ourselves to that awe we experience when we are fully and truly known. This is the naming on the level of experience. We find ourselves as the beloved whom God desires and calls.

We find ourselves being called "loved sinners." This is the naming on the level of concept. This echoes the Easter Vigil liturgy, which sees the sin of humanity, rendered archetypically in Adam and Eve, as "O happy fault," because it brings into our lives the human embodiment of God in the form of Jesus Christ.

We can find our naming in the response we now offer to the love that has found us. This can be manifest in an attitude of humility and gratitude towards this awesome mystery, whose sole desire is that we come to life and its fullness. Humility emerges from the profound awareness of our limitations, blindness, and destructive actions. Gratitude comes from that profound awareness that we are always held and loved into being.

We may also find our naming in what we do. The life that names us also defines us by what we do. The choices we make define our identity. As the famous prayer of Fr. Pedro Arrupe, a recent Father General of the Jesuits, puts it,

Nothing is more practical than finding God,
that is, than falling in love
in a quite absolute, final way.
What you are in love with,
what seizes your imagination,
will affect everything.
It will decide what will get you
out of bed in the morning,
what you will do with your evenings,
how to spend your weekends,
what you read,
who you know,
what breaks your heart,
and what amazes you with joy and gratitude.
Fall in love; stay in love,
and it will decide everything.

(attributed to Pedro Arrupe, former Father General of the Society of Jesus)

Finally, we can live love, in all of its mysterious complexity and simplicity. We let love name us and guide us in the very depths of our being. Of particular use here is the eight-fold noble path of the Buddha. Centuries before Jesus, the Buddha, following his enlightenment, devoted his life to promoting his insights into living correctly. We adapt the Buddha's insights here for a Christian context, because those insights represent eight interrelated approaches that create a wholesome spiritual path. To live an integrated life, one must have the following: right view; right thinking; right mindfulness; right speech; right action; right effort; right concentration; and right livelihood. We examine these here to clarify those aspects of our lives that are out of sync with who we are called to be. That clarity will inform our prayers to experience God's compassionate mercy.

The Eight Practices of Wisdom

• *Right view* reminds us that we are rooted in God's love: that we are all lovable and capable of loving, no matter what situation we find ourselves in. St. Paul puts it this way: "Nothing, neither death, nor life, nor angels, nor principalities, nor things present, nor things to come, nor powers, nor height, nor depth, nor anything else in all creation, will be able to separate us from the love of God in Christ Jesus our Lord" (Romans 8:38-9).

• *Right thinking* refers to the process of reflection that arises from the experience of God's love for us, as opposed to those negative tapes of conditioning that debilitate us and alienate others. Right thinking does not ignore the real presence of evil, but knows — as Julian of Norwich knew — that "all shall be well and all manners of things shall be well." It knows that good overcomes evil and transforms it. It knows that fundamentally we are aligned to good. It knows that forms of evil, because they have separated themselves from the creativity of God, are basically deceptive.

• *Right mindfulness* is being attentive to the truth, and so discerns truth from illusion. It seeks to find God in all situations and to live in the love the Christ has for the Father. In practising right mindfulness, we have the same focus and desire as the Christ, and live fully in the gift of this presence.

• *Right speech* speaks the truth lovingly. Truth without love is a lie; and love without truth is sentimentality.

• *Right action* manifests itself in a reverence for life through generosity, responsible gestures (a gesture is an act of homage to God performed in this world), and the way we place our body as incarnate spirit. We practise right action conscious that we are the beloved of God.

• *Right effort* examines how we spend our energy. We can achieve correct effects by incorrect means. To live out of the right effort is to use correct means. As evil seeks to ensnare us ever more tightly in the webs of narcissism, right effort struggles against those ego-limitations to embrace ever more comprehensive and life-giving relationships within our communities.

• *Right concentration* is a spiritual calm that acknowledges both what passes and what abides at the same time. It is the Ignatian "indifference" that values everything as a response to God's love.

• *Right livelihood* is having an occupation that fosters our vocation to be a witness to that love.

Along with these practices is *right community*. We are not isolated individuals, but need the support of others who share our vision. The above eight practices of wisdom allow for the creation of community, which is not a given – like an address or a selection of cronies – but allows unity in diversity.

We can make a fundamental option to live in this way, but how that will be concretely and existentially realized in our daily life will emerge in the path of intimacy we are walking. At the moment it is enough to acknowledge, joyfully and gratefully, that we have let ourselves be found by God. We can relish the delight in being found. This is the first stage of intimacy.

Questions for Prayer and Reflection

1. Where has your prayer led you?

2. Using each element of the eight-fold noble path, examine your life to see where you stand; where you are called to grow; where you are invited to be disciplined; where you need – because you may still be trapped – God's help and mercy.

3. What has been the consolation of this set of prayer periods? What does that tell you?

4. What were the desolations? What does that tell you?

The Movie
THE HURT LOCKER

Director: Kathryn Bigelow (2009 – 131 mins.)
Starring: Jeremy Renner, Anthony Mackie, Guy Pearce, David Morse

1. Synopsis

Disarming bombs amid combat in Iraq is a very dangerous job. When a new sergeant, James, takes over an elite bomb disposal team he sends his two subordinates, Sanborn and Eldridge, into a deadly game of urban combat. The city falls into chaos and James' true character is unveiled.

Note: Rated R for violence and language.

2. About the Movie

1. This film "is the best nondocumentary American feature made yet about the war in Iraq. This may sound like faint praise and also like a commercial death sentence, since movies about that war have not exactly galvanized audiences or risen to the level of art. The squad of well-meaning topical dramas that trudged across the screens in the fall of 2007 were at once hysterical and noncommittal, registering an anxious, high-minded ambivalence that was neither illuminating nor especially entertaining. And the public, perhaps sufficiently enervated and confused by reality, was not eager to see it recreated on screen." (A.O. Scott, *The New Yorker*, June 26, 2009)

    Though the film won an impressive number of awards – at the Academy Awards it won six Oscars including best picture and best director (Kathryn Bigelow, the first woman to win this award) and was on every critics' Best Films of 2009 – it was not a box office success. Budgeted at $15 million – most Hollywood film budgets start at around $90 million – *The Hurt Locker* brought in less than $49 million worldwide. Why do you think more people did not go to see it? Do people really not want to see the reality of Iraq re-created on screen?

2. It has been said that you leave the film shaken, exhilarated, and drained, but you will also be thinking. What did you feel after seeing the film? And what were you thinking about?

3. "*The Hurt Locker* focuses on three men whose contrasting temperaments knit this episodic exploration of peril and bravery into a coherent and satisfying story. The wild card is Staff Sgt. William James who joins Delta after its leader is killed and who approaches his work more like a jazz musician or an abstract expressionist painter than like a sober technician. A smoker and a heavy metal fan with an irreverent, profane sense of humor and a relaxed sense of military discipline, he approaches each new bomb or skirmish not with dread but with a kind of inspired, improvisational zeal …. to quote a Robert Frost poem, James is a man whose work is play for mortal stakes." (A.O. Scott, *The New Yorker*, June

26, 2009) How would you define the character of the other two men – Sgt. Sanborn and Staff Sgt. James – and what do they contribute to this diverse trio?

4. "Free of liberal hand-wringing and quasi-political subtext, *The Hurt Locker* is an adrenaline-drenched war thriller which, like *Point Break*, *Near Dark* and *Blue Steel*, uses a conventional genre format to explore and expose issues of violence, compulsion and masculinity. Alternatively, you can just ignore all that, sit back and enjoy a perfectly paced two-hour thrill-fest." (Keith Stuart, *Filmstar Magazine*, August, 24, 2009) Is the film free of any "liberal hand-wringing and quasi-political subtext"? Or does it have something significant to say about war? How does the film use the genre of the war film to explore "violence, compulsion and masculinity"?

5. The film's "immediate concerns are more concrete – the intricacies of the dismantling process, studied up close; the second-by-second choices that must be made in the explosive environment of terrorist turf. Yet those concerns are dramatized so astutely, and balanced so adroitly – the tone is neither militarist nor pacifist – that *The Hurt Locker* takes on the dimensions of a meditation on war and human nature." (Joe Morgenstern, *The Wall Street Journal*, June 25, 2009) What is the end result of such a "meditation" as presented in this film?

3. The Relationship of the Movie to the Theme of the Exercise

1. The film opens with a quote from Chris Hedges, a former war correspondent for *The New York Times*, declaring that "war is a drug." Do you think this is true? What does he mean? For whom is the war a drug? Does the film portray the men who fight in this war as being "drug" addicts? Is it this "drug" that prevents these men from accepting the gift of self-recognition?

2. The Exercise speaks of a "right community." The bomb disposal team constitutes a real community. Which of the eight practices of wisdom quoted in the Exercise are found in this community? Go through the eight practices and consider how different this community would be if even some of the "right" was in place.

3. In this Exercise we find some five ways of "naming." Which of these five ways applies best to the member of the team whom you believe comes closest to "self-recognition"?

4. The Relationship of the Movie to One's Self in the Exercise

Repetition – review – in this Exercise calls on you to look at what has gone before. Think back, for example, to the way that small acts can have huge effects.

1. When have your small acts gone on to have huge effects, in your own life or in the lives of the people around you?

2. What small act in this film has serious consequences? At what point in your own life have you gone after something that led you away from God, thinking that it was just a small thing, simple and close to the truth?

Hell

Whatever overcomes a person enslaves that person.
(2 Peter 2:19)

I shall also thank God for this, that up to this very moment He has shown Himself so loving and merciful to me. (Sp. Ex. #71)

"I should ask for what I desire. Here it will be to beg for a deep sense of the pain which the lost suffer, that if because of my faults I forget the love of the eternal Lord, at least the fear of these punishments will keep me from falling into sin." (Sp. Ex. #65)

Understanding Mysteries

This is a meditation on hell. We are asked to enter as fully as possible, imaginatively, into the realm of hell from our present perspective on life, and to use our senses to become aware of the pain that the lost suffer. From medieval times to today, popular preaching uses graphic depictions of hell as a motivation for upright behaviour. Ignatius is no different. He notes that "if because of my faults I forget the love of God, at least the fear of the pains of Hell will keep me from falling into sin." The question is this: How can a loving God allow hell to exist? The following question is similar: How can a God of love allow evil to exist and allow the effects of evil to attack the innocent? These are big questions. They raise the very real issues of our image of God, our understanding of love, and, even more radically, the limitations of our understanding to comprehend these mysteries.

Before we can enter into this meditation, we need to examine the ways we experience hell on earth. Wars and famine abound. Oppression and the brutality of self-righteous power are rife. People torture each other and treat others with disregard and prejudice. Some people find their food in garbage dumps. People experience despair, self-pity, and meaninglessness. Anger, malice, confusion, abuse, and neglect are rampant. Some practise idolatry by expecting the world to be God and by sacrificing themselves to that world. We do not have to conjure up some Gothic scenario to know this. It is part of our world, our culture, our lives, and, if we dare acknowledge it, even our own hearts.

This exercise attempts to bring to light those areas in our own lives, in our own hearts, in our predispositions that prefer to accept the disorder of a fallen world and its implications rather than accept and live out of the mercy of God. Inasmuch as we live in this world, and we accept this world as it is, we not only live in hell (and, at times, hell can be comfortable), but also we contribute to it. When we experience love and reject it, or manipulate its free gifts for our own ends, we are in hell. Hell is nothing but the rejection of love. The passion of God's love is everywhere. Hell is filled with the love of God, but the lost refuse to acknowledge that love, and thus experience their rejection and the torments of that rejection. The mystery is not that hell exists, but that we can prefer to live out of such a rejection. And that is the mystery of the freedom that God offers us in his love. In fact, on whatever level it happens, falling in love is the path to becoming free.

Those Without Love

In this exercise, Ignatius asks us to consider those who have never experienced love; those who have been offered love but have chosen otherwise; and those who have been offered, have accepted, and have experienced love, but later reject it. One might want to consider child soldiers, whose only experience of life is brutality; or those in our culture who prefer success to relationships; or those who become afraid of intimacy and so retreat into the self-destructive security of narcissism.

But, more important, we can consider how these three dynamics operate in our own lives and looking at the effects of living in such destructive ways. The prayer attempts to flush out any residual resistance we might have to accepting God's love. Of course we resist. If we are honest, we will realize that we will always resist and continue to live destructively in ways beyond our control. We can admit this. In the end, we fall upon the mercy of God, who is always willing to embrace, support, encourage and purify us to a continually deepening love.

In becoming aware of this mercy, of allowing ourselves to experience and accept it, and in opening ourselves up to it at deeper and more comprehensive levels, we increasingly occupy the posture of gratitude and thanksgiving.

Ignatius suggests that we conclude this prayer period by allowing ourselves spontaneously to express that thanksgiving to the mystery of God we call "Abba," and to conclude with the recollected praying of the "Our Father," which expresses our relationship to the One who loves us.

Questions for Prayer and Reflection

1. Where is hell in your life?

2. How do you experience it?

3. How do you respond to it?

4. What happens when you find yourself in contact with it?

5. How does it affect you?

6. Are you helpless in those moments and situations?

7. What can you do?

8. Where is Christ in all of this? (Here you may want to recall Elie Wiesel's story of the Jewish prisoner being beaten to death in one of the prison camps while the rest were forced to watch. In one of the lines a voice whispered, "Where is God now?" Another voice answered: "Here He is – He is hanging here on this gallows.")

9. Where is the Father in all of this? Why don't you ask him where he is?

10. Have you ever experienced the mercy of God? Where? How?

11. How do you experience the mercy of the Father now?

12. How does that mercy feel?

The Movie

PRECIOUS: BASED ON THE NOVEL PUSH BY SAPPHIRE

Director: Lee Daniels (2009 – 109 mins.)
Starring: Gabourey Sidibe, Mo'Nique, Mariah Carey

1. Synopsis

Claireece Precious Jones endures unimaginable hardships in her young life. Physically and mentally abused by her mother, twice raped and impregnated by her father, she grows up poor, angry, illiterate, fat, unloved and generally unnoticed.

The family resides in a Harlem tenement and subsists on welfare. Her first child has Down's syndrome and is being cared for by Precious's grandmother. After Precious becomes pregnant for the second time, she is suspended from school. Precious fights to find a way out of her traumatic daily existence through imagination and fantasy.

Note: Rated R for child abuse including sexual assault, and pervasive language.

2. About the Movie

1. *Precious: Based on the Novel* Push *by Sapphire* is like a diamond – clear, bright, but oh so hard. To simply call it harrowing or unsparing doesn't quite cut it; *Precious* is also courageous and uncompromising, a shaken cocktail of debasement and elation, despair and hope. Everyone involved deserves credit for creating a movie so dangerous, problematic and ultimately elevating… this is, for all its scorched-earth emotion, a film to be loved. (John Anderson, *Variety*, January 18, 2009) This is, without a doubt, a difficult film to watch. Why does the critic call it both "dangerous and uncompromising" as well as "a film to be loved"?

2. "Part of the great power of movies is that they can take us perilously close to the life of someone we might otherwise feel perilously far from. The title character of *Precious: Based on the Novel* Push *by Sapphire* is a hushed, damaged, morbidly obese 16-year-old African-American girl from the lower depths of Harlem. It's 1987, and Claireece Precious Jones is poor and ignorant, a depressed, withdrawn shell of a human being, with a face so inexpressive it might be a visor clamped down over her features." (Owen Gleiberman, *Entertainment Weekly*, November 19, 2009) What happens to us when we do get this close to someone we "feel perilously far from"?

3. "Yet [director] Daniels mixes up the harsh urban drama with episodes of magical realism, moments when the title character cuts away from the horrors of abuse into a fantasy world of glamorous photo shoots and red-carpet schmoozing. In that realm, she's adored. In the real world, she's raped and reviled." (Amy Biancoli, *San Francisco Chronicle*,

November 13, 2009) How does the contrast between the idealized and the real emphasize the unforgiving grittiness of Precious' life? How does it also show us the resilience of a girl who hasn't yet given up on loving or being loved?

4. "But *Precious* is, in any case, less the examination of a social problem than the illumination of an individual's painful and partial self-realization. Inarticulate and emotionally shut down, her massive body at once a prison and a hiding place, Precious is also perceptive and shrewd, possessed of talents visible only to those who bother to look …. Ms. Sidibe, perhaps the least-known member of this movie's unusual cast, is also the glue that holds it together. Nimble and self-assured as Mr. Daniels's direction may be, he could not make you believe in Precious unless you were able to believe in Precious herself. You will." (A.O. Scott, *The New York Times*, November 6, 2009) What is it about Ms. Sidibe's performance that makes us believe in Precious herself?

5. There is no question but that this film melodramatizes everything, and yet its overall effect is something more than melodrama. What is it about this film that allows it to move beyond melodrama?

3. The Relationship of the Movie to the Theme of the Exercise

1. It is clear from this Exercise that hell involves alienation. In the film, most of the characters are as alienated from each other as it is possible to be. What are some examples of this alienation?

2. The Exercise asks us to consider the three dynamics of love in our lives. Which characters in this film have never experienced love? Were offered love but chose otherwise? Were offered love, accepted it, and then rejected it? What do these people show us about our own acceptance of God's love?

3. Precious finds a way out of her traumatic daily existence through imagination and fantasy. In her mind, there is another world where she is loved and appreciated. How does this help her escape from a world in which her only experience of life is brutality?

4. The Relationship of the Movie to One's Self in the Exercise

1. Jean Paul Sartre, in his play *No Exit*, says that hell is other people. This is, in the briefest form possible, Sartre's definition of humanity's fundamental sin. If, as in the play, you were to be confined for all eternity with two other people in one room, which two characters from *Precious* would you least like to be with? Why? And which two people from your own life would you least like to be with? Why?

2. In some way, each of the characters in the film contributes to the Hell in which they live. Look at the way three of the characters do this, and reflect on how you also experience some of this in your own life.

3. At the end of *The Thin Red Line* – another movie about Hell – this question appears on the screen: "Where does the Love come from?" What is your response to this question?

Death

God so loved the world that He gave his only Son that whoever believes in him should not perish but have eternal life. For God sent the Son into the world, not to condemn the world, but that the world might be saved through him. (John 3:16-17)

This is to consider how God works and labours for me. (Sp. Ex. #236)

To experience oneself deeply as a loved sinner.

Death Is Our Friend

Ignatius suggests two other exercises to help us experience the loving mercy of God: one on death and one on judgment. These two exercises reinforce the graces of the First Week and so are included here.

We will all die. In fact, we are dying at this very moment. Heidegger says we are being thrown towards death, and nothing can stop that process. Often our life is an attempt to ignore or deny death. Our exaltation of youth as the standard for beauty, accruing power as symbolic of life, and our refusal to recognize how we deplete resources while we try to sustain extravagant and vital lifestyles are just three ways that human beings, individually and collectively, maintain a deliberate blindness to the life cycle in nature. Such blindness leads to aggression, then frustration, and then despair. Out of that despair comes the malice of self-hatred and of vindictiveness towards others.

But we need not regard death as an enemy. Constant awareness of death allows for a calm indifference to "the slings and arrows of outrageous fortune." It allows us to examine our values and to commit ourselves to the most important ones. It helps us to relish the beauty in what is transient. It encourages us to seek for what abides under the transient. Death shows us that, ultimately, we cannot hold on to life. In Western mythology, the vampire is the one who, in trying to hold on to life, instead becomes a living death, corrupting everything and everyone who crosses its path.

But if we enter into the mercy of God, we discover that death can be a friend. Rather than being the final destination of an inconstant life, death becomes a doorway towards a greater life – resurrection, even. Moreover, as we relax more fully into the mercy of God, we begin to discover the many smaller deaths that are stations in our life so far. For example, each stage of our spiritual development involves rites of passage. In each of these pivotal moments, we leave behind the old and enter into the unknown and its uncertainties. We risk our very lives in those transitions, because we do not know what will emerge. But we emerge from that darkness and slowly become familiar with a new state of life. We establish relationships according to that new state of life. And then we are called once more to give up what was familiar and to journey forward again into the darkness, becoming light. Our spiritual journey into intimacy calls us ever forward beyond ourselves into greater life. That calling turns us always to the darkness and the deaths it contains.

Transition Points

In this meditation, you can consider any one of those transition points in your life, and the ways you have negotiated the significant moments in that transition. You may even want to re-enter prayerfully into that time, especially if it was a difficult one, or if it left you with scars that are not yet signs of the resurrection. When you re-enter these moments, do so conscious of the mercy of God present there. Ask to be held and transformed by that mercy as you allow those images, sensations, and memories to emerge.

One significant way of entering this contemplation is to imagine our own death. We can imagine our fading powers and our growing dependence upon others; we can imagine moving beyond their phsyical help; we can imagine our own abandonment to our helplessness; we can imagine the body's struggle beyond our will to maintain itself; we can imagine its exhaustion; we can imagine it stopping. Death. But we can also imagine being surrounded by God's love, manifested in God's tangible mercy. We can imagine being supported by the saints and angels and all the powers of good, by all the people we know and love who have gone before us. They all encourage us to become one with that love and that sense of compassionate presence, which desires only the fullness of life for us.

In this prayer, we can sink into that sense of presence that shows us that no one dies alone, and that this death is a time to lay down all our burdens. It is time to trust that the Divine Presence, who has cared for all from the beginning of creation, will kindly take care of all our unfinished business. We dwell in this warm, embracing sense of presence, with its sense of light entering into the depths of our being. We allow what emerges at this time of simple dwelling to be the matter for reflection and discussion with God, who desires only that we come to the fullness of life.

Questions for Prayer and Reflection

1. How do you deal with death?
2. What experiences of death have you had?
3. How do you experience death in your world?
4. How do you react to that experience?
5. In what ways has your denial of death shaped the way you live? How has it influenced your projects and plans?
6. How have you negotiated the significant transition points of your life?
7. Is there a common pattern of behaviour to those experiences?
8. Is this the way to deal with your death?
9. What would you wish to be different? What would you keep the same?
10. Is death a friend for you? Or an enemy?
11. How can you make death a friend?
12. What happens when you imagine yourself surrounded and penetrated by God's love and light as you lie on your deathbed? Is there any unfinished business that you want God to take care of for you? Is there anything you would like to tell God or the people in your life, past and present? Is there anything you wish you had done? or left undone?
13. How do you experience God's mercy touching those areas in your prayer?

91

The Movie
BIG FISH

Director: Tim Burton (2003 – 122 mins.)
Starring: Albert Finney, Ewan McGregor, Billy Crudup, Jessica Lange, Helena Bonham Carter, Alison Lohman, Steve Buscemi, and Danny DeVito

1. Synopsis

The movie tells of the final days of Edward Bloom and the strained relationship he has with his son, William, who has not spoken to him for three years, the result of growing animosity over the tales his father used to pass as truth to family and friends. But when Edward is dying of cancer, William comes to his father's bedside in Alabama, and the stories of Edward's youth are told one more time.

2. About the Movie

1. "Bloom is a mixture of Odysseus, Candide and your long-winded uncle, and just when the movie seems in danger of veering off into sentimental, Burton pulls it back." (Lynn Hirschberg, *The New York Times Magazine*, November 9, 2003, p. 52.) There are many examples of this happening in *Big Fish*. How does this take place during the extraordinary ending when Bloom's son, William, finally gets to tell his own story?

2. Director Tim Burton: "*Big Fish* is about what's real and what's fantastic, what's true and what's not true, what's partially true and how, in the end, it's all true. To show those contrasting elements was the challenge." (Quoted in Lynn Hirschberg, *The New York Times Magazine*, November 9, 2003, p. 52.) How well do you think Burton succeeds in what he is trying to do? What got you involved with the movie? Or – What stopped you from becoming involved in the movie?

3. "*Big Fish* argues that sometimes it's better to accept the truth you want to believe about yourself. In effect, you need to get in touch with your inner deceiver." (Peter Howell, *The Toronto Star*, December 10, 2003) Why is it difficult for you to accept this interpretation of the movie?

4 "Will, a journalist who has made his career by serving facts straight, hates his father for constructing myths to hide behind. It's the myths, of course, that most reveal the real Edward. And Burton wisely builds his movie around them." (Peter Travers, *Rolling Stone*, December 11, 2003) What do the myths reveal about the real Edward?

5. How do William's final lines in the movie explain the theme of the movie?

3. The Relationship of the Movie to the Theme of the Exercise

1. The Exercises show us how the denial of death can turn us towards the malice of self-hatred and vindictiveness towards others. How does Edward react to his death? How do the stories he has told prepare him for death?

2. Perhaps it is William who regards death as an enemy. Death will rob him of the chance to find out just who his father is. William – a journalist – looks for the factual truth about his father, not the emotional truth – a very different thing. Do you think that Edward ever said a single true thing? Perhaps he never did, but also perhaps every story he told had a deeper level of truth behind it. What is one scene that shows this possibility to you?

3. Edward is well aware that he is dying – and he believes he knows just how he will die. He has no need to contemplate his own death for he has often contemplated his life's ending, which he saw as a child. How does the story that William tells to the dying Edward ensure that this will all come to pass?

4. The Relationship of the Movie to One's Self in the Exercise

1. The Exercise speaks of the many smaller deaths that are stations in our own life so far. It is very evident what these stations are in the lives of both Edward and William. But what are these smaller deaths – these significant moments – in your own life and what have you learned from them?

2. Towards the end of the Exercise, there is a list of the steps that we can take in contemplating our own death. In prayer, you have tried to do this. In the movie we have seen how Edward handles these steps. What is the most difficult of the steps for you to accept?

3. No one dies alone. The movie shows us the many people from Edward's life who come to be with him as he dies. But the Exercise does not speak of the presence of people around us as we die. It speaks to us of the comforting presence of God within us at that time. What comes to your mind when you acknowledge and reflect on this simple but powerful fact of God's love for us?

8th Exercise
Judgment

Now the word of the Lord came to me saying:
Before I formed you in the womb I knew you,
And before you were born I consecrated you.

(Jeremiah 1:5)

The lover gives and shares with the beloved what he possesses, or something that he has or is able to give; and vice versa, the beloved shares with the lover.

(Sp. Ex. #231)

To experience God's healing love pouring into the broken and damaged places of our life transforming them and integrating them into the community that is the fullness of our life.

The Lies of Evil

God has an abiding judgment of us. God judges that we are lovable and capable of loving. In all of his dealings with us, God has never deviated from that judgment. God creates in love, with love, and through love. At our very essence we are love incarnate, for we are made in God's image and likeness.

It is evil that judges us as other than God's creation, God's creatures, God's delight. In the beginning of the book of Job, Satan is described as "the accuser." It is the evil one – or, as Ignatius so aptly calls him, "the enemy of our human nature" – who judges us negatively and asks us to judge ourselves as incapable and unworthy of love.

From the life we have lived on earth, the choices we make show whether we agree with God or with Satan. In Christian mythology, at the judgment we encounter after death, we find ourselves in the presence of God. There we experience the freedom and the self-image that we have shaped with our choices in this life. We may experience ourselves as a mass of obsessive-compulsive behaviours that manifest our narcissism, or we may find ourselves as acknowledging with our very lives that we are children of God, seeing God in everything and in each other and in ourselves. We may be astonished at this self-revelation and ask, "But Lord, when did we see you?" And he will reply, "When I was hungry and you fed my hunger; when I was lonely and you became community; when I was with the oppressed and you struggled to set them free; when I was with the joyful and you celebrated life with us; when I was with those who risk themselves in creating and you did not abandon me." For truly God is in all places and all times and with all peoples. Nothing and no one is left out, for God chooses freely to be committed to us.

What we see now and at the judgment emerges from who we are. At that judgment, we shall experience God as God, and we shall experience ourselves as we truly are. We can rejoice because we are finally found and are finally coming home, or we can be like Adam and Eve in the garden after they ate the forbidden fruit, hiding from themselves and from God.

Even there we can trust either in our egos or in the mercy of God.

Surrounded by Saints

For this meditation, imagine that you are already dead and are surrounded by the dynamic, compassionate love of God; surrounded by all the saints and the powers of good who pour out their energy and love into us; surrounded by all those whom you love and who love you and desire only what is best for you. Allow yourself to enter into that embrace, and allow that embrace to enter into the very depth of yourself. Deeper and ever deeper. Just remain in that state of acceptance and see what happens, and how you respond. Allow whatever emerges in your awareness to come, and, without holding onto it, offer it up to that mercy who transforms everything into life. Stay with that state of presence until it ceases.

Have a conversation with the Father about what happened in that prayer period. Allow yourself to express all the things that you experienced, and discuss what you experienced with the Father. Close with the "Our Father."

Questions for Prayer and Reflection

1. What self-image do you hold now?

2. Where does that self-image come from?

3. The medieval mystic Meister Eckhart says, "The eye by which I see God is the eye by which God sees me." What do you think he means?

4. How do you experience God seeing you?

5. How do you experience God?

6. What was significant in the prayer?

7. Why was this significant?

8. What does it tell you about your relationship to God? Your relationship to yourself? God's relationship to you?

9. What are the crucial elements in a relationship for you?

10. Do you experience God trusting you? How do you experience that? How does it feel?

11. How do you respond?

12. How did the prayer experience reveal you to yourself?

The Movie
THE LOVELY BONES

Director: Peter Jackson (2009 – 136 mins.)
Starring: Saoirse Ronan, Stanley Tucci, Mark Wahlberg, Susan Sarandon

1. Synopsis

On December 6, 1973, in Norristown, Pennsylvania, on her way home from school, fourteen year-old Susie Salmon is approached by a neighbour, George Harvey, who persuades her to visit an underground den he has recently built. There he rapes her and stabs her to death.

Based on the critically acclaimed best-selling novel by Alice Sebold, the story is told from the point of view of the murdered Susie who watches over her family – and her killer – from heaven. She must weigh her desire for vengeance against her desire for her family to heal.

2. About the Movie

1. "Director Peter Jackson certainly is familiar with the challenges of satisfying filmgoers' expectations, having helmed three films derived from J.R.R. Tolkien's immensely popular *Lord of the Rings* novel[s] and a second remake of the iconic film *King Kong*. So Alice Sebold's best-selling novel *The Lovely Bones*, published in 2002, should be right in his wheelhouse. In this case, though, he has changed the focus and characters to such a significant degree that his film might resonate more with those who have not read the book .... Sebold's otherworldly meditation on unspeakable tragedy and hard-earned healing has been transformed by Jackson into something akin to a supernatural suspense thriller. A philosophical story about family, memory and obsession has regrettably become a mawkish appeal to victimhood." (Kirk Honeycutt, *The Hollywood Reporter*, November 24, 2009)

Adapting a novel to film is always a difficult process. They are two very different forms of art. Why would Jackson transform Alice Sebold's startling, unique novel about the aftermath of a terrible murder into a story more focused on crime and punishment?

2. "How do you literalize heaven? It's a problem moviemakers have struggled with forever, and Jackson hasn't solved it. Sebold's notion was that everyone creates a heaven to fit her fantasies and wishes. Jackson creates the afterlife of a 14-year-old raised on '70s teen life and pop culture – a kitsch universe of greeting-card imagery and Renaissance Faire clothes. The tackiness, intentional or not, is jarring. Even worse is the vision of Susie and the other murdered girls as a happy, gamboling clan of free spirits." (David Ansen, *Newsweek*, December 01, 2009)

What would your heaven look like if Sebold's notion is correct?

3. "There are all sorts of ways to botch a book-into-film adaptation: A filmmaker can be too cavalier about changing an author's character conception or meaning, or he can be so slavishly respectful of those things that he fails to make a work that resonates cinematically. He can rely too heavily on the use of voice-over; he can miscast one actor, or every actor; he can simply fall down on the job of capturing the lyricism or muscle of a particular writer's prose, as plenty of great directors have done. Adaptation is an art, not a science, and it's a thankless job to boot: Not even the most graceful filmmaker can escape the carping of the 'Movies are always inferior to the books they're based on' crowd." (Stephanie Zacharek, *Salon*, December 10, 2009)

If you have read Sebold's novel, do you think Jackson has made some/all of the above fatal errors in his adaptation? And if you haven't read the novel but only have the film to judge by, then do you think the film works? Why or why not?

4. "The foundation of the film is emotional. The devastation of losing a child; the nervous titter of puppy love; the frenzied pursuit of justice; the icy calm of a killer: Jackson builds and conveys it all with unswerving certainty. There are moments of heartrending grief in *Bones*, and of sickmaking dread, and of breathless exhilaration. And in all, as ever, Jackson proves himself a born filmmaker." (Shawn Levy, *The Oregonian*, January 15, 2010)

Why does Levy call emotion the foundation of the film? How is emotion portrayed in the film?

3. The Relationship of the Movie to the Theme of the Exercise

1. It is the evil one, this Exercise tells us, who judges us negatively and who asks us to judge ourselves as incapable and unworthy of love. In the film, do any of the main characters see themselves as incapable and unworthy of love? Why? Why not?

2. As the film begins to come to an end, Susie is shown finally entering her wide heaven. She addresses the audience in her final sentences: "My name is Salmon; like the fish, first name Susie. I was 14 years old when I was murdered on December 6, 1973. I was here for a moment and then I was gone. I wish you all a long and happy life." What does she teach us about love at that moment – given all that has gone before in the film?

3. Film critic Roger Ebert was critical of the film's portrayal of heaven, which he compared to a "happy gathering of new Facebook friends." Would you agree with Ebert's criticism? Why? Why not? What is your view of heaven?

4. The Relationship of the Movie to One's Self in the Exercise

1. In some of the characters in the film, we find something of ourselves. What do they have that can help us to find that we are both lovable and capable of loving?

2. Who is judged in this film? What is the judgment and how is it delivered? How often have we judged someone? How often have we judged wrongly but never admitted it? What leads us to leap into such judgment?

Overview of the First Week

"We know that all things work for the good of those who love the Lord." (Romans 8:28)

The Spiritual Exercises have "as their purpose the conquest of self and the ordering of one's life in such a way that no decision is made under the influence of any inordinate attachment." (Sp. Ex. #21)

To ask the Father to show you your life as He sees it, and to rejoice in the life and in the path that is one's life.

Finding the Pattern

You have just been through the rather intense experience of the First Week of the Spiritual Exercises of St. Ignatius of Loyola. Before we continue on this spiritual journey, it is helpful to reflect on what has happened and how it has affected you. A simple way of doing this is to ask yourself the following questions:

• What has changed in me because of this experience?

• How was I before entering this journey? How am I now?

• What accounts for the difference?

• What have I learned from this experience?

• What are the graces I was given by God by opening myself up to these exercises?

Take some time to reflect on these questions before you proceed to the outlook presented below. Write your responses in your journal.

The aim of the First Week is to experience the mercy of God and achieve some self-awareness about being a sinner and yet being loved at an intimate and personal level.

This conversion dynamic seeks to liberate the self from the constraints of the ego as defined by sin operating on cosmic, human, and personal levels. What is brought to light are the illusions of the illusion that we hold to be the self. Those illusions encompass our self-image and our deeply rooted ways of seeing the world, our relationships, and even God. Some of the ways that this false self, which we hold instinctively to be ourselves, are deconstructed include the questioning of the self that is part of every exercise. This allows the prayerful reconstructions of a self exposed to God's love. What follows is our growing self-acceptance as defined by God, rather than by the traumas that create self-consciousness. Thus we pray to see, know, and love ourselves as God sees, knows, and loves us. While God calls us back to be faithful lovers, we experience ourselves as loved sinners.

People experience this pattern differently. Some find the experience of confronting themselves to be a source of desolation; others find it a relief finally to abandon the project of creating the self, and to rest in God's creative mercy. Many move from desolation to consolation in this set of exercises. At first, we tend both consciously and unconsciously to resist the transformation that occurs as we open ourselves to God's love. We experience the ways the self is imprisoned, and we resist accepting those unredeemed areas of our lives. The love we encounter challenges the sense of comfort and the habitual, by which we maintain our ego.

When the prayer invites us past these boundaries, we often experience as threatening or overwhelming the fear of what is "other." At the same time, we have a profound sense of entrapment and bewilderment. We are asked to remain in that sense of the unknown until we realize that we are neither destroyed nor overwhelmed by it. If we can do this, we experience both a liberation of those trapped energies and the consolation of being loved and accepted beyond ourselves. We sink into God's love and discover a renewed sense of being alive and of being amazed at the life that is given to us.

But what does all of this mean in terms of grace? First, we discover the truth of our very self, and the dynamic context of love in which all of our lives are held. We find ourselves falling in love with a God who has fallen in love with us even before we knew it. This awareness of being loved also makes us realize that we are not God, and so we become aware of our boundaries, limitations, and our constant need for God's mercy. Moreover, as we sink into that love, we are invited to continue that journey towards even greater intimacy. The journey is both inward and outward at the same time. Inwardly, we discover more and more aspects of ourselves being loved into life. Outwardly, we are invited to share in the work of that creative love seeking to transform the world. What we discover in all of this is how we are relationship: we are related to everything, and everything is related to us. St. Ignatius demonstrates this insight when he notes that in saving others, we save ourselves. The journey into intimacy encompasses all of creation opening out to God, and experiences the love of God unceasingly at work in that creation.

Questions for Prayer and Reflection

1. How helpful was the description of the First Week for you?

2. How has it illuminated your experience and self-understanding?

3. What was different from the description, in your experience?

4. How do you explain this difference?

5. In what ways does the mystery of God remain a mystery?

6. How comfortable are you in living in such a mystery?

7. What do you feel called to do next?

The Movie
THREE COLORS: BLUE

Director: Krzysztof Kieslowski (1993, 98 mins.)
Starring: Juliette Binoche, Benoit Regent, Florence Pernei

I. Synopsis

Three Colors: Blue is the first film in Kieslowski's trilogy on France's motto: Liberty, Equality, Fraternity. *Blue* shared the Golden Lion at Venice in 1993; *White* earned Kieslowski the best director prize in Berlin, 1994; and *Red* brought him an Academy Award nomination for best director in 1995.

After Julie's husband and young daughter are killed in a car accident, she tries to start a new life, free of personal commitments, belongings, grief, and love. Her aim is to withdraw from the world and live independently, anonymously and alone in Paris. But as various people find their way into her life, the healing begins.

Note: If at all possible, watch the subtitled version. Much of an actor's art lies in the use of voice to express emotion, mood, and character. Dubbed movies can never have the full impact of the original.

2. About the Movie

1. "For Kieslowski, subtlety is a religion. He hints or implies – anything to keep from laying his cards on the table. With *Blue*, you never feel he's shown his whole hand; not even after the game is over." (Hal Hinson, *Washington Post*, March 4, 1994.) What are some of the examples of how Kieslowski uses this subtlety in *Blue*?

2. Kieslowski told an interviewer: "I can identify with what [Ingmar] Bergman says about life, about what he says about love. I identify more or less with his attitude towards the world ... towards men and women and what we do in everyday life ... forgetting about what is most important." How do the characters in *Blue* forget about what is most important in their everyday lives?

3. Kieslowski's *Blue* examines the meaning of liberty, not as political or social concepts, which, he says, have already been achieved in France, but in terms of the individual. And Julie is no ordinary individual. She may be one of the most important composers of the 20th century. Yet the film does not explore this except in very oblique terms. Rather, *Blue* is more concerned with Julie's attempt to liberate herself from her sorrowful love and to establish a new life. How successful do you think Julie is in actually finding liberty? What steps does she take to achieve this goal?

3. The Relationship of the Movie to the Theme of the Exercise

1. The First Week is not the easiest to get through – it is very intense and leads us down the path of

self-awareness. How much self-awareness does Julie achieve in the course of the movie?

2. The First Week helps us see the illusions of the illusion we hold to be the self – as the exercise tells us. Where in the movie do any of the principal characters come to see the illusion they hold to be their selves?

3. Through the First Week we have learned to deconstruct our false selves by:

   • self-questioning,

   • imaginative reconstructing of ourselves as exposed to love, and

   • the growing self-acceptance of ourselves.

   Who are the characters in the movie who help Julie work through such a deconstruction?

4. The Relationship of the Movie to One's Self in the Exercise

1. Some people find facing up to themselves to be sheer desolation – others find it to be a relief. In the film, we see how Julie reacts to facing up to herself. How do you react – now, at the end of the First Week – to this facing up yourself?

2. The Exercise reminds us that we often experience the fear of what is other to ourselves as threatening or overwhelming. We know that this happened to Julie. What is the "other" for you that is the most challenging as you come to the end of the First Week?

3. With acceptance of self comes a liberation of energies and the consolation of being loved and accepted beyond ourselves. *Blue* is a lyrically studied, solemn, sometimes almost abstract consideration of Julie's attempt to liberate herself from her sorrowful love and to establish a new life. At the end of this First Week, how have you found yourself being loved and accepted beyond yourself?

Part 2
The Second Week – The Path of Spiritual Intimacy

1st Exercise
The Kingdom

Happy is the one whose help is the God of Jacob,
Whose hope is in the Lord, our God,
Who made heaven and earth ...
Who gives food for the hungry.
The Lord sets the prisoners free;
The Lord opens the eyes of the blind.
The Lord lifts up those who are bowed down;
The Lord loves the righteous.
The Lord watches over those who journey;
He upholds the widow and the orphan
But the ways of the wicked he brings to ruin.

(Psalm 146)

Eternal God of all things, in the presence of your infinite goodness, and of Your glorious mother, and of all the saints of Your heavenly court, this is the offering of myself which I make with Your favour and help. I protest that it is my earnest desire and my deliberate choice, provided only it is for Your greater service and praise, to imitate You in bearing all wrongs and all abuse and all poverty, both actual and spiritual, should Your most holy majesty deign to choose and admit me to such a state and way of life. (Sp. Ex. #98)

Here it will be to ask of our Lord the grace not to be deaf to His call, but prompt and diligent to accomplish his most holy will. (Sp. Ex. #91)

Becoming Engaged

We are all called to love. It is our very nature. Our very nature – who we truly are, and how we are situated in relationship to God, to others, and to the rest of creation – finds its fulfillment in loving and in being loved. It is only when that first step is radically settled and affirmed in our lives that the next step on our spiritual journey appears. How are we to manifest the love that we have received and that calls forth our own loving in our daily lives?

At this point we may be tempted to think we can make that decision by ourselves. We figure: I have experienced the love that loves me no matter what, so whatever I do will be all right because I am doing it in love. This temptation is very subtle and insidious, because there is much truth and value in it.

But it is not the whole picture. Think of yourself as driving a car that is a wreck. You take it to a garage where it is fixed, serviced, and refuelled. Now you are on the road again. "The open road ... freedom ... yes, this is the life!" you might say to yourself. This analogy might describe your situation when you discover you are loved. But just because the car is now roadworthy doesn't mean your worries are over. You can still have engine trouble. You can still hit potholes. You can still fall asleep at the wheel. The idea that whatever you do will be okay is problematic for three reasons. First, it presumes that you no longer need God's grace. Second, you do not know the route that will make more effective your new-found desire to be more loving. Third, you do not yet know how to communicate with the God who loves you into an ever fuller life. Now that you are in relationship with God, you need to consult God on how to live the rest of your life. This present stage in your spiritual journey is like a formal engagement between a couple who have fallen in love, but who still need to figure out how to live that love concretely.

During the engagement period, each learns more about the other, and accommodates plans and projects to include the other. In this stage of our journey, we risk our new-found lives to God, and God risks his fullest manifestation in creation to us. The grace we seek at this time is to enter into this developing relationship as deeply as possible. Ignatius puts it this way: "Here it will be to ask of God the grace not to be deaf to His call, but prompt and diligent to accomplish His most holy will" (#91). This is very much the stance of the lover asking the beloved, What do you want? What do you want of me? What do you want with me? What do you want for me? What do you want us to do together in this world in which we find, and lose, ourselves? We desire to give of ourselves in any way that might help.

The Cost of Loving

To enter into this contemplation, Ignatius asks us to consider how we might respond to someone who is obviously doing God's work. Ignatius believes that such a person must be "chosen by God Our Lord Himself" (#92). Many projects and enterprises claim to be from God. Many leaders use spiritual, religious, moral, and ethical arguments to validate their ways of proceeding. Often these seem persuasive; they may have the weight of public opinion or tradition on their side. But this does not necessarily make them God's chosen. In fact, when we read the scriptures, we discover God often chooses those who run counter to establishment values. The prophets were such people, as was Jesus. Ignatius insists that it is God who must do the choosing, not humans. Humans might try to conscript God into their own projects and dramas, but God's ways are not human ways, and the Spirit blows where it wills. The qualities we consider important in service to God – gender, religious tradition, political subscription, intellectual acuity, ethnic nationality, economic or social status – do not matter to God. Indeed, the history of God's choices shows a significant indifference to race, creed, colour, academic giftedness, sexual orientation, or economic status. What that history does show is how the chosen people give witness to the same values as God's chosen, the Christ.

All of God's chosen leaders offer a sharing of the life of service to the Father. This life of service follows the same pattern as the life of Jesus Christ. It is a life of creativity that labours and suffers, as Christ did, to allow people to experience themselves as lovable and capable of loving. Ignatius knows that such a labour, while it gives a joy the world cannot offer, also involves suffering as we work against the forces of disorder present in ourselves, our circle of relationships, our culture, and our world.

Indeed, Ignatius does not cover up the cost of engaging in such an enterprise. This kind of love in action is not sentimental or occasional. It is battered by forces from within and without. It is hopeful without being naive, faithful without being self-serving, compassionate without being weak. It is human with all the flaws and glories of being human, when being human asks us always to go beyond ourselves, and to move from sincerity to authenticity. We are sincere when we trust ourselves and remain within ourselves; we are authentic when we trust beyond ourselves in such a way that we are brought to a deeper and truer sense of ourselves. Our spiritual journey calls us beyond sincerity to authenticity. A spiritual leader, such as Moses guiding the Israelites out of Egypt, is one who leads us to authenticity.

Love calls us to authenticity. Love calls us to love. Love calls us to God, who is manifest in love.

Such authenticity is not possible by ourselves. We need friends, companions, partners, lovers, spouses. We need others who are committed to the same path. But more than them, we need God.

We cannot respond to God and offer ourselves to God by ourselves. We need God's constant presence and the constant presence and support of the company of those who have committed their lives to God's service. We can then make that offering of ourselves, knowing deeply and passionately that we are never alone in the struggle to bring life to a disordered time and a disordered world.

Ignatius asks us to contemplate those whose lives witness to such a dedication. He asks us to consider how we feel when we take some time to examine one such life. He also asks us to experience our sense of a common mission with such a life, and the resulting sense of community that involvement in a common mission gives to us. He suggests that we conclude our reflection with a prayer offering ourselves to be part of that mission and community.

O most gracious God, source of all life, I can only make this offering with your grace and your help. I make it aware of your constant loving goodness and in the presence of all those who have dedicated their lives to you – all the forces of good in all times and in all places throughout creation, and all the saints of every tradition. My deepest wish and desire, only if it serves to build up the community of all creation infinitely open to your never-ceasing love, is to become an intimate companion of your Son, the Christ. Then, I desire to be with him wherever he is and goes, and to share his life, his joys and sorrows, and, like him, bear all injuries and wrongs, all abuse and poverty, actual as well as spiritual, if doing that helps build up your community of loving. I desire this only if you desire to choose for me such a way of life, and to receive me into that life, and, because I am weak and fickle, only if you be with me strongly in such a life.

Questions for Prayer and Reflection

1. What do you value now at this stage of your life? How are those values expressed in what you do, whom you associate with, how you plan for the future? Do you find any tension in your values?

2. What elements in your life are in conflict with your deeper values?

3. How do you resolve these conflicts?

4. What happens when you let yourself experience the desire to do something of greater value with your life?

5. What stands in the way of your doing this?

6. When you contemplate the Christ speaking to you, what does he say and do?

7. How do you feel about that?

8. How do you see yourself as a companion of Christ, as one who shares his vision and work of being the compassionate and creative presence of the Father in the world?

9. What would your prayer of self-dedication be? (Let this come out of your prayer, rather than out of some idealized way you might see yourself or want to see the world.)

10. What is possible given your real circumstances?

The Movie

HARRY POTTER AND THE DEATHLY HALLOWS
PART ONE AND PART TWO

Director: Peter Yates (2010 and 2011)
Starring: Daniel Radcliffe, Emma Watson, Rupert Grint, Ralph Fiennes

Note: The final book in the Harry Potter series has been split into two movies to give proper closure to each character's story and to the series as a while. The first part was released in November 2010, the second part in July 2011. Ideally, both parts one and two should be watched for this exercise. However, many of the questions for reflection will apply to either film.

1. Synopsis

Harry, Hermione, and Ron set out from Hogwarts on a quest to find and destroy the Horcruxes – the mysterious objects that hold the secret to Voldemort's power and immortality. On their own, without the guidance of their professors or the protection of Professor Dumbledore, the three friends must now rely on one another more than ever. But there are dark forces in their midst that threaten to tear them apart.

Meanwhile, the wizarding world has become a dangerous place for all enemies of the Dark Lord. The long-feared war has begun and Voldemort's Death Eaters have seized control of the Ministry of Magic and even Hogwarts, terrorizing and arresting anyone who might oppose them. But the one prize they still seek is the one most valuable to Voldemort: Harry Potter. The Chosen One has become the hunted one as the Death Eaters search for Harry with orders to bring him to Voldemort... alive.

Harry's only chance is to find and destroy the Horcruxes before Voldemort finds him. But as he searches for clues, he uncovers an old and almost forgotten tale – the legend of the Deathly Hallows. And if the legend turns out to be true, it could give Voldemort the ultimate power he seeks. The Hallows are revealed to be three sacred objects: the Resurrection Stone, a stone with the power to bring others back to life; the Elder Wand, an unbeatable wand; and an infallible Invisibility Cloak.

Little does Harry know that his future has already been decided by his past, on that fateful day when he became "the Boy Who Lived." No longer just a boy, Harry Potter is drawing ever closer to the task for which he has been preparing since the day he first stepped into Hogwarts: the ultimate battle with Voldemort.

2. About the Movie

1. "We love Harry and the rest, and are touched over and over again by the strength of their friendship. We have watched them grow up, felt their flaws and admired their bravery, and will willingly read about them through their times of trouble, even without the distraction of Hogwarts. Rowling's genius is not just her total realization of a fantasy world, but the quieter skill of creating characters that bounce off the page, real and flawed and brave and lovable." (Alice Fordham, *Times Online*, July 21, 2007)

   Who are your favourite characters in the Harry Potter series – either in the books or as seen in the films based on the books? What attracts you to them?

2. Four themes common to all the books and films are the heroic journey, choice, self-sacrifice, loneliness, and loss. Uniting them all is one theme that J.K.Rowling has been very clear about: "My books are largely about death."

   How do you see these four themes linked to the unifying notion of death in this film?

3. The seven Harry Potter books have been published in 64 languages and have sold 400 million copies. The first six films earned $5.4 billion. "I am convinced that the fundamental reason for the astonishing popularity of the Harry Potter novels is their ability to meet a spiritual longing for some experience of the truths of life, love, and death taught by Christianity but denied by secular culture." (James Parker, *The Atlantic*, July/August, 2009)

   How much do you agree with Parker's reasons for the books' – and films' – extraordinary popularity and success? What other reasons might there be for this?

4. Throughout the series – in the books and on the screen – Harry has one major weapon in his battle against evil as personified in Lord Voldemort. In *The Half Blood Prince*, Harry's mentor Dumbledore solemnly tells him that, "You are protected by your ability to love." In their final confrontation, Voldemort asks Harry "Why do you live?" and Harry replies, "Because I have something worth living for."

   How is this simple capacity for love, for human tenderness, seen as the "weapon" that will ultimately defeat Voldemort? Is it possible that expressing this love might be seen as a distraction or, worse, a weakness? Or is it that in finally accepting the power of love in his life, Harry comes to understand the importance of love as the antidote to fear? What scenes from the film best exemplify your choice?

5. Author J.K. Rowling's *Harry Potter* books have always dealt explicitly with religious themes and questions, but until *Harry Potter and the Deathly Hallows*, they had never quoted any specific religion. As Rowling said, "To me [the religious parallels have] always been obvious," she said. "But I never wanted to talk too openly about it because I thought it might show people who just wanted the story where we were going." (quoted in an interview with Shawn Adler, "Harry Potter author," mtv.com/news/articles, October 17, 2007)

Indeed, at its most simplistic, Harry's final tale can in some respects be boiled down to a resurrection story, with Harry venturing to a heavenly way station of sorts after getting hit with a killing curse, only to return to his earthly home.

On his parents' tombstone Harry reads the quote, "The last enemy that shall be destroyed is death," while on another tombstone (that of Dumbledore's mother and sister) he reads, "Where your treasure is, there will your heart be also." The second is a direct quote of Jesus from Matthew 6:19, the first from 1 Corinthians 15:26. As Hermione tells Harry shortly after he sees the graves, his parents' message means "living beyond death. Living after death." It is one of the central foundations of resurrection theology.

"[But] I think those two particular quotations he finds on the tombstones at Godric's Hollow, they sum up – they almost epitomize the whole series." (J.K. Rowling, quoted in an interview with Shawn Adler, "Harry Potter author," mtv. com/news/articles, October 17, 2007)

From viewing either the first and/or the second part of this film, where do you see references to religious parallels? How important do you think they are as a final explanation of the series?

3. The Relationship of the Movie to the Theme of the Exercise

1. The fifth of the key concepts of media literacy indicates that all media contain, explicitly or implicitly, values messages. What human values – especially those given in this Exercise – are found in the Harry Potter novels and films, especially in these last two films?

2. In the Exercise we learn that it is important to see how even flawed characters can risk and in so doing change their world. What are Harry's flaws – especially as seen in the last two films?

3. This Exercises call us to "love in action." How is this manifested in these films?

4. The Relationship of the Movie to One's Self in the Exercise

1. Love in action, as we learn in this Exercise, is also "human with all the flaws and glories of being human." What are the "flaws and glories" that we see in Harry Potter that are reflected in our own lives?

2. We need the help of others in this endeavour. As the Exercise puts it, we need "that constant presence of God, and that constant presence of the company of those who have committed their lives to God's service." So many people – his friends, his teachers, his godfather, Sirius Black – serve as this force for Harry. Thinking back to *The Chamber of Secrets*, we remember that it was the phoenix – a classic symbol of Christ's passion, who dies and rises again – who helps Harry by weeping in his wounds to heal him.

More importantly for us, how is God coming to be constantly present in our lives? And who are the "others" who help us so that we are never alone in our struggle and our journey?

2nd Exercise
(1) The Incarnation

This exercise has two parts: the Divine Presence's concern for the world and their decision to do something at the right time, and the human response of Mary at the Annunciation.

Who is like the Lord, our God,
Who is seated on high,
Who looks far down
Upon the heaven and the earth?
He raises the poor from the dust,
And lifts the needy from the ash heap,
To make them sit with the rulers,
With the rulers of his people.
He gives the barren woman a home,
Making her the joyous mother of children.
Praise the Lord!   (Psalm 113)

The Three Divine Persons look upon the whole expanse or circuit of all the earth, filled with human beings. Since they see that all are going down to hell, They decree in Their eternity that the Second Person should become man to save the human race.   (Sp. Ex. #102)

This is to ask for what I desire. Here it will be to ask for an intimate knowledge of our Lord, who has become human for me, that I may love Him more and follow him more closely.   (Sp. Ex. #103)

Imagining the World

The Spiritual Exercises of St. Ignatius expand our understanding of how we are present to ourselves, to others, and to the world. One of the most significant ways it does this is by expanding our imagination and allowing us to experience it not just as the producer of fantasy and images, but as the producer of all that is. If we look around, even where we are now, everything we see or feel or hear was first a product of the imagination. The process of transforming that imagined entity to a sensible reality also requires an imaginative process. When our imaginations are frozen, we end up with the notion that reality cannot be changed. When our imaginations are subverted by evil, we create distorted forms of reality. But when our imaginations are liberated by God, we imagine as God imagines, and create as God creates.

When we are trapped by sin, all we can see is sin, and the way we imagine we can free ourselves is in itself sinful. Ignatius starts his Exercises by showing us how sin traps us in ways beyond any form of self-help. One of the first steps in our liberation is realizing our radical helplessness. The work of love is to liberate those trapped energies of our imagination so that we can see and experience ourselves as God sees and experiences us.

This liberation is present in the first part of this second exercise, where we are asked to imagine being in the very presence of God as the three persons of the Trinity contemplate the disordered state of our world. The divine energies of love, manifest in the Father, the Son, and the Holy Spirit, are not detached, dispassionate omni-powers. They are the fullest manifestations of an involved and concerned Love that creates constantly, sustains without ceasing, and redeems always by entering into the traps of sin and death to bring all, in their patient wisdom, to the process of resurrection. God knows that we, and our worlds, are still being created. We are invited to co-operate in that creation. That process transforms evil into good by entering into the afflicted dimensions of creation.

Seeing as God Sees

In this contemplation, we are asked to share the perspective of the three Divine Persons of the Trinity as they look at the state of the world. They are not filled with moral disgust at the desperate state of humanity; rather, they determine that the best way for us to be saved is for one of them to become one of us. In this way we can see that it is still possible – despite the terrible straits we are in, and the illusions to which we enslave ourselves – to realize our union with God. The deceptions we are mired in either suggest to us that this is not possible, or offer erroneous ways to achieve that reality. These only increase our frustration and despair. As we have already discovered, we cannot liberate ourselves. How can we be human without being mastered by sin? The question is this: How can we be ourselves and yet be beyond ourselves?

The Trinity's solution to this question is the Incarnation. God enters into the human condition, into created history, to show us that we can enter into God's condition, God's creativity, and God's very life. The Trinity offer us the gift of themselves, and they offer the way for us to receive and open, live and share that gift. They show us how to be most fully human.

Because of this action of God, we are given the opportunity to become most truly ourselves by going beyond how we see ourselves. We see ourselves with the possibilities God always sees in us and calls us to. The gift of love, when we accept it, makes us truly loving. In love we grow in our connection to ourselves, to all others, and to God.

Questions for Prayer and Reflection

1. How do you receive gifts?

2. How do you open gifts?

3. How do you use gifts?

4. How do you share your gifts? Have you ever been given a gift that you did not know existed? That you did not know how to ask for? What was it?

5. Have you ever been in love?

6. Have you ever loved anyone – not for yourself, but just for that other person?

7. What is/was it like?

8. How does it keep changing your life?

9. In this prayer period, what does it feel like to enter into the imagination of God?

10. How do you feel as you become a part of the Trinity's decision not to give up on humankind? If you were to talk to the Trinity about their decision, what would these conversations and your concerns be about?

The Movie
WINTER'S BONE

Director: Debra Granik (2010 – 100 mins.)
Starring: Jennifer Lawrence, John Jawkes, Kevin Breznaham
2010: Grand Prize: Sundance Film Festival

1. Synopsis

Despite her father's absence, seventeen-year-old Ree Dolly is trying to keep her family together in a poor rural area of the Ozark Mountains. Then she finds out that her father put up their house as collateral for his bail. Unless he shows up for his trial in a week, they will lose their home.

Ree knows her father manufactures crystal meth, but no one will help her find him. She risks her life to get at the truth.

2. About the Movie

1. "The gritty, desperate Ozarks milieu of *Winter's Bone* feels so real, so right, that you only slowly realize you're watching a detective movie. It's those noir bones that give this social-realist drama its punch, as if Humphrey Bogart had been recast as a 17-year-old girl and dropped into the poorest corner of America." (Ty Burr, *Boston Globe*, June 18, 2010)

Film noir is a cinematic term used primarily to describe stylish Hollywood crime dramas, particularly those that emphasize cynical attitudes and sexual motivations. Hollywood's classic film noir period is generally regarded as stretching from the early 1940s to the late 1950s. Film noir of this era is associated with a low-key, black-and-white visual style that has roots in German Expressionist cinematography. Many of the prototypical stories and much of the attitude of classic noir derive from the hard-boiled school of crime fiction that emerged in the United States during the Depression.

How does this film fit into the film noir genre? Consider how, despite warnings and beatings, Ree – like any good film noir hero – takes it and keeps on going, burrowing deeper into the mystery of her father's whereabouts. Consider the ending in the swamp and how she reacts. Does she earn respect? Or does she convince the others of the self-respect she already has? To paraphrase Raymond Chandler (whose novels were the basis for many a film noir): Down these mean roads a girl must go.

2. Author Daniel Woodrell's work has been described as "country noir." "Director Granik's film fits the basic requirements of that label. In her search for the truth, her heroine follows a circuitous, precipitous path. But Granik has no taste for noir archness, opting for a chilly, shot-on-decaying-locations naturalism that feels as

lived-in as Lawrence's performance. When her brother, after squeamishly learning to gut a squirrel, asks if they eat the organ meat, she quips darkly, 'Not yet.' While her siblings frolic with the stray dogs and newborn kittens that find their way to the cabin beneath the perpetually overcast skies of early winter, Lawrence carries herself like someone who knows the rules of the world and the cost of breaking them." (Keith Phipps, *The Onion A.V. Club*, June 10, 2010)

Ree Dolly is indeed a fascinating character and Jennifer Lawrence inhabits her completely. What five words would you use to describe Ree Dolly? What gives Ree the strength to carry on not only caring for the family but also searching for her father in the face of all the obstacles that are put before her?

3. "*Winter's Bone* isn't a liberal sociological study of poverty; nor does it rely on genre conventions. We feel so apprehensive for Ree because we have no idea which way the story will go: Mafia behavior is predictable; the Dollys are unfathomable. We look to the older Dolly women for clues. They work at protecting their mangy, surly men, but they know how to get around them, too, and, when they have to, they do the dirty business of cleaning up crimes. Ree is the only hope amid this sordid life. She's not just the most interesting teen-ager around, she's more believable as a heroic character than any of the men we've seen peacocking through movies recently. In its lived-in, completely non-ideological way, *Winter's Bone* is one of the great feminist works in film." (David Denby, *The New Yorker*, July 5, 2010)

How would you defend Denby's statement that this film is "one of the greatest feminist works in film." Use scenes from the film to explain your response.

4. "So it falls to Ree to do what male heroes from Jason and the Argonauts seeking the Golden Fleece to Galahad searching for the Holy Grail have done: She goes on a quest. More than that, she sets out to find her father in a world where women acting independently is actively discouraged. When someone asks her, 'Ain't you got no men folk to do this?' the answer is clearly no. Ree undertakes this classic genre exercise in an especially dangerous, convincingly brutal world. Though she is related by blood to many of the people she will be asking for help, the pervasive drug culture that has wreaked havoc in the area has made everyone even more close-mouthed, suspicious and not averse to mayhem. Ree may be proud to be 'a Dolly bread and buttered,' as she puts it, but Dollywood this is definitely not." (Kenneth Turan, *Los Angeles Times*, June 11, 2010)

The theme of quest is one we are familiar with in movies from *Star Wars* to *The Lord of the Rings*. There are "rules" for such journeys. Based on what you know of the theme of "quest" from other films and from this one, what are some of these rules and how are they exemplified here?

3. The Relationship of the Movie to the Theme of the Exercise

1. "This is a world out of time and, despite the trappings of flinty realism, the film too unfolds like an elemental myth from the stormy past – a Greek tragedy driven by dark fates and strug-

gling toward a catharsis." (Rick Groen, *The Globe and Mail*, June 17, 2010)

The Second Exercise speaks of the importance of imagination in our lives and of what happens when our imaginations are liberated. How does a liberated imagination allow us – with the help of this film – to enter into a world that few, if any of us, have ever experienced?

2. Ree is smart, tough, and pragmatic. She has what most everyone around her lacks: a profound and determined sense of justice. Her quest is not only a real one – to track down her father – but also a symbolic one – to locate in the heart of the community a sense of rightness and decency.

   How does Ree deal with the opportunity in these two quests to become more truly herself by going beyond what she and others see of her? How successful is she in completing her symbolic quest? What is the biggest help to her in this? What is the biggest hindrance?

3. Where does hope fit into this film? Is it the women – who function like a Greek chorus – who offer Ree the only faint hope of success she has? Where does that hope surface? And what does that hope actually bring to Ree? Perhaps that hope is found in the musical family jamboree Ree stumbles upon? Does that jamboree offer a moment of hope that suggests tradition can nurture and sustain those within it? And consider Ree's belief that the hardship that informs life need not corrupt it, and that selfless love is a drug worth taking. Remember the scene in which she, as a sister, says to the children she keeps, "I'd be lost without the weight of you two on my back. I ain't going anywhere."

4. The Relationship of the Movie to One's Self in the Exercise

1. We want to change to the "sensible reality" called for by the Exercise. What is it that is subverting our imagination and not allowing us to "imagine as God imagines, create and God creates"?

2. As Ree goes on her quests, it is soon clear to her that not only is she somehow different from the people of her community, even her relatives, but also that they see her as different from them. At this point in the Exercises, what is your own understanding of how you are present to yourself and to others?

3. This Exercise encourages us to expand our imagination, seeing it not only as the producer of fantasy and images but also as the "producer of all that actually is." In your own life, on your own journey, what use do you make of the mass media – particularly TV and film – and how do they help you to expand your imagination?

(2) The Annunciation

Mary's prayer:

You come to me, O mysterious One, as Desire
O, My deepest Desire

and I, thus found, am lost
in Your Love
You take from me

All I know
except your Love
calling me beyond my life
into Your darkness
to trust you and you alone

You open my life
as a beggar's bowl
and I am attentive to what is daily given

Such riches
I have not imagined

I offer what is given
the life that flows
through my emptiness
water to the thirsty
food to the hungry
a home to the dispossessed

all because I said yes
to your, first, Yes.   (adapted from Luke 1:46-55)

Consider what the persons on the face of the earth do, for example, wound, kill and go down to hell. Also what the Divine Persons do, namely, work the most holy Incarnation, etc. Likewise, what the Angel and our Lady do; how the Angel carries out his office as ambassador; and how our Lady humbles herself, and offers thanks to the Divine Majesty.   (Sp. Ex. #10)

Here it will be to ask for an intimate knowledge of our Lord, who has become human for me, that I may love Him more and follow Him more closely.

The Risks of God

In the narratives of the Bible, God constantly risks his plans and desires with his human collaborators. This begins in the Old Testament with Adam and Eve, then moves through Abraham and Sarah, Isaac, Jacob, Joseph, Moses, David, and the chosen people. They all agreed to the covenanted relationship, but they all broke it. God chose each of them in love, and kept on risking his life with each of them. Nevertheless, God did not give up on them, and God does not give up on us. God also constantly risks his plans and desires with each of us.

In the New Testament, God's risk-taking reaches new levels. The Three Persons of the Trinity commit all of their creative plan to the free response of a politically, socially, and culturally insignificant young woman in a small village in a war-torn and occupied territory in the Middle East. They desire that she become the mother of the Word made Flesh. This has never happened before in human history. The God of all creation asks Mary, who is engaged but not yet married to Joseph, to break all the codes of orthodox religious behaviour and consent to a plan that challenges the boundaries of established sanity and conventional wisdom. The story is told in Luke 1:26-38.

In today's contemplation, you are asked to enter into the dynamics of this mystery.

The iconic depictions of Mary's response presented in Luke's gospel have been refined in order to express post-resurrection theology. But imagine a young girl's crisis when she finds herself unmarried and pregnant. How can she explain the pregnancy to her betrothed? To her family? To his family? To the village? Historically, young girls have from time immemorial become suddenly pregnant. The excuses have varied, but the reality has remained the same, and the punishments in the Middle East, as in many other cultures of the world, for bringing such shame upon one's clan are brutal.

Even before Mary agrees to co-operate with God's plan, the implications of such an act weigh in. Mary has the freedom to accept or to decline. God neither seduces nor rapes. For Mary, this is not a moment of reckless romantic abandon that no after-life of prudent consideration will compensate for. She does not hurl herself into this act unthinkingly. Neither does she bargain. What shapes her answer is her own love story with God. Her love for God frees her to trust her entire being, and her future, to that One from whom she has accepted the gift of being the beloved. She agrees to become the mother of the Messiah.

Opening to Love

In this contemplation we are asked to do two things. First, we are asked to be as fully present as possible to God's incredible vulnerability and trust in offering the deepest mystery of his love to one of his creation. Second, we are invited to enter into Mary's profound sense of self-offering as she says yes to God's invitation. In doing so we may feel ourselves being opened by love to our very depths. We may choose in the prayer to behold Mary with God's eyes, and find ourselves profoundly grateful for that love that says yes to what it does not understand, a yes to an intimacy that will carry it to places beyond its imaginings. We may even choose to enter into the role of the angel who mediates between God and Mary, and experience what it means to be missioned and to find one's life, joy, and meaning in that service. Our entry into our annunciation is to let the desire that is our life encounter the Desire who desires us to the depths of our being. We, like Mary, or God, or the angel, experience annunciation as the expression of desire. We are asked to allow ourselves to acknowledge ourselves as that desire that wells up in us and manifests itself as the profound longing to love, and to give our lives in service to that Love that passionately and profoundly desires us. When our deepest longing encounters that simple and all-encompassing love, we enter the state of intimacy called annunciation.

To facilitate this contemplation, you might want to read the passage in Luke's gospel that describes this scene (Luke 1:26-38). Spend time with the encounter. Allow the energies of the Annunciation to touch your own energies in their desire to be part of the ongoing incarnation that occurs when we open ourselves to God in love.

The love affair that we are invited to here is willing to risk itself for us and in us. It invites us to respond – not impetuously, but freely. Where we are free, we experience love. Where we are not free, we experience the tug of compulsion. We can offer only what we have. This love, which has waited since the beginning of time for Mary to appear and to be ready, now waits for us.

Questions for Prayer and Reflection

1. Have you ever felt called in love to do something?

2. How was this different from being compelled?

3. Do you know the difference between passion and intensity? Passion calls us beyond our egos; intensity inflates those egos.

4. Have you ever waited on someone in love?

5. What is it like?

6. Have you ever experienced someone waiting on you in love? What was that like?

7. Our lives are filled with moments of annunciation. Identify some of these moments and enter into those experiences again.

8. What was the prayer you just experienced like?

9. What did it reveal to you about yourself? about God? about your path in the world?

10. If you were to have a conversation with Mary about her experience of annunciation, what would you say? What do you think she would say to you?

To say yes to love opens us up to an incredible level of vulnerability – both God's and our own – and often in contexts that are destructive. Here we are asked to trust in the Divine Providence that does not seek to have us destroyed. We must be discerning so that we can distinguish between what is good and what only appears to be good. In saying yes, we maintain our integrity in the face of the seductions towards the lesser good.

In the Nativity, we see God's providence at work in a world alienated from the greater good that desires the fullness of life for all.

The Movie

JUNO

Director: Jason Reitman (2007 – 96 mins.)
Starring: Ellen Page, Michael Cera, Jennifer Garner, Jason Bateman

1. Synopsis

One autumn, sixteen-year-old Juno, a high school student, discovers she's pregnant after a one-time sexual encounter with her best friend, Paulie. Neither Juno nor Paulie consider themselves ready to be a family complete with a child. Paulie is there for Juno, but leaves the decision about the baby up to her.

In the waiting room of an abortion clinic, Juno makes the decision to have the baby and to give the child up for adoption. Her parents support her decision and the search is on for prospective parents for the child. In the Pennysaver ad section of the paper, Juno finds Mark and Vanessa Loring, a yuppie couple living in the suburbs. Juno meets with the chosen parents, and, finding that she likes them, signs adoption papers – a closed rather than open adoption contract, meaning she will have no contact with the baby after she gives it up. Juno carries on with school, treats the pregnancy with care but detachment, and the year unfolds.

2. About the Movie

1. "Pregnant as a beachball and vulnerable as a child, Juno crashes hard against the brokenness of everything. It's not just one marriage breaking down because the husband is foolish and selfish. It's how everything breaks down – marriages, friendships, truths we once held with certainty. Juno at sixteen has to figure out how to live in this world full of divorce, cowardice and disaster. Isaiah could have written the rest of the script. The hope of the world is that a young woman is with child and shall bear a son." (Michael Swan, *The Catholic Register*, February 10, 2008) How does the child Juno bears become a solution to begin the putting together that which has been broken in her world? How does this seem to be a script written by the prophet Isaiah?

2. This film "not only gives us a superb new cast of believable characters, it transcends its own genre. Only superficially a teen comedy, the movie redounds with postmodern – but emotionally genuine – gravitas." (Desson Thomson, *Washington Post*, December 14, 2007)

   What gives this film "postmodern gravitas"? Is it the memorable banter among the characters, all of whom feel real? Is it Juno – a charming, complex and witty personality who uses irony to cope with overwhelming issues? What are some examples of the irony in this film?

3. "The screenwriter, Diablo Cody, knows the limits of this story and, better still, the limits of our

patience for its sentimental possibilities, and Jason Reitman, the director, is also a cool operator. He's much more a wry observer than an over-eager manipulator of our emotions. One example: almost every time Juno is on the street, a team of uniformed runners goes jogging silently past. They symbolize, I suppose, the fact that there are other people in the world, lost in their own preoccupations, benignly indifferent to the issues absorbing Juno, absorbing us. It is a smart reminder that the story any fiction relates is arbitrarily chosen and dependent for its effect on the ability of its tellers to enlist our interest – no special pleading, no emotional cheap shots permitted." (Richard Schickel, *Time*, December 7, 2007)

What are some other examples of Reitman's wry observations? What do they symbolize?

3. The Relationship of the Movie to the Theme of the Exercise

1. Building on the notion of developing the imagination, which you examined in the last Exercise, how does this film takes us beyond being just another teen angst film to deal with issues of love and caring?

2. Love, in many forms, is at the centre of this film. Juno herself searches for love on different levels, knowing that, as the Exercise tells us, it will carry her "to places beyond imagining." Where does Juno's love take her and what happens to her as she travels to these places?

3. In the Exercise we see how what God asks of Mary challenged "the boundaries of established sanity and conventional wisdom." How does Juno's search for love also challenge everything that we might have come to expect from the Juno we first meet?

4. The Relationship of the Movie to One's Self in the Exercise

1. We can only imagine the loneliness that Mary felt when she accepted the call of God. There was no one who would believe her if she were to tell them what had happened. When Juno sets out on her quest, she also experiences loneliness. In your own response to God's call, to whom do you turn when you find yourself falling into loneliness? Who gives you the strength to continue and how do they do that?

2. The love to which this Exercise calls us invites us to respond freely but not impetuously. What is it in your own life that causes you not to be able to respond in this way?

3. The love that is God asks only that we offer what we have. What is it that Juno has to offer on this journey to find love? What is it that you have in your own life to offer what waits for you?

117

The Nativity

She gave birth to her first-born son and wrapped him in swaddling cloths, and laid him in a manger, because there was no place for them in the inn. (Luke 1:7)

Consider what [the Holy Family] are doing, for example, making the journey and labouring that our Lord may be born, in extreme poverty, and that after many labours, after hunger, thirst, heat, and cold, after insults and outrages, He might die on the cross, and all this for me. (Sp. Ex. #116)

This is to ask for what I desire. Here it will be to ask for an intimate knowledge of our Lord, who has become human for me, that I may love Him more and follow Him more closely.

The Illusions of Christmas

We have sentimentalized Christmas. We have made it pretty and politically correct. We are trapped in the tug of unreality this creation imposes upon us with its saccharine depictions of peace, family harmony, Victorian cheer, and nativity crèches of pious and frozen poses. Prayer does not support such illusion; instead, it puts us in touch with the truth, of which those illusions are fragmented distortions. The contemplation on the nativity of Christ allows us to experience the mystery of the divine love, and of various forms of human love present to each other in mutual dependence in the most difficult of circumstances. It invites us to share in that reality as we now read and contemplate prayerfully Luke 2:1-14.

Between the Annunciation and Jesus' birth, Mary's life has not been settled. She has told Joseph of her condition. He decides to break their engagement quietly, and is only dissuaded from this plan by a dream. He has not been involved in Mary's original decision; yet his life, too, is turned upside down by these unique events, about which he has to make choices and commitments. Then Mary leaves to visit Elizabeth, her kinswoman, who has become pregnant in her old age. Mary cares for her and then returns home, only to set out for Bethlehem to register in the Roman census with her husband and his family. Her baby will be born soon. There, in spite of the cult of hospitality, her condition and the shame it brings upon them affords her and Joseph no space in his family homes. There is no mention of care or concern from those quarters. There is not even room in the inn. In the place where animals are stabled, the Christ is born.

Caring for God

Ignatius asks us to enter into that human drama of struggle and sacrifice so that love can be born. In our contemplations of the sequences leading up to and including the birth, he suggests that we make ourselves "poor, little, and unworthy servant[s] [of the holy family] gazing at them, contemplating them, and serving them in their needs ... with all possible respect and reverence" (#114). In this poverty, we imitate the Divine Word, who "did not count equality with God as something to hold onto, but emptied himself, taking on the form of a servant" (1 Philippians 2:7). That second person of the Trinity becomes poor and humble in the service of a love that desires to save us and all of creation. As we enter into that love, we find ourselves taking on its characteristics.

Mary and Joseph also take on those characteristics of self-emptying. One of the points of this contemplation, Ignatius tells us, "is to behold and consider what they are doing; for example, journeying and toiling that the Lord may be born in greatest poverty; and that after so many hardships of hunger, thirst, heat, cold, injuries, and insults, he may die on the cross! And all this for me!" (#116).

In this contemplation we witness that self-emptying love in Mary and Joseph and in their relationships with each other. Mary gives up her own personal interests and desires because of that love. God does not abandon her after the moment of annunciation. His love remains active in her world. When Joseph wants to dismiss her, God intercedes with him in his dreams, and Joseph takes Mary as his wife. That same God protects the family in their trials when the political forces of the day seek to destroy Jesus. But even with this help, their lives are not easy; rather, their lives are rooted in a love for God that goes beyond their self-interests. They respond to God's love, which, in its mysterious ways, chose them to be part of its merciful providence.

When we enter into this contemplation, we enter into all the aspects of that journey to birthing God in this world. We go with Mary and Joseph on their journey, and make it our own journey. We are present to the perils and the uncertainties of that journey, present to the care and concern they show to each other. We are present at the birth of Christ, the miracle of seeing God fully human and fully vulnerable, needing us. We can ask to hold that child and that love in our arms, in our hearts, and with our lives.

We conclude this prayer period with a conversation to the Trinity, to the Christ, or to Mary about what stirs in us during the contemplation.

Questions for Prayer and Reflection

1   How did you find this contemplation?

2.   What happened to you in this contemplation? Where did it take you?

3.   What was deeply personal for you in this prayer?

4.   How did it feel to hold the child Jesus?

5.   What did the prayer confirm in you?

6.   What was the conversation at the end of the contemplation like?

7.   Is there any part of the prayer that you feel called to return to because you know there is more in it for you?

8.   Did you find any part of the prayer difficult or dry? Why do you think that was so? What does it tell you about yourself?

119

The Movie
CHILDREN OF MEN

Director: Alfonso Cuaron (2006 – 99 mins.)
Starring: Clive Owen, Julianne Moore, Michael Caine

1. Synopsis

In 2027, after no child has been born for eighteen years, a peace activist named Theo Faron and his ex-wife Julian join forces to save humankind by protecting a young woman, Kee, who has mysteriously become pregnant. Leading Kee on a dangerous trip across England to reach the Human Project, Theo must learn whom to trust.

Note: Rated R for strong violence, language, some drug use, and brief nudity.

2. About the Movie

1. "The idea of the world redeemed by a helpless infant is a specifically Christian one, but here it shines out from a landscape that is bitterly stripped of faith. The people I know who have seen *Children of Men* have admired its grip, but they had to be dragged to the theatre; it's a film that you need to see, not a film that you especially want to. I guess it should it be logged as sci-fi, yet by 2027 mankind is clearly beyond the reach of science, and the roughened pace of the film – photographed by Emmanuel Lubezki – leans away from fiction and toward the natural stutter of reportage." (Anthony Lane, *The New Yorker*, January 08, 2007)

Why should you have to be "dragged to a theatre" to see this film? Why is Lane telling us that this is a film we "need to see ... not especially want to?"

2. "Owen carries the film more in the tradition of a Jimmy Stewart or Henry Fonda. than a Clint Eastwood or Harrison Ford. He has to wear flip-flops for part of the time without losing his dignity, and he never reaches for a weapon or guns anyone down. Cuaron and Owen may have created the first believable 21st-century movie hero." (Ray Bennett, *The Hollywood Reporter*, January 08, 2007)

What is your concept of the typical hero of an action film? How is Clive Owen's portrayal different from what one might expect from a young Harrison Ford?

3. "*Children of Men* is clearly more than a thrilling chase movie: it's meant to hold a barely distorted mirror to the world we're living in now. But the characters are too sketchy for the political metaphors to resonate .... What exactly will it accomplish to get Kee out of the country? Since the future of mankind rests on this pregnant girl, we want details. *Children of Men* leaves too many questions unanswered, yet it has a stunning visceral impact. You can forgive a lot in the face of

filmmaking this dazzling." (David Ansen, *Newsweek*, December 18, 2006)

Why should this film be expected to answer all the questions? Doesn't the mirror the film holds up to us show us enough that we accept the premise just as the director has. Is it not enough to accept the situation as a given, that the film actually puts us alongside the characters on their journey, and go from there?

4. "Cuarón has a gift only the greatest filmmakers share: He makes you believe." (Peter Travers, *Rolling Stone*, December 25, 2006)

What is it that Cuaron makes you believe? How does he do this?

3. The Relationship of the Movie to the Theme of the Exercise

1. We've looked at the importance of the use of the imagination in the Exercises. This film uses imagination to interpret what might be called transcendental themes – life and death, alternate worlds, appearance and reality, love and betrayal. Which of these themes appeals to you and how does the movie reveal them to you?

2. The Exercise speaks to us about the human drama of struggle and sacrifice that must take place before love can be born. In this film where do we find such a struggle and sacrifice? And what is it that is waiting to be born?

3. Darkly poetic throughout, the film starts with an explosion and ends drifting in fog with no clear resolution in sight. How brave and oddly satisfying this is. Along the way we meet people whose lives are rooted – as the Exercise says – in a love that goes beyond their self-interests. Who are some of these people and how do we see this love expressed in the film?

4. The Relationship of the Movie to One's Self in the Exercise

1. When we are present at the Birth of Christ we are asked to note the perils and uncertainties of the journey as well as the care and concern those involved show to each other. How is this type of care and concern reflected in this film and how is it reflected in your own journey of love? What are the perils and uncertainties of your journey? What stops you from fully entering into your journey?

2. Theo must learn to overcome his doubts and to understand that he is the one chosen to protect and lead to safety the woman who holds the key to the existence of the human race. The Exercise refers to such a process as working towards "self-emptying." What prevents you from such an act?

3. Just as we learn in the Exercise that Mary must give up her own personal interests and desires, and – as we've seen – Theo also must do likewise, so now it is your turn to discover the personal interests and desires that you are being asked to give up.

4th Exercise
The Early Life of Christ (I)

Jesus increased in wisdom and in stature, and in favour with God and man. (Luke 2:52)

I will make myself a poor little unworthy slave, and as though present, look upon them, contemplate them, and serve them in their needs with all possible homage and reverence. (Sp. Ex. #114)

This is to ask for what I desire. Here it will be to ask for an intimate knowledge of our Lord, who has become man for me, that I may love Him more and follow Him more closely. (Sp. Ex. #104)

The First Ones to See Jesus

Ignatius divides the early incidents of the life of the Christ child in the following sequence: the angels' announcement of the birth of Christ to the shepherds (Luke 2:8-20); the circumcision of Christ (Luke 2:21); the visit of the three kings (Matthew 2:1-12); the purification of Our Lady and the presentation of the Infant Jesus (Luke 2:22-38). Normally, each one of these incidents would be a prayer period in itself. The intent of each section, and of the whole sequence, is to proclaim God's mercy to the human condition. In our contemplations we are asked to find ourselves in that mercy, and so we always pray during this Week of the Exercises for that grace of "an interior knowledge of Our Lord, who became human for me, that I may love Him more and follow Him more closely" (#104).

It is helpful to unpack the gift we are asking for in these prayer periods. We seek an intimacy with the Christ first of all. That intimacy goes to the source of our being, where we are rooted in God. It is out of this rootedness that love flows, and it is out of this love that we discover how to follow Christ in service. The love does not create the intimacy; the prior intimacy manifests itself in love. Ignatius believes we are all mystics since we are all rooted in the mystery we call God. Sin deceives us into living out of the false notions of who we truly are. But as we enter the path of the Incarnation, we return to our depths, and there we discover our union with God, who has always been united to us. The journey through the Exercises is the path to an intimacy that includes, but goes beyond, the sensible, the emotional, the social. It is a journey that allows us to seek and find God in all that we encounter. The God we discover excludes nothing and no one.

A Politically Incorrect God

The shepherds were the first to be shown the birth of Christ. Shepherds, in Christ's time, were regarded as depraved, corrupt, and outside of the Law. They were social outcasts and considered to have less value than the animals they protected. Shepherds were the poorest of the poor. When you are poor, no one believes in you; you do not even believe in yourself. Yet it is to these that the angels came with the news of Christ's birth, and they were the first outsiders to see him in the flesh. At this point it is helpful to remember the gift of the First Week, when the divine mercy comes to those who are alienated from themselves and from others. The love we experience in this contemplation is the same love that goes out to the shepherds. Divine love desires that nothing and no one is left out of its embrace.

That divine mercy calls to all: poor and rich, wise and unlearned. It calls to the magi – those wise ones from a religious tradition other than the Jewish faith. Following their hearts' desire and using the knowledge available to them, they, too, encounter the Christ child; they worship and they offer their gifts to this tiny human manifestation of the divine. On their journey to Bethlehem, they also encounter Herod, the duplicitous, who seeks their knowledge for his own ends. But because they are under the divine mercy, they escape his wiles.

For Ignatius, God's love is not exclusive or other-worldly. It concerns itself with everyone, no matter what their state of life. The nativity story reveals a God who touches the lives of a variety of people to affirm, protect, or rescue them, or to answer their needs. Inasmuch as we, too, are touched by that divine mercy, we see, as the Trinity does, everyone in need of love. In our desire to be one with that love, we offer freely to all, here and now, what has been given to us freely and joyfully. That love is the witness of the intimacy we share with God. The witness does not come from obligation or compulsion or ideology. It flows out of a covenant – a *cum-venio* – the coming together of God and ourselves.

Circumcision is the sign of the covenant between the Jewish people and God. When Christ is circumcised, he witnesses to that covenanted love. In being named "Jesus," he becomes the embodiment of that naming that "God saves." Where we place our bodies witnesses to what we value, and how we place our bodies incarnates those values. Among the Christmas names of Jesus is "Emmanuel" – God is with us. In the Christ child, we see a God who is one with humanity, who in human form is still the second person of the Trinity. We experience the value God places in us: he enters our human condition so that one day we can enter into God's own life. In these prayers, we ask to experience ourselves as ones who are so valued. The contemplation asks us to enter into that experience of being so valued – not just intellectually, but intimately and with all of our senses and desires. It asks us to relish that intimacy and to rest in it.

The Patience of Hope

It is this intimacy that Simeon and Anna relish when they encounter Joseph and Mary as they bring Jesus to present him in the temple. Both Simeon and Anna were devout people. They had lived through the trials of a Roman occupation and through the corruptions of Herod's religious politics without abandoning hope that one day they would experience the deliverance of Israel. They always remained faithful to God's promise, not knowing when it would be given or in what form it would take. God is gracious to them in their patience and humility and long-suffering. That long waiting on God teaches them discernment. It lets them see what is from God and what is not from God. Because their eyes are so opened, they can see in the ordinary baby the promise of God. That day at the temple, God rewards their patience and fidelity. They know Jesus to be that lived answer to their hope and their faith. They feel, touch, see, and hold their hearts' desire. Too often we give up our heart's desire. We accept what the world has to offer as the only reality. But our desire never gives up on us, for to do that is to die. If, in this contemplation, we can open ourselves to our deepest desires, to the pain and the longing, and to its promise, we, like Simeon and Anna, discover in our patient waiting a gift that answers that longing. It is the Christ. Let us relish that gift in this contemplation.

Questions for Prayer and Reflection

1. In the contemplation, which particular incident was particularly meaningful for you? Why?

2. How does it feel to enter into Christ's life in your contemplations?

3. How does it feel to have Christ enter into your life during these contemplations?

4. What does this tell you about your developing relationship with God?

5. What comes up as significant in your conversations with God, or with Mary, or with Jesus at the end of the prayer period?

6. Does anything disturb you in the prayer? What? Why do you think that happens?

7. How is your prayer influencing the rest of your day or week?

8. How is the time out of prayer affecting your contemplations?

9. Do you think you are getting the grace of an intimate knowledge of the Christ from your prayer?

10. How does that grace affect you?

The Movie
A PROPHET

Director: Jacques Audiard (2009 – 155 mins.)
Starring: Tahar Rahim, Niels Arestup, Adel Bencherif

1. Synopsis

Nineteen-year-old Malik, a French Arab, is beginning a six-year prison sentence. He hopes to serve his time peacefully, with no problems. But César Luciani has other ideas. He conscripts Malik to take part in criminal activities both within and outside the prison.

The other Corsicans don't like it: they think Malik is just a dirty Arab. The Muslims, meanwhile, no longer trust him. Malik just carries on, trying to save himself while in prison and to set up his future life on his own terms.

Note: Rated R for strong violence, sexual content, nudity, language, and drug material.

Note: If at all possible, watch the subtitled version. Much of an actor's art lies in the use of voice to express emotion, mood, and character. Dubbed movies can never have the full impact of the original.

2. About the Movie

1. "Movie history is full of charismatic criminal antiheroes, from Edward G. Robinson's Little Caesar to Al Pacino's Scarface. But Malik El Djebena, the young convict … brings something new to the party. When baby-faced Malik enters a tough French prison at age 19, sentenced to six years for an assault against a police officer he says he did not commit, he seems more like an innocent or a feral child than a hardened criminal. We learn virtually nothing about his life to that point, except that he can neither read nor write. He offers prison authorities only baffling non-answers to questions about his family and childhood. It's as if Malik were just born, a test-tube hybrid spawned in the underbelly of the new France." (Andrew O'Hehir, *Salon*, February 25, 2010)

Why (or why not) would you call Malik less an antihero than an old-fashioned hero who triumphs over his appalling circumstances and never loses the audience's sympathy?

2. *A Prophet* could easily have been a very depressing film, but it isn't. It is quite enthralling not only in its technical brilliance but also from our sense that Malik's rise to power stems from something mysterious within himself, an inexplicable moral centre that may be related to his premonitory visions. Does this make the title at least half-ironic? Is Malik a real prophet, and if so, what is his message?

3. Director Audiard isn't much interested in the story's pop-psychological aspects or ethnic politics. He gives us a crime film that, as Andrew

O'Hehir points out, "stretches the form to its outermost limits, resisting the most familiar kinds of characterizations or narrative clichés." How does the director accomplish this? How does he turn the movie into something much more than just a crime film?

4. In an interview at Cannes (quoted in Kenneth Turan, *Los Angeles Times*, February 26, 2010), director Audiard explains that he not only believes in this style of storytelling in and of itself, he values it for what it can clandestinely say about larger issues. "What interests me about genre," he said in an interview, "is that the public connects immediately with it. I like that it's a popular form of cinema with mass appeal. Art cinema aspects and elements can be inserted and reach the widest audience.'" What other examples can you offer of films that have done the same thing – taken a popular genre and inserted a very powerful message?

3. The Relationship of the Movie to the Theme of the Exercise

1. Like the shepherds in the Exercise, Malik is an outcast to many – even perhaps regarded as less than human. The Exercise also tell us that we have to experience ourselves as valued. In what ways does the movie show us that Malik is valued by God?

2. How is Malik a prophet? Does this role play a part in the way he comes to accept the various groups he meets in and out of prison? The Exercise tells us that love desires that nothing and no one is left out. How does Malik show love to the people around him?

3. The intent of this part of the Exercises is to manifest the witness of proclaiming God's mercy within the human condition. Do you see what is happening throughout the film as proclaiming God's mercy? Why? Why not?

4. The Relationship of the Movie to One's Self in the Exercise

1. What kind of love motivates Malik? What is there in your life that is motivated by love? What stops you from acting solely out of love in return for the love God gives you?

2. It is clear that Malik refuses to accept what the world has to offer as being the only reality. How willing are you to give your all for what God calls you to? What is the "reality" in your life that the world offers you in place of that love?

The Early Life of Christ (2)

An angel of the Lord appeared to Joseph in a dream and said, "Rise, take the child and his mother, and flee to Egypt, and remain there till I tell you; for Herod is about to search for the child, to destroy him."

(Matthew 2:13)

It is characteristic of God and His Angels, when they act upon the soul, to give true happiness and spiritual joy, and to banish all sadness and disturbances which are caused by the enemy.
It is characteristic of the evil one to fight against such happiness and consolation by proposing fallacious reasonings, subtleties, and continual deception.

(Sp. Ex. #329)

This is to ask for what I desire. Here it will be to ask for an intimate knowledge of our Lord, who has become man for me, that I may love Him more and follow Him more closely.

(Sp. Ex. #104)

The Human Cost of Love

Until the beginning of Jesus' public life, the scriptures mention only three incidents after the presentation of Christ in the temple. Ignatius cites these as the flight into Egypt (Matthew 2:13-18), the return from Egypt (Matthew 2:19-23), and his discovery in the temple at the age of twelve (Luke 2:41-50). All three show the human cost of love: the way those who commit themselves to the Divine Life are treated in the world. Innocents are slaughtered because they are suspected of being a political threat. Jesus and his family become refugees and lead lives abandoned to Divine Providence. The contemplations based on these scripture passages destroy the notion of a sentimental God as a divine Santa Claus. They show, instead, the power of love in hard times, in the face of absurdity and worldly malice. The focus of that love is always on the primary call of the divine.

The Powers of the World

In secular terms, where reality is understood only as a worldly construct, any claim to power or authority is a challenge to the rulers of the time. Such is the case with Herod when he hears the news of Christ's birth. He is dominated by his desire to eliminate what he sees as a challenge to his authority. As local king, he orders the death of any male child born in and around Bethlehem around the time of Christ's nativity. Christ escapes that slaughter because Joseph is told in a dream to take his family and flee into Egypt. Here Matthew's story echoes the story in Genesis of Joseph the dreamer, who is sold by his brothers into slavery in Egypt. There he eventually rises to power and rescues the Israelites in a time of famine. Egypt, as we note in the book of Exodus, is place of exile and slavery. Matthew's Joseph and family become refugees, aliens in an alien land. Their commitment to God, and God's commitment to

127

them, prevents them from being destroyed, but it does not prevent them from suffering loss, hardship, and exile. Moreover, the story also tells us the tragic cost to those families with children around Jesus' age. The presence of God's mercy in this world provokes the powers of this world to act with outrageous cruelty. No one, not even the innocent and the unwitting, are uninvolved in this cosmic human drama. All are involved; all are consumed. We, too, find ourselves in this sphere of action.

In this contemplation we encounter the forces of the divine and the energies of the despotic. We can ask, in the midst of human suffering "Where is God?" God can also ask, "Where are you in all of this?" God shows us where he is: he is the life in the midst of death. We are asked to follow the Christ.

The return from exile occurs when Herod dies. But the hope for homecoming is dashed when Herod's equally corrupt son assumes the throne. Instead of being able to return home, Joseph, once again warned in a dream, withdraws with his family to Nazareth in Galilee, where Jesus grows up.

The Sacred Space in Every Exile

Every exile dreams of returning home. Exiles define themselves by memory. They long for the place and the people they remember as their own. They suffer from a homesickness caused by too long an absence from all that roots them and gives them their identity. That dream and that desire become a passion – at times, even an obsession. This passion provokes a fanaticism for a homeland free of foreign influences. In Joseph's case, despite that dreadful and raw need, he remains faithful to the covenant promise of the Messiah who will restore the fortunes of Israel. He waits, open to the mystery of God's provenance. His new home, he discovers, is within the relationships of Mary and Jesus, and not within the pre-established norms of clan, culture, and land.

When we enter into this contemplation, we enter into a sacred space where our own dreams and energies are realigned from clan and culture, ethnicity or ego-orientation, to our deepest passion: to be one with God. We acknowledge both what we desire from our human point of view and what God is giving us.

Even Mary and Joseph endure this human tension. They have sacrificed everything for the sake of the one they call Jesus. Yet, at Passover, when it is time for his ritual entrance into adulthood, the twelve-year-old Jesus leaves them behind to stay in the temple. As he later tells them, "Did you not know I must be in my Father's house?" (Luke 3:49). Jesus' passionate desire is always for the Father; everything else finds meaning only in that relationship. The story foretells another Passover, some 21 years later, when the Christ's passion for his Father, and the Father's passion for the Christ, reaches through the boundaries of human life and human relationships – death. – to resurrection. The focus on Divine Providence that underlies the early life of Jesus, as well as his family, sets the stage for his public life and ministry.

If the earlier parts of this prayer period reveal the focus of love in a corrupt and cruel world, the prayer ends with that focus bearing in on the intimate relationships within a small family centred on the Christ. The pattern is the same: the relationship with God is of the utmost importance. It is only that intimacy that allows us to live a life of love in situations that mock the reality of a God who cares. The prayer does not lead us away from those terrible situations. Rather, it invites us to seek and find God in those places where Jesus finds himself, and us.

In this prayer you are asked to enter more and more deeply into that relationship by contemplating the early life of Christ in the world of his time.

Questions for Prayer and Reflection

1. In these prayer periods, you have been asking for the grace of "an interior knowledge of Our Lord, who became human for me, that I may love him more and follow him more closely" (#104). How has this grace been given to you?

2. What has been revealed to you about the nature of the world? How do you react to that spontaneously? How do you react to it when you travel with Christ?

3. What was the most consoling thing about this prayer? What does it tell you about yourself and about your relationship with God?

4. What has been the most negative thing about this prayer? When did it occur? What does it suggest about your values and relationships?

5. Have you ever had an experience of being alienated or separated from the people or the places you loved? How did you survive that separation?

6. Are any aspects of your life like being in exile, being a refugee, or being the pawn of forces greater than you? What are they? What forces exile you?

7. How do you deal with those aspects and those forces?

8. Can you bring those forces and those aspects to your contemplation, or to your dialogues with God?

The Movie
THE YOUNG VICTORIA

Director: Jean-Marc Vallée (2009 – 165 mins)
Starring: Emily Blunt, Rupert Friend, Paul Bettany, Miranda Richardson

1. Synopsis

Tumultuous historical incidents around the accession to the throne, the early reign of Queen Victoria of England (who reigned from 1819 to 1901), and her marriage to Prince Albert are the basis for this film. Victoria, now a teenager, refuses to give her mother and her consort, Conroy, the power to act as her regent in the last days of the reign of her uncle, William IV.

Albert, a Saxon Prince and her German cousin, is encouraged to court Victoria for political reasons. But when she ascends the throne at the age of eighteen, he falls in love with her and is dismayed by her reliance on prime minister Melbourne. Victoria's loyalty to the prime minister nearly results in a constitutional crisis; Albert helps her regain self-confidence. They marry; Albert becomes a devoted spouse and an agent of much-needed reform, and helps Victoria find her purpose.

2. About the Movie

1. "What filmmaker Jean-Marc Vallée has done in this delicious historical romance is capture that hot blush of pure emotion that comes before kisses, sex, heartbreak and the rest can dilute it. Vallée understands the power in the promise of things to come, and though kings and queens might abuse the power, the director uses it wisely." (Betsy Sharkey, *Los Angeles Times*, December 18, 2009)

   Less is more. Unlike other historical romances, there is no "bodice ripping," or even a lurking vampire or two. What is that "hot blush of pure emotion" that Sharkey refers to, and how does the director manage to capture it?

2. "What young girl doesn't dream of being a princess?" asks Queen Victoria in a voice-over from the British period drama *The Young Victoria*. Those who do have such dreams have had any number of films – *The Princess Diaries*, *The Princess Diaries 2*, *Enchanted*, *The Princess and the Frog* – and an astonishing array of dolls, games, and other products to help fulfill their dream.

   The princess craze parallels a trend for grown-up movies about female royalty – dramas that focus less on tiaras and gowns than on the complex problems of women wielding power in a man's world. What are some of the more recent films that deal with this?

3. The movie follows Victoria through a series of conflicts with powerful men – her mother's comptroller, Sir John Conroy; her first prime minister, Lord Melbourne; and finally Albert – as she learns the art of politics and gradually gains control of her own fate.

How does Victoria gain control over these men? Does this make her a feminist heroine? Isn't she an unlikely choice as a role model for women, given her sexual conservatism and rigid gender codes?

4. From the start, Victoria and Albert's relationship is bound up in the exercise of power. As they play chess together Victoria asks Albert, "Do you ever feel like a chess piece yourself, in a game being played against your will?" When Albert advises her to master the game herself, Victoria asks, "You don't recommend I find a husband to play it for me?" Fixing her with a stare, Albert replies, "I should find one to play it with you, not for you."

This is an implicit offer of partnership and is carried through after their wedding. Why then, later on, does Albert try to take over control from Victoria? How does she not only take back power but also keep Albert's love? How fair is it to say that this film speaks not of regal triumphs but of grown-up compromises and accommodations?

3. The Relationship of the Movie to the Theme of the Exercise

1. The Exercises directs us to contemplate three episodes in the life of Christ – The Flight into Egypt, The Return from Egypt, and The Finding in the Temple. All these episodes show the cost of love. How do the various episodes that make up this film show the cost of love? Consider the various stages of the young Victoria's life that we see portrayed.

2. For much of her young life, Victoria was truly alone and unable to let others into her emotional life. This Exercise speaks to us of the presence of God in the midst of human suffering. Where is God in this movie? Do we have to intuit his presence? Or does the filmmaker clearly present God to us?

3. The Exercise reminds us of the power of love in hard times, in the face of absurdity and worldly malice. Where is the power of love in the hard times, the absurdities, and the malice that make up this film?

4. The Relationship of the Movie to One's Self in the Exercise

1. Victoria, despite the face she must put on in public, is very alone and uncertain of many things. What "face" do you present to the public? Does it show what you are really feeling? What stops you from reaching out to the love you know is offered you by God?

2. The Exercise tells us that God is life in the midst of death and suffering. All of us undergo a variety of suffering in our own lives. Where is God in the midst of your own suffering? What keeps you from opening to him so that he may show you his love?

3. As the Exercise tells us, Mary and Joseph endure this " human tension." The film reveals a great deal of this human tension, not only between Victoria and Albert, but also between Victoria and many others who would use her for their own purposes. In your own life, where is your human tension and how do you "endure" it?

The Hidden Life

In the beginning was the Word, and the Word was with God, and the Word was God. He was in the beginning with God; all things were made through him, and without him was not anything that was made. In him was life, and the life was the light of men. The light shone in the darkness, and the darkness has not overcome it.

(John 1:1-5)

In souls that are progressing to greater perfection the action of the good angel is delicate, gentle, delightful. It may be compared to a drop of water penetrating a sponge.

The action of the evil spirit upon such souls is violent, noisy, and disturbing. It may be compared to a drop of water falling upon a stone. (Sp. Ex. #335)

This is to ask for what I desire. Here it will be to ask for an intimate knowledge of our Lord, who has become man for me, that I may love Him more and follow Him more closely.

Waiting for God

The following exercise may well be one of the most enigmatic of the prayer periods that St. Ignatius asks us to engage in. We are asked to contemplate the hidden life of Christ from age twelve to the beginning of his public ministry, when he sets off for the Jordan and is baptized by his cousin John. Nothing is written of these years except a general statement in Luke: "Jesus increased in wisdom and stature, in favour with God and man" (2:52).

People have different prayer experiences when they ask Jesus to reveal that hidden life. What is fairly common to all is that what is given deepens their personal relationship with Jesus. Each person receives what he or she needs to continue this spiritual journey to intimacy with God.

Up to now, the material of the Exercises has been contained in scripture or in a personal history. Now you are asked to enter the contemplation, in the hope that something will be given to you. This must come from God: it cannot be created by the one doing the Exercises, and yet it must completely involve that person's particular energies and concerns. It is just like someone falling in love saying to the beloved, "Tell me about yourself; tell me what you have never told anyone else." What is given is not conjecture to be verified against possible historical evidence. Its truth lies in the intimate weaving of the personal with the divine within the depths of the psyche, and is experienced through the contemplative imagination.

There is a level of intimacy in love that allows personal questions to be asked. The level of trust established allows those questions to be answered in such a way that the answer reveals both the lover and the beloved.

Here the unknown becomes known; here God makes the incarnation personal.

The relationship with God requires trust. This contemplation is about trust. From the time of the finding in the temple, when Christ announces to his world that he is about his Father's business, Christ waits on the Father to reveal how that business is to take place. At a time when young Jewish men first assume the responsibilities of their maturity – having a job, a vocation, a family of their own – Jesus waits on the Father to reveal to him the next step. He waits eighteen years. He learns to wait. This is an experiential learning that allows him to withstand the temptations in the desert and to wait on the Father's will; this learning continues on the cross, when, in his passion and death, Christ waits on the Father to reveal his love. That revelation is resurrection. But here, in the hidden life, we contemplate a young man's waiting. And we enter into our own waiting.

Learning to Be Ready

There are many ways to wait. We can "kill" time with distractions; we can freeze time in boredom; we can suffer time in anxiety as we search for meaning, purpose, fulfillment. We can slowly learn that the patience of God is time, and so, like Simeon and Anna, become attentive to time, to what is daily given. We learn to cherish each moment without grasping it. In this we learn indifference, that basic stance of doing what we can to the best of our nature, and trusting that what we do reveals our acceptance of the constant mercy of God. Through this learning, we become instruments of God, attuned to God's will. This is what it means to be contemplatives in action. It is not pious and sentimental, or intense and willful. We learn to be flexible and open so that we can delight in what is joyful, mourn with what is sorrowful, revere what is holy, shun what is destructive. We learn to live fully in the world without becoming trapped by the world and its values and judgments.

In this contemplation, we discover how Jesus learns and how he grows into that state of readiness that will allow him to hear and accept his call by the Father at his baptism in the Jordan.

What is happening to Jesus is also happening to us in this contemplation and in these Exercises. When we become intimate with Christ, we share his relationship with the Father. Like him, we grow in awareness of what that relationship is.

Questions for Prayer and Reflection

1. What happened when you entered into this contemplation? What surprised you about it?

2. What were the consolations and desolations of this contemplation?

3. How did the grace of intimacy with the Christ manifest itself to you?

4. How do you generally wait?

5. How do you view the future? with trepidation? with worry? with calm? with curiosity? with joy? How do you feel when you wake up in the morning?

6. How have you experienced time? Your history?

7. How do you find your relationships with people?

8. How do you find your relationship with that mystery we call Father?

9. How do you experience your sense of sinking into an intimacy with God?

10. How does that affect you?

133

The Movie
LET THE RIGHT ONE IN

Director: Tomas Alfredson (2008 – 115 mins.)
Starring: Kåre Hedebrant, Lina Leandersson

1. Synopsis

A fragile, anxious boy, twelve-year-old Oskar is regularly bullied by his stronger classmates but never strikes back. The lonely boy's wish for a friend seems to come true when he meets Eli, also twelve, who moves in next door to him with her father. A pale, serious young girl, she only comes out at night and doesn't seem affected by the freezing temperatures. Coinciding with Eli's arrival is a series of inexplicable disappearances and murders. One man is found tied to a tree, another frozen in the lake, a woman bitten in the neck. Blood seems to be the common denominator. But by now a subtle romance has blossomed between Oskar and Eli, and she gives him the strength to fight back against his aggressors.

Note: Rated R for some bloody violence including disturbing images, brief nudity, and language.

Note: If at all possible, watch the subtitled version. Much of an actor's art lies in the use of voice to express emotion, mood, and character. Dubbed movies can never have the full impact of the original. Also watch the original Swedish film rather than the 2010 Hollywood remake.

2. About the Movie

1. "Director Tomas Alfredson, working from John Ajvide Lindqvist's novel and screenplay, shoots (the film) as a quiet drama with a muted score – an approach that unsettles the viewer's mind much as Kubrick's overly composed interiors did in *The Shining*. The snowbound Swedish setting and close-up camerawork between Oskar and Eli (beautifully played by the ferociously calm child actors) give the bursts of violence a terrifying, sometimes comic impact. This approach extends to the movie's muted color palette, which is mostly white and light blue offset by carefully placed bits of red." (Mike Russell, *The Oregonian*, November 13, 2008)

How patient and unflinching is this approach in building up dramatic and atmospheric detail? How does it contribute to making this film what many critics called one of the great horror films of the decade?

2. "Mr. Alfredson takes a darkly amused attitude toward the little world he has fashioned with such care, he also takes the morbid unhappiness of his young characters seriously. Both are achingly alone, and it is the ordinary fact of their loneliness rather than their extraordinary circumstances that makes the film more than the sum of its chills and estimable technique. Eli seizes on Oskar immediately, slipping her hand under his, writing him notes, becoming his protector, bar-

ing her fangs. 'Are you a vampire?' he asks tremulously at one point. Her answer may surprise you, but it's another of his questions – 'Will you be my girlfriend?' – that will floor you." (Manohla Dargis, *The New York Times*, October 24, 2008)

What was Eli's answer to Oskar about whether or not she is a vampire? Did it surprise you? As much as his other question and her answer?

3. "Some will classify *Let the Right One In* as a horror movie, and I suppose that's technically accurate. To me, however, this is much more of a coming-of-age/friendship movie. There is blood and gore, but it's not excessive, and director Tomas Alfredson is more interested in touching emotional chords than in creating 'boo!' moments or layering the atmosphere to the point where it is ponderous and impenetrable. That's not to say the film doesn't have a specific look and feel – there's a lot of darkness, snow, and ice – but those things aren't the production's primary reasons for existing. Despite the presence of monsters, the best word I can come up with to describe *Let the Right One In* is 'sweet.' Its portrayal of the relationship between two improbably alike pre-teens is more believable than what we see in many 'realistic' dramas." (James Berardinelli, *Reel Views*, October 24, 2008)

How is it possible for a movie to be a horror film, a coming-of-age film, a friendship film and still be described as "sweet"? What one word would sum up what you think about this film?

3. The Relationship of the Movie to the Theme of the Exercise

1. Despite the horror and the tragic violence that this film protrays, how much of the innocence of childhood is still to be found in the film? The innocence that we have as children disappears when we become adults. We grow up and our hearts break in two. How does this Exercise help us to preserve some of that innocence?

2. Eli's advice has given Oskar some real power to deal with the bullies at school. She is an ironic saviour. But, as the Exercise says, we must trust the unknown to become known. Oskar has done this. Is this only on a human level or is there something spiritual about this?

3. It could be said that this film is about a "redemptive" love that is so haunted that you are never sure if it can lead to anything but more evil. How true do you think that notion is? How would it be possible for this relationship to lead to something good?

4. The Relationship of the Movie to One's Self in the Exercise

1. This contemplation is about trust. Eli and Oskar must learn to trust each other – Bobby's need for the presence of his absent father and Eli's need for someone to understand her are part of the reasons for this. Whom do you trust? Trust completely? What might be preventing you from having such trust in God's love for you and all that follows from that?

2. At the end of the film we sense a kind of calmness – as well as excitement – about what comes next. This is true for Oskar, even though he knows the future will not be pleasant. What is it that you most fear about the future? Where will you go to try to relieve this fear?

7th Exercise
The Two Standards

Beloved, do not imitate evil but imitate good.

(3 John 1:11)

St. Ignatius recommends that
1. We should approach our Lady asking her to obtain for us from her Son and Lord the grace to be able to follow Him.
2. We then ask her Son to obtain the same favour for us from the Father.
3. We beg the Father to grant us the same graces.

(Sp. Ex. #147)

This is to ask for what I desire. Here it will be to ask for 4 things. 1. a knowledge of the deceits of evil and how I am caught by them, 2. help to guard myself against them, 3. a knowledge of how to live truly, as shown by Christ, and 4. the grace to be like Him. (Sp. Ex. #139)

The Human Struggle

In the middle of the Exercises, when we contemplate Jesus' life and how he operates in his world, Ignatius pauses to ask us to consider how we, individually, operate. He states, "While continuing to contemplate His life, let us begin to investigate and ask in what kind of life or in what state the Divine Majesty wishes to make use of us" (#135). He suggests that we do this by first looking at the ways Christ operates and the ways "the enemy of our human nature" operates. To this end Ignatius proposes a meditation on "Two Standards" (#136). First he looks at the way we are seduced and trapped by evil. Then he looks at the way Jesus operates, and asks us to follow that way. When we do evil, we operate under the Standard of Satan; when we do good, we operate under the Standard of Christ. Ignatius adapts this military image from his years in the army, when soldiers declared their allegiance to a cause by serving under its flag or standard.

This is not an abstract process of reflection. Ignatius realizes that we need help in discovering these things. We cannot abstract ourselves either from our good or our bad orientations to achieve these insights. To hammer home the individual patterns of our personality dynamics, he names four graces to pray for during this period: (1) a knowledge of the deceits of the evil leader; (2) help to guard myself against them; (3) a knowledge of what gives genuine life as shown in Jesus; and (4) the grace to imitate him.

People of the Lie

The simplest way of arriving at these insights is to consider how you behave when you feel vulnerable. We have two opposing ways of being in such situations: the way of the evil one and the way of Christ. The way of the evil one appeals to our strengths, so that we achieve the prestige and honour that the world bestows because of our own strength; this reinforces the pride of our egos. For example, when I enter a social situation where I feel uncomfortable, I withdraw into a posture of witty cynicism that comes easily to me. People react to my comments and I become the centre of attention. This justifies my belief that I need only depend on myself.

Ignatius says that we are tempted first to covet riches, so that we might more easily attain the empty honours of this world, and thus develop overweening pride. "Riches" may be material wealth. But riches also include any talent or gift, or any other created thing that we have or desire and that we can use for our own ends in order to live in a way that maintains our ego. For Ignatius, the movement to narcissism keeps us from being fully human. No one is ever free from this temptation. Ignatius does not claim that riches, strengths, or gifts in themselves are bad. But holding onto them and using them to boost our self-image is dangerous. This movement and direction, which we find in ourselves and which carries us to a self-enclosed ego-maintenance, is destructive. For Ignatius, there is no such thing as a static state of being; we are all moving either to spiritual intimacy or to more and more radical forms of self-enclosure and fragmentation.

In the meditation on the Two Standards, evil is shown to operate by terrorizing us and then offering us a way of coping with our terror by seductive techniques of ego-maintenance. This meditation offers us a way of discovering how our own personality dynamics respond to being presented with situations that elicit our fear.

It is very useful here to examine our personal histories to see the pattern of our basic disorder at work, and to discover how we become complicit in destruction. Awareness of this dynamic can help us overcome it. But we also need to learn other techniques to counteract these spontaneous tendencies. Ultimately, we realize that we cannot do this by ourselves; we need God's constant help and mercy.

Ignatius knows, from personal experience, that this help and mercy is constantly and freely given. He knows that we are loved even when we sin, and even when we are trapped and blinded by sin. This love stops us from further self-destruction.

The Hard Road

Opposed to the seductions, manipulations, and entrapments of evil is the hard road to freedom offered by Christ. Ignatius's Christ and his followers "spread His sacred doctrine" to all, "no matter what their state or condition" (#145). Religion is not just for the rich, or just for the poor. It is for all. Everyone needs God's love. Christ's teaching and ways of life cut across any form of exclusivity. The sacred doctrine he presents is God's incarnate mercy. There is a pattern to embodying this mercy, and it all depends on God's own desire. For Ignatius, nothing should be done unless God desires it. The principle of all human action, in freedom, is God's desire. Such freedom is different from liberty. Liberty is doing what we like; freedom is living in a relationship that carries us to the fullness of life. That relationship is with God. What is to be done? The answer is "Inshallah" – "as God desires."

Within the scope of that desire, the path Christ offers is through spiritual poverty, which leads us to desire exactly what this world does not desire. In response to a life lived as the desire for God rather than for the world, the world offers insults and contempt. Rejected by the world, we discover humility (#146). Humility is not spiritual self-abuse. Humility is living out our life in the right relationship we have with God – living in constant intimacy with a God who has created us, sustains us, protects us, loves and redeems us.

137

From a worldly perspective, humility, where we reject the affirmation of the world, and spiritual poverty are difficult to desire. We are so caught up in this world that even asking for them seems masochistic, inhuman, unnatural. The truth is we are totally and utterly dependent on God. But as our time in the First Week showed, we generally live our lives away from this basic truth. We come to that truth when we realize our radical spiritual poverty. Too often, we are so caught up with running from that understanding of ourselves that we also forget the God who creates, sustains, and redeems us. This Love does not desire our harm, but only that we be happy and become fuller and yet fuller manifestations of that love. The way we can witness to that love, and to our loving and trusting that love, is by living out of the poverty in our lives, should God so desire it. As Ignatius puts it, the call Christ makes to those who love him is that they "seek to help all, first by attracting them to the highest spiritual poverty, and should it please the Divine Majesty, and should it please Him to choose them for it, even to actual poverty" (#146).

Living Our Poverty

We do not offer to God the gift of our poverty, spiritual or material. The reality of our spiritual poverty is the human condition; the gift of actual poverty is what God also offers to some. This gift is not the imposition of poverty through personal misfortune, social injustice, the economic imbalance of nations, or the results of global imperialism. Those are evils. Actual poverty is the choice of a lifestyle we make freely, desiring only God's love and to live out of God's loving providence in this world. We choose this only if we are confirmed that God desires this for us. Anything else is spiritual pride masquerading as poverty. Should God desire it, we are offered the option of choosing actual poverty. We do not let poverty choose us. In freely choosing actual poverty, we witness to the world that we are willing to be radically dependent on God for all we need to live joyfully in this world, knowing fully well that such poverty leaves us open to be trampled by those forces that strive to dominate the world.

When we live out of the very poverty that is the centre of our being, we quickly discover that we do not live out of the values of this world. In fact, our path becomes offensive to the world. The world responds with pity, condescension, contempt, insults, mockery, neglect, abuse, abandonment. Instead of the trappings of honour and prestige that the world so delights in, some wear the tatters of humiliation. In this they identify with Jesus, who was also insulted, treated with contempt, humiliated. This identification with the beloved is important. We do not choose insults and reproaches; we choose Christ. We choose to be as Christ was and is in this world. We choose to be with the poor of Christ in this world. They are our community, because they share with us the vision and the desire of a radical intimacy with God.

To look for insults and injury while we maintain purely worldly values is to be sick and self-destructive. That is not what God desires. God desires that we be holy. That holiness comes when, instead of fleeing from the full awareness of our poverty, we embrace it, and through it see our path to God with new eyes. We have, in the examples of saints and holy people of all spiritual traditions, this rejection of the values of the world while living in the world. And we have the long tradition of their ill treatment at the hands of the world throughout human history in various cultures and religions.

That ill treatment from the world engenders a profound humility. In humility, the ego does not

138

have to defend itself. In humility we live every day totally and intentionally dependent on God and on the compassionate manifestions of goodness in the world. We wait on God, and on the providence of God. We see everything given as a gift to be opened. We discover the presence of God. Every moment offers an entry into the divine. Then our lives become an open space through which God enters into the world, and the pain of the world encounters the compassionate mercy of God. In humility, we accept that we are God's beloved and we live our lives in that love. In the eyes of the world, this is sheer folly. But we celebrate our gift of being God's fools.

The Pattern of Our Choices

The meditation on the Two Standards allows us to see graphically in our own lives the choice that opens to us at every moment of our life, whether we are conscious of it or not. In our vulnerability, we can take up either the standard of evil or the standard of Christ. If we take up the standard of evil, we are led through coveting riches to honour and pride. If we accept the standard of Christ, we are offered poverty and, through that, the displeasure of the world, and so reach humility. The choice is ours.

Ignatius realizes that this is a difficult and subtle meditation. He suggests that we do it four times so we can realize the graces we are asking for in this prayer. Those graces are first, to understand truly how we get trapped; secondly, to receive help to escape those traps; third, to understand how Christ behaves; and, fourth, to ask for and receive the grace to follow him.

This prayer is not a pious exercise. It seeks to reveal the dynamic core of our being and our behaviour patterns. The resistance to this revelation is strong. God's love for us, however, is stronger.

We need to draw on all the help we can to achieve the graces we seek in this prayer. The Spiritual Exercises suggests that we seek the help of Mary, the mother of Jesus, then Jesus, and finally the Father, by discussing with them what we need and what arises when we enter fully into this prayer.

Questions for Prayer and Reflection

1. How do you spontaneously react when you are vulnerable?

2. What are your "riches," "honour," "pride"? How do they manifest themselves?

3. What is your "poverty"? How do you deal with your poverty? Have you ever found God in your poverty?

4. What happens when you pray to be identified with Jesus as he is insulted and held in contempt?

5. How do you live your humility? How does it shape the way you see and deal with others?

6. How does it affect your relationship with the things you possess?

7. What happened in your prayer that was consoling? What does this tell you?

8. What happened in your prayer that was negative? What does this tell you?

9. What happened in your conversations at the end of the prayer with Mary, Jesus, and the Father?

10. As you prepare to repeat this prayer, what areas do you feel the need to focus on?

11. Were the graces you prayed for given? How? How did you receive them?

12. How does this prayer relate to your earlier prayers of this Second Week?

The Movie
THE INFORMANT!

Director: Steven Soderbergh (2009 – 108 mins.)
Starring: Matt Damon, Scott Bakula, Eddie Jemison, Rusty Schwimmer

1. Synopsis

A rising star at agri-industry giant Archer Daniels Midland (ADM), Mark Whitacre suddenly turns whistleblower. Even as he exposes his company's multi-national price-fixing conspiracy to the FBI, Whitacre envisions himself being hailed as a hero of the common man and handed a promotion. But before all that can happen, the FBI needs evidence, so Whitacre eagerly agrees to wear a wire and carry a hidden tape recorder in his briefcase, imagining himself as a kind of de facto secret agent.

Unfortunately for the FBI, their lead witness hasn't been quite so forthcoming about helping himself to the corporate coffers. Whitacre's ever-changing account frustrates the agents and threatens the case against ADM as it becomes almost impossible to decipher what is real and what is the product of Whitacre's rambling imagination. The movie is based on the true story of the highest-ranking corporate whistleblower in US history.

2. About the Movie

1. By the time the movie was released, the real Mark Whitacre had served his time in prison, been released, and had rejoined his family. He is gainfully employed as a senior executive. How do you think the following people would react to seeing the movie – his family, his co-workers, his clients, his friends, Mark Whitacre himself? How would you respond if you saw your illogical actions and serial lies presented in a feature movie?

2. Sinner or saint – or a little of each – Mark Whitacre's story sounds relentlessly serious. But is that how the movie presents it? The trailer for the movie plays down the "based on true events" angle and plays up the wacky satire angle. Would you say that the movie is a very satirical, very black comedy?

3. Black comedy is found in existentialist theatre and in modern American fiction from Joseph Heller's *Catch-22* to Kurt Vonnegut's *Slaughterhouse Five*. The history of film is filled with wonderful examples of black humour – think of Kubrick's *Dr. Strangelove* – a terrifying comic treatment of the dropping of an atomic bomb. Black comedy makes us pay attention to issues we'd rather forget. Can you name some other black comedies?

4. The film contains many elements of black comedy. The first time you saw the movie, which of the following did you notice: the use of the inner voice, the absurdity of a faked kidnapping, the reference to the movie *The Firm*, Mark telling his gardener he is agent double 0014 because he is twice as smart as 007, the casting of stand-up comics throughout the movie?

5. Speaking about the real Mark Whitacre, Dean Paisley, an FBI agent, said, "Had it not been for the fraud conviction, he would be a national hero. Well, he is a national hero." Not everyone would agree that Mark Whitacre is a national hero. Some might say he is but one more black mark on corporate America's report card.

   Mark Whitacre blew the whistle on price fixing in his company, and worked with the FBI to collect criminal evidence. Plagued with a bipolar disorder, Whitacre handled the stress badly, becoming manic and suicidal, trusting no one. He embezzled millions and received a ten-year prison sentence.

   Those are the facts. But we can only know the Mark Whitacre that the movie offers us. The movie presents Whitacre's words and actions, but also his inner monologues, to show what is going on beneath the surface. Because Whitacre can't seem to distinguish between imagination and fact, his story becomes very curious, even absurd. Who do you think Mark Whitacre really is?

6. We count on narration in a movie to tell us what is happening. But here, not only is the narration unreliable, it doesn't necessarily refer to the scene unfolding on the screen. It's more like a stream of consciousness. The narrator might be in the middle of a crucial conversation when something triggers an inner monologue that can spin off in any direction: neckties, polar bears, frequent flier miles — whatever. In the midst of one intense scene, we hear his internal voice saying: "Polar bears hide their noses during hunting because seals can recognize them if they see their black noses on their white faces."

Near the end, when Agent Sheppard asks Whitacre, "Why do you keep lying?" Whitacre responds, "I think I need to go back to the hospital." But his inner thought response — which only the audience hears — is "I don't know." What does this narrative tell us about Whitacre? Did Whitacre lie because of the stress of the covert work, or was he always compulsive?

7. A brilliant biochemist as well as an astute businessman, Whiteacre is — as one character says — "Just a little more out there than the rest of us." That's putting it mildly. We cringe at what he does, but he is also very charismatic. Is this why you find yourself forgiving him when he says, "That's it, I've told you everything," even though we know he's never told us everything?

8. Soundtrack music is carefully selected or composed to create a mood, set a tone, define a character. Movie music is most often subliminal, or hardly noticed, as it supports the action and dialogue. It is frequently played at the beginning of new scenes, but also through and over dialogue.

   In *The Informant*, award-winning composer Marvin Hamlisch used music very purposefully to set the tone of the film and to put the audience in a comedic frame of mind. For example, the hoedown bluegrass music during Whitacre's lie detector test shows the audience how absurd it is to give a truth test to a compulsive liar.

   How many of the following popular genres of music did *The Informant* use and what kind of tone do they set for the movie: polka, bluegrass, big band, jazz, chart toppers, themes from secret agent movies, TV game show themes?

3. The Relationship of the Movie to the Theme of the Exercise

1. As a former soldier, Ignatius visualizes us as choosing the standard – the flag if you want – of one of two kings: one good, one evil. The choice is not only always ours, but we will often have to make such choices in our lives. Remember what Dumbledore tells Harry Potter: "It is our choices, Harry, that show what we truly are, far more than our abilities." Mark Whitacre's life is filled with choices. Which standard – that of the good king or that of the evil king – do you think that Mark ultimately chooses? What scene in the film best demonstrates this?

2. As the Exercise tells us, evil operates by terrorizing us and then offering us a way of coping with our fear in the face of such terror by seductive techniques of ego-maintenance. Where is there a point in the film where Mark is truly afraid of what he has done and is about to do? How does he overcome this fear and move beyond the evil to what he perceives as good?

3. The Exercise tells us that discovering for ourselves how we become complicit in destruction is one help to overcoming the problem. Where does Mark see himself as being aware of this? Or does he ever? Does he remain firm in his belief that what he has done and is doing is the correct thing to do?

4. The Relationship of the Movie to One's Self in the Exercise

1. The Two Standards looks at the ways in which we are seduced by evil and the ways in which Jesus asks us to follow. Mark is being tempted to embezzle money from his company. At the same time he feels the need to expose the corruption that is rampant in the same company. Which way does he choose to follow? In your own world, you must choose – as must we all – the standard of good or the standard of evil. What tempts you to evil in your own life? What or who in your life shows you the way of the good – the way of Christ?

2. Mark has many strengths. It is how he uses them that causes difficulties. As the Exercise says, the way of the evil one appeals to our strengths, so that we achieve the prestige and honour that our strengths give us and we reinforce the pride of our egos. What is the gift which you have (or want to have) that would tempt you to live in the world in a way that maintains and boosts your ego and shuts out the good that is God?

3. Throughout the film, it becomes clear that Mark sees himself as many different people – a national hero, a spy, a faithful husband and father – but he never truly understands who he is. He is, as the Exercise tells us, caught up with running from that understanding of himself that he needs. We also do this all too often. What is it that you are afraid to face? What is it that you are running from that will not allow you to remember the God who creates, sustains, and redeems us?

4. What are the temptations of "riches," "honour," and "pride" which Mark must face? Does he manage to overcome any of these temptations? Which of your "riches" or "honour" is the most difficult for you to overcome? Why?

8th Exercise
The Three Classes of People

Behold, I have set before you an open door, which no one is able to shut; I know you have but little power, and yet you have kept my word and have not denied my name.

(Revelation 3:8)

Here it will be to behold myself standing in the presence of God our Lord and of all His saints that I may know and desire what is more pleasing to His Divine Goodness. (Sp. Ex. #151)

Here it will be to beg for the grace to choose what is more for the glory of His Divine Majesty and the salvation of my soul. (Sp. Ex. #152)

Our Choices Define Who We Are

In spiritual terms, people can be divided into three groups: a) those who do not care one way or the other about God, b) those who want God to support them in their schemes, and c) those who desire to follow God. Each of us combines elements of all three types. Depending on the circumstances, we behave in one of these three ways. This is because our lives are fragmented. The path of intimacy that we are walking seeks to orient all aspects of our lives in one direction: facing God. In the choices we make, each of us must decide how we will relate to God. It is not what we have, but the choices we make with what we have, that define who we are. Those choices show how we embody our deepest desire in our daily lives.

Let's look a little more closely at these three different types of people. The first group does not pursue a relationship with God, for a variety of reasons, some of which are valid ones. So the relationship never gets expressed. It is rather like being in love with someone and not admitting it to yourself, not declaring your love to that person, not doing anything about it. The relationship remains unacknowledged and undeveloped. People who live this way are not concerned with sincerity or authenticity. They operate according to an existential pragmatism that asks and answers these questions: What is the next step? What is to be done? Other people function simply to facilitate that next step.

The second type of person admits to being in love, but that love is defined only by personal needs. This person is sincere, and so, being true only to the self, lives to satisfy those needs and demands. The beloved must do and live only as the person in love wants the beloved to live. This type of love manifests itself in jealousy or narcissism. The beloved has no individual life, but instead must live as the lover's idealized projection. Abusive relationships often arise from such selfishness. This second type of person treats others, and God, as objects to be manipulated for immediate satisfaction. Often, we think God treats us in that same way. This is because we do not allow ourselves to experience the freedom God gives, which includes the choice to turn away from God. If it seems like God acts as this second type of person does, this means we are the same type, and have projected upon God our own notions of relationship and intimacy. We avoid, then, the mutuality of a love that allows both God and ourselves to be free.

The third type of person is committed to the beloved and lives out of that commitment in a responsible way. People of this type "seek to will or not will as God our Lord inspires them, and as seems better for the service and praise of the Divine Majesty" (#155). Because of the mutuality of the intimacy they share with God, they enter the process of discernment about their choices. They seek to love responsibly in the concrete circumstances of their lives so that neither they, nor anyone else, nor the witness to God's love are destroyed as a result of their choices. Their intimacy with God gives them a spiritual literacy. They discover how they speak to God, and how God speaks to them. Together they develop ways of communicating with each other and of being together that allow choices that build up the community of love we call the kingdom of God.

Of course, all of us would claim that we want to love in a way that brings life to those involved with us. Love is a much overworked word. It means different things to each of these three types of people we have been reflecting on. Each would claim to act lovingly. For each, the greater good has different connotations. It really is difficult to achieve true self-awareness of what we mean by "love" in our daily lives. Ignatius suggests that instead of looking at love, we look at how we would use riches – money or talent – that we have received. Cunningly, Ignatius suggests that we consider the means by which we have acquired those riches, to be disposed for the love of God, to be somewhat suspect (#150). Those riches are not ours by natural right or by law. Ignatius knows that our gifts are just that. They are not us.

They are distinct from us, and the distance between us and them means that we have to make conscious choices about how to use them. We know we should use them for good, because we do not want to be selfish. Having completed the First Week of the Exercises, we know that selfishness traps and destroys us, and we want to avoid that trap. But we also know that we are not free from the tendencies to selfishness.

Facing Selfishness

The first type of person, who is unable to decide how to avoid being selfish, does nothing and so remains selfish. The second type of person makes the decision to be selfish and seeks to have God justify that selfishness. The third type of person is concerned only with making the best use of the gift. If the best use is seen as selfish by others, that is not their concern. If that best use is seen as wonderfully philanthropic by others, that also is not their concern. That person wants only to better serve and praise God as a gesture of gratitude for the love freely given and received. The person here does not act out of contractual obligation or moral duty. The intimacy in the relationship sees the giving and receiving as a gift.

This exercise is not about making a decision. It is about the intimacy needed in order to make a correct decision. St. Augustine sums up this attitude in his precept "Love and do what you will." St. Ignatius asks, "But what do you love?" What you will shows what you love. Your will-ing is your love in action. When you see where your will has led you, then you will see who and what you love.

Whom you love and what you love may not love you. In fact, the expression of your desires may even destroy you. This is what happened to Christ. Why you love what you love is crucial. Jesus loves us as an expression of his love for the Father. In his love for the Father, who loves us to the depths of our being, Jesus is willing to be fully present to the alien forces of creation that seek to destroy us. He chooses a path that leads through death, not out of a love for death, but out of his passionate desire to show us that this same path through death leads towards the fullness of life. So it is not just a question of loving, but of loving for the right reasons. We love as an expression of spiritual intimacy. The grace we seek in the present stage of the spiritual journey we are on is for "an intimate knowledge of our Lord, who has become man for me, that I may love Him more and follow Him more closely" (#104). This intimacy manifests itself in a love shown in concrete acts of service.

If we are passionate for God and allow God to be passionate for us – as Christ is passionate for the Father, and the Father is passionate for Christ, and for us – then we become indifferent to all created things. We desire only what God desires. This does not mean that we are passive or wishy-washy. It means that we see and hold all things within the dynamism of that love that loves us intimately and totally.

While we may agree wholeheartedly with this approach, and find it very moving, it is very difficult to give up our self-will and to value things and other people only within the mutual love between God and us. St. Ignatius suggests that when we find this difficult, we should beg God to give us the freedom and the grace to work against those desires that limit us, and to come to the position of loving as God loves.

Questions for Prayer and Reflection

1. When have you been unable to make a decision? Why did that happen? How did it affect you?

2. When have you spontaneously expected the world, others, and even God to agree with your plans and desires? How did you try to manipulate those situations to meet your own needs? What happened when things did not go according to your plan?

3. When have you given yourself over unreflectively to a mood, a situation, another person, a political position, or social or cultural values because you felt it was the right thing to do?

4. In what ways have you loved? In what ways have what you loved not been in your best interests?

5. Have you ever loved in a way that you found life and brought life to one or more persons?

6. Did that loving involve any sacrifice? How did you deal with that sacrifice?

7. If you are in a relationship now, how do you communicate with each other? How do you make decisions together? What are the tensions in that relationship that create difficulty in making decisions together? How do you resolve those tensions to make good decisions?

The Movie
BROKEBACK MOUNTAIN

Director: Ang Lee (2005 – 134 mins.)
Starring: Heath Ledger, Jake Gyllenhaal, Michelle Williams, Randy Quaid

1. Synopsis

Based on the E. Annie Proulx story, the film takes place in the summer of 1963 in the Wyoming mountains. Two young men, Ennis, a ranch hand, and Jack, a rodeo cowboy, are hired to work the summer on Brokeback Mountain. During the long months of isolation, a bond develops between them of which they are only vaguely aware, until one night it rises to the surface in a passionate encounter.

It is only when the summer ends and they go their separate ways that they realize the true depth of their feelings. For the next nineteen years of their lives, through marriage, through raising children, and through the confines of society's expectations of what it means to be a man, the two men struggle with their connection, and ultimately provide a testament to the endurance and power of love.

Note: Rated R for sexual content, nudity, language, and some violence.

2. About the Movie

1. In most classic Westerns, the relationship between cowboys is depicted as something special – and it has been said that it is a relationship deeper and more spiritually sustaining than the love between a man and a woman. *Brokeback Mountain*, which screenwriters Larry McMurtry and Diana Ossana expanded from the celebrated 1997 short story by Annie Proulx, makes explicit the sexual undercurrent that, rightly or wrongly, not a few critics have at times detected in the intense masculine bonds of these strong, silent types.

How does the relationship between Ennis and Jack change from the first time they meet until they come down from the mountain?

2. "Gyllenhaal has a rare ability to bring out the youthful ardor in his characters without seeming callow. It is a gift that stands him in good stead because we must believe that the smitten Jack, over a period of two decades, is capable of sustaining a deepening passion. Ledger does something even more difficult: He gives us a full-scale portrait of a man who is so imprisoned by tradition and inhibition that he can never break out. Ledger's underplaying is a sign of grace. It is an acknowledgment that, for some men, there is pain too deep for words." (Peter Rainer, *The Christian Science Monitor*, December 9, 2005)

What attempts does Ennis make to break out of the tradition and inhibition that prevents his love from happening? How successful are these attempts? How does he react when these attempts fail?

146

3. There is a difference in how Jack and Ennis cope with modern life. Jack finds compromises – selling farm equipment for his father-in-law, soliciting back-alley men in Mexico. But it is very different for Ennis. "[H]e's a walking anachronism, a poor fit for the world he lives in. Where once being a 'cowboy' signified freedom and mastery, the horse and the gun, it is now synonymous with 'ranch hand,' a menial occupation, a life with shovel in hand. And try as he might, he can't escape the discomfort of civilization .... (He lives in) a trailer in the middle of nowhere. And yet not quite nowhere. In the film's final, moving scene, Ennis nearly breaks down as he looks at a postcard of Brokeback Mountain that he's tacked to his closet door; beside it, the trailer window looks out on a field of corn that extends to the horizon. It's a juxtaposition of beauty and barrenness, but also of idiosyncratic wilderness and domesticated land, acres upon acres that've been flattened out and made uniform until they no longer have any place in them for men like Ennis Del Mar, gay or not." (Christopher Orr, *The New Republic*, April 18, 2006)

This is a love story, but it is also just a cowboy movie, a wistful, elegiac meditation on a vanishing archetype of American masculinity. In what ways has civilization itself pushed aside this archetype?

4. " Ennis, we are made to believe, is the Old West while Jack, who imagines they can have a life together, is a precursor of the New West. But both are in the wrong place at the wrong time. *Brokeback Mountain* is a tragedy because these men have found something that many people, of whatever sexual persuasion, never find – true love. And they can't do anything about it." (Peter Rainer, *The Christian Science Monitor*, December 9, 2005)

How much emotional damage do Jack and Ennis undergo? Who else suffers because of their love? Whose fault is it? Why is it fair to say that no one is a villain, and that no one is spared from sorrow?

3. The Relationship of the Movie to the Theme of the Exercise

While it is true that we all have some elements of each of the three classes, it could be said that Ennis and Jack belong in one class more than another. Using the following summary statements from the Exercise, choose which class is most suited to Ennis and to Jack. Use specific scenes and/or dialogue from the film to prove your point:

(1) The First Class of people: those who do not care one way or the other about God. It is rather like being in love with someone and never telling yourself that you are in love or never telling that person, or never doing anything about it. The relationship remains, on your part, on the level of friendship. It's comfortable and safe and easy. The first type of person, unable to decide how to avoid being selfish, does nothing and so remains selfish.

(2) The Second Class of people: those who want God to support them in their schemes. This person is in love, but that love is defined only by their needs. The beloved must do and behave and live only as the person in love wants. Such is the love that manifests itself in jealousy or nar-

cissism. The beloved has no life of her own, but instead must live out her life as the idealized projection of the lover's desires. This second type of person does not have a problem with decision.

(3) The Third Class of people: those who desire to follow God, commit themselves to the other, and gives their life over to that relationship. Such people ask themselves how to love responsibly in the concrete circumstances of their lives so that neither they nor any others, nor the witness to God's love, is destroyed by what they choose to do. This third type of person is not concerned with selfishness, but rather is concerned only with what is the best use of the gift.

4. The Relationship of the Movie to One's Self in the Exercise

1. As individuals, Ennis and Jack each have many different character traits. Which of these character traits do you find in yourself? How do they manifest themselves in your daily life? Would you want to change what you see? How would you begin to make the changes?

2. As the Exercise tells us, the three classes of people can be summed up by how we embody our deepest desires in our daily life. In the film, Ennis and Jack each attempt to do this either alone or with someone's help. How do you try to live your daily life based on your deepest desire? Who do you turn to for help in this? How do these people help you?

3. The Exercise points out something we all feel deeply. It is very difficult to give up our self-will, to value things and others only within the mutual love between God and oneself. In the film, Jack and Ennis each have some strong part of their self-will which they cannot give up. What part of your self-will do you find most difficult to give up? Where do you turn for help to do this? Is this an ongoing process or will you be able to give up that part of you in time? Why? Why not?

9th Exercise
The Three Degrees of Humility

Have this mind among yourselves, which you have in Christ Jesus, who, though he was in the form of God, did not count equality with God a thing to be grasped, but emptied himself, taking the form of a servant, being born in the likeness of men. And being found in human form he humbled himself and became obedient unto death, even death on the cross. (Philippians 2:5-8)

I desire and choose poverty with Christ poor, rather than riches; insults with Christ loaded with them, rather than honours; I desire to be accounted as worthless and a fool for Christ, rather than be esteemed as wise and prudent in this world. So Christ was treated before me.
(Sp. Ex. #167)

They should beg our Lord to deign to choose them for this third kind of humility, which is higher and better, that they might the more imitate and serve Him, provided equal or greater praise and service be given to the Divine Majesty. (Sp. Ex. #168)

Being Human

The word "human" comes from the Latin word *humus*, meaning earth or soil. The word "humility" comes from that same root. To be human is to be humble. To be demonic is not to be humble, for then one is filled with pride and sets oneself up as a god. To be humble is to understand ourselves profoundly as creatures, born of the soil but loved by God. How we live as humans depends both on our awareness of ourselves as creatures and on how deeply we love.

Ignatius asks us to consider this exercise as a development of the previous one, where he had asked us to pray for the grace to love. In this exercise, he asks us to pray for the grace to love as deeply and passionately as Christ loves. He sees this approach, which he calls the third degree of humility, as the most perfect way of being human.

Love and Goodness

The first degree of humility is to love as a good person. That person lives with integrity, is respectful of other people and of creation, and loves God. Such an individual is ethical, moral, and upright; does not do wrong but lives in a way that maintains essential relationships; admits limitations and boundaries and lives within them. This, admittedly, is a very high standard of morality, and most of us, if we are honest with ourselves, reach this level of commitment only in certain areas of our lives and at certain times. For the rest, we find ourselves caught in ambiguity and compromise. We acknowledge that we are sinners and that, in spite of our occasional best efforts, we get trapped by our own disorders and by the disorders of the world. We can even acknowledge that we are so trapped as to be blind, for the most part, to the ways we destroy ourselves, others, or the world. For example, we can maintain a standard of living that does violence to the resources of the planet, or live a stressful lifestyle that damages our bodies and our spirits, and think that this is normal or mature or acceptable. This is not to say that we are not good people. We are. We are good people living at the first level of humility.

Love and Detachment

The second degree of humility moves from a certain lack of reflectivity that ignores a greater spiritual good. It seeks to become aware of what blinds us at the first level, and to try to become indifferent to those things that we would normally value as good. Ignatius gives us some examples of these. He says, "As far as we are concerned, we should not prefer health to sickness, riches to poverty, honour to dishonour, a long life to a short life" (#23).

Now this is quite radical. No one wants to be sick or poor or despised or to die without having lived enough. What Ignatius knows, from his own life, and what we know from examining the lives of the saints, is that illness can be a blessing. It was only when Ignatius fell ill that he started his quest for God; indeed, illness shows us the radical limitations of the self to control and maintain life. Similarly, we can learn that riches cannot buy happiness, and that in poverty we may discover a freedom to use our energies in more life-giving ways. We will also find, as we mature spiritually, that loving relationships, not the prestige of the world, establish our identity, and a loving relationship with God takes away our fear of death.

Here Ignatius is not asking us to choose poverty, or sickness, or dishonour, or a short life. He is merely asking us to be indifferent to these things. To be indifferent is to be so passionate only for God that we desire only those things that will maintain that loving relationship. We value whatever we have only inasmuch as it helps that relationship deepen. It might well be that riches or health foster a vital relationship with God. In that case, we should actively cultivate them. The second degree of humility describes the attitude of mind that seeks only God, and seeks everything else only as it can help that relationship with God. This sensitivity is not just theoretical: it manifests itself actively in what we do and how we live.

Love and Passion

The third degree of humility is grounded on the first and second. It asks us not to be indifferent to poverty or dishonour, but to choose them: not for themselves (since they are just "creatures"), but in solidarity with Christ's poor and suffering, and in a lover's identification with the condition of the Beloved, the Christ, in this world. Moreover, that choice is made only if it gives greater praise and service to God.

This third way of loving is more than just a witness for God in a socially conventional manner. It means showing with our very lives our abiding trust in Divine Providence that the love to which we give ourselves will not abandon or destroy us. It means putting our lives where the beloved has put his life. Christ, the beloved, lives a passionate intimacy with the Father. In his daily life, public or hidden, he waits on the Father for all he needs. Similarly, in that mutual self-giving, the Father gives the Christ all that is necessary for him to walk his human path back to the fullness of life. We, too, in this third degree of humility, are invited to a similar path and a similar passion.

In the great hymn in Philippians 2:1-11, we are told that the Christ did not count equality with God as something to be held onto, but rather emptied himself, "taking on the form of a servant," and became one like us. He went even further, because as a human he "humbled himself and became obedient even unto death" – that shameful death on a cross.

Ignatius does not present an incarnate Christ who is a triumphalistic or autocratic human being. Rather, he presents a Christ who manifests himself in humble service to the mystery we call Father. He suggests that the highest form of human love happens in identifying with the beloved in a similar manner. He offers to us the possibility of praying for that identification in the third level of humility, which says, "I want to be so like you that I am willing to live as you lived, love as you loved, suffer as you suffered." It says, "I am willing to share your life with those who are poor and suffering and dishonoured, neglected, mocked, ignored." It says, "I am willing, if you want me to, to become one of them and to live the fate of one of them because you loved me that much and because I, too, love you as you have loved me." This is not the path of the hero or the masochist. This is the path of the saint and the mystic. We are all called, every one of us, in our own ways, to be saints and mystics, for they express most fully what it means to be human and our response to having every aspect of our being loved totally, intimately, and passionately.

Questions for Prayer and Reflection

1. Have you reached even that first level of humility?

2. How do you respond to God's love knowing that you are a sinner?

3. Does an awareness of your sinfulness stop you from loving as fully as you dare?

4. How do you experience the urges to love more? How do you embody them without being imprudent or naive?

5. How does your culture condition you to accept yourself as it defines you? How do you break out of that conditioning? What helps you move beyond those definitions of yourself? How does it feel to live in those spaces beyond cultural definition?

6. Who are the saints that inspire you? How do they do that?

7. Who do you know who lives (or tries to live) that third level of humility today?

8. What happens to you when you consider living radically out of God's love?

9. What happens to you when you ask someone – such as Mary, the mother of Jesus, then Jesus himself, then the mystery Jesus calls his "Father" – for the love to live and love as fully as they love you?

10. What do Mary, Jesus, and the Father say to you in that prayer? How do you experience that prayer?

The Movie
ATONEMENT

Director: Joe Wright (2007 – 123 mins.)
Starring: James McAvoy, Keira Knightley, Saorise Ronan, Brenda Blethyn

1. Synopsis

At thirteen, Briony Tallis sees her older sister Cecilia and the son of a family servant, Robbie Turner, together, and misunderstands what is happening between them. When Briony later reads a letter intended for Cecilia, the younger sister concludes that Robbie is a deviant. Her misinterpretation of what is going on between Cecilia and Robbie ends up having long-lasting repercussions for all concerned.

Note: Rated R for disturbing war images, language, and some sexual content.

2. About the Movie

1. Any number of critics have called *Atonement* one of the most beautiful films ever made. There was even a comment that the film illuminates our minds like J.M.W. Turner's paintings. What other films can you name that might also be called "beautiful"? What does "beauty" add to *Atonement*?

2. "Each period (of time) in the film packs a seismic revelation, the ultimate one is both devastating and cleansing." (Richard Corliss, *Time*, December 3, 2007) What are the various revelations in each period and what makes the ultimate one not only devastating but also cleansing?

3. "Breathing fresh life into a stuffy genre, this ambitious literary epic of love and war is the best of its kind since *The English Patient*." (Brian D. Johnson, *Maclean's*, December 31, 2007) What film genre is Johnson talking about? Why would he consider films of this genre to be "stuffy"? How does this film avoid that appellation?

4. *Atonement* "gives us a romantic Good Friday with no Easter. The little girl whose lie set the tragedy in motion spends 50 years writing fiction about good lives lived to good purpose. She bears her guilt through her whole life, and certainly suffers for it, but this atonement does not bring younger lovers back to life and we can't accept the idea she has given them back their lives in her novels. Redemption has to be real." (Michael Swan, *The Catholic Register*, February 10, 2008) What does Swan mean by his last statement that "redemption has to be real?" Does Briony not believe in anything that could redeem her? And why is there no Easter after the Good Friday that is the film?

5. "Regret is everywhere in Ian McEwan's 2001 novel *Atonement*, like the air the characters breathe or the water they keep tumbling into. It seeps into cracks, weighs people down, turns them brittle and exhausted. It's the stuff of life and the

clay of fiction. How do you make a movie out of this? How do you photograph a black hole of sorrow for things not done and wrongs not righted? Joe Wright's sweeping, ambitious reduction of McEwan's meticulously written book has one answer: Pretend you're making an impeccably acted period piece – the sort of thing that wins Oscars for costumes at the very least – and then go deeper, into mysteries of authorship, art, and human connection." (Ty Burr, *The Boston Globe*, December 7, 2007)

In the end, how far does what director Wright presents on the screen go towards showing us the "regret" that the novelist made the "stuff of life"?

3. The Relationship of the Movie to the Theme of the Exercise

1. Films such as *The Go-Between*, *The Closer*, and now *Atonement* say "… we are creatures of our wills; it's what makes us human. *Atonement* says we can sink into sin and lift ourselves out. That's the message of this wise, beautifully acted parable of vengeance and contrition." (Richard Corliss, *Time*, December 3, 2007). In what sense is this film a parable? And is it a religious parable or – if such a thing exists – a secular parable?

2. Consider the three degrees of humility. In which degree would you place Briony? Or does she belong in any of the three degrees? Does this change over the 50 years of her life that the film covers?

3. The Exercise tells us that to be human is to be humble. How we live as humans depends on our awareness of our creaturehood and on how deeply we love. Are there any examples of humility in Briony's life? Consider her confession to Cecilia and Robbie. What causes her to confess what she has done? Why has she kept the truth hidden for so long?

4. The Relationship of the Movie to One's Self in the Exercise

1. If Briony is to move forward in her own life, there are many obstacles to overcome – not the least of which is herself. How does she come to understand what she has to do and find the motivation to do it. What motivates you as you attempt to move from one degree of humility to another? What stops you from moving from one degree to another? And what can you possibly do to overcome this?

2. What is it that causes Briony to try and right the wrong that she did and which had such tragic results? Does this happen because she is drawn to something more than herself – something higher? What draws you to live a higher standard of morality than that of the world? What are some examples in your own life of areas and times when you have reached the high level of commitment that the Exercise talks about?

3. What do you think Briony thinks of herself? Does she see herself as a "good" person? Why? And what about yourself? What is it that stops you from seeing the goodness that is in you and that calls you to something more?

10th Exercise
Discernment

None of us lives to ourself, and none of us dies to ourself. If we live we live to the Lord, and if we die, we die to the Lord; so then, whether we live or whether we die, we are the Lord's. (Romans 14:7-9)

In every good choice, as far as depends on us, our intentions must be simple. I must consider only the end for which I am created, that is, for the praise of God our Lord and for the salvation of my soul. Hence, whatever I choose must help me to this end for which I am created. (Sp. Ex. #169)

To seek to find and serve God in all things. (Sp. Ex. #233)

Seeking a Heart to Understand

We all want to love passionately and choose rightly. But we realize that not only do we lack all the facts necessary for the perfect choice, our perceptions of the facts can be biased by our disorders. Still, we must choose. Every day we make myriad decisions – major and minor – that determine the shape of our lives. With major ones, we become a little more conscious of the decision-making process. Each of us has our own way of making a decision. We collect facts, get insights, have intuitions, weigh the pros and cons, look for signs of rightness, ask friends for advice, or pray for God's help. We try to get into the right "space" to make a correct choice.

Sometimes, the right decision comes to us clearly and simply. Sometimes we have to find a quiet place and settle down to see what emerges from our deliberations. Sometimes we must project ourselves imaginatively into living that decision and foreseeing the outcome. Sometimes we ask God to show us the way. Whatever we do, every decision is a risk and a creative moment. We set out on a path we have not walked before.

What is a discernment and how does it differ from a decision? The two are different, even though the result might look the same. A decision is not necessarily a deliberate, self-conscious choice, and it does not necessarily occur in the context of prayer. Discernment does both. With discernment, we enter into a dialogue with God after establishing a right relationship. In that mutual sharing and trust, an answer emerges. Then we not only see as God sees, but we act as we believe God would want us to act.

So far in these Exercises, we have been establishing that right relationship with God, discovering how God communicates with us personally through our feelings and our history. We are becoming aware of how we operate, so that we know when we are being tempted to narcissism or being invited to self-transcendence. Now Ignatius is asking us to discern a life path, or a step on our pilgrim journey through life.

154

Making Correct Discernments

For St. Ignatius, correct discernments always move us towards God, community, and each other, as well as integrating the different aspects of ourselves. But, like any other discernment, we need to check them out to see whether they are valid or illusory. This takes time. The time given to us is the time of the retreat. If we have a decision we want to discern, we can take it with us as we journey through the rest of these Exercises. We can bring that decision into prayer and into the reflection questions. Does that decision hold up to the relationship we form with Christ as we continue our journey? A good decision will draw us closer to Christ and identify us with him. A bad decision will alienate us from the Christ, put us at odds with our deepest desires, and separate us from the best elements in our community.

If we are called to make a decision at this moment, we might want to use some of the suggestions found at the beginning of this exercise. If we have made a decision and want to verify it, we can bring it along as we journey through the rest of the Exercises. This will transform the decision into a discernment. If there is no decision to make or verify, we can still deepen our intimacy with God as we continue. What we need to remember is that, as we are searching for God, God is searching for us. We will experience God's search for us in terms of that mercy and concern we can acknowledge in our path. Whatever decisions we make, we are always held in God's loving mercy. That mercy has the power to transform the deadly effects of bad decisions into opportunities for resurrection. It has the power to affirm good decisions by celebrating the life it brings.

Questions for Prayer and Reflection

1. How do you generally make decisions? How have they differed from the discernments you have made? Has involving God made a difference?

2. How have you made significant decisions in your life so far?

3. Of those significant decisions, how have you made the ones that have brought you life? How have you made those that have been destructive?

4. What does this tell you about the way to make good decisions?

5. Is there any discernment that you need to make with God now? How will you two go about it?

6. Where does God feature in that process? How has God featured in your good decision-making process? Can you approach God in the same way this time?

7. When you pray about your life, what is God telling you about it?

Discernments and the Path

We are on a spiritual journey. On that journey, different paths open to us. When we look back on our lives, we see that the choices we have made, and the choices that have been made for us, have led us to this moment. Those choices have made us who we are, and we are unfinished business. We are still in the process of being created. We can co-operate in that creation by what we do. Often our doing is not conscious. We operate by habit and by conventions. They set our attitudes, and our attitudes determine the possibilities open to us. At almost every moment of our lives we make choices, unaware that we are doing so. Sometimes our paths are determined by one of those moments. Only later do we see the significance of that moment.

At other times we are very aware that we have come to a place where we must make a choice. Choice implies risk. Because we then enter unknown territory, we become very attentive to the things around us and within us in order to ascertain the right decision. We know that whatever we choose means giving up certain things and accepting others. Each possible path has advantages and disadvantages from our present perspective. But sometimes we do not even know whether something is an advantage or a disadvantage. Then we try to reach a level of awareness that allows us to see correctly, judge wisely, and choose what will satisfy our deepest desire. The choice is a door into the darkness. We do not know what we will encounter on the path that opens to us, and there is no turning back. We can and do make mistakes. But we know from experience that some of these choices have brought us life, joy, and freedom. So what do we do? How do we choose? What are we to hold as most valuable when we assess the pros and cons of possible decisions?

We know that ultimately God can transform even the effects of bad decisions, and we have already experienced the mercy of God in saving us even when we were in situations that were destructive. So what are we doing when we discern?

What discernments do, first of all, is witness to the relationship we have with God. They are covenant moments. The choices we wish to make will be the expression of our intimacy with God. We might simply think that what we are seeking is what is best for us. But the best for us is what satisfies our deepest desire in concrete situations. These choices give "praise, reverence, and service" to God, but not in an ideological or programmatic manner that has as a propaganda slogan "This is being done for God!"

Rather, such choices reveal my attitude of being disposed to God and for God. As such they give praise. The praise they offer is that of a being willing to be disposed by God. The choice is a gesture towards God, acknowledging that I am a sinner. I can and do make mistakes. I often fall from the path. But I love you. What I choose to do in this situation, I do out of that love for you, knowing that you will not allow me to destroy myself. The gesture arises out of humility and a sense of dependence on God. It is carried out trusting God for whatever I need to live out the discernment. This attitude arises from the intimacy I have with God. The discernment is the expression of gratitude at having been found by God in this particular moment in my life.

This attitude manifests itself in a stance of reverence and respect for God. The reverence here is a posture of seeking God in all things, and seeking to please God in all things. Like the widow putting her mite in the treasury, what we do is very little, but how we do it is important. How we behave in the world and in our daily life reveals our disposition to God. This creation is maintained by God's goodness. As creatures, we who are a part of that creation reveal our intimacy with God by the way we relate to his creation. The level of intimacy creates the posture we spontaneously assume. This is not a matter of liturgical correctness or cultural decorum. It is an act of adoration. It witnesses to the passion we, like Christ in the world, have for the Father.

We demonstrate that passion in acts of service that build up the community of love that is the Body of Christ. These acts of service that are the discernment in action say, "I am doing this because I believe that you, my God, have shown me this is the best thing to be done at this time in history in the ongoing struggle of good against evil." They manifest our commitment to that struggle as co-creators of the kingdom of God.

God's commitment in a discernment is to maintain the relationship with us as we live out our choice. This is the fidelity of God. We cannot undertake to live out our discernments by ourselves. That is impossible. Our commitment is also to maintain that relationship so that the discernment can take root and open further the path of intimacy. Sometimes we make a discernment, but do not maintain the intimacy with God in which the decision was made. Like Israel in the Old Testament, we break the covenant. We stray from that relationship or from the ways in which we might help maintain it. As a result, our commitment ceases, and our way of living changes. In this new state, we again find ourselves living in circumstances that call for God's mercy. Then we again seek to be redeemed. We may seek a new covenant in our changed circumstances.

We can make and live out correct discernments only in freedom, and those discernments can be effective only if we maintain the relationship with God in which they were made. When we discern, we have expectations about the way the discernment will work out in our lives. We often find that what happens as we live out of the discernment is quite different from what we imagined. This does not mean that the discernment was wrong. The meaning of the discernment changes at different stages of our journey.

We may fall in love and decide to live our life in a certain way. As we walk in that way, we change. We find that, from one stage to the next, we give up how we understand ourselves, or how we saw God, or even how we understood the meaning of the discernment. But we hold on to the relationship that allowed the discernment to happen. As the relationship changes, even our understanding of relationship changes. The intimacy of friends is different from the intimacy of lovers, and that is different from the intimacy of newlyweds. Their intimacy is different from that of a married couple with children, and an old couple understand and express their mutuality in ways that are different still from those bringing up a family. The same is true for the spiritual journey. The discernments that manifest themselves in covenant moments do not reveal their full meaning at those moments. As the journey progresses, the understanding of those moments changes.

Discerning does not guarantee us success in the eyes of the world, nor security, nor acceptance. Discernments do not make our path through the world any easier than Christ's. Discernments do not take away God's freedom or our own. What they do is open the path to intimacy where we discover, in new and often surprising ways, how we are God's beloved.

Questions for Prayer and Reflection

1. Can you recall covenant moments in your life? How have they defined your spiritual path?

2. Have these moments led to a greater intimacy with God?

3. How has your sense of intimacy changed because of them?

4. How does this manifest in your understanding of yourself? in your relationship with others?

The Movie
THE MOTORCYCLE DIARIES

Director: Walter Salles (2004 – 126 mins.)
Starring: Gael Garcia Bernal, Rodrigo De la Serna, Mercedes Morán

1. Synopsis

The Motorcycle Diaries is based on the journals of Che Guevara, leader of the Cuban Revolution. These journals describe adventures that Guevera and his best friend, Alberto Granado, had in the early 1950s as they rode across South America by motorcycle to do their medical residency at a leper colony.

The two young students are looking for women and adventure before they have to settle down and take life more seriously.

Note: If at all possible, watch the subtitled version. Much of an actor's art lies in the use of voice to express emotion, mood, and character. Dubbed movies can never have the full impact of the original.

2. About the Movie

1. The film is about "two lives running parallel for a while." The two best friends start off with the same goals and aspirations, but by the time the film is over, it's clear what each man's destiny has become.

   What are the goals they both start out with? And what is their destiny at the end of the film? How different are their destinies at the end of the film?

2. "But one reason to explore the past is to try to rediscover an elusive sense of forgotten possibility, and in Mr. Salles's hands what might have been a schematic story of political awakening becomes a lyrical exploration of the sensations and perceptions from which a political understanding of the world emerges." (A.O. Scott, *The New York Times*, September 24, 2004)

   The diaries were found long after Guervara's death. Their author did not know who he would become, even as the notebooks themselves dramatize a crucial stage in his development. How does this allow the filmmakers to create a film that is not about "political awakening"?

3. "When he was murdered in Bolivia in October 1967 by the local army in association with the CIA, Ernesto 'Che' Guevara immediately took his place alongside Bolivar, Pancho Villa and other heroic Latin American revolutionaries. Comparable in popular appeal to Jack Kennedy, he immediately became for young people what TE Lawrence and Leon Trotsky had been for their parents, the contemporary model of the intellectual as man of action. Like Lawrence he was an irregular soldier who took up the cause of others. Like Trotsky he was a communist intellectual and second in command of a revolution

that confounded political theory. Like both of them he was physically unprepossessing, but made up for this in charisma, and like them too, he died a violent death." (Philip French, *The Observer*, August 29, 2004)

What hints of such a man do you find in the film? Can you describe some scenes that show some of the qualities that foreshadow the Che that he will become?

4. After watching the film one might say that it is really a love story in the form of a travelogue. The love it chronicles is no less profound – and no less stirring to the senses – for taking place not between two people but between a person and a continent.

What role does this "love" play in the quickening of Ernesto's youthful idealism, and the gradual turning of his passionate, literary nature toward an as yet unspecified form of radical commitment? Consider the birthday toast Ernesto makes near the end of the film. In it he evokes a pan-Latin American identity that transcends the arbitrary boundaries of nation and race. Perhaps as A.O. Scott points out in his review of the film, "In an age of mass tourism, it also unabashedly revives the venerable, romantic notion that travel can enlarge the soul, and even change the world." (*The New York Times*, September 24, 2004)

3. The Relationship of the Movie to the Theme of the Exercise

1. Following Che through his first tenuous steps towards self-identity, the film is nominally a story about a bike ride, but it is really about the transformation such journeys engender so magnificently. Why is the journey metaphor important in the film?

2. Of the two ways to arrive at a decision that are given in the Exercise (it comes to us suddenly with such clarity that we know it is right, or it comes only after quiet deliberation), which applies to Che in this film? Where do we see examples of this?

4. The Relationship of the Movie to One's Self in the Exercise

1. The journey offers a look at moments in Che's life that will become very significant for him. When you look at your life, can you list the significant moments that led you to where you are now? How many of those moments were beyond your control? How many started off as something else? In how many were the choices yours?

2. In the Old Testament, the young king Solomon is devastated by the death of his father David. He does not know how to proceed and he calls on God. He does not ask for riches or a long life. He asks only for the heart to understand how to discern the difference between good and evil (1 Kings 3:9). What is the "good and evil" in your life that you are asking God to help you discern?

11th Exercise
The Baptism of Jesus

This is my beloved Son with whom I am well pleased.
(Matthew 3:17)

It is more suitable and much better that the Creator and Lord in person communicate Himself to the devout soul in quest of the divine will, that He may inflame it with His love and praise, and dispose it for the way in which it could better serve God in the future. (Sp. Ex. #15)

This is to ask for what I desire. Here it will be to ask for an intimate knowledge of our Lord, who has become man for me, that I may love Him more and follow Him more closely. (Sp. Ex. #104)

Living out of a Love that Trusts

All that any spiritual discipline does is dispose us to God. It signals to God that we are willing to enter into a relationship with the divine. It cannot compel that relationship to happen. Similarly, spiritual techniques and rituals can facilitate the relationship with the holy, but they can never substitute for the holy. They cannot compel the holy to be present to us in ways we find useful. The same thing can be said about the Spiritual Exercises or any other prayer. They do not make God present; they are merely a way of presenting ourselves to God. This is what happens to Christ. He loves the Father and disposes himself to the Father, but he cannot compel the Father to act before his time or in ways that are opposed to his mystery. Love does not force love; love trusts love and expects love to be loving. Christ lives out of that trust and that love.

After his presentation in the temple at age twelve, when he declares he must be about his Father's business, Christ receives no confirmation about what he is to do for the next eighteen years. He waits on God for the next step. He waits for God. We do not know just how that waiting shapes him. We can imagine him learning patience; putting up with the growing concern of his relatives that "he has not found himself"; and even working to understand what it means to be a just person in his religious tradition, without ever having affirmed at the root of his being what he intuits about himself. Because he is human, we can relate to his questioning who he is, his brooding about what others have told him about himself, his self-doubts, his sense of being special.

And then, one day, something happens. Jesus goes down to the river Jordan where his cousin John, an itinerant preacher, is preaching and baptizing. Jesus is baptized and experiences an epiphany. He receives his call when the Father says, "This is my beloved Son, with whom I am well pleased" (Matthew 3:13-17). The call is given not in terms of a plan of action, but as a relationship of love, of generation. Jesus is acknowledged as the Father's son, and as the beloved who pleases his Father well.

When we are called to love, we are called to relationship. Each of us is loved for who we are, and not for what we do. It is the other in the relationship who acknowledges us. This is pure gift. We can dis-

160

pose ourselves to the possibility of its happening, but how it happens, and when, where, why, and how, are beyond our control. We fall in love with someone and discover we are loved in return. We discover that we are in love with God and we experience God loving us.

What's in a Name?

Only after we have received that gift and accepted it can we name it, for it occurs at the core of our being. It takes time before we even realize what has happened. It takes more time to accept it and to live out of that wonder. It takes even more time to let that love name us and to discover our own name for that love, which now nourishes and enlightens us. It affirms that the core of our being is united to the source of all life, the Mystery Jesus calls "Father." That Mystery roots us. We know that we are created by God, sustained by God, and transformed by God. But to be rooted is to be carried to deeper levels of relationship that struggle for words to express them. This is what Christ experienced at his baptism in the Jordan; God declares Jesus to be "my beloved Son." This is what we experience when God calls us by name. This naming does more than the names our parents and families bestow on us – it establishes our place in the structures and dynamics of creation. For this reason, names are sacred in spirituality: they tell us how we are holy.

In our lives, various incidents name us. When we are born, we receive not only our family name but "given" names – the names of ancestors, saints, or other significant people. We may have a confirmation name; friends may give us nicknames. Society names us with professional titles. The ones we love have pet names for us, intimate endearments that have secret codes of meaning. God also names us,

and in that naming is our call. Thus, in Genesis, "Abram" is named "Abraham" by God; that naming publicly establishes their relationship (Genesis 17:1-14). A call is a vocation. Our naming shows us how we are to act in the world. Abraham's naming, for example, makes him the father of the Jewish people.

In Christ's baptism, he is named not only "Son" but also "Beloved." In the Second Week of the Exercises, the grace we pray for is a growing intimacy with Christ. As we are given that grace, we discover that we, too, are called "Beloved" and named as God's living Word in the world.

Rite of Passage

That naming is a transitional point in our lives. In biblical topography, the Jordan was the river that the Israelites crossed to the Promised Land, the place where they could live out their covenanted relationship with God in community and in a land they could finally call their own. When we hear our call, we reach a transition point in our lives. At times that transition is difficult, as the Jordan was difficult to cross and treacherous in places. Often when we hear our call, when we experience our baptism, we find ourselves in a difficult place. We must give up the comfort of an old way of life. We must risk setting off on a new path that was not open to us before. When we do, we find ourselves.

As you enter this contemplation of Christ's baptism, remember the times and places when you were named and given an identity. Recall the times when you were misnamed, given a false identity, and so lived in servitude. True naming emerges only in love and out of love. As you immerse yourself in the dangerous waters of transition, immerse yourself also in that love that surrounds you, cherishes you and calls you "Beloved," in the passionate intimacy that each of us uniquely shares with the one we call "God." Ask for the grace to hear your naming.

Questions for Prayer and Reflection

1. What happened in this contemplation as you asked to share Christ's baptismal experience?

2. What has named and shaped you? How did these manifest themselves in your life?

3. What are your experiences of being known truly and lovingly?

4. Whom do you love so much that they learned to accept themselves, which changed the way they behave to others?

5. What risks do you take in loving, in giving love, and in sharing that love with others? Why do you take those risks?

6. What is the life you find as you risk in love? Does it sustain you? How?

7. When Jesus goes to the Jordan, he leaves home in such a way that he can never go back again. Have you ever left home that way? How did you deal with the resulting emotions? How can you bring those emotions to the prayer you are entering into?

8. How do you live out your being named "Beloved"?

The Movie
C.R.A.Z.Y.

Director: Jean-Marc Vallée (2005 – 127 mins)
Starring: Michel Côté, Marc-André Grondin, Danielle Proulx

1. Synopsis

Love is at the heart of this movie: a father's love for his sons, and one son's love for his father. That son is Zac Beaulieu, born in 1960. The next 20 years lead Zac on a surprising journey; in the end he is able to accept himself for who he is and his father does the same. A story of a modern-day Christ-like figure, this film reveals the many complexities and contradictions of the human spirit.

Note: If at all possible, watch the subtitled version. Much of an actor's art lies in the use of voice to express emotion, mood, and character. Dubbed movies can never have the full impact of the original.

2. About the Movie

1. The title of the film looks like a mistake. Were you able to figure out the meaning of the title before the end of the film? What clues did you have to follow to do this?

2. "Just like his father, for whom Patsy Cline and Aznavour are the twin deities of song, music is the gateway to Zac's highly developed fantasy life, and Vallee is at his most creative when he's got a pop song blaring on the soundtrack. An exuberant levitation scene in church, to the accompaniment of the Rolling Stones' 'Sympathy for the Devil,' marks 15-year-old Zac's entry into his confused yet idiosyncratic teen years. Vallee's feel for music, from Patsy Cline's 'Crazy' to David Bowie's 'Space Oddity' is one of the pic's most enjoyable features; Helmer reportedly took a salary cut to pay for the numerous song rights." (Jay Weissberg, *Variety*, September 13, 2005)

How does the soundtrack propel the story through time? Whether it's Patsy Cline or the Stones or Bowie or Pink Floyd or Jefferson Airplane, how does the music prove essential, anchoring the film in its time and providing a powerful sense of reality?

3. "One of the film's subtexts is the waning influence of the Catholic Church in Quebec society; at one point, Zachary's father remarks that he's 'getting sick' of the local priests. When his faith in Catholicism buckles and his relationship with his father suffers, a teenaged Zachary turns to Bowie as a religious figure. 'In that scene, *Space Oddity* really becomes like a prayer,' says Vallée. '[Zachary]'s praying to God. He's using rebellious music to talk about the fact that he's different, but that it's okay. He's struggling with his place in the world, and Bowie speaks to him. These are spiritual rock songs.'" (Matthew Hays, cbc.ca, October 14, 2005)

What are some of the examples that we see in the film of the "waning influence" of the Catholic Church? What replaces religion for the members of this family?

3. "In the movie's most uplifting moment, literally, Zac levitates in church while the entire congregation sings along to 'Sympathy for the Devil.' It's his moment of clarity, but it won't be long until his fairy-fearing father drags him to a shrink and then refuses to accept him when the truth finally comes out at the disastrous and alcohol-soaked wedding of one of his brothers. Zac and his father are now estranged, and Zac heads off to the Holy Land to look for answers." (Don Willmott, AMC Filmcritic.com, December 28, 2006)

Zac was born on Christmas Day 1960, a fact that tightens the film's religious themes. What happens when Zac literally follows in the footsteps of Christ? What is he hoping to accomplish by doing this?

4. "At times it's an ugly watch – Vallée doesn't balk at the plain nastiness that can arise in even the most loving families – yet C.R.A.Z.Y. emerges as a warm, thoughtful vignette that offers a refreshing new take on problems as old as the human race." (Liz Beardsworth, *Empire*, 2006)

Zac's story and his relationship with his father are central to the film. What roles do the mother and Zac's brothers play in this relationship?

5. "Though Vallée doesn't see his film as a coming-out movie ('It's really about anyone who's different,' he says), he feels Quebec society has had an easier time accepting gays. 'Since we're alone in Quebec, surrounded by English Canada and English-speaking America, we feel different in our environment,' Vallée says. 'Perhaps that makes it easier for us to accept the different ones. Because we do feel different because we're speaking another language.' And that, reports Vallée, is the main reason he spent 10 years making C.R.A.Z.Y. 'I wanted to show my sons [Émile and Alex] that everyone has something to offer. I wanted to show them that acceptance of people who are different is the way to go.'" (Matthew Hays, cbc.ca., October 14, 2005)

When you came to the end of the film, how well did you think the director achieved what he was trying to do – show us (as well as his sons) that "acceptance of people who are different is the way to go"?

3. The Relationship of the Movie to the Theme of the Exercise

1. It is certain that both Zac's mother and his father would say that – as the Exercise says of the young Jesus – "he has not found himself." Zac also wonders about himself and how others see him – especially his own family – and about his relationships with Michelle and Toto. Would you say that there is a point in the film when Zac realizes that he has a call – a call to what he sees as love and a call to what he sees as a relationship?

2. Zac, who was born on Christmas day, seems to follow in the footsteps of Christ during the time he spends in the Holy Land and specifically in the desert. How does his time in the wilderness make him conscious of his vulnerability? What are the choices that follow this realization?

3. In this Exercise we are immersed in the danger-ous waters of transition, helped along mostly by the love that surrounds us and cherishes us and calls us. By the end of the move, Zac has grown and changed. This transition from boy to man has been turbulent – often terrifying for him. What sustains Zac during this time? Is there any one scene that brings out this aspect for you?

4. In many ways, Zac's relationship with his father is stronger than anything else in his life. How important is this in Zac's journey to understand-ing himself. How does this lead him, as a notice-ably older man, to be able to narrate, "I don't know if it was Raymond's passing, or if time heals all wounds, but my father had become my father once more. Although, it took him 10 years to allow me into his home with a lover, and we've never mentioned our differences since nor Patsy Cline"?

4. The Relationship of the Movie to One's Self in the Exercise

1. In our lives, as the Exercise tells us, there are incidents that name us – being born results in being given at least two names; perhaps another at confirmation and another if we are a "profes-sional"; our friends give us a nickname, while we may have pet names for those we love. Zac is given many names by his family and his friends. What names have been given to you thus far in your life? Who gave them to you? For what rea-son? Do you accept such naming graciously?

2. One of the key concepts of media education tells us that the audience negotiates meaning. Simply put, this means that everything that makes us who we are – everything that names us – plays a role in how we look at media. What have you brought to the movie – what is it of you – that causes you to think as you do about this movie? What is it within you that makes you like or dis-like this film? What makes you open to under-standing it or makes you closed to what the movie has to say to you?

3. According to the Exercise, enlightenment is an accident; what the Exercises do is to make us accident-prone. Certainly Zac exemplifies this in the film. What incidents have happened in your life that have resulted in enlightenment about yourself? How did you react to these situations?

165

12th Exercise
The Temptations in the Desert

Blessed be the God and Father of our Lord Jesus Christ, who has blessed us in Christ with every spiritual blessing in the heavenly places, even as he chose us in him before the foundation of the world that we should be holy and blameless before him. He destined us in love to be his own through Jesus Christ, according to the purpose of his will, to the praise of his glorious grace which he freely bestowed on us in the Beloved. (Ephesians 1:3-6)

It is the mark of the evil spirit to assume the appearance of an angel of light. He begins by suggesting thoughts that are suited to a devout soul, and ends by suggesting his own. For example, he will suggest holy and pious thoughts that are wholly in conformity with the sanctity of the soul. Afterwards, he will endeavor little by little to end by drawing the soul into his hidden snares and evil designs. (Sp. Ex. #332)

This is to ask for what I desire. Here it will be to ask for an intimate knowledge of our Lord, who has become man for me, that I may love Him more and follow Him more closely. (Sp. Ex. #104)

Living Vulnerably

Something dramatic happens in Jesus' life immediately after his baptism: "The Spirit immediately drove him out into the wilderness. And he was in the wilderness forty days, tempted by Satan; and he was with the wild beasts; and the angels ministered to him" (Mark 1:12-13). It is easy to think that when we are called and are filled with the Spirit, experiencing a profound confirmation of our identity, life will become easy and we will be spared its terrors. But that is simply not true. Rather, we immediately come in contact with malign forces – within us or outside of us – that try to make life unbearable, and we discover that we are vulnerable to those forces. Yet we do not encounter those forces alone. Just as it is human nature to help someone who is in need or in trouble, it is God's nature to go to the endangered aspects of creation. When we are tempted, the illusion offered us is that we are alone. This is not true. Whether we feel it or not, we are held then, as always, in God's love. We are asked to rely on that love, rather than on our own abilities.

In the wilderness, Jesus is tempted to use his new-found identity to satisfy his ego. What the wilderness does for Jesus – as it does for each of us – is make us conscious of our vulnerability. In that vulnerability we have choices. We can rely on ourselves; or we can rely on God. The evil spirit suggests to us that we rely on ourselves. God asks us to trust in that Divine Mercy we have experienced constantly loving us.

More Than an Animal

Thus, when Jesus is hungry, he is tempted to turn the stones into bread. He has the ability to do this, and he has a real need. But he responds by saying that we do not live on bread alone but by every word that proceeds from the mouth of God. That all-creating word of the Father makes both stone and bread,

166

but, even more important, it manifests itself in the mercy of Divine Providence. Jesus is willing, in his hunger, to trust Divine Providence rather than his own gifts. In terms of the Two Standards, he chooses poverty rather than riches.

More Than a Social Creation

Next, Jesus is offered the honour of the world (Luke 4:5-7). This he rejects by remembering that his basic identity comes from his relationship with God, rather than with any aspect of creation. He affirms his basic stance of "praise, reverence, and service" to God rather than accepting the "authority" and "glory" of all the kingdoms of the world. Often we, too, are seduced by our own needs to abandon that intimacy with God and to substitute for it the approval of others or the definitions of ourselves that the world tries to impose upon us.

More Than Self-Determined

In the final temptation, Satan wants Jesus to throw himself from a high place, the pinnacle of the temple in Jerusalem. He reasons that if Jesus is the Son of God, God will save him. But Jesus knows that he cannot flaunt the Father's gift to him as his right. He can only operate out of it as a merciful dispensation from the Father. Moreover, he knows who he is; he does not have to prove it to anyone. He replies, "You shall not tempt the Lord your God."

The temptations ask Jesus to be less than who he is. They ask him to rely on his own gifts, to use the things of the world to maintain his own identity, and to use God to affirm himself. The temptations attempt to deny or distort his relationship with the one who has just called him his "beloved." In rejecting the temptations, Jesus shows himself content to wait on God to feed him, to affirm him, and to save him. Such waiting he learned in his hidden life; it will manifest itself again when he is on the cross.

To enter into a contemplation of Christ's temptations in the desert is to discover how our energies, now being woven together with Christ's energies, enter into temptation. We find, as we found in the Two Standards, that we are tempted by riches, honour, and pride. We want to rely on ourselves, to seek the approval of the world, and to set ourselves up as the centre of our universe. But if we journey with Jesus, we find that we can overcome those temptations because our relationship with the Father, like that of Jesus, is stronger than our selfishness. We discover that, like Jesus, we are nourished and affirmed, and we find ourselves in that relationship. This manifests our call as companions of the Christ.

Questions for Prayer and Reflection

1. What happens when you read and contemplate the temptations of Christ in the desert?

2. What are your deserts? in your work? your family? your relationships? the society you live in? the world?

3. Is there a pattern to the way you are tempted?

4. How does the prayer affect the way you encounter temptation and deal with it?

5. What have been the consequences in your life of falling in love with God and allowing God to express his love for you?

6. What have been the consequences of not falling in love with God and of ignoring his relationship with you?

7. How does your intimacy with God express itself in your daily life?

8. How do you distinguish between being pious and being spiritual in your life?

The Movie
CORALINE

Director: Henry Selick (2009 – 100 mins.)
Starring: Dakota Fanning, Terri Hatcher, Jennifer Saunders, Dawn French

1. Synopsis

Eleven-year-old Coraline Jones moves with her parents into an apartment in a dilapidated pink Victorian house called the Pink Palace Apartments. On a walk, Coraline meets Wybie Lovat, whose grandmother grew up in the house. But Coraline is lonely, for she has moved far away from her friends. She also feels bored and neglected by her parents, who are busy writing a garden catalog.

Exploring the old house, Coraline finds a hidden door with a bricked up passage. When she makes her way through the passage, she discovers a parallel world that turns out to be a trap. She must draw on all her resourcefulness and courage to make her way home and save her family.

2. About the Movie

1. "Henry Selick, the mad-genius puppetmaster behind Tim Burton's *The Nightmare Before Christmas* and *James and the Giant Peach*, has brought Neil Gaiman's 2002 cult novella to the screen with almost all its playful psychodrama intact. This is *The Corpse Bride* with teeth, Bruno Bettelheim retooled for the multiplex, a nightmare of daft and creative consequence." (Ty Burr, *Boston Globe*, February 6, 2009)

Bettelheim suggested that traditional fairy tales – like those of the Brothers Grimm – with the darkness of abandonment, death, witches, and injuries, allowed children to grapple with their fears in remote, symbolic terms. If they could read and interpret these fairy tales in their own way, he believed, they would find a greater sense of meaning and purpose, and they would experience emotional growth that would better prepare them for their own futures. How does Bettleheim's theory apply to this film?

2. "Coraline is a beautifully designed, rather scary answered-prayer story: the little girl longs for more attention than she's getting from her parents, so she enters a parallel world in which her parents are very attentive indeed – so attentive that they want to take control of her, sew buttons into her eyes, and turn her into a ghost child. All her neighbors are there, too, in slightly altered form, and the movie is filled with both sinister and enchanting transformations, as when the two portly, retired British music-hall performers who live in Coraline's house burst out of their shells of voluminous bosom and elephantine waist and fly through the air as slender, graceful young maidens. Animation is the art in which all wishes, sweet and sour, eventually

come true." (David Denby, *The New Yorker*, March 2, 2009)

How possible would it have been to present creatively the parallel world in a live action film instead of an animated film?

3. "Most animated films are parables about growing up, often in the absence of one or both parents; this one goes a dark step further to suggest that the woman who gave you life may take it away by smothering you to meet her insatiable needs .... The story borrows liberally from other fantasy sources, including *Spirited Away* (a girl rescues human parents who have been transformed) and *The Matrix* (deluded happiness comes from abandoning not only responsibilities but freedom of choice)." (Lawrence Toppmann, *The Charlotte Observer*, February 05, 2009)

What other dramatic and /or fantasy sources can you find in this film?

4. "Scratch its colorful loop-de-loop surface, and the story is both elemental and rare: an epic psychic battle between a mother and her daughter for acceptance, recognition, and space. The Other Mother is eventually revealed to Coraline (and us) as the evil harridan all teenage girls know their moms to be right after they've slammed the bedroom door, but there's a pathos to the older woman's neediness that's unexpectedly moving. Better, Coraline's real mother is proved to be just that: real, flawed, loving." (Ty Burr, *Boston Globe*, February 6, 2009)

How does the director convey this elemental emotion and theme? Why does the reviewer call it "rare"?

5. "Selick's script plays up the colorful fantasy possibilities of Gaiman's perfect world, in a series of amazing sequences where mechanical mice, independently mobile flowers, and hideously near-naked old ladies perform for Coraline's pleasure. But he also taps into a playfully Burton-esque streak of delicious dread that's as much *Beetlejuice* as *Nightmare*. Gaiman poised the story — one of his tightest and slyest — at the nightmarish border of traditional fairy tales, and Selick expands it while respecting its strong characters and eerie tone. He brings it to life as a piece of stunningly mobile art, a lovingly detailed, beautifully constructed clockwork contraption with CGI fluidity and handmade soul." (Tasha Robinson, *The Onion AV Club*, February 5, 2009)

Stop motion is an animation technique to make a physically manipulated object appear to move on its own. The object is moved in small increments between individually photographed frames, creating the illusion of movement when the series of frames is played as a continuous sequence. How does Selick use the technique to enhance the comedy and horror that mingle in his more "family-friendly" version of Gaiman's dark story?

6. "The first contemporary film in which the 3-D experience feels intrinsic to the story instead of a Godforsaken gimmick, *Coraline* is a remarkable feat of imagination, a magical tale with a genuinely sinister edge .... Selick is the preeminent practitioner of stop-motion animation, which makes *Coraline* the first 3-D film to be made in that painstaking, labor-intensive process that involves the frame-by-frame manipulation of three-dimensional models. Stop-motion and 3-D

may seem like strange bedfellows, but in fact they complement each other beautifully. To bring this complex, unexpected world to the screen required a punishing investment of time and energy. *Coraline* spent two years in preproduction and then shot for 83 weeks on more than 50 small stages." (Kenneth Turran, *Los Angeles Times*, February 6, 2009)

Whether you watch Coraline in 3-D or not, are you aware of technique that was used to make the film or are you aware of none of that? Instead, are you captured completely by what is going on? How rare, and how wonderful, is that?

3. The Relationship of the Movie to the Theme of the Exercise

1. Coraline Jones, the brave, clever, curious protagonist and self-proclaimed eleven-year-old explorer, is aggravated by crazy adults (as they all seem to be), by not being taken seriously because of her young age and outgoing demeanor, and by people who constantly mistake her name for Caroline. As the Exercise tells us, the evil spirit tells us to rely on ourselves. How much does Coraline rely on herself to try to save her parents? What role does Wybie play in this? How would you describe the relationship between Coraline and Wybie? Could it be described as a slight "love-hate relationship"?

2. The Exercise tells us that when we believe we have confirmed our identity and are ready to deal with the world, then that is the time the world fights back to make life unbearable. There is a point at which Coraline is ready to accept the Other World. During one visit, Coraline encounters the black cat from her own world. Having the ability to talk in the Other World, it warns Coraline of the dangers of the place, but Coraline pays him no mind. What tempts Coraline to want to stay in the Other World? How is her treatment in the Other World different from her treatment by others in the real world?

3. In the Other World, Coraline has her own desert experience complete with temptations. What are the riches, honour, and pride that she is tempted to accept?

4. The Relationship of the Movie to One's Self in the Exercise

1. In the Other World, Coraline is tempted to be less than who she is. What temptation do you face regarding your personal integrity? How do you work to overcome this temptation?

2. God is never mentioned in the movie, yet our media literacy key concepts tell us that all media texts contain implicit or explicit values. The Exercise tell us that Jesus overcame the temptations because his relationship with the Father was stronger than his selfishness. In the midst of these Exercises, what is it about this Exercise that gives you hope that you can overcome the temptations to riches, honour, and pride that are being offered you?

3. The film presents a number of characters who tend to rely on themselves rather than readily accepting the help of others. Where, in your life, do you see yourself tempted to "go it alone," to rely on your own gifts and not seek the help and love of God?

13th Exercise
The Call

The Spirit of the Lord is upon me,
Because he has anointed me to preach good news
*   to the poor.*
He has sent me to proclaim release to the captives
And recovery of sight to the blind,
To set at liberty those who are oppressed,
To proclaim the acceptable year of the Lord.

(Luke 4:18-19)

If a devout soul wishes to do something ... that may be
for the glory of God our Lord, there may come a thought
or temptation from without not to say or do it. Apparent
reasons may be adduced for this, such that it is moti-
vated by vainglory or some such other imperfect inten-
tion, etc. ... He should act against the temptation.
According to St. Bernard, we must answer the tempter, "I
did not undertake this because of you, and I am not
going to relinquish it because of you." (Sp. Ex. #351)

This is to ask for what I desire. Here it will be to ask for
an intimate knowledge of our Lord, who has become man
for me, that I may love Him more and follow Him more
closely. (Sp. Ex. #104)

The Nature of a Call

In the temptations in the wilderness, Jesus discerns how to behave in the world and returns to the world with that knowledge. He knows he is in the community of the Father and has the support of his family and friends. He knows he is not alone. But he realizes that if he is to share the mercy of the Father with the world, he needs others who are like him – who have seen the misery of this world and have encountered the traps and illusions the world uses to ensnare people. He needs others, who, like him, seek to do something, however small, to relieve that burden of mindless suffering, to enlighten the deceived, and to celebrate the life that comes from knowing one is rooted in love. First he calls people he trusts. Interestingly, he does not approach religious figures, but ordinary people, like you and me.

Each of us is, at the root of our being, a manifestation of love. This is our identity and we experience a sense of it only when we are in loving relationships. But, as we all know, there are levels to loving. There is the love that is not expressed, and there is the love that is expressed. After that there is the love expressed and received. Then there is the love shared. Finally, there is the love that is the expression and work of that shared love. Our call emerges when the love that is given to us is received, lived out, shared, and acted upon. Every call contains the forces of attraction, response, engagement, and commitment.

If we look at what we do with our life, we will see we live this way because of a call. Our behaviour is a response to that call. This call may be a basic call to survival. It may be difficult or monotonous, but we endure it because we care about our family, or a particular cause, or a particular talent. Every call shows itself in what we value, because what we value is where we put our lives.

The call of Jesus to his disciples, and to each of us, asks us to put our lives beyond ourselves in trusting in a relationship with him. When we enter into that relationship, we are given a deeper access to the Father's mercy. But, like every relationship, it contains an element of risk. We give up our security to achieve our authenticity.

An Authentic Call

There is a story of an acrobat in a small circus whose single act was to walk a tightrope without a safety net. Above the middle of the high wire was suspended a ring made of rope, soaked in gasoline and set alight. At times he would climb the ladder to the roll of the drums and start his walk, only to turn back. The crowds would jeer. At other times, he would leap through the flaming circle. He said he was always afraid, and he turned back when his fear got the better of him. But when asked why he would attempt it in the first place, his answer was simple. He would say, "I know my life is on the other side."

When we follow our call, we give up our security, because our life is on the other side, in the living out of that call.

But how do we know we are called? In fact, we are called by many things, so the question is knowing what is the true call. A true call engages us fully, carries us beyond ourselves. It connects us, on a whole range of levels, with a reality that is both inviting and mysterious, compassionate and uncompromising. It is profoundly personal. It brings out the best in us and gives us a new and more realistic understanding of ourselves. But in answering a call, we also face our demons, as Christ did in the desert: we learn our limitations. We begin to appreciate what is given to us on our path and to be grateful for that path and for the companions and adventures we have along that way.

So how can we distinguish a true call? By the fidelity of the One who calls us. That One is true to our relationship in good times and in bad; does not judge us as anything less than lovable and capable of loving; respects our individuality; celebrates with us what is good in life; works along with us in transforming what is damaging in our world; gives us the strength and the courage to hold what is suffering or damaged; lets us experience our freedom to be creative. The one who calls us truly shares with us all that he has and is. When we are called by Christ, he shares with us the life and spirit he has with the compassionate and creative mystery he calls "Abba" … "Father."

Questions for Prayer and Reflection

1. When have you felt called to do something that you saw as significant? What were the stages of that experience? Looking back, what affirmed you? How did that happen? What forces worked against you? How did they manifest themselves? How did you overcome them?

2. Do the same exercise for two or three other significant life-changing experiences. Can you see a common pattern in the way you are called and the way you respond?

3. Read the call of apostles in the gospels (John 1; Mark 1; Luke 5; Matthew 4). Enter prayerfully and imaginatively into one of those scenes, giving the characters and yourself the freedom to say and do as they wish. What was significant in that scene for you?

4. Who in your world lives out such a calling within a family (such as a parent), a job (such as an artist), the community (such as an advocate

172

for human rights), the international scene (such as a world leader), or a religious tradition (such as a saint, the Buddha, Rumi)? Have a conversation with that person about what moves you and what moved them to lead such a life.

5. Are you experiencing a call now? What form does it take? What are you doing about it?

6. In what ways are you a witness to life for others?

7. Not all of us are asked to be religious, but we are all spiritual by nature. In what ways does your intimacy with the spiritual manifest itself?

The Movie
JULIE & JULIA

Director: Nora Ephron (2009 – 123 mins)
Starring: Meryl Streep, Amy Adams, Stanley Tucci, Chris Messina

1. Synopsis

It is 1949 and Julia Child, the wife of an American diplomat in Paris, is wondering what she is going to do with her time. Her attempts at hat making and bridge are not successful, and it is not until she takes cooking lessons at Cordon Bleu that she discovers her passion.

It is 2002 and Julie Powell, about to turn 30, is an underemployed and unpublished writer. She comes across Julia Child's first book, *Mastering the Art of French Cooking*, and decides not only to cook her way through it in a year but also to blog about it.

The movie goes back and forth between these stories of two women and their cooking experiences.

2. About the Movie

1. "*Julie & Julia* is one of the gentlest, most charming American movies of the past decade. Its subject is less food as something to cook than food as the binding and unifying element of dinner parties, friendship, and marriage." (David Denby, *The New Yorker*, August 24, 2009)

   List some scenes in this movie that prove that Denby is on the right track towards understanding what the film is all about. Or list some scenes that show he is totally wrong.

2. "Both women are unstoppable forces searching for something worth their involvement, and both find that cooking completes them, makes them feel alive in ways wonderful and unforeseen. …. It's also worth noting that these two stories are tales, so to speak, of sisters doing it for themselves. Though both women have loyal and encouraging husbands (played by fine actors Stanley Tucci and Chris Messina) who are crucial to their success, this is the rare Hollywood film where it's the men who are the support team, not the women …. *Julie & Julia* is very much a female coming to power story, which is one of several reasons why the producers were fortunate to get Ephron to write and direct." (Kenneth Turan, *Los Angeles Times*, August 7, 2010)

   Consider other films has Ephron written and/or directed (*Bewitched*, *You've Got Mail*, *Sleepless in Seattle*, *Hanging Up*, *When Harry Met Sally*). Where do they fit in with this idea of a "female coming to power story"?

3. "The impact of that first volume of *Mastering the Art*, and of Child's subsequent television career (which is mostly tangential to the movie's concerns), is hard to overstate. The book stands with a few other postwar touchstones – including Dr. Benjamin Spock's *Baby and Child Care*, the Kinsey

Report and Dr. Seuss's *Cat in the Hat* – as a publication that fundamentally altered the way a basic human activity was perceived and pursued." (A.O. Scott, *The New York Times*, August 7, 2010)

How does this film indicate the importance of Julia Child's *Mastering the Art* so that it ranks up there with the other books Scott mentions?

4. "And generosity is what *Julie & Julia* is about: the generosity of the earth and the generosity of effort required to make good food; the generosity of spirit that goes into a good dinner, and the generosity of investment that goes into a life's calling. It's about the recipe for the good life, how one woman finds it and how the other one couldn't, even with a map." (Mike LaSalle, *San Francisco Chronicle*, August 7, 2009)

Is LaSalle taking this a little far? Isn't the movie just meant to be a pleasant little comedy and not a treatise on "generosity"?

3. The Relationship of the Movie to the Theme of the Exercise

1. The Exercise lists a number of elements of a true call. How do each of these apply to the call that is made to Julia and Julie?

   • A call that engages us fully.

   • A call that carries us beyond ourselves.

   • A call that connects us on a whole range of levels with a reality that is both inviting and mysterious, compassionate and uncompromising.

   • A call that is profoundly personal.

   • A call that brings out the best in us.

   • A call that give us a new and more realistic self-understanding.

2. Certain factors, listed below, will lead us to believe in the one who calls us. Who calls Julia? Who calls Julie? And how are these factors present as the two women respond to their calls? The one who calls us

   • is true to the relationship in good times and bad;

   • does not judge us as anything less than lovable and capable of loving;

   • respects our individuality;

   • celebrates with us what is good in life;

   • works with us in transforming what is damaging in our world;

   • lets us experience the freedom to be creative;

   • shares with us all that he has and is.

4. The Relationship of the Movie to One's Self in the Exercise

1. If, as the Exercise states, we look at what we do with our life, we will see we live the way we do because of a call. This is true of both Julia and Julie. What are you called to? How should your response to this call have changed your life?

2. Every call shows itself in what we value, as the Exercise tells us, because what we value is where we put our lives. We see quite clearly what Julia and Julie value. What value is shown in what you are called to? How to you react to this call?

175

14th Exercise
The Cost of Discipleship

If anyone would come after me, let him deny himself and take up his cross and follow me. For whoever would save his life will lose it; and whoever loses his life for my sake and the gospel's sake will save it. For what does it profit a man, to gain the whole world and forfeit his life.

(Mark 8:34-36)

They will strive to conduct themselves as if every attachment ... had been broken. They will make efforts neither to want that, or anything else, unless the service of God our Lord alone moves them to do so. (Sp. Ex. #155)

This is to ask for what I desire. Here it will be to ask for an intimate knowledge of our Lord, who has become man for me, that I may love Him more and follow Him more closely. (Sp. Ex. #104)

The Challenge of Living Authentically

A script we sometimes buy into suggests that implementing decisions is easy. But this is not so. Often the values of the world deride the decisions we make because this world's illusions are fickle and superficial. When we make a radical decision, even though we still live in the world, we do not live as the world proposes we should live. For example, to enter into a life commitment flies in the face of overwhelming self-indulgence; to love what is broken transcends the lure of perfectionism; to believe in the power of truth destroys the convenient lie; to live spiritually exposes the shallowness of the materialism that surrounds us.

The Poor in Spirit

A call invites us to a deeper relationship with the divine. As we discovered in the First Week, when we encounter the divine personally and intimately, we discover our creaturehood. We experience that we are nothing in ourselves, and exist only because of the relationship God maintains with us, even though we might not be conscious of it most of the time. To exist consciously in that awareness is both liberating and terrifying. It is rather like discovering that the ground we have built our lives on, and our egos, with all of its assumptions and projects, is not solid after all. Until we learn intimately to trust the love that creates us, maintains us, and delights in us, what we hold to be real is merely the product of habit and blindness. But when we love, we discover reality is mysterious. It challenges and delights. And, as we learn to trust that relationship with God, we discover that we are not destroyed by our sense of our nothingness. In fact, we become more joyful and free in learning that we are cared for by a Love that is bigger than we can ever imagine. That awareness allows us to see every moment as an entry into the divine.

Walking Through Our Deaths

That perspective is the basis of our discipleship. As we enter the journey to a closer union with God, we meet forces that prevent us from fully experiencing that love. To reach the life we desire, we must acknowledge and mourn the many deaths that keep us prisoner: the loss of innocence; loss of loving relationships; destruction of our ideals and hopes; despair that goes with accepting as reality that "things cannot change"; cynicism that is suspicious of any form of good. We have to find ways not to submit to these deaths. How do we do this? First, we can acknowledge them for what they are. They are moments in our path. They do not define us. Only God does. That awareness takes power away from them. Second, we need to be open about how they affect us. Often we close down in those situations that drain us of life. When we do that, we deny God the access into our lives to change them. Third, we can enter consciously into those deaths in prayer and ritual, and offer them up to that transforming power of love found in resurrection. That love seeks us just as we seek it. To be a disciple is to offer the deaths we experience to God, and so witness to our intimacy with the sacred.

Daily Gifts

In so doing, we discover humility. We experience our powerlessness in the face of the powers of this world and of our own disorders. We become sensitive to the forms of malign absurdity that seek to control even the most common and simple good. But we also become increasingly attentive to what is given to us daily and to the quiet and, often, small good that can be found and shared and celebrated in our lives. We discover that this is enough for the day and for our needs.

Hungering for Life

Yet we long for a just world, a good and meaningful life. We wish we could see, know, and love the world and ourselves the way the Father sees and knows and loves us. This "more" that we hunger for as we grow into discipleship becomes the consuming passion that God the lover has for us, the beloved. This passion shows itself in mercy.

A Compassionate Mercy

In our world, we strive to be merciful with our slender means as the Father is merciful to us. We give what has been given to us. We do this out of compassion, because we know what it is to be lost and lonely and unloved. But we also do it because the one who loves us behaves that way, and we desire to be one with the beloved in the ways that the beloved deals with the world. The disciple seeks at first to imitate the God who calls us all. In responding to that call, we discover that the journey to love slowly transforms the way of the pilgrim from imitation into identification. The mercy that finds us and that we accept slowly becomes our own life. The lover becomes the beloved in the world.

A Practical Love

In sharing the heart of God, we manifest Christ's love for the Father and the Father's love for his Son. This is not pious sentimentality or an otherworldly relationship of unnatural intensity. It is simple, direct, and practical. It sees what must be done and does it. It sees what needs to be done and does what it can. It manifests the quiet, ongoing creativity and the constant patient suffering of God. It says, as Paul says, "It is no longer I who live, but Christ lives in me" (Galatians 2:20).

Reweaving the World

The life of Christ that disciples witness to with their own lives is one of a growing spiritual intimacy. That intimacy creates community on ever-more encompassing levels of relationships. There is the inner work of uniting the separated parts of the self, and, at the same time, the outer work of creating and maintaining bonds within families, communities, society, and nations. That intimacy reaches out to the broader dimensions of community, including the ecological and even the cosmic. This sense of unity is fostered by right relationships. The work of the disciple is to establish, preserve, and support relationships that give life and are rooted in the mystery of God's creativity.

But to live this way requires courage and a conscious rootedness in God's love, for such a life has to loose the bonds of oppression and unmask the lies that trap the human family. So we must be willing to speak for those with no voice and to share the life of these little ones in a way that convinces them of their worth and their goodness. Too often, such a life leads to suffering and persecution. The disciple knows that anyone in this intimate following of Christ will be treated in this world just as the Christ was treated.

Yet we are asked to live this way and on this path if we are to help transform this world into a place where good can be seen and cherished, truth known and upheld, and love become the basis of all action. The call to discipleship is primarily a call to such a deep intimacy with God that our lives manifest this intimacy in all we do and hold. Each of us is offered that call and that path. It is the path of the Beatitudes (Matthew 5:1-16).

Questions for Prayer and Reflection

1. This contemplation is a path through the Beatitudes and describes the life of a disciple. The Beatitudes were central to the First Week, to lead us to a spiritual freedom. Here the Beatitudes foster a deeper sense of intimacy with the Christ. This is the grace you are praying for. You might wish to pray your way through the Beatitudes as if Christ is journeying with you. Stay with each one until it moves you to the next.

2. In your journey through this contemplation, where did you find yourself stopping because something moved you, either positively or negatively? List those moments and go back to them one at a time, staying with each moment until you feel ready to move on.

3. Have a conversation with Christ about how your life resembles his. Ask him to show you how this is so.

4. What fears do you have about developing a closer intimacy with God? Where do these fears come from? What do they suggest about what you should do next? How will you deal with them?

5. What do you find attractive when you contemplate a closer intimacy with God? How do you know if this attraction is deceptive or not? How will you find out? What will you do next?

6. At the end of your prayer periods, do you find yourself being consistently called to pray about something? What? How will you pray about it? (Ask God to show you.)

7. At the end of your prayer periods, have a conversation with the Father, or Jesus, or his mother, or one of your favourite saints about what happened in the prayer.

The Movie
TOY STORY 3

Director: Lee Unkrich (2010 – 103 mins.)
Starring: Tom Hanks, Tim Allen, Joan Cusack, Ned Beatty

1. Synopsis

Andy is now seventeen and his toys are given away to the Sunnyside Daycare Center by mistake. Woody, Buzz, Jessie and the others are glad to be played with again, until they see what's really going on at the daycare. They must work together one more time to break out and make their way home to Andy.

2. About the Movie

1. "In providing sheer moviegoing satisfaction – plot, characters, verbal wit and visual delight, cheap laughs and honest sentiment – *Toy Story 3* is wondrously generous and inventive. It is also, by the time it reaches a quiet denouement that balances its noisy beginning, moving in the way that parts of *Up* were. That is, this film – this whole three-part, 15-year epic – about the adventures of a bunch of silly plastic junk turns out also to be a long, melancholy meditation on loss, impermanence and that noble, stubborn, foolish thing called love. We all know money can't buy it, except sometimes, for the price of a plastic figurine or a movie ticket." (A.O. Scott, *The New York Times*, June 18, 2010)

How does this film deal with loss and impermanence? Which of the characters in the film come to mind when we meditate on these?

2. "Upon arrival (at the daycare center), they meet a new batch of playthings, who look like they belong on the Island of Misfit Toys. They also meet the stuffed animal who runs the place, a drawling Lots-o'-Huggin' Bear named Lotso, who explains that they will now be played with every day by an eager crop of kids. It sounds a little too good to be true – and it is. Besides, they'll no longer be Andy's toys. They know, in their synthetic joints, that they're being put out to pasture, and the awareness that they are not wanted creeps up on them, and us, like a giant swelling teardrop. All of a sudden, a Pixar movie has the poignance of a Tennessee Williams play, and that sense of fragility – of once-loved, now-outdated toys fighting for dignity and survival – haunts the entire movie." (Owen Glelberman, *Entertainment Weekly*, June 18, 2010)

How does an animated film such as this manage to convey such a sense of fragility? What are some of the scenes that show this?

3. "Deep into *Toy Story 3*, there's a moment where some of the toy protagonists realize that in spite of all their cleverness and determination, there's

no way out of the fatal trap into which they've fallen. In any other children's film, this would be a time for comedic panic, long-withheld personal confessions, or dramatic statements that would immediately turn out to be ironic. In any other children's film, the moment would quickly peak and pass. But *Toy Story 3* director Lee Unkrich (*Finding Nemo, Monsters Inc.*) holds for long, excruciating moments on the silent characters, as they pass from disbelief into sorrowful resolve, then take each others' hands and wait. And wait. And wait." (Tasha Robinson, *The Onion A.V. Club*, June 17, 2010)

Time and again, the film finds other real resonant emotional moments. How does the film find these places of deep emotion and explore them without blunting them, over-explaining them, or passing them off with a laugh?

4. "[John] Lasseter (creative director at Pixar), whose office at the company's Lego-like headquarters in Emeryville, Calif., is crammed with hundreds of gewgaws from his films, is an expert on the secret life of toys. 'If something inanimate were to come to life,' he posits, 'it would want to do what it's been manufactured to do. A toy wants to be played with by a child, to make that child happy. If it's not played with, that causes severe anxieties. If a toy is lost, it can be found. If broken, it can be repaired. The one thing toys are most anxious about is being outgrown, because there's no way that can be fixed.'" (Richard Corliss, *Time*, June 14, 2010)

How are these qualities of toys demonstrated in this film? Is it possible that there is an analogy between toys and people in what Lasseter says?

3. The Relationship of the Movie to the Theme of the Exercise

1. To be a disciple is to offer the deaths we experience, as the Exercise tells us, and witness to the relationship that we hold with the sacred. How is this shown in this film? How do each of the main characters show it, each in their own way?

2. Well into the film, the moment arrives when some of the toy protagonists realize that in spite of all their cleverness and determination, they are caught in a fatal trap. What is their response to this situation? How does this show the cost of discipleship for them?

4. The Relationship of the Movie to One's Self in the Exercise

1. There comes a point where the toys feel that they have lost the love of Andy, but then something happens to fill that emptiness. How has God done this in your own life?

2. How is God present in this film? What does he ask of his disciples here? Do they see God in their lives? Have you seen God in your life? Where? Think of the saying "God is in the details."

15th Exercise
Christ Walks on the Water
(Matthew 14:22-33)

All things are possible with God. (Mark 10:27)

God our Lord knows our nature infinitely better [than we do] ... He often grants us the grace to understand what is suitable for us. (Sp. Ex. #89)

This is to ask for what I desire. Here it will be to ask for an intimate knowledge of our Lord, who has become man for me, that I may love Him more and follow Him more closely. (Sp. Ex. #104)

The Impossible Happens

In this gospel sequence, Jesus has just heard about his cousin John's execution by Herod. He withdraws to a quiet place to reflect on this news, but when the crowds see where he is going, they follow him. Feeling sorry for them, he heals the sick among them. In the evening, seeing that they have nothing to eat, he feeds them all from the little food they brought. Then he goes up into the mountains to pray. Late that stormy night, the disciples are in a boat on the lake. They see Jesus walking on the waters towards them and are afraid, but Peter says, "If it is you, let me walk on the waters to you." Jesus says, "Come." Peter climbs out of the boat and walks on the water, but, when he feels the force of the wind, he is afraid and starts to sink. He cries out to be saved. Jesus stretches out his hand and saves him, and they get into the boat. When the others see what

Jesus has done, they acknowledge that he is truly divine.

When we enter into this contemplation, we feel very much as Peter did. In the midst of living out of our call, we are surrounded by alien forces beyond our control. The world situation teeters into instability, ecological catastrophes, nation in conflict with nation. Closer to home, we experience family tensions, health concerns, financial stress. No one is immune to these issues, and the security we struggle to maintain is always fragile. In the midst of worries that sometimes threaten to overwhelm us, we forget our relationship with Christ, and try to save ourselves. When this happens, we do become overwhelmed. In desperation, we cry out for deliverance. When we do so, we see that help is at hand. God does not promise us security. He offers us a relationship that is not broken, no matter what dangers surround and infect us. In holding onto that relationship, we realize we are rescued from despair. We experience that ever-present mercy of God that calls us to go beyond ourselves and our resources to trust in him. He sustains and saves us.

Unfortunately, it often seems that we must find ourselves in such situations before we can accept that we are looked after. And, to be honest, in every new situation where we are surrounded by destructive forces, we forget the life lessons of being saved, and so we sink again. We sink until we cry out again in desperation to be saved, and again we are saved.

In following the path of the disciple, the ego never disappears; in situations of vulnerability it tries to rely on itself. It is the fallen human condition to rely on our own abilities in dire circumstances. We lose touch with that more deeply human aspect of ourselves that knows we live only in relationship and are most fully alive only in relationship with God.

Depending on God

To consider Jesus in his humanity and to see what he does in dire circumstances is also personally transforming. He had started his public ministry following John's example, but here Jesus sees what can happen when people witness in that way. The forces of the world destroy them. Herod kills John.

Jesus is grieved by the murder of a family member, but he also realizes the consequences of the path he walks. He withdraws, as in a retreat, to enter more self-consciously into that relationship with his Father, to be more deeply rooted and to take heart.

His desire for self-renewal is frustrated by the needs of the crowd. He puts aside his own ego needs in compassionate imitation of his Father. He heals the sick. Gathering the little food they have, he prays to the Father and experiences once again that mercy passing through him into the world. The loaves and fish are multiplied and all are fed. Even in his extreme need, Jesus depends on his relationship with the Father to sustain him and his mission. That love, which names him, as it names us, as the beloved, comes through. The people are satisfied.

It is only then that Jesus continues on his own project. He goes off into the mountains to commune with his Father. As we experience in the practice of these Exercises, he realizes that he needs time to maintain his bond with the source of his life. He takes the time to do that. Out of this, he is renewed to continue his mission. He returns to those whom the Father has given him as companions for the journey, and he finds them in need. They are surprised at his mode of coming to them (as they will be surprised in the resurrection sequences) and wonder if it is not a figment of their frantic imaginations. Peter asks him to identify himself through his powers. Jesus accepts and calls him. In that personal calling, Peter is given the power to do what Jesus does. He walks on the water. When we accept our call, we are given the same power to do as Jesus does, and to live as Jesus lives. We set out, like Peter, with our eyes fixed on the Christ. It is when we leave our habitual forms of security and totally depend on Jesus that our faith falters and we become aware of our situation. We turn towards ourselves and break the relationship we have with the one who calls us. We sink.

We are rescued when we turn in desperation once again to God. The first time we turn is for proof; the second time we seek a deeper level. That first time is like the occasion when we make a discernment and some plan of action gets confirmed. The second time is like setting out on that plan, becoming overwhelmed by what we have to do, and falling back on our own resources. We discover that they are not enough. We panic and cry out to God as our last resort. By those saving acts, we recognize that neither ghosts nor illusions save us, but the Christ.

Many things happen to us in this contemplation. We recognize that the one who loves us is divine, and that this does not take away from his humanity, since he, too, suffers. We also learn to distinguish between the illusions that look like God and the real God, since only God can save us. We find out how vital is our relationship with God in living out our call, because we cannot do this on our own. We discover God's constant fidelity in taking the little we have and making it enough for what we must do. We learn that the Christ works to maintain his relationship with his Father, and that just as Christ responds to our needs, the Father responds to Christ's needs. We enter more deeply into that creative mercy that witnesses to the Father's love for us and to Christ's love for us. We live out and share that creative mercy in our lives.

As we enter into this contemplation and open ourselves to being transformed by God's love, we become the disciples that Christ gathers around him, as we are given that intimate knowledge that makes us his continuing presence on earth.

Questions for Prayer and Reflection

1. Read Matthew 14:22-33. Enter into a contemplation of it. Where were you? Were you an onlooker? One of those fed? A disciple on the boat? Peter? Jesus? What did the contemplation reveal to you about yourself? About your relationship to God?

2. Have you ever been in dire straits and then, through matters beyond your control, triumphed over that situation? When you relive such situation, what does it say about your life and about God's presence in your life?

3. Are you in a desperate situation now? What is happening? What are you doing to emerge from this situation? How is God helping you to emerge?

4. In what ways can you be creative and joyful in your life in the midst of the unsettling times in which we all live?

5. When you read this exercise, what are the things that strike and move you? Stay with one of these and see how that gift opens. Stay with the others, one at a time, and see what emerges when you give yourself time to think about them.

6. After you have reflected and prayed through these questions, how is your relationship to God changed? Deepened? What areas of growth and challenge remain?

7. Are you still willing to walk with God in the midst of your incompleteness and your questions? Why? How?

The Movie
SLUMDOG MILLIONAIRE

Director: Danny Boyle and Loveleen Tandan (2008 – 120 mins.)
Starring: Dev Patel, Freida Pinto, Anil Kapoor, Irfan Kahn

1. Synopsis

All of India has its eyes on Jamal, age eighteen. He has to answer one more question correctly to win the princely sum of 20 million rupees on India's version of *Who Wants to Be a Millionaire*. Then he's arrested for cheating: no poor street kid could know the answers on his own!

To show that he is innocent, Jamal tells the colourful story of his life in the slum where he and his brother grew up alone, of their many adventures, of close calls with local criminals, and of Latika, the girl he loved and then lost to another.

Note: Rated R for some violence, disturbing images, and language.

2. About the Movie

1. "Great movies transport the audience, and this one left me floating on air after two viewings. I can't wait to see it again – and share it with others. It's actually one of those movies that are best approached with as little advance knowledge as possible." (Lou Lumenick, *The New York Post*, November 12, 2008)

   This film cost $8 million to make, took in over $360 million at the box office and won many awards (including 8 Oscars – Best Picture and Best Director among them). There have been grumblings that the film's just too pretty, and that a movie about India directed by an Englishman can't be taken seriously. How did you react after you had seen it? Is it possible that all the advance buzz spoiled the film for audiences who went in expecting something that wasn't there?

2. "It doesn't happen often, but when it does, look out: a movie that rocks and rolls, that transports, startles, delights, shocks, seduces. A movie that is, quite simply, great. *Slumdog Millionaire*, the epic yarn of a Mumbai street urchin who grows up and goes on the Indian version of *Who Wants to Be a Millionaire* – and then keeps getting the answers right, one stunner after another – is that movie. It's exhilarating. It's life-affirming. (Am I gushing enough?) It's about true love and destiny, about raging poverty and vast wealth, about the global powerhouse that is India in the 21st century. And it's about a scrappy hero – a guttersnipe with resiliency and smarts – who would do Charles Dickens proud." (Stephen Rea, *The Philadelphia Inquirer*, November 21, 2008)

   Is Rea indeed "gushing? Which of the many themes he mentions do you think best fits this film? Why? What is another theme that he might have missed?

3. "You've never heard of the actors. A third of the film is in Hindi. Much of it takes place in the most fetid, poverty-ridden corners of the Indian subcontinent, and most of it isn't nice. Yet this sprawling, madly romantic fairy-tale epic is the kind of deep-dish audience-rouser we've long given up hoping for from Hollywood. *Slumdog* is a soaring return to form for director Danny Boyle (*Trainspotting*), but mostly it's just a miracle of mainstream pop moviemaking – the sort of thing modern filmmakers aren't supposed to make anymore. Except they just did." (Ty Burr, *The Boston Globe*, November 12, 2008)

Why do you think that Hollywood stopped making such films? After this film, how many similar films can you name that came out of Hollywood?

4. "Running is a constant motif in *Slumdog Millionaire* – and the element most reminiscent of Boyle's breakthrough film, *Trainspotting*. The most exciting scenes in *Slumdog Millionaire* are a series of high-adrenalin chases through the swarming slums of Mumbai. From the opening chase (accompanied by the Sri Lankan-English pop artist M.I.A.) through the pervasive Indian soundtrack by A.R. Rahman, the music has a fierce momentum, and the camera work from Anthony Dod Mantle – in slow-motion, step-motion and wild camera angles – is completely immersive." (Liam Lacey, *The Globe and Mail*, November 12, 2008)

In an interview, Director Boyle said: "In this case, the style is that there is very little control that you can have in Mumbai. There is no precision.

You cannot specify or control a bit of life, and then repeat it for the camera. It's there for you to capture if you can do it. But it won't repeat itself; there is no such thing as continuity. It is a wave and you have to ride it. If you do, if you trust it in the right way, the film will come back to you. It can be quite alarming sometimes, but the city will give it back to you. For me it was like the city was alive." (Andrew O'Hehir, *Salon*, November 12, 2008)

How do you think that the "life" of Mumbai made Mumbai itself a major character in the film? How is some of this reflected in all the running scenes Lacey refers to in the quote above?

5. "*Slumdog Millionaire* does the neat trick of making us both ignore and subliminally enjoy the melodramatic manipulation, distracting us with its multistrand plot and caffeinated editing, before resolving on a predictable but satisfying conclusion. Less obviously, the film also has an ace up its sleeve in the performance of Patel, the sad-eyed, gentle British-born actor who plays Jamal. In the spotlight of the TV cameras, the police interrogation or slipping into the world of the wealthy as a subaltern, he has a quiet observant presence. The story may stretch credibility until it's ready to pop its seams, but Patel conveys the simple confidence of a prodigy who has learned everything important in life, except how to lie." (Liam Lacey, *The Globe and Mail*, November 12, 2008)

This may be a melodrama or a romance or an action film or a modern version of *Oliver Twist* but it is always held together by an intriguing social conscience. What is that social conscience all about? How might Jamal's inability to lie be at the centre of it?

6. "As I said to (director Danny) Boyle, it's a cliché for critics to call a social-realist drama with a large cast of characters that depicts class conflict Dickensian, but in this case the shoe fits pretty well. 'It's because of the extremes,' he said. 'There are such extremes in Mumbai. Dickens' source material was really Victorian London, wasn't it? You think of a burgeoning city that is creating massive wealth on a base of incredible poverty and endurance, stocking this great machine. Mumbai is like that now. But they have this extra thing, I think, in that they don't separate their extremes. Everything and everyone is involved and included. That is why it is such an exciting place to go as a storyteller. You can push the extremes to both ends, yet you still stay involved in the society.'" (Andrew O'Hehir, *Salon*, November 12, 2008)

Critic after critic refers to this film as Dickensian. What elements of this film remind you of Dickens' novels? Consider the Dickens-like contrasts between rich and poor, good and evil; the Dickensian attention to details and the extremes of poverty and wealth within a culture; the way the story unfolds with the scope and brisk energy of a Dickens novel; what Boyle himself says in the interview with O'Hehir.

7. "After the dust has settled, the Bollywood dance scene that explodes under the closing credits feels both incongruous and earned: Young India kicking up its heels. You may even feel like dancing in the aisles yourself. Sure, the real world doesn't always work this way. Have you forgotten that this is one of the reasons why we go to movies in the first place?" (Ty Burr, *The Boston Globe*, November 12, 2008)

Why do you go to the movies? Is forgetting the real world one reason? And what do you think the critic means by saying the Bollywood dance sequence is both "incongruous and earned"?

3. The Relationship of the Movie to the Theme of the Exercise

1 Jamal tries so hard to be self-reliant in each situation but he knows he is not. In situations of vulnerability, he tries to become his own person. What happens to him because of this? Is there any awareness of God's presence in the things that happen? Indeed, is God even mentioned in the movie? Or is God implicitly present? How?

2. Almost all of the main characters in the film are confronted with love in one form or another. How does each of them react when the opportunity for love is offered them?

4. The Relationship of the Movie to One's Self in the Exercise

1. Does Jamal ever "sink" like Peter does? Do you? What is it that causes you to turn in on yourself and to break the relationship with the one who calls you?

2. Jamal must learn, as the Exercise urges us, to distinguish between illusions that look like God and the real God. What illusions have appeared in your life that you have thought were God — with the easy answers? How did you distinguish between what is real and what is illusion?

186

16th Exercise

Jesus in the Temple

(John 2:13-22)

This people honours me with their lips, but their heart is far from me; in vain do they worship me, teaching as doctrines the precepts of men. (Matthew 15:8-9)

Consider how [the enemy of our human nature] summons innumerable demons, and scatters them, some to one city and some to another, throughout the whole world, so that no province, no place, no state of life, no individual is overlooked. (Sp. Ex. #141)

This is to ask for what I desire. Here it will be to ask for an intimate knowledge of our Lord, who has become man for me, that I may love Him more and follow Him more closely. (Sp. Ex. #104)

Facing Hypocrisy

There is something dreadful happening when elements in religious organizations preach fear, control access to God through exclusivity, and set themselves up as the sole purveyors of salvation. It is even sadder when those same forces distort and restrict the message of God's compassionate mercy into systems of law, ethics, and theology. But saddest of all is the lack of the spirit of love, and the self-imposed blindness to that lack, when such figures present themselves to the world as authoritative voices for religious belief.

Then we have death masquerading as life. The same is true of social and political organizations that claim to maintain justice but create and uphold laws that favour the powerful, or that claim to search for and speak the truth but manipulate image and word for expedient ends. Jesus is fearless in the face of this hypocrisy. He condemns it.

And what about us, who see these things so clearly and are disgusted by them? What do we do? What do we do with ourselves when we find that we are no better than the institutions and structures we condemn?

This is a subtle and pervasive temptation in our time. Seduced by moral disgust, we either despair and do nothing, or react in a violent and destructive manner. If the previous exercise shows us how fear stops us from being intimate with Christ, this exercise shows us how both clarity and power are enemies of a full relationship with the One who invites us to share his life. With clarity we can see things as they are, but we react in a worldly way to what we see so clearly. With power we become presumptuous, and act out our desire to change in a worldly manner what we perceive to be wrong. Our journey now invites us not only to walk with the Christ, but to live and act as he does.

Creating a Sacred Space

In this contemplation, Jesus cleanses the temple by driving out those who corrupted that sacred space where people meet God. How are we supposed to act when we discover our sacred spaces are despoiled?

We do not slavishly imitate Jesus' actions in his time, but put on the mind and heart of Jesus. This crucial distinction points to the importance of a deep and lived personal intimacy with Christ. In that intimacy he reveals to us and shares with us his relationship with the Father, and invites us to be like him in living out of that relationship. So we act not out of our own perceptions and insights and inclinations, even though these may be valid, but rather out of the stance of being one with the source of all creation and creativity. This becomes our principle for discernment and action. Our role in the world when we act out of this stance is to maintain right relationships between everything and God. What Jesus did in the temple was to display the energy of righteousness against those who had made religion a business transaction rather than the expression of mercy.

In fact, all of Jesus' actions in the Temple – from his being found there by Mary and Joseph as a child, to his preaching there, to this final act – are manifestations of being about his Father's business. That business is love – not a sentimental or pious love, not an escapist or exclusive love, not a passive or self-indulgent love, but a love that enters the world to bring everything and everyone into loving relationships with each other. This love has a reverence for life; it practises generosity by sharing time, energy, gifts, and resources; it sees itself as responsible for all of creation, human and otherwise; and it is full of care in the way it relates to others. In so doing, it acts as the Father acts towards creation. God has lovingly brought this creation into being; he maintains it and desires to transform it into a habitat where the destructive effects of sin are transformed into creativity and life.

Jesus turns his attention to the temple, because, for him, the temple is the meeting place between God and humanity. That meeting place had been turned from a spiritual, open space where the sufferings of humanity met the compassion of God into a place where transactions were commercial, political, and worldly rather than.

Because the mercy of God refuses to be constrained by disorder, the Father creates a new temple to embody that compassionate love. Christ is that temple, and he calls each of us to become that sacred place where the world's pain and brokenness can, in humility, be met by compassionate mercy and held up to healing: to liberate the oppressed and to celebrate community.

The Holiness of Everything

In his life, Christ restores sacredness to the desecrated. Our intimacy with Christ carries us along that same path. When we walk that path, we discover that everything that exists is open to the holy, and that everything we meet can invite us to encounter God in a deeper way. Evil, no matter how it is disguised as good, even as religious good, effectively tries to stop us encountering God. But when we have travelled a while with the Christ, as we have done in praying though these Exercises, we see through the illusions that pretend to be holiness. In relating to them for what they truly are, we take away their power over us and over those we care for and whom we are now committed to cherish into the fullness of life. Like Christ, we are invited in love to restore a right order to creation.

When Christ cleanses the temple, he acts as a peacemaker. What is the difference between a peacekeeper, a peace-lover, and a peacemaker? A peacekeeper sacrifices everything to make sure that there is no disturbance in what is accepted as habitual. Fear and co-dependency underlie that position. A peace

188

lover wants peace, but is not willing to commit to any actions that would remove or transform the forces that block right relations between different aspects of creation – people, classes, cultures, and nations. A peacemaker commits to establishing those right relations, which are found only when we take on the perspective and the work of the Creator. In cleansing the temple, Christ acts as a peacemaker, because his deepest desire is to do the will of his Father, and the deepest desire of the Father is that everything be seen as it is: holy. We are holy, our deepest identity is to live that holiness, and our mission in this world, no matter what we do, is to allow the holiness of everything to manifest itself in celebrating life.

Questions for Prayer and Reflection

1. How do you confuse religion with holiness? How does that restrict your deepest desires? How does it stop you from encountering God?

2. Pray through those manifestations of religion in your life that create a false image of God, yourself, and others by offering them up to the transforming spirit of the Father. What happens when you do this? How are you liberated?

3. How can you distinguish between your anger and God's transforming energy in the face of the world's oppressive forces?

4. How do you distinguish between self-indulgence and freedom in your life and in the world?

5. How do you feel when you discover that your growing intimacy with Christ asks you to take a stance in the world? In practical terms, what does that stance look like? (Remember that we are not asked to be seduced by our idealisms, our fears. We are simply asked to be where Jesus is.) When you ask the Christ in prayer where you are to be with him, what answers do you receive?

The Movie

THE GIRL WITH THE DRAGON TATTOO

Director: Niels Arden Oplev (2009 – 150 mins.)
Starring: Michael Nyqvist, Noomi Rapace, Peter Haber, Lena Andre

1. Synopsis

Journalist Mikael Blomkvist and computer hacker Lisbeth Salander are on a mission: to investigate the forty-year-old disappearance of Harriet Vanger. Her body was never found. Harriet's uncle suspects that a member of his own dysfunctional family is responsible. As the investigation proceeds, Mikael and Lisbeth uncover a terrible family secret and test their own limits to survive.

Note: Rated R for disturbing violent content including rape, grisly images, sexual material, nudity, and language.

Note: If at all possible, watch the subtitled version. Much of an actor's art lies in the use of voice to express emotion, mood, and character. Dubbed movies can never have the full impact of the original.

2. About the Movie

1. Lisbeth Salander "has her own problems, too, most notably a new court-appointed guardian who is a sexual deviant, a brutal and imperious creep. The rape and torture scenes, a vivid (and necessary) component of Larsson's book, are rendered with fearless detail in the film. They are neither exploitative nor gratuitous, but they are certainly not easy to watch …. There's a gloomy Scandinavian current running beneath the surface of the mystery here: disturbing stuff about abuse and misogyny, Nazis and anti-Semitism, the rot at the heart of the civilized, socialist state. Like Thomas Harris' novels (and subsequent screen adaptations) *Red Dragon* and *The Silence of the Lambs*, *The Girl with the Dragon Tattoo* is rife with nightmarishly violent and horrific behavior. It's intense, graphic, frightening. And, yes, exhilarating." (Steven Rea, *The Philadelphia Inquirer*, March 19, 2010)

The rape and torture scenes are indeed graphic and terrible to watch. Rea speaks of them as a "necessary" component of the book. Reading such scenes is quite different from watching them on the screen. Do you see them as necessary to the film? Did they have to be presented "with fearless detail"? If you were the director would you have handled the scenes differently? Could you have left them out completely? Why? Why not?

2. "*The Girl with the Dragon Tattoo* balances character development with plot, and that's crucial to its

success. The average thriller is interested in advancing the narrative with little concern for whether the protagonists become cardboard cut-outs. Here, Mikael and especially Lisbeth are as intriguing – if not more so – than the mystery they are investigating. Viewers don't mind when director Niels Arden Oplev takes a break from the main story for a tangent. Lisbeth's interaction with her parole officer could be excised from the movie without damaging the investigation, but its value comes in what it reveals about her. Will the Hollywood remake (which is in the works) contain it? If not, we will lose a critical component of understanding this character." (James Berardinelli, *Reelviews*, March 19, 2010)

Given that the film is adapted from Stieg Larsson's 2005 bestseller, it ought not to be a surprise that it unfolds not with the breakneck velocity of a typical film of this sort, but with the gradual, unforced, character-based focus of a novel. How are the characters – especially Mikael and Lisbeth – developed in this film? What is shown that allows us to see them as real three-dimensional people and not cardboard cut-outs? And what are the main characteristics of Mikael and Lisbeth? How well do the actors portraying them help us to understand the characters?

3. "The film makes excellent use of the cold Scandinavian landscape to emphasize the story's gloomy loneliness. And Rapace and Nyqvist have compelling chemistry. The two stars have shot the next two movies in Larsson's trilogy – and I look forward to them with a combination of squeamish fear of what tortures I'll see and queasy excitement about how Lisbeth Salander will handle the next skeevy guy." (Lisa Schwarzbaum, *Entertainment Weekly*, March 19, 2010)

How does the Swedish landscape help bring out the theme of loneliness? Do Mikael and Lisbeth come together only in an attempt to overcome the loneliness in both their lives? Why would – or would not – you look forward to the next two movies in this three-part series?

4. "However you respond to it, the fraught sexual and investigative chemistry between Mikael and Lisbeth is the most powerful ingredient of *Girl with the Dragon Tattoo*. The movie's second half is a capably executed but mostly by-the-numbers procedural." (Andrew O'Hehir, Salon.com, March 18, 2010)

How did you respond to the chemistry between Mikael and Lisbeth? Do you agree with O'Hehir that this chemistry is the most "powerful ingredient" of this film? Why? Why not?

3. The Relationship of the Movie to the Theme of the Exercise

1. "Beneath the sadistic surface, there is a strange cultural masochism in (Steig) Larsson ... It is as though (he wants) not merely to disassemble the reputation of their homeland as a model – the model – of benign social democracy but to dig backward in a bid to prove that the past, too, was not one of liberal health and justice but a sump of buried transgressions and moral disease .... In a rare reflective interlude, Lisbeth says, 'You choose who you want to be,' but the rest of the film belies that view, seeing most people, Lisbeth included, as prisoners sealed in their past. It's a true conundrum, for those who devise mysteries:

if the sins of the fathers, or the crimes of the motherland, are always to blame, what happens to pure evil? It could be out of a job." (Anthony Lane, *The New Yorker*, March 29, 2010)

What does happen to "pure evil" in this film? Is it possible for any of the characters to choose who they want to be? Do you think that Lisbeth chose what she became? Why? Why not?

2. "But even the ending is peripheral to the Point: where and how is it possible to find both Truth and Love in the urban squalor of a commodified world, in which everything has a price and nothing has value independent of the krona? It is a point that John the Evangelist would have recognized: does the ultimate Goodness come from above or from within – or maybe a bit of both? … Not since *Schindler's List* have I left a film so much in need of a long walk; and not since *Shawshank* have I felt so redeemed." (Paul O'Reilley, SJ, Thinking Faith.org, March 26, 2010)

Why would one feel the need for a long walk after seeing this film? And what is it about the film that would make one feel redeemed?

3. The Exercise speaks of groups who claim to maintain justice, who claim to search for and speak the truth but who manipulate image and word for their own ends. How is this evident in this film? Though set in Sweden, how possible is it to draw an analogy to the current situation in our own country?

4. Relationship of the Movie to One's Self in the Exercise

1. There is – we learn in this Exercise – a subtle and pervasive temptation in our time. Seduced by moral disgust, we either despair and do nothing or react in a violent and destructive manner. Why do you think that Lisbeth reacts as she does in response to her situation?

2. It can be argued that Lisbeth strives to do as the Exercise says – to act out of the stance of being one with the source of all creation and creativity. While she may have no knowledge that this is what she is doing, she has been influenced by Mikael. What has been the strong influence in your life that leads you towards the love that is God in all that you do and say? What stops you from following that influence completely?

3. The way that the politicians and the police act in the film is a good example of how power makes us presumptious and makes us want to change in a worldly fashion what we perceive to be wrong. How is this a danger in your own life? How is this a danger when you come to discern how you ought to act?

17th Exercise
The Raising of Lazarus
(John 11:1-45)

God shows his love for us in that while we were yet sinners Christ died for us. (Romans 5:8)

Reflect how God dwells in creatures: in the elements giving them existence, in the plants giving them life, in the animals conferring upon them sensation, in humans bestowing understanding. So He dwells in me and gives me being, life, sensation, intelligence; and makes a temple of me, since I am created in the likeness and image of the Divine Majesty. (Sp. Ex. #235)

This is to ask for what I desire. Here it will be to ask for an intimate knowledge of our Lord, who has become man for me, that I may love Him more and follow Him more closely. (Sp. Ex. #104)

Waiting on the Father

The scriptures tell us that Jesus raised the son of the widow of Naim and Jairus's daughter from the dead. Jesus did not know either of these two people or their families. He simply acts out of compassion. Jesus also raised Lazarus. Lazarus was his friend, and Jesus knew the family very well. The odd thing about the raising of Lazarus is that Jesus knew that Lazarus was sick, and although he was not far away, he did not go and heal him. After Lazarus died, Jesus waited several days before even going to comfort the family, which seems unusual for someone who embodies the compassion of God. Jesus knew that the religious authorities were trying to kill him; was he afraid for his life? His previous actions indicate that he was not afraid of those authorities and often challenged them to their faces. We also know that his mission was to be compassionate even in the face of bodily destruction. So why did he delay going to Lazarus until it was too late?

In our own lives we experience instances of need. Even though we know that God is fully aware of our needs, nothing seems to be done. Others experience this as well. This is the reason many people do not believe in God. So at this stage of our spiritual journey through the Exercises, we raise this question: If this is the way you treat the person whom you say you love and whose life you share, how will you treat us, whom you say you love and ask to journey with you?

The answer lies in Jesus' relationship with the Father. Jesus does nothing apart from the Father's will, and his whole life is a manifestation of that will. He waited to be called at his baptism. He waits now until the Father tells him to go to Lazarus's tomb. He will wait for the Father to raise him from the dead. It grieves him to wait to rescue his friend and to comfort the family. In his waiting, he manifests that first commandment to "Love the Lord your God with all your heart and with all your soul and with all your mind, and with all your strength" (Mark 12:30).

In our deepening intimacy with the Christ, we, too, are asked to wait on the Father's will. It may grieve us to do that, for there are things we know we can do, and things we know need to be done. To seem to be doing nothing while others suffer and die, and to claim at the same time to love them, cause the Christ's followers to be deemed irrelevant, mindless, passive, or alienated from reality.

But Christianity is more than a program of social action. Waiting on the Father is not equivalent to inactivity. It is first and foremost a profound witness of our creaturehood. It is also a profound act of faith, hope, and love to wait in that relationship, knowing that something will be done, that it will be the right thing, and that what will be done and how it will be done will more deeply reveal God's selfless, constant, caring compassion. To wait like this in love is not apathy. It is leaning passionately into a relationship committed to making us fulfilled, comforted, and cared for. We expect it. We live out of it. And it comes.

The Greatest Gift

When Jesus goes to Bethany to Lazarus's home, Martha and then Mary meet him. Both upbraid him for not using his powers to save their brother from death. Yet Jesus' call is not to manifest his powers, but to live out his relationship with his Father. Jesus can raise Lazarus from the dead, as he raised two others. Like those two others, Lazarus will eventually die again. Jesus' own relationship with the Father allows for his resurrection, not resuscitation. That relationship manifests a love so strong that death cannot overcome it. Jesus enters into death, journeying towards a love beyond name and imagining, and that love enters into death to bring the beloved into that new creation called resurrection. That new creation is not the cyclical return of natural rhythms, nor is it the miraculous raising up of the dead back into earthly life. It is something new, and it attests to the transforming creativity of the Father. In the Lazarus story, Jesus gives some indication of that greater gift the Father has for us. This is not the gift of a life repeated. It is the gift of such intimacy that we will be like the Christ – not that we will bring the dead back to life, but that we will be resurrected. The gift does not ignore the wretchedness of a disordered world or the ravages of sin and death and their effects on all of us. Instead, it enters into those places of crisis and takes away their power, making them doorways – however painful and powerful – into new life. This greater gift empowers us to be in the disordered places of our world as a transforming presence.

The risk the Father takes with Mary and Martha in denying them immediate access to Jesus' power is the risk the Father takes with each of us. If we are indulged with instant gratification because we know God loves us, and we love God, we reduce God to being a magician and ourselves to a narcissism that ignores the world's suffering. This approach overlooks God's mysterious will to enter into that suffering as a human being, and to endure it even to a humiliating and painful death on a cross. Reducing God to a magician does not admit that we are invited to follow Christ in living out his passion for the Father. Neither does it admit that our intimacy with Christ makes us *more* human, not less. So we are more aware of the destructiveness of evil, but also more aware of the depths of God's love.

When Jesus raises Lazarus from the dead, he does it not to manifest his power, but to show the dimensions of his relationship with the Father. He says, "Father, I thank you because you have heard me. I know that you hear me always but I have said this on account of the people standing by that they may believe you sent me" (John 11:41). He calls on the Father and the Father answers. Now he can act. In front of that tomb that holds a man four days dead, he cries out in a loud voice, "Lazarus! Come out!" The gospel tells us what happens next. "The dead man came out, his hands and feet bound in bandages, and his face wrapped with a cloth." Jesus said to those around him, 'Unbind him, and let him go.'"

Setting the Captured Free

Now we can see our task. It is God who raises up the dead. Our work is the unbinding and the letting go. If we let God be God, we find ourselves co-operating with him. We cannot overcome sin, or its first fruits: death. Only God can do that. But we can do our part of the relationship and allow those who have been set free to live freely. Too often we are unwilling to unbind and set free, because we cannot believe that new life is given to a situation or to people. Our lack of faith in the power of God's love stops us from seeing what is right in front of us. But if we accept the power of the relationship that Christ has with the Father, a relationship he offers to each of us, we can see as he sees, and then do our part. As Jesus says elsewhere in John's gospel, "Receive the Holy Spirit. If you forgive the sins of any, they are forgiven. If you retain the sins of any, they are retained" (John 20:23). It is only when we share in the relationship that Jesus has with the Father – that is, share their Holy Spirit – that we can unbind and forgive. That is liberation and life.

Questions for Prayer and Reflection

1. When you entered this contemplation, what happened to you? Where did you find yourself? What was your relationship to Jesus? to Mary and Martha? How did you deal with Lazarus?

2. When have you been in a dire situation beyond your control and had to wait for God to act? How did you wait? How did you relate to God at that time? What happened?

3. Are you in such a situation now? How are you relating to God?

4. When you look at your culture and the world, your family, your partner, your relationships, and yourself, where do you find God bringing the dead to life? How do you co-operate with that?

5. Do you ever, like Jesus did, wait on the Father's moment to act, even though you could do something about a situation that needs remedying? How did you discern what to do and when, or not do it? What was your prayer then?

6. When have you been liberated from a situation you considered hopeless?

7. When have you liberated others from situations they found hopeless?

8. When have you experienced your sins being forgiven so that you felt like a new person?

9. When have you forgiven someone in such a way that that person came "alive" again?

The Movie

AMERICAN BEAUTY

Director: Sam Mendes, 1999, 121 mins.
Starring: Kevin Spacey, Annette Bening, Thora Birch, Wes Bentley

1. Synopsis

Take an apparently perfect marriage, an apparently perfect family, in an apparently perfect neighbourhood. Then add the fact that the father, Lester Burnham, is in the midst of a mid-life crisis that deepens as he realizes that he is infatuated with one of his daughter's friends. His daughter Jane is in love with the shy boy next door whose father is a homophobic ex-marine, and Lester's wife is slowly becoming aware that she no longer has any control over the family. Each of these people is in search of that elusive thing known as American beauty in a variety of forms.

2. About the Movie

1. "*American Beauty* is a film that shows the hunger for God in our modern Western cities is by no means dead. It proclaims that God can be found in our post-modern secular lives. It argues that ordinariness by no means signifies the absence of the divine. It challenges us to open our eyes and look for the God who is present to us in spite of and even in the midst of our messiness." (John O'Donnell, SJ, *National Jesuit News*, February/March 2000) What are specific examples from the movie which would prove – or disprove – this critic's thesis about the movie?

2. "As these characters struggle viciously – and hilariously – to escape the middle-class doldrums, the film also evinces a real and ever more stirring compassion. As it detects increasingly vital signs of life behind the absurd surfaces that Mendes presents so beautifully, the film takes on a gravity to match its evil zest." (Janet Maslin, *The New York Times*, September 15, 1999)

Would you classify this movie as a comedy or a drama? Or can there be both elements in a movie? If both are present here, how does that affect the impact of the movie on the viewer?

3. "The real targets here are a shopworn pair of twin heroes – the American Dream and the American Family, that once-dynamic duo whose health has waxed and waned over the past century." (Rick Groen, *The Globe and Mail*, September 17, 1999)

How are these two groups targeted in the movie? How does the director make these two groups – partly seen in the character of Lester – so pathetically comic and yet so profoundly tragic?

4. "It's also essentially two films in one, analyzing the angst of both middle age and teenage and comparing the dashed hopes of both." (Peter Howell, *The Toronto Star*, September 17, 1999)

What is the "angst" we see in Lester and Carolyn, and in Jane and Ricky?

5. A major component of any movie is the music. In *American Beauty*, music plays an important role. Not only the theme music, written by Thomas Newman (you may recognize it from the TV series *Six Feet Under*, which he also wrote, along with the music for many great movies, including *Finding Nemo*, *White Oleander*, *Erin Brockovich*, *The Green Mile*, *The Three Kings*, and *The Player*) but also the songs chosen for various scenes – from "Because" (by the Beatles) to "American Woman" to "Don't Rain on My Parade." How does the director use this music? To create mood? To advance the plot? To underline the theme of a scene? Choose two examples of the music to talk about.

3. The Relationship of the Movie to the Theme of the Exercise

1. In his first words of narration, Lester introduces himself and tells us that in less than a year he will be dead. And then he says, "Of course I don't know that yet, and in a way I am dead already." Lester's year to come is a resurrection – he sets himself free and lives freely. What scenes show us how Lester has been set free?

2. As the Exercise tells us, God's gift does not ignore the wretchedness of a disordered world or the ravages of sin and death. It enters into those places and makes them doors – painful ones – into new life. How does this apply to Lester? To Carolyn? To Ricky? To Jane?

3. All of the characters in the movie are waiting for something to happen – for something that will give them new life. But they are looking in the wrong place – they are looking in the world. How do you think that their awareness of the presence and love of God in their lives would make a difference to what each of them do at the end of the movie?

4. The Relationship of the Movie to One's Self in the Exercise

1. Consider Lester's last narrative note to the viewer: that if you don't share the film's piercing vision of what really matters, someday you will. It took death for Lester to realize this. Do we – do you – have to face death before we realize that we "feel gratitude for every single moment of my stupid little life", and that "it's hard to stay mad when there's so much beauty in the world"? What does opening yourself to God's love do to bring forward the understanding of what Lester is saying? What will cause your own resurrection in life?

2. It is often in the very ordinary that we find God – that we see the joys of a new life that God gives people. For Ricky this occurred in two places: his film of a floating plastic bag, and the look in the eyes of a dead homeless woman in which he saw God. Where do you find God in the ordinary parts of your life?

3. Our lack of faith in the power of God's love makes us unable to see what is in front of our eyes. Lester may be the only one who has any inkling of what more is out there, but even he sees only through a glass darkly. And try as he might, Ricky does not appear to see an image of God reflected in Lester's eyes at the end of the movie. What is lacking in your faith that stops you from seeing God's love in your life?

197

18th Exercise
Palm Sunday
(Matthew 21:1-17)

The true light that enlightens everyone was coming into the world; he was in the world, and the world was made through him, yet the world knew him not. He came to his own home and his own people received him not.

(John 1:9-11)

We must carefully observe the whole course of our thoughts. If the beginning and middle and end of the course of thoughts are wholly good and directed to what is entirely right, it is a sign that they are from the good spirit. But the course of thoughts suggested to us may terminate in something evil, or distracting, or less good than the soul had formerly proposed to do. Again it may end in what weakens the soul, or disquiets it; or by destroying the peace, tranquillity, and quiet which it had before, it may cause disturbance to the soul. These things are a clear sign that the thoughts are proceeding from the evil spirit, the enemy of our progress and eternal salvation.

(Sp. Ex. #333)

This is to ask for what I desire. Here it will be to ask for an intimate knowledge of our Lord, who has become man for me, that I may love Him more and follow Him more closely.

(Sp. Ex. #104)

A Servant King

Whom do you look for when you look for God? What do you see when you look at death? This final exercise of the Second Week asks both of these questions. Underlying the contemplation of Christ entering Jerusalem and being treated as a king and a secular saviour is the difference between what the world calls redemption and what God offers. The Second Week of the Exercises begins with a meditation on "The Kingdom." There we are asked to reflect on a king, chosen by God, who invites us to live under his standard. By the time we have journeyed through this Second Week, we discover what that means for us: to be poor with Christ in his poverty, humble with Christ in his total dependence on the Father, to labour with Christ as he labours to build a community of life and love.

But what the crowd wants when it gathers palms and celebrates Christ's entry into Jerusalem is a hero who will right their every wrong, a liberator who will overthrow the tyranny of the Roman imperial power and its brutalities, a magician who will cure their every ill, a religious preacher who will offer a way of life free of stultifying legalism and hypocrisy. When, in their dreadful need, they see Jesus – who raised the dead; cured the sick; challenged the religious leaders; consorted with the poor, the dispossessed and the outcast; fed a multitude from the little they could offer – and when they hear his preaching and his claims to be the chosen one of God, they see this son of Mary as the answer to their dream of a messiah. A new, just world order, so long promised by prophets and so long the passionate and desperate dream of humankind, was to be fulfilled in their time and in their world.

They take off their cloaks, strip the palm trees of their leaves and celebrate the entrance of Christ into Jerusalem, the holy city, so long despoiled by corruption at every level. Now is the time of transformation. And it does become a time of transformation. The Christ is the Messiah, the warrior saviour of God – but as God sees and enacts this, not as the crowd desires it.

Even here, even now, we need constantly to ask ourselves: Who is God for me? How does God act in our world? Is that God the one we want? Is the God of our needs the same as the God who reveals himself in our prayer and in our lives? Which God do we commit ourselves to follow and to be intimate with?

A New Human

When we look at the scriptures, we see an interesting development in the way Christ presents himself. In the beginning, he heals the sick, cures ills, raises the dead, transforms water into wine, feeds the multitudes with almost no food, performs miracles, preaches with power. But when Peter acknowledges him to be more than a miracle worker and more than one of the earlier prophets come back from the dead – when Peter declares him to be the Messiah, the Special One of God – Jesus begins to present himself differently and to talk about his suffering and death.

Peter tells him that this is not how a god behaves. Christ rebukes Peter, saying he speaks as a human who knows nothing of how the true God acts. But after Peter's declaration, Jesus performs fewer miracles, and when he raises Lazarus, he does so in a way that informs the witness that the significant point of his ministry is to reveal who the Father is and how the Father operates. His kingship, though it is *in* this world, and is firmly concerned with the way the world operates, is not *of* this world. Christ does not act as the world wants him to act. His behaviour always manifests his relationship with the Father. So, even though he enters Jerusalem with all the ritual allusions of a worldly liberator, he understands those signs differently. He is entering the contest where the powers of the world are overthrown: he becomes the prototype for the new human who can be so intimate with God, and who can allow God to be so intimate with us, that the values of this world are no longer the most important.

Facing Death

The world's values revolve around coping with death. Death ultimately devalues the world. On the one hand, people flee from death by maintaining the ego and subscribing to forms of ambition. Such people give the world an importance it cannot maintain. They become overinvolved in this world and overcommitted to the values it manifests. On the other hand, there are people who, confronted with death's reality, despair about the world, which radically limits their scope in the world. They refuse to become involved.

Even if we accept the reality of death and the absurdity it casts on the human project from a purely natural perspective, we are left with a hollow stoicism or the angst of existential absurdity. The nonspiritual death provides the outer limit of the human condition.

Jesus entering Jerusalem faces his death. He realizes that it will be horrible, shameful, and painful, and he wonders if he will break under it. The test for him, as it was in the temptations in the desert, is to see if he will abandon his relationship with the Father and his trust in that relationship. But as he enters

Jerusalem, he sees death as a door through which he must go to meet the Father. For him, death is not an ending – it is a step on the path of his return to the Father. He will enter into death. He will wait for his Father to rescue him in whatever way the Father sees best.

We, too, will die. In fact, each of us is dying at this moment. We can try to avoid thinking about it by hurling ourselves into the world, or we can become so obsessed by it that we are useless in this world. But we have another choice. We can see it as Jesus sees it. We do not know the circumstances of our end, but we know that we can face that end: not as an end in itself, but as a new beginning. How we live shapes how we die, for we die as we live. Like Jesus, we can live in relationship with the Father; like Jesus, we can die maintaining that relationship.

Questions for Prayer and Reflection

1. Out of what self-image do you live? How is this manifest in what you do each day?

2. Do you feel confident enough of your relationship with the Father to trust your life with him? How could this be a foolish question? Why is this not a foolish question?

3. How does the Father trust you? How do you know this? Is this any different from any other relationship of trust you have?

4. What do you need to do to grow in trust?

5. In a conversation with the Father, ask what he needs to grow in trust of you. What does he say?

6. How do you face your death? How does this shape the way you live?

7. How have we dealt with the imminent death of someone close to us?

8. In your prayer, how do you deal with what Christ is doing? Where are you in relation to Christ in this?

The Movie
A SERIOUS MAN

Director: Ethan Coen and Joel Coen (2009 – 96 mins.)
Starring: Michael Stuhlbarg, Richard Kind, Sari Lennick

1. Synopsis

Larry Gopnik is a serious-minded physics lecturer whose life is imploding. His children are using him and his brother Arthur has descended on him. Before they know it, Arthur and Larry have to move to a motel when Larry's wife, Judy, moves her lover, Sy, into the house. Sy ends up dying in a car accident, but Larry and Arthur are still living in the motel.

As the trials and tribulations mount, Larry is tempted to give one of his students an illegal pass mark on an exam in exchange for a bribe. Larry consults rabbis but doesn't find the answers he seeks. Where is God in all this, Larry wonders, when he has tried to be a serious man?

Note: Rated R for language, some sexual content/nudity, and brief violence.

2. About the Movie

1. "For perhaps the first time in a Coen film outside *No Country for Old Men*, we are asked to authentically empathise with a realistic character in a realistic setting, and yet he and the landscape around him suffer the same lampooning slings and sardonic tone as the characters of *Raising Arizona* (1987), *Barton Fink* (1991), *Fargo* (1995) and *O Brother, Where Art Thou?* (2000). *A Serious Man* is a sincerely sympathetic portrait of an American family man in crisis – even as it insults its characters and derides their culture. It's an old complaint about the Coens, that they cruelly observe their hapless characters as they would pratfalling ants in an ant farm." (Michael Atkinson, *Sight and Sound*, December 2009)

How does this film show the Coens' comic spirit, which – for better or worse – has been consistent and sharply observed, by allowing melancholy and sensitivity to sneak in naturally like the back flavours of strong red wine? Argue if you like that this movie's philosophical inquiries are answered by the Coens' ridicule – that life, like the film, is merely a thin joke by a cruel God or gods. What respect could the cosmos have for Larry and his world if the film-makers have little or none?

2. "As his woes increase biblically, Gopnik tries with increasing desperation to find out why this is happening to him. He consults a divorce attorney … three rabbis, and he hears a fantastical story about a Hebrew cry for help engraved on a goy's teeth, only to come to fear that what he guessed all along might be the case: It's not always easy to find out what God is trying to tell us …. On the one hand, *A Serious Man* is rife with specific Jewish references …. Yet it's impossible to watch Larry Gopnik's travails without feeling

that they will speak to everyone who's been battered and blindsided by life's tormenting crises and wonders why …. 'I've tried to be a serious man. I've tried to do right,' Gopnik laments. Haven't we all, this unexpected film, at once comic and haunting, asks. Haven't we all?" (Kenneth Turan, *Los Angeles Times*, October 2, 2009)

What are some of the Jewish references that turn up in the film? How is the paradox – that Larry is Jewish yet also Everyman – resolved? Or is it?

3. "Can art come from jadedness? Will the brothers ever 'mean it'? *A Serious Man* forces the issue in ways that will either floor you or drive you batty. There are Coen movies that are inconsequential goofs, and there are the ones that count. This is one of the ones that count, and it's a work of cruel comic genius, in some ways even crueler than *No Country for Old Men*. Some have already labeled the film despicable. I think it's Jewish Bergman and one of their very best movies – a pitch-black Old Testament farce in which God is either absent, absent-minded, or mad as hell. It's a film to haunt you for a long time to come. … *A Serious Man* has a bigger, even cosmic heft to its rhythms and images, though – a gravity that tends equally toward Kafka and the Bible." (Ty Burr, *The Boston Globe*, October 9, 2009)

Would you label this film "despicable" or see it as a "black Old Testament farce"? Why? Why not? Consider the question that ends the prologue – and then gnaws at us for the rest of the film. Which one of us is possessed? Do we live in an unjust universe or are we fools, unserious men, to think it could ever be otherwise?

4. "Larry … does not exactly fear the divinity whom he, like other devout Jews, calls Hashem ('the name' in Hebrew). It's more that he's puzzled, beleaguered, perplexed. What does God want from us? What should we expect from him? As weird inconveniences spiral into operatic miseries, Larry dutifully searches for clues, answers, signs. He talks to learned rabbis and listens to recordings of famous cantors. What he encounters, apart from haunting music and drab suburban sacred architecture, is silence, nonsense and – from that metaphysical zone beyond the screen, where the rest of us sit and watch – laughter. (A.O. Scott, *The New York Times*, October 2, 2009)

So a question that *A Serious Man* asks you is whether it makes the case for atheism or looks at the world from a divine point of view. Are the Coens mocking God, playing God, or taking his side in a rigged cosmic game? What's the difference?

5. "As Fate keeps stomping (Larry), he embraces Heisenberg's Uncertainty Principle. What he tells his class about the theory – 'Even if you can't figure it out, you're still responsible for it on the midterm' – applies, in spades, to his crumbling life. And yet for most of the movie he hangs in there, behaving honorably, seeking the wisdom of his ancestors, trying to observe the Jewish concept of Hashem. 'Receive with simplicity everything that happens to you,' says Elie Wiesel's Rashi. To absorb God's body blows, this disquieting, haunting movie says, is to be fully alive. To do otherwise could kill you." (Richard Corliss, *Time*, September 12, 2009)

How does Larry react to insults? How does he react when he finds that what he believes to be true is all lies? Why does he just suck it up and take it? Do we really have to just absorb all that life sends us to be truly and fully alive?

3. The Relationship of the Movie to the Theme of the Exercise

1. For the world, as the Exercise says, death leaves either a hollow stoicism or the angst of existential absurdity. At the end of the film, what are the main characters left with in the face of impending death? Consider Larry's urgent summons to see his doctor and the situation with the children at Hebrew school.

2. As the film progresses, so do the misfortunes which befall George. They do so to the point where you see Larry as a modern-day Job, and you wonder just how much more he can take. The life he once had is now dead to him. How does George react to each of the "deaths" in his life?

3. The Exercise also asks what you see when you look for God. Larry's sufferings cause him to look for God, but the two rabbis he consults are either obtuse, oblivious, or obscure. What does George see when he looks for God? How does God respond to George's plea for help?

4. The Relationship of the Movie to One's Self in the Exercise

1. Death always affects us. This film is not about the death of some thousands of people on the terrible scale of 9/11. It is about the death of one man and the probable death of a man we have come to admire. As the preface for the dead reminds us – life is changed not ended – and so death is a new beginning. This is easy to say. How easy do you find it to believe when you experience the death of a loved one? Why? Why not?

2. Watching the children of the victims of 9/11 gather on each anniversary to read out the names of the dead can be a very emotional experience. This reading of names is one way the USA – as a nation – has coped with these deaths. It has more impact than any homily or speech or poem. Yet there is a finality to this – as there is in the film – that seems without hope. What gives you hope about those whom you know who have died? What gives you hope when you consider your own death?

3. We know what Larry saw when he set out to look for God. What happens to you when you set out to look for God? Who helps you with this search? What is the most difficult part of this search for you?

19th Exercise
Overview of the Second Week

Set me as a seal on your heart,
As a seal on your arm;
For stern as death is love,
Relentless as the nether world is devotion;
Its flames are a blazing fire.
Deep waters cannot quench love,
Nor floods sweep it away.
Were one to offer all one owns to purchase love,
Such a person would be roundly mocked.

(Song of Songs 8:6-7)

Let him desire and seek nothing except the greater praise and glory of God our Lord as the aim of all he does. For everyone must keep in mind that in all that concerns the spiritual life his progress will be in proportion to his surrender of his self-love and of his own will and interests.

(Sp. Ex. #189)

This is to ask for what I desire. Here it will be to ask for an intimate knowledge of our Lord, who has become man for me, that I may love Him more and follow Him more closely.

(Sp. Ex. #104)

The Journey So Far

If the First Week of the Exercises is falling in love, the Second Week is the engagement period. What distinguishes this Week is the growing intimacy between God and ourselves as lovers. The grace we ask for is "an intimate knowledge of our Lord who has become human for me, that I may love Him more and follow Him more closely." In this intimacy, God reveals himself through the Christ, and the Christ reveals his secret self, his relationship with the Father. He invites us to share that relationship; through that union we discover what it means to love him and to follow him out of love for him.

The First Week of the Exercises begins within a fallen creation ruined by the malice of evil, but as we journey through it, we discover a path to love that allows us to live in this world in a liberated way. The Second Week invites us deeper into that love, to put on the perspective of God and to see the world as capable of redemption. It further invites us to unite ourselves with God in working for that redemption. In this we not only enter God's world, but we allow God to enter into our world, for it is in our world that this redemption takes place.

To work concretely towards that redemption we need to know ourselves, as well as Jesus; we need to know how Jesus comes to us as well as how the enemies of our human nature lure us away. The easiest way of reflecting on this is to see how we react when we are vulnerable.

With Christ we can accept our vulnerability and the social shame that comes along with living in such an exposed way. This leads to the humility we identify with in Christ. Living from this stance creates community. Or we can flee from our vulnerability into forms of social approval that reinforce the walls around our ego. Then we remained trapped in narcissism. To live freely in our vulnerability, we need the humility to ask God not only for help to recognize the pattern of our disorders and to resist them, but also for the grace to love and follow Jesus intimately in our daily life.

To do this we contemplate the life of Christ and the way that Christ's life operates in the world. We see what it is to have love enter our world in a vulnerable way and watch it grow to be mature and responsible. We see that this life operates not out of self-interest but out of an authenticity that constantly calls it beyond itself to risk in the world, trusting God's mercy to protect and sustain it in its needs and relationships. We see this love building relationships and trust; we see it challenging the forces of disorder that tend to deny or subvert the witness of God's love. As this Second Week draws to a close, we see this love, of which we are now a part, walking steadfastly into the face of a death arranged by those forces of disorder, eyes and heart fixed firmly on the love of the Father, whom it trusts to redeem it from death.

When we reflect on this Second Week, we review the way we have journeyed to the place we are at now. We can use our journal to see the path we have taken.

Walking to the Beloved

We look to see how the freedom we felt at the beginning of this Week became focused and mature and grounded in our life. We see if the decisions made to follow Christ more concretely in this world really allow us to do that. We can determine this by noting, as we continued to pray and reflect on Christ's life, whether we are closer to him or farther away. Whether we are making a decision or not, upon reflection we may see if we are rooted in our daily life in a way that allows us to face uncertainty more calmly and creatively. Are we enjoying life more, celebrating what is good, and facing more responsibly the things we find destructive or debilitating?

If we find ourselves rooted in the Father's love, we can continue our journey with Christ and be with him in his suffering and death – the time of the naked and intimate embrace of God and the world. It is a time of God's embracing us and our embracing God, as Jesus stretches out his hands on the cross to embrace both us and his Father.

The Embrace

Imagine someone running to God with arms full of gifts to give him, and God running to that person with arms full of the gifts he, too, wants to bestow. They meet, but they cannot embrace because their arms are full. If God puts down his gifts to embrace the beloved, God is seen as naked and vulnerable. This is not a God of power and might, but one who is empty, humble, despised by the world. Often this is not the God we want to follow or get close to or even recognize. We turn away.

Instead of God putting down his gifts, imagine that we put down our gifts to embrace God. Then we see ourselves in our abject nakedness, with our deceptions and fears, our selfishness and our disordered passions, and we turn away, ashamed, from that embrace.

The embrace can only happen if God puts down his gifts and we put down our gifts. We must both have empty arms. In that emptiness is the intimacy of the lover with the beloved. The embrace is possible only if we experience deeply the commitment the Father has for us, and we trust and lean into what is offered in love. In the Third Week, we will enter that loving embrace.

Questions for Prayer and Reflection

1. As you review this whole phase, what was your most life-giving moment? As you reflect on it, what does it mean in your life's path?

2. What was your most desolate moment? What does it signify to you?

3. How does the pattern of riches, leading to honour and then pride, operate in your life?

4. How does the pattern of poverty, leading to social dismissal and then to humility, operate in your life?

5. What things would you like to do with your life, if you were free to do them? Would those things make you a better person and this world a better place to live in? What would be the cost of doing those things?

6. How do you share life with those you care about? How do you let them share life with you?

7. How do you deal with death in your life, in your world? How do you deal with the forces of death around you?

8. How do you celebrate life in the midst of a busy and chaotic world?

9. How do you find your rootedness? How do you maintain your relationship to that rootedness so it can support you in your daily life?

The Movie
IN BRUGES

Director: Martin McDonagh (2008 – 107 mins.)
Staring: Colin Farrell, Ralph Fiennes, Brendan Gleeson

1. Synopsis

The Irish hit men Ken and Ray are sent by the London mobster Harry Waters to the medieval Belgian city of Bruges at Christmastime after a job in a London church goes awry. While Ken, fascinated by the medieval, enjoys the historic city, Ray feels completely bored and misses his home. This changes when Ray meets the small-time drug dealer and crook Chloë, who sells drugs to the cast and crew of a movie that is filmed in Bruges.

Note: Rated R for strong, bloody violence, pervasive language, and some drug use.

2. About the Movie

1. "Gleeson's older, more settled character wants to experience the haunting medieval architecture, while Farrell's loudmouthed lad is bored stiff by the sightseeing. The movie gradually deepens from odd-couple comedy into Catholic-themed drama, but it remains marvelously funny throughout. Instead of hitting the easy notes of black humor, McDonagh skillfully modulates between broad character laughs and the men's piercing anguish as the story nears its bloody conclusion." (J.R. Jones, *Chicago Reader*, February 6, 2008)

What are some of the Catholic themes that are in this film? Give examples of where you find them.

2. "What the hit man and his baggage mean to most moviemakers is a shortcut to sorely conflicted humanity. What they mean to writer-director Martin McDonagh is an opportunity to take pot shots at the system. The dramatic system. The system that says a movie must go this way, then that, and leave us in a comfortable place. Many filmmakers have become intoxicated with the chance to alter formula, and stumbled …. Those who know McDonagh's work know a vein of darkness will run deeply through the comedy. It has seldom been darker. Or funnier. He has made a hit-man movie in which you don't know what will happen and can't wait to find out. Every movie should be so cliched. (John Anderson, *Washington Post*, February 8, 2009)

What prevents McDonagh from "stumbling" as he works to alter the formula of hit men films? How successful do you think he is in what he attempts?

3. "*In Bruges* is full of contradiction: for a very quiet film, it has some explosive moments and a mounting death toll; it's out to shock you but is, in its own way, rather moral. About two hitmen

who are sent to the Belgian city to cool their heels after a botched job, Colin Farrell's character insists throughout that 'Bruges is a shithole' while all the visual evidence tells you the complete opposite – the place is gorgeous. The local tourist board must be delighted." (Rob Mackie, *The Guardian*, August 8, 2008)

Does morality have to be shocking to get the attention of the filmgoer? Would it be possible to present the moral theme of this film without the shock and violence of the film?

3. The Relationship of the Movie to the Theme of the Exercise

1. The Exercise tells us that accepting our vulnerability will lead to humility and that this will lead to community. Who is the more vulnerable person in this film – Ken or Ray? Using examples from the film, trace the progress of Ken or Ray from his lack of true knowledge of himself to his acceptance of his vulnerability. What type of community results from this for him?

2. "There's a certain instability, or even derangement, about this story of two Irish hit men (played, marvelously, by Colin Farrell and Brendan Gleeson) on an enforced vacation in the medieval Belgian city of the title. Despite its scabrous, gutter-poetry dialogue and elements of Tarantino-style grotesque, *In Bruges* is also a fable about morality, self-sacrifice and religious doubt." (Andrew O'Hehir, *Salon*, February 8, 2008)

How is this film a "fable about morality, self-sacrifice and religious doubt"? In answering, consider the partly serious Christian symbolism running under the surface of the picture.

4. The Relationship of the Movie to One's Self in the Exercise

1. What are the "riches, honour, and pride" that Ken and Ray have put together for themselves? How similar are these to your own pattern on "riches, honour, and pride"? How do Ken and Ray deal with them? How do you plan to deal with yours?

2. Both Ken and Ray are, in different ways, very vulnerable people – partly because of what they do and partly because of how they have come to see themselves. They must learn to accept this and deal with it. What is it in your life that makes you vulnerable? What allows you to accept this vulnerability? What happens when you do accept it?

3. Although they are not aware of it right away, both Ken and Ray are on a journey that will cause them to reflect on themselves in many different ways. This Exercise is an overview of the Second Week – a time which was meant as a voyage of discovery for you. Looking back on this week and on what you have written in your journal, what has been the most significant thing about yourself that you have discovered in your relationship with God?

Part 3
The Third Week – A Passionate Love

1st Exercise
Preparation for the Third Week

O Lord my God in you do I take refuge;
Save me from all my pursuers, and deliver me,
Lest like a lion they rend me,
Dragging me away with none to rescue.

(Psalm 7:1-2)

Consider how the divinity hides itself; for example, it could destroy its enemies and does not do so, but leaves the most sacred humanity to suffer so cruelly.

(Sp. Ex. #196)

This is to ask for what I desire. Here it will be to ask for sorrow, compassion, and shame because the Lord is going to His suffering for my sins.　　(Sp. Ex. #193)

Sharing the Beloved's Pain

In the Third Week we follow Christ from the Last Supper to his entombment. We pray for the grace to be as present as possible to him as he journeys through loneliness, pain, humiliation, and death to the Father. It is a huge grace to be simply present to another's suffering without running away, falling back into ourselves, or trying to remedy the situation. The Christ has chosen to walk to the Father. The circumstances of his life and times have conspired to make this part of his journey as destructive as humanly possible. Yet, in the face of that horror, he does not turn away. We ask for the grace to be with him as we would be with a loved one who is betrayed by friends, wrongfully accused by the religious and political authorities, mocked and tortured by their underlings, and then shamefully left to die on a cross. In being present to him as he endures all of this, we share his pain and sorrow.

It is not our pain and sorrow we hold, but his. This phase of the journey is not about us – it is about going out of ourselves in compassion to embrace the beloved in his time of greatest need.

What is awe-full about the drama of the Third Week is the destruction – of human good and of the best about human nature – by sin, as manifested in personal, social, and cultural relationships. Sin moves to make life meaningless. We need to walk through those deserts of meaninglessness to discover that there is an indestructible base to human nature: God's love for each one of us. This is the most difficult human journey we can make, but we know it is possible because Jesus has made it, as a human being, before us. In making this journey, he breaks the tyranny of the fear of death, and destroys the fatal human illusion that insists we are determined fully by our social conditions and even by the stories we tell ourselves. He shows that, even when everything is stripped away and we remain as naked desire, even beyond emotion, that desire leans into the Love who creates it, sustains it, and now redeems it. This love does not ignore any of the brutal realities of sin or reduce its consequences. Rather, it demonstrates a love that is stronger than any evil, a light that refuses to be put out by any darkness, a compassion that will not turn aside from any horror. This loves manifests the intimacy out of which it springs.

Entering Mystery

When we enter into situations that reflect this constant reality, we are carried beyond ourselves into silence and stillness. Here we enter a mystery that is so personal and so beyond our own imagining that we feel we have entered a sacred space. We sense our unworthiness and finitude, which manifest in the graces of shame and confusion that Ignatius asks us to pray for at this time. This is not breast-beating or a guilt trip that subtly affirms the ego. It is simply the mode of felt experience of finitude in the presence of the holy.

For St. Ignatius, spirituality is very practical. He asks what we ought to do and suffer for Christ now that we have become intimates with him. We are invited to share in the work and the path of the beloved in the concrete circumstances of our lives. This is not a form of masochism or some contract of repayment. Here we might want to consider how Moses, after encountering God in the burning bush (Exodus 3:1-12), is invited to share in God's work of liberation. We can only respond to that invitation if we ourselves are free, for we cannot give others what we do not have ourselves. Intimacy with the divine makes us free; it is that freedom we see when we follow Jesus as he freely chooses to hand himself over to the Father's will. In these prayer periods, we can exercise our freedom by being as present as we can to that witness of freedom. It leads to resurrection, a life that encompasses and transcends the powers of this world.

Questions for Prayer and Reflection

1. Have you ever been present to the dying of someone you loved? How did you feel? What stages of being present did you go through?

2. How was God present to you at that time? How were the people who are close to you present? How were you present to yourself?

3. How did you survive that experience? How has it shaped the rest of your life?

4. When you consider the significant people of your time, or in your life, who have struggled for justice, freedom, human rights, or for a more human and loving life, how does your spirit react? Stay with that feeling and see what it brings to you.

5. How do you enter the quiet heroism of daily living and the quiet martyrdoms it calls forth?

6. When have you had an experience when your circumstances caused you to behave in ways that took you out of yourself? As you re-enter that experience, now in a more self-conscious and prayerful manner, what does it tell you about yourself? What does it tell you about the forces around you? What does it tell you about your God?

7. Sit with this reflection. What parts move you particularly? Go back to each of these moments and stay with them. What else can you find there? What is revealed to you?

210

The Movie
DANCER IN THE DARK

Director: Lars Von Trier (2000 – 140 mins.)
Starring: Bjork, Catherine Deneuve, David Morse, Joel Grey

1. Synopsis

A single mother, Selma has emigrated with her son Gene to America from eastern Europe in 1964. Because of a genetic defect, Selma will inevitably go blind. To prevent the same thing from happening to her son, Selma struggles to make money working in a factory not only to make ends meet but also to save money to get an operation for Gene.

2. About the Movie

1. "... this film won the Palme d'Or at the Cannes Film Festival. Since it is impossible to take the plot seriously on any literal level, it must be approached, I think, as a deliberate exercise in soap opera. It is valid to dislike it, but not fair to criticize it on the grounds of plausibility, because the movie has made a deliberate decision to be implausible: The plot is not a mistake but a choice .... *Dancer in the Dark* is a brave throwback to the fundamentals of the cinema – to heroines and villains, noble sacrifices and dastardly betrayals. The relatively crude visual look underlines the movie's abandonment of slick modernism." (Roger Ebert, *Chicago Sun-Times*, October 20, 2000)

What an unusual movie this is! People either like it or hate it. But either way, it is a movie with something to say and a certain style in the way it says it. What do you think the director was attempting to say with this movie?

2. "Over the course of more than two hours the viewer is thrown from moments of harrowing realism – scenes whose jumpy rhythm and raw immediacy make you feel as if you're peeking through the window at a moment of private misery – to flights of fantastic absurdity. The one constant presence, and the single force that keeps the movie from collapsing under its contradictory ambitions, is Selma." (A.O. Scott, *The New York Times*, September 22, 2000) What is it that attracts us to Selma? How is the fact that Selma is "mentally challenged" – as is her friend Jeff – handled in the movie? This is the first time that Bjork has acted in film. What is it about her person, her performance that keeps our attention?

3. "The musical numbers, which grow organically out of the near-blind Selma's detection of music and rhythm in the pounding thrum of factory noise, are affirmations of the magic in the ordinary – railway workers may swing hammers like canes and kick like Kelly, but they remain railway workers. And when people sing, they sing of the flight-giving wonder of singing itself: 'We'll

211

always be there to catch you,' goes one particularly apt lyric, while another forgives Selma of the crime which will eventually seal her tragedy: 'You just did what you had to do.' This is fantasy firmly grounded in the soil of the everyday, and fully aware of its populist power of denial. Leave Kansas – but we wouldn't have to: Dorothy would find the end of the rainbow in a hog-trough." (Geoff Pevere, *The Toronto Star*, September 22, 2000)

There is no way to avoid talking about the use of musical numbers in the movie – they are so much a part of what the movie is all about. They speak of what is happening. How are the musical numbers integral to the movie? What, for example, is Selma saying to us about herself in "I've Seen it All"?

3. The Relationship of the Movie to the Theme of the Exercise

1. How does the movie correspond to the Passion of Christ? Consider Selma's love for her son and what she does for him, consider her betrayal, her capture, her trial, her sentence, and – finally – the horror of her death. And then ask yourself how ready you are to follow Christ in his journey.

2. In our Third Week, we will exercise our freedom by being present as we can to Christ. How are Selma's two friends – Cathy and Jeff – present to her during her passion and death?

3. The horror and brutality of the act of crucifixion is mirrored in the horrific and realistic portrayal of the hanging that ends the movie. We know why we are moved by the death of Christ, but why are we moved by the death of Selma?

4. The Relationship of the Movie to One's Self in the Exercise

1. During the Third Week you will follow Christ through the terror and horror of his Passion and death. In this movie, you will probably turn away from the horror of Selma's death. If the death of a woman can have such an impact on you in a movie, where will you find the strength to follow Christ and be there for him in his Passion and death during this Third Week? This is not a movie but reality. Will you be able to face this reality?

2. Selma was betrayed and left alone by those she thought were her friends; Christ was also betrayed, and though he was abandoned by his friends, he was not alone. God was with him on this terrible journey. In your own life, has there been a "passion" that you have had to go through – like the loss of a loved one? Who was there for you at this time?

3. Selma's love for her son, Gene, is one that is, as we read in this Exercise, a love that is stronger than any evil, a light that refuses to be put out by any darkness, a compassion that will not turn aside from any horror. She gives her life for her son. Where in your life do you find such a love?

212

2nd Exercise
The Last Supper
(Matthew 26:20-30; John 13:1-30)

While we were still helpless, at the right time Christ died for the ungodly. Why, one will hardly die for a righteous person — though perhaps for a good person one will dare even to die. But God shows his love for us in that while we were yet sinners Christ died for us.

(Romans 5:6-8)

Consider what Christ our Lord suffers in His human nature. (Sp. Ex. #195)

This is to ask for what I desire. Here it will be to ask for sorrow, compassion, and shame because the Lord is going to His suffering for my sins. (Sp. Ex. #193)

Celebrating Freedom

In Western culture, our ideas of the Last Supper are strongly coloured by religious paintings of the event and by the piety that surrounds the eucharistic liturgies that derive from it. From these we have received such a formal notion of that meal that we have lost sight of its profoundly passionate celebration of life. The meal celebrates Passover, when the Israelite people gained their freedom from their oppressors, the Egyptians, and started their long journey through the desert to form a religious identity. At that meal, families and friends gather to remember and retell that story, to celebrate God's particular and practical concern for them. That gathering celebrates who they are – God's chosen – and celebrates their intimate relationship with God, which is manifest in what God has done for them.

In the Passover meal Christ shared with his friends, he celebrates what it means to be God's chosen: to bear witness to God's mercy, to hope even when there is no cause for optimism, to serve even the self-interested, to give over one's life to make sure that others receive life. In living this way, Christ takes up the meaning of the Jewish Passover and transforms it into something that reveals more of God's intimacy with us. He reveals to us at a deeper level who we really are and what we are capable of.

Jesus does not deny the past. As a Jewish man, and a rabbi, he has a profound sense of his religious history. But he does not understand himself totally in terms of the past, or its texts. He understands himself most fully through his relationship with his Father. The Lord becomes Abba, and Jesus is willing to share that relationship with us. The God who saves the Israelites becomes the one who saves each of us and all of us.

What Jesus does at the Passover meal is what we all do at family celebrations. We remember the past with the ones who share life with us, and each year we bring what has happened to us, and we tend to discuss these happenings so they become part of that occasion.

The ritual gathering on that particular evening becomes more than a celebration of surviving another year under Roman occupation, more than the

213

revival of the hope of yet another liberation from foreign oppression. For Christ, it allows the entry into a new dispensation that allows us freedom in the world, but not the freedom of worldly standards and methods. With the meal he offers, he gives the way of being united with God in more than just memory and ritual. In the bread and wine, he blesses real manifestations of himself; he ensures that his essence remains with those who share his life and mission. We become what we eat. We become partakers of the same relationship he has with the Father. This relationship gives a peace the world cannot give, and a rootedness that transcends this world's limitations.

In that rootedness lie freedom and focus. When we love someone, we open ourselves to that person. We give our very selves over to the beloved. We become the beloved, and the beloved, in accepting our gift, becomes us. In Jesus' founding of this new ritual using the elements of the Passover meal, our unity with God is established in a way that is as real and as physical as our own bodies.

The Gift of Mercy

Christ accomplishes this under the most trying circumstances. The people he had gathered around him, with whom he had worked and had trained, with whom he had celebrated life, and to whom he had revealed all that was given to him to reveal, had not been converted. He is intimate to them. He has revealed who he is to them. They have not been intimate with him simply because they do not know themselves the way he knows them. One would betray him; the rest would abandon him in his hard times. Yet he sees past how they act to what they are capable of. He sees, knows, and loves them in ways they do not yet see and know and love themselves. So what he offers to them, he offers in hope. He

hopes what he is doing will make them aware of their deepest identity and that they will live out of that deepest identity. Then, through their lives, they would be able to witness God's love for the world. He knows that, even after being with him for three years, his followers are riddled with self-interest and ambition. They do not yet understand that love is an attentive and disinterested service in the world.

So he serves them. At that Last Supper he washes their feet. Normally this was the role of a servant. This is humble service, never performed by the master of the house. While Christ humbles himself, the disciples are concerned with prestige and with who will be the first in Christ's new kingdom. They do not understand this kingdom in terms of loving service to the Father and to each other. They can't comprehend that Christ's whole life was one of service, of returning a fallen and dismayed world to its true identity. So, even with his heart breaking and with the awareness of what is coming next, Jesus performs an act that shows them how to act: he washes their feet. This is not the posturing of honour and pride, nor is it the abjection that comes from a corrupt self-image and false humility. It is the response to a question: How do we celebrate our neighbour?

Offered to All

How do we act in this world to bring it life, and to share that life? What do we do to create and maintain the common good? Jesus' answer is humble service. Peter cannot understand or accept this humility. He refuses to have his feet washed until Jesus replies that, unless he allows his feet to be washed, Peter cannot know whom he follows, and thus cannot be one with him. It takes humility to offer a gift; it also takes humility to receive a gift, accept it, open it, and live it. It is this gift of transforming life that Jesus offers and Peter finally accepts. This is the gift that the mercy of God offers to all.

But in the story of the Last Supper, one person refuses that gift and that mercy. Judas leaves the community Christ is establishing and goes to betray him. The gospels tell us that Judas Iscariot kept the community's money and stole from it. In Ignatian terms, of the Two Standards, Judas chose riches rather than poverty. Scholars have suggested that the relationship between Jesus and Judas fractured because of Judas's ideology. He may have been a zealot who wanted Jesus to use his powers to overturn the political oppression and social corruption of the day. He understood the Messianic rule in secular terms. He was unwilling to follow Jesus' trust in the Father to bring about that new creation. He preferred Jesus to follow him. When it became clear to Judas that Jesus' way was not what Judas wanted, his bitter disappointment led to his rejection of Jesus. We may wonder why Jesus tolerated Judas in the first place. We may wonder about his skills of discerning his disciples. We may even wonder about how this manifests today. But Jesus' position is that no one is to be lost. He offers himself to all without reserve. When we look at the other apostles, we discover that they are equally venal and self-serving. We may even find ourselves among them.

What Christ offers to his companions at the Last Supper, he also offers to us. We may wonder at his choice. But he knows us better than we know ourselves. He knows how fickle we are; but he also knows that we are capable of being one with him, following him, and sharing his life, joyfully and simply. He knows we are capable of love.

Questions for Prayer and Reflection

1. What are your moments of deepest meaning when you reflect on the Last Supper in one of the gospels (e.g., John 13:1-30)? Why do those moments touch you in this way? How do they reflect on your life's journey?

2. Think of an incident where someone close to you gave his or her life so others might have a better life. How did that sacrifice affect your life?

3. When have you sacrificed something for someone you love? For someone you didn't know? For someone who betrayed you afterwards?

4. When has someone hoped in you even when you did not hope in yourself? How do you think that changed your life?

5. How do you feel at family celebrations? How do you contribute to these gatherings? In what ways do they bring the clan together? If there are tensions, where do these come from? How do you live with them during the gathering?

6. When you contemplate the Last Supper, where are you in the action? Are you an onlooker, one of the disciples, Peter, Jesus, Judas? Did you get your feet washed? What stories were told at this gathering?

7. Have you ever been offered a gift you could not pay back? How do you deal with gratitude?

8. Think of some times when your humility brought you a great deal of freedom. What happened?

9. Think of a situation that did not go according to what you had planned or hoped. How did you discern what to do next?

10. Think of a time when you betrayed yourself or someone else. How did you find forgiveness?

11. What happens if you do not find forgiveness? Can you allow yourself to be held in God's mercy even then?

The Movie
WHERE THE WILD THINGS ARE

Director: Spike Jonze (2009 – 101 mins.)
Starring: Max Records, James Gandolfini, Catherine O'Hara, Paul Dano

1. Synopsis

An adaptation of Maurice Sendak's classic children's story, where Max, a disobedient little boy sent to bed without his supper, creates his own world. This world, an ocean away, is inhabited by ferocious wild creatures who crown Max as their ruler after he proclaims himself a king who can magically solve all their problems. And then, well, as Max says: "Let the wild rumpus start."

2. About the Movie

1. In 1963, when *Where the Wild Things Are* was published, the initial adult view was that these "Wild Things" were monsters who symbolized fear and anxiety and would be frightening for children. What worried adults weren't just the wild things, with their unreadable expressions and steak-knife teeth, but also the boy, Max, with his wild behaviour, his wild emotions, his refusal to listen to his mother. "I'll eat you up!" he shouts at her.

2. People now see the book as presenting something positive for children, giving them a way to cope with their angers and fears. The monsters have come to represent the "fears, anxiety and vulnerability of children and their struggle to make themselves 'King of All Wild Things.'" The book reflects what it's actually like to be a child. It's a book that could be respected by children for it gets to the heart of everything you feel growing up.

3. Which of these two views do you is more likely to be held today? Has childhood changed so much that one view is more correct than another?

4. One critic said "It feels like a movie that was written by a child who knew what he was doing but had never seen a movie before." That this compliment would sound in another context like a criticism is telling: people who dislike the movie will probably say that the story was poorly crafted, and people who love it will praise its childlike quality. Which side do you fall on and why?

5. Director Spike Jonze wanted the movie to have a tone of its own. He wanted it all to feel true to a nine-year-old viewer. There are no big movie speeches where a nine-year-old is suddenly reciting the wisdom of the ages. He hadn't set out to make a children's movie so much as to accurately depict childhood. Everything he did, all the decisions that he made, were to try to capture the feeling of what it means to be nine years old. How well do you think he succeeded?

6. There are – no doubt – as many themes in the movie as there are commentators. Could the movie be about true empowerment and survival, or about confronting emotions, or maybe it is about children's understanding of life. Which theme do you think is the main one in the film?

7. This movie challenges its audience. Some may think its lack of Hollywood-style structure makes it childish, while others may see its authentic childishness as its greatest asset. The director and writer do invent many things, but it all feels extremely honest and very much in the spirit of the book. Would you agree – and if so why, and if not, why not – that the movie is also apologetically bittersweet, bizarrely beautiful, and very much an adult story?

8. Mythologist Joseph Campbell said that the adventure you are ready for is the one you get. Max is ready for an adventure where his "mischief" becomes a "wild rumpus." But his adventure over, Max heads home to the cozy normality of his nine-year-old world where he "found his supper waiting for him – and it was still hot!" Does the movie triumph – as does the book – in that it gives children a way to cope with their angers and fears by taming them?

3. The Relationship of the Movie to the Theme of the Exercise

1. When we love someone, as we learn from the Exercise,

   • we open ourselves to that person,

   • we give ourselves over to the beloved, and

   • we become the beloved, and the beloved, in accepting us, becomes us.

Max loves the wild things on the island unconditionally. How is he open to them? How does he give himself to them? How do they accept him?

2. Within Christ's own group of disciples was the one who would betray him. One who chose riches rather than poverty. Are there any betrayers in this film? If so, what are the "riches" each of them choses over "poverty"? Whose is the greatest betrayal? Why?

4. The Relationship of the Movie to One's Self in the Exercise

1. What do the Wild Things represent? And what do they teach Max about himself and about coming to terms with some of the more difficult things he is facing in his life – his parent's separation, the growing distance from his older sister to whom he was once so close? What are the Wild Things in your own life and what do they teach you? Do you find excuses not to listen to them?

2. In the film, does Max take sides in the disputes among the Wild Things – even in the midst of the wild rumpus? Have you taken sides? On what issue? In doing this, do you put on a face to meet the faces that you meet? What is the main obstacle to being who people think you are? More important, perhaps, what is the main obstacle to your being who you really are?

217

The Agony in the Garden

(Matthew 26:30-46; Mark 14:32-44)

Abba, Father, all things are possible to you; remove this cup from me; yet not what I will but what you will.

(Mark 14:36)

Take, Lord, and receive all my liberty, my memory, my understanding, and my entire will, all that I have and possess. You have given all to me. To You, O Lord, I return it. All is Yours, dispose of it wholly according to Your will. Give me Your love and Your grace, for this is sufficient for me. (Sp. Ex. #234)

This is to ask for what I desire. Here it will be to ask for sorrow, compassion, and shame because the Lord is going to His suffering for my sins. (Sp. Ex. #193)

Freedom and Liberty

As we saw earlier, there is a difference between freedom and liberty. When we are free, we can make choices that affect our lives, even though we might not be at liberty. This is because we are connected to the source of our life. On the other hand, we might have liberty but not be free: even though we are able to move around, we might be trapped in compulsions and oppressive systems. Often we confuse license, liberty, and freedom. License is using our prerogatives to behave in selfish ways; liberty is the right given to us to behave according to social norms; freedom is living out of our deepest desire as relationship with God. When Christ leaves with his remaining companions after the Last Supper and goes to the Mount of Olives, he experiences his last moments of liberty and the agonizing tension between freedom and liberty.

If he keeps his liberty, he must give up his freedom, his union with the Father, which allows him to be indifferent to the things of this world. If he keeps his liberty, he could escape those coming to capture and kill him, but then he would no longer be true to his deepest sense of identity. If he keeps his freedom, on the other hand, he will be captured and killed. The tension is agony for him: he prays for the strength to be true to himself and to the God he loves. The choice is between security and identity: he has reached the intensely emotional stage where he must make an existential choice. In handing over his life to the Father, he knows that he is handing his body over to torture and death.

Struck by Terror

We, too, are faced with moments of radical choice in which we are asked to abandon familiar and established ways of doing things and to strike out on our own. Like Christ, we find that our friends and companions are not with us. They might like us and be generally sympathetic to us, but ultimately we are alone. Even when we turn to God in prayer, we find emptiness and an absence of consolation. We are struck by terror.

This terror undermines our courage, our connectedness with ourselves and with others; it erodes our self-confidence, and we find ourselves in a no man's land where our very sense of identity erodes. What are we to do in that situation? Like Christ, we must abandon ourselves to divine providence. We wait. We pray desperately in that darkness. We hand over our lives to the forces beyond our control. We act with integrity, being kind when we can and being patient when we must. We accept that suffering as it is received, whether through the indifference of our friends or through the realization that, in our present state, we have fallen through the bombed-out constructions of the world and its illusions of security. There is no comfort there. We go through the motions of living. As the psalmist says, "O my God, I cry by day, but you do not answer; and by night, but find no rest" (Psalm 22:3).

Christ enters this intensely human and dark space at Gethsemane. All over Jerusalem, families and friends are celebrating Passover; he has finished his. Oppressed by what awaits him, he goes to one of his favourite places to pray with his close friends. The place offers no comfort; his friends grow tired and fall asleep. Even Peter, who promises to remain with him and who vows never to betray him, cannot stay awake. Jesus is alone. He prays to his Father, in the intimacy of this relationship, that the upcoming trial be taken from him, but affirms that he wants to do the will of that mysterious one he calls "Abba." As he prays, he comes to the understanding that if redemption is to be achieved, then he must go through with what lies ahead.

Leaning into the Darkness

He embraces his Father's will, and in this embrace his prayer moves from seeking an escape from suffering to accepting that suffering. In that acceptance he moves from being resigned to Divine Providence to actively participating in that providence. Within this movement, we do not see the Father's presence. Christ receives no assurances that things will turn out right. Throughout his life, Christ has always actively participated in the workings of the divine providence of the Father. To reach that level of co-operation, he has learned to wait on the Father. His waiting here in this pain is not hopeless. He leans into the darkness, painful though it is to say yes to what will happen, because he trusts the Father. His "yes" is more than a passive acquiescence to fate. Instead, it says, "I will maintain that integrity that has been my life path." That integrity has been manifested in his three years of public ministry. It has been a constant and loving dependence on the Father's mercy. That integrity will be maintained now, even in the face of God's silence.

Jesus arrives at this hard-earned moment and returns to his companions to find that Judas and a band of soldiers have come to arrest him. The public drama of his passion is about to begin. His liberty is taken away and he is prey to the whole range of human evil, from malicious brutality to the cowardice of political authority. In the presence of all these, he maintains his freedom, his relationship to the Father.

Questions for Prayer and Reflection

1. When you read and prayed the scripture passages, were you able to stay with Jesus? What kind of resistances came up? What do they suggest to you?

2. When you spent time with the reflection on Christ in the garden, what aspects struck you? Did they cause any aspect of your life to rise to

219

your awareness? What was significant about those aspects? How do you deal with them? Can you bring them now to God and stay with those moments? What happens when you do that?

3. How do you live your freedom? What would you consider to be areas of freedom in your life? What would be areas of unfreedom? How do they manifest themselves in terms of this prayer exercise?

4. Recall times when you risked your life in some moment of self-transcendence even though you knew that it would be painful. Is there a common pattern to those moments? What does that pattern tell you about your relationship to God?

5. What areas of your life or your world do you despair over? Does that despair make you frozen or resigned? How can you start to move within that despair? Can you move from resignation, to passive acceptance, to active acceptance? Can you imagine that movement? What does it do to your sense of rootedness?

6. When have you been present to others as they made critical decisions about their lives? How did you find them? How did you find yourselves with them?

7. After reflecting on and praying through these questions, what sense do you have of yourself? Can you accept that sense of self?

The Movie
SOLITARY MAN

Director: Brian Koppelman and David Levien (2009 – 90 mins)
Starring: Michael Douglas, Susan Sarandan, Danny DeVito, Mary-Louise Parker.

1. Synopsis

Ben Kalmen is a 50-something New Yorker and former successful car dealer, who, through his own bad choices, watches his personal and professional life hit the skids because of his business and romantic indiscretions.

Note: Rated R for language and some sexual content.

2. About the Movie

1. "In Ben's world, there is only one person who really counts: Ben. He's selfish, self-centered and a heel to everyone he comes into contact with. And yet … Douglas treads a careful line, in that he (and directors Brian Koppelman and David Levien) don't make Ben sympathetic, exactly – he's too boorish for that. But Douglas allows the salesman to shine through a bit, even in disgrace. The disarming smile, the smack on the shoulder – it's all as insincere as the promises he makes. … But Ben, and what we really mean here is Douglas, won't be ignored. Douglas excels at this kind of role. You don't root for Ben, certainly. But you do wish that he could maybe turn things around a bit, stop the slide a little." (Bill Goodykoontz, *Arizona Republic*, June 9, 2010)

What are your feelings about Ben? Is there any scene in which you might have some sympathy for him and his situation?

2. "Ben – liar, cynic, compulsive womanizer and all-around jerk – makes no apologies for his behavior, and *Solitary Man* presents him in a remarkably evenhanded way, refusing to celebrate, to excuse or to judge his behavior. Just about everyone in Ben's life takes care of that. There are women who fall for him against their better inclinations, friends and colleagues who treat him with affection and respect, and also more than a few people who find the things he does completely unforgivable." (A.O. Scott, *The New York Times*, May 21, 2010)

Why is it possible to say that Ben, for all his manifold flaws, is never dishonest – his mistake is to place a higher value on candor than he does on decency? It may not be easy to like this solitary man. It may be impossible. But by the end of this trim and satisfying movie, you know him. And is this enough to satisfy you at the end of the movie – that you know what such a man is really like?

3. "There is nothing noble in failure," says Ben Kalmen, the protagonist of the dark comedy *Solitary Man* …. Happily, Ben's dictum about failure doesn't apply to movies. Failure itself isn't

noble or heroic or innately interesting; it's just a human condition like any other. But because mainstream American cinema tends to cower in fear of any behavior it considers unsympathetic and any circumstance it considers unhappy, a film about failure possesses a small degree of nobility right out of the gate. You just don't see that kind of film every day." (Matt Zoller Seitz, *Salon*, May 21, 2010)

What other films have you seen that deal with failure and have become successful films?

3. The Relationship of the Movie to the Theme of the Exercise

1. The Exercise tells us that in our lives we are faced with moments of radical choice. What is the "radical choice" with which Ben is faced in the film? What happens to his relationship with people around him that causes him to be confirmed in the need to make this "radical choice"?

2. "It's not often that a movie offers up a sinner who is fully aware of his sins and their corrosive consequences, yet is uncomplaining when they arrive because, on balance, he prefers the excitement of vice to the tedium of virtue …. Ironically, then, the film may be a victim of its success. The gem at the centre is so multifaceted, so knowingly selfish yet incapable of self-deceit, that the movie resists a conventional plot's easy turns. We don't want him redeemed, nor do we need him punished beyond what he inflicts on himself." (Rick Groen, *The Globe and Mail*, July 1, 2010)

This "radical choice" requires that we abandon familiar things and strike out on our own. Even our friends are not with us. How alone is Ben at the end of the movie? Recall his statement: "At your highest moments, and your lowest, you're alone."

3. This "radical choice" eventually causes us to turn and abandon ourselves to Divine Providence. Is there any sign in the film that might be construed as a symbol of Divine Providence that Ben turns to?

4. The Relationship of the Movie to One's Self in the Exercise

1. The Exercise helps us to see the difference between freedom and liberty. Look back in the exercise to review the difference between the two. Does Ben have freedom or liberty? Or does he have either? What is one moment of "radical choice" in your life? How did you approach it? In liberty? In freedom?

2. How does Ben react to one of his moments of radical choice? At one of your own moments of "radical choice," when you felt alone and without any self-confidence, what did you do? Did you even consider just abandoning yourself to Divine Providence? If you did so, what happened?

3. Who in the film offers to help Ben as he makes his radical choice? Have you ever been in a situation where you've watched a friend or lover make a "radical choice"? What have you done/ would you do in such a situation to offer support to that person?

4th Exercise
The Betrayal
(Matthew 26:47-58; Luke 22:47-57; Mark 14:44-54, 66-68)

If we say we have no sin we deceive ourselves and the truth is not in us. If we confess our sins, he is faithful and just, and will forgive our sins, and cleanse us from all unrighteousness. (1 John 1:8-9)

We must carefully observe the whole course of our thoughts. If the beginning and middle and end of the course of thoughts are wholly good and directed to what is entirely right, it is a sign that they are from the good angel. But the course of thoughts suggested to us may terminate in something evil, or distracting, or less good than the soul had formally proposed to do. Again, it may end in what weakens the soul, or disquiets it; or by destroying the peace, tranquillity, and quiet which it had before, it may cause disturbance to the soul. These things are a clear sign that the thoughts are proceeding from the evil spirit, the enemy of our progress and eternal salvation. (Sp. Ex. #333)

This is to ask for what I desire. Here it will be to ask for sorrow, compassion, and shame because the Lord is going to His suffering for my sins. (Sp. Ex. #193)

Intimate Acts of Violence

After the intense inner journey to freedom in the Garden, Jesus is taken captive by the temple guards. When Judas identifies him with a kiss, Jesus is seized. Someone tries to defend Jesus by striking out at the high priest's servant. In the ensuing conflict, a young man runs off naked. The guards bring Jesus to the courtyard of the high priest where, as he waits, he hears Peter deny him three times. The sequence revolves around the shame of betrayal and of Jesus' response to that betrayal.

Betrayal is an intimate act of violence. The integrity of the person betrayed is shattered: the betrayer has entered a personal sacred space through trust and has violated it. Betrayal destroys the bonds of human relationships and undermines those connections that make us who we are. The betrayals Jesus endures eat away at his confidence in human nature to maintain the sense of community he strove to witness to. He sees clearly, as the prophet Jeremiah does, that there is nothing so devious and desperately corrupt as the human heart (Jeremiah 17:9). But even here he holds on to what the Father sees of the human heart, rather than what he is experiencing.

The Father sees the human heart as lovable and loving. He sees it in the human heart that is Jesus'.

It is this Jesus whom Judas identifies with a kiss to the crowd arriving with clubs and swords to seize him. Judas's despair has turned to malice, and his kiss reveals the opposite of what it symbolizes. It is a lie. Lies destroy relationships; it is no wonder that Satan is called the prince of lies. He stands for the destruction of community, as the Christ stands for the creation of community. Judas's kiss betrays the spirit of community. Yet Jesus does not react by rejecting

Judas. He still calls him "Friend." What Jesus sees in Judas, Judas cannot see in himself. It is because he is so caught in this false self-image that he later destroys himself. He cannot live with what he has done. He cannot conceive of a love that can forgive him. God's mercy asks us to live out of God's image of us. It says that no matter what we have done, we are forgiven. We need to learn to accept that forgiveness. In this Exercise we can do that by being as present as we can to Christ as he manifests the extent of that forgiveness. His fidelity to the Father and to us, even in his suffering and death, shows that we will not be abandoned. We are asked to dare to believe this and to live out of that belief. It is the path to liberation.

Often we think, and sometimes it is true, that we need to fight for what is right, and that those acts of resistance bring liberation. But in this story, the person who defends Jesus by cutting off the servant's ear is using violence in reaction to violence. Jesus has accepted his path; the violence enacted here tries to stop Jesus from walking his path.

As Ecclesiastes says, there is "a time for war and a time for peace" (Ecclesiastes 3:8). How can we know the right thing to do at a particular time? That knowledge comes from doing as Christ does. His face is turned steadfastly towards the Father. In our path to intimacy, as we face what Jesus faces, we can also face who Jesus faces. It is the Father. Here, at his arrest, Jesus does not resist his capture. The one who tries to defend him is not one with Jesus. This is another type of betrayal, no less significant than that of Judas. As with Judas, such behaviour claims to know the best way for God to act. Once again, self-will displaces obedience to God's will.

If we are making a discernment at this time, we must see if our choice allows us to be present to Jesus as he is, rather than attempting to conscript him to our cause. If the latter is true, we will find ourselves alienated from Jesus in the prayer. We will either be trapped in a self-righteousness that brings desolation, or we will be exposed the way the young man in the story is exposed.

Naked to My Enemies

Mark's gospel tells us this story: "A young man followed him, with nothing but a linen cloth about his body; and they seized him, but he left the linen cloth and ran away naked" (Mark 14:51-52). Had the young man allowed himself to be seized, he would not have been thus exposed, but he chose his own security and his own shame rather than accompany Jesus. It may be a very short story, but it contains the same dynamics as that of Cardinal Wolsey. Wolsey sacrificed his integrity and his vocation to serve his king, Henry the Eighth (1485–1547), a contemporary of Ignatius and the early Jesuits. After Wolsey had served Henry's worldly purposes, Henry had him deposed for high treason. Wolsey is reported to have said, "Had I served my God with half the zeal I had served my king, He would not have left me thus naked to mine enemies." This betrayal occurred, Wolsey realized, because the values he held did not arise from a living, passionate, and intimate relationship with God.

The Long Last Night

When Jesus is taken, he is carried to the high priest. There, many false witnesses testify against him, but since they do not agree among themselves, the high priest asks Jesus directly if he is equal to God. Saying yes would convict him of blasphemy under Jewish law, since no one was the equal of God. The punishment for such blasphemy was death. Knowing the law, Jesus refuses to betray his relationship with the Father. He is true to that intimacy even

224

though he is humiliated by being spat upon and beaten up by those in the high priest's house.

Outside in the courtyard, though, is one who had followed him so far. It is Peter, with whom Jesus had an especially close relationship. It was Peter Jesus had appointed as his right-hand man; Peter who first recognized him as the Messiah; Peter who saw his transfiguration; Peter who was rescued walking on the water. That same Peter had said he would never betray Jesus, no matter what. Yet, when those in the courtyard ask whether he is a follower of Jesus, Peter denies this relationship three times. At the third time, when a cock crows twice, Peter remembers that Jesus had said to him, "Before the cock crows twice, you will deny me three times" (Mark 14:72). He breaks down and weeps. He realizes that, despite his special intimacy with the Christ, he is no different from the other disciples. He betrays himself in his denial of Christ. His self-image cannot withstand the pressures of the social situation. It is not that he does not know and love Jesus. He does. But he is a coward. Up to this point, Peter has been brash, impetuous, charismatic. But he lacks courage, a heart bonded to Jesus' heart. As Ignatius points out later, love is demonstrated more in deeds rather than words. Where we put our lives and our bodies shows what we value.

The Passover meal was celebrated at sundown. Morning has not yet broken. Jesus waits. He has waited for the betrayer to arrive; he waits for the trial and the verdict of the high priest; he waits for his Father. He waits for the next move. In the midst of this waiting, he is focused, not knowing exactly what will come next, but knowing that, when all is being taken away from him and his mission is in ruins, he is still committed to the Father.

Questions for Prayer and Reflection

1. As you prayed the scripture passages, which part of the contemplation struck you the most? Where were you in the action? What does this suggest to you?

2. When you read the above reflection, what moved you the most? How does that aspect connect to your life and your path? Does it bring back memories? If you go back to those memories with Christ as your companion, what happens?

3. When have you felt betrayed? How did you cope with it? How do you cope with it now?

4. When have you betrayed another person, an ideal, or the way you saw yourself? How did you experience forgiveness? How do you live with those areas where you have not experienced forgiveness? What can you do now about those situations?

5. Do you experience tension in your life between your religion and your spirituality? If so, how does it express itself?

6. How are you rooted in these prayer periods? How does it feel?

7. How are you distracted in these prayer periods? How can you dispose yourself to be rooted?

8. Sometimes the temptation is to try to persuade Jesus not to walk the path he has accepted. Have you experienced this temptation? How does it manifest itself in your life?

9. What happens to you when you stay, simply, with Christ?

10. What are your conversations with Mary, Jesus, or the Father like at the end of these prayer periods?

The Movie
THE DARK KNIGHT

Director: Christopher Nolan (2008 – 152 mins.)
Starring: Christian Bale, Heath Ledger, Aaron Eckhart, Michael Caine

1. Synopsis

It has been less than a year since what happened in *Batman Begins*. Now Batman, Lieutenant Gordon, and district attorney Harvey Dent are rounding up the criminals that have been holding Gotham City in their evil grip. Then the Joker arrives, and fresh chaos is unleashed on the city. Batman's battle with the Joker gets personal, and Batman must "confront everything he believes."

2. About the Movie

1. *The Dark Knight* is a morality play about power – wanting it, having it – about the difference between the two, and about the ethical questions raised about the complications of having power versus aspiring to power. What is the traditional definition of a "morality play" and how does *The Dark Knight* fit in that tradition?

2. Batman has a very strict moral code about what he will and won't do. The Joker – who has no morals – uses this to his advantage. He tempts Batman to cross the line, to bend the rules without breaking them, all in the name of cleaning up crime in Gotham. He tempts Batman to do the right deed for the wrong reason.

Batman tells the Joker that he has only one rule. The Joker replies, "Then you'll have to break it." What is Batman's rule? Why must he break it to defeat the Joker?

3. Director Christopher Nolan has made it clear that a thread running through the movie deals with anarchy as being the most frightening thing there is. And he has said that for him, in this day and age, chaos and anarchy are the things he is fears most. The Joker represents that anarchy. The Joker is an anarchist – pure and simple – with no limits and absolutely nothing to lose.

Where the Joker's pain – the pain we see reflected so clearly in his eyes – comes from, we never learn. The director and writers decided not to explore the origins of the Joker but to portray the character as a massively full-formed destructive anarchic force. What difference would it make if we did see the background of the Joker?

4. Batman and Joker in some ways need each other; they occupy a space set apart from the mainstream of their society, a space defined by its own rules. While Batman and Joker are indeed enemies in a real sense, they are more intimate and more involved with each other than either Bruce Wayne is with his friends or the Joker is with his own gang. Perhaps it is only in con-

fronting each other that they can be completely themselves. Would you agree? Why? Why not?

5. Director Christopher Nolan told the Los Angeles Times that "the foundation of the film is the transformation of Aaron Eckhart's Harvey Dent from a crusading prosecutor to Two-Face, a maniac whose face is ravaged on one side by a horrible injury." Why would he say that? Is this not a film about Batman?

3. The Relationship of the Movie to the Theme of the Exercise

1. Comic books are produced for entertainment. In actuality, comic books look at society, look at us and the world around us, and, through narration, make us see our world through the eyes of the characters, the artist, and the writer. Comic books mirror our world. What elements of our world are mirrored in *The Dark Knight?*

   This film is about discernment. It holds a mirror to our lives. It asks of us the question: What is the basis of our discernment as we walk the path to a fuller life?

2. The struggle between good and evil is not between two equals. The resurrection shows that evil has been overcome. Order wins over chaos. Community over narcissism. Self-sacrifice over self-interest. That much is simple. What is difficult is the process by which this happens. The issue of discernment becomes crucial here. The film is about masks. How do we read those masks? There is an instructive moment late in the film when common people must make a choice to preserve themselves. We should note our bias as we watch that sequence on the ferry boats. It brings to the fore this question: How do we read people? What do we understand is behind the masks? Why are masks significant as signifiers of our identity? What happens when we are reduced to our masks – the social faces we put on for society?

4. The Relationship of the Movie to One's Self in the Exercise

1. The film has much to say about the law and justice. What is the relationship between the law and justice? How do you respond when you encounter unjust laws, such as those that promote discrimination, or where you encounter a system of justice that does not deal with the evil in the world?

2. Christopher Nolan's films are concerned with questions of identity and duality. Of *The Dark Knight*, Nolan says that moral ambiguity is a theme that interested him. Batman exists in this very precarious state of someone who has very negative impulses but tries to channel them into something good. This is a truly human dilemma, and in this film we see those impulses infect more and more people. The Joker is the catalyst for this infection. How are people infected in the film? Why are they infected? What is the infection in your own life?

5th Exercise
Jesus Before Pilate

[Pilate said to Jesus] "Do you not know that I have the power to release you, and power to crucify you?" Jesus answered, "You have no power over me unless it had been given to you from above." (John 19:10-11)

Consider all blessings and gifts as descending from above. Thus, my limited power comes from the supreme and infinite power above. (Sp. Ex. #237)

This is to ask for what I desire. Here it will be to ask for sorrow, compassion, and shame because the Lord is going to His suffering for my sins. (Sp. Ex. #193)

Politics and Religion

In the previous contemplations, we saw Jesus betrayed by his companions and by the corruption of some religious authorities. The destructiveness found in venal religious figures is one of the shocking realities of human history. It has set people against people; thrown countries into civil war; divided families; alienated individuals from their deepest selves; exploited to justify the pillaging of the earth; and even separated people from the merciful love of God. Yet religious institutions have not disappeared from the face of the earth. We are created to be spiritual, but we need religion to incarnate that spirit. And so we struggle with the institutionalization of the Spirit, which gives it expression, but which at times seeks to repress it for institutional reasons. That Spirit is not to be denied; it blows where it will. Jesus embodies that spirit as the manifestation of God in the world. The Spirit led him to a profound appreciation of the law, which he does not deny but transcends in his one person and in the living community to whom he gives it. For Jesus, the fullness of the law is summed up in two basic principles: the total, shameless, passionate love of God, and the love of one's neighbour as oneself. We belong to each other; in that belonging we are the community of the Christ longing for the Father.

The political world embodies the rules for belonging, just as the religious world embodies the rules for the spirit. The religious leaders turn Jesus over to the political powers not because they respect those powers, but because they do not have the authority to put anyone to death. Because Jesus has shown with his life their lack of spirit, they claim he does not belong and should be treated like an outcast. But their malice goes even further than a tribal or cultic expulsion of a heretic. He must be eradicated in such a way that will leave no doubt in people's minds that a spirit like his will never be tolerated — by the public humiliation and the torture of death on a cross. For this, they need the collusion of the Roman authority, who alone have the right to execute criminals.

Jesus is taken to Pilate, the Roman governor of the province. The religious authorities must decide how to use the Roman law to accomplish their goal. The charge they bring before Pilate is this: "We have found this man perverting our nation and forbidding us to give tribute to Caesar, and saying that he himself is Christ a king" (Luke 23:2). Under Roman law there was one emperor, Caesar. All the lands under Caesar paid taxes or tribute. The accusation against Jesus, then, is that of treason; the penalty for treason is death by crucifixion. Jesus does not reply to the charges.

It is the way of a soiled world to rationalize its needs. Against those forces, innocence and truth are crushed. Perhaps it is naive to expect more than the politically expedient in corrupt and duplicitous social systems. Pilate chooses pragmatically. Even though he can find no fault with Jesus from the charges brought against him, and even though he judges that "nothing deserving death has been done by him" (Luke 23:9), he is trapped by the insistent demands of the chief priests, the rulers, and the people, and hands Jesus over to his death. The horror of what he has done is compounded by the fact that, instead of releasing Jesus, he is forced to release Barabbas, a man "who had been thrown into prison for murder and insurrection" (Luke 23:25). It may be a scriptural irony that the name "Barabbas" translates as "son of the Father." Jesus also calls himself the "Son of the Father," yet his world will accept only a murderer and a rebel by that name.

Victim and Oppressor

In our own world, we have seen the innocent brutalized and crushed by political and religious forces that seek only their own ends, not caring who is destroyed in the process. Many starve in a world that can feed all; many have no voice or power in their own country; many commit violence after being swayed by the lies of their leaders; many have souls that are deformed by generations of hate; many disappear, unnoticed. This is the fate of the victim. But every single one of these is a member of the human family, a community that extends across time and place. Each one has been uniquely named a child and the beloved of God, just as Christ was. In Christ, each has an identity. Even though the world has denied or ignored or subverted this identity, in the suffering of Christ, each is carried to the Father. Our own lives and identities are carried there, too. What Christ suffers, we suffer; what anyone suffers, we suffer, too. We are all one.

We are all one with the oppressor, also, for the oppressor is a victim, too. In denying part of his or her humanity to maintain a position of privilege, the oppressor lives a crippled, wounded life. In fact, it is because of one's hurts that one hurts others. The malice of the chief priests of Christ's day; the self-destructive hate of the Roman soldiers; the animal passions of the crowd; the confusion of Pilate; the circus curiosity of Herod; the self-absorption of Judas — these are all forms of hell. Christ walks through those hells without losing his integrity, even though he is battered and scarred by these encounters. He does not engage those powers at the level on which they operate. He maintains his silence in the face of lies and his humanity in the face of inhumanity. He keeps his focus on the Father, even as he is treated as an object.

It is often hard for us to see how we damage ourselves and others. Such awareness is usually too painful to bear. When we hurt others, we tend to rationalize our actions so we can live with ourselves. When we are present to Jesus in his suffering, we face the suffering of the world as both victim and oppressor. But we are also liberated from the passivity of the victim and from the aggression of the perpetrator. We start seeing things as they are. With the integrity of Christ, we behold a world in pain, needing to be redeemed. We also see that the work of redemption lies in embracing that suffering with a love that comes from the Father and returns to the Father.

Questions for Prayer and Reflection

1. As you contemplate Christ's journey from the house of Annas to the House of Caiaphas, and from there to Pilate, then to Herod and back to Pilate, what strikes you as most compelling? As you stay with those moments, what is revealed to you?

2. What stops you from being seduced by moral disgust? How does that affect your relationship with modern religious institutions? How does that affect your understanding and involvement in the political world around you?

3. Where do you find the face and the person of Christ in the world today? How does that presence engage you?

4. In what ways are you a victim? In what ways does the role of victim rob you of your integrity? How do you cope with that? What happens when you pray about your sense of being a victim?

5. In what ways do you identify with the powers of the world? How does this manifest itself in your daily life, in the choices you make, in the values you adopt? How do you justify that perspective? How do you feel moved when you realize your depth of complicity in that world?

6. How do you find your integrity? How do you maintain it? What are the costs? What is its value?

7. In your prayer, what emerges in your conversations with the Father and with Jesus?

8. Who, in the world today, is Jesus for you? How?

9. Who, in the world today, are you Jesus for? How?

The Movie
THERE WILL BE BLOOD

Director: Paul Thomas Anderson (2007 – 138 mins.)
Starring: Daniel Day-Lewis, Dillon Freasier, Paul Dano, Sydney McCallister

1. Synopsis

Daniel Plainview, an oil prospector of the early 20th century who will stop at nothing to get what he wants, is fuelled by his hatred of other people and his need to see anyone who is competing with him fail. When he moves to a new site in California that is said to be full of oil, he finds ways to strip the locals of their land for his own ends.

Note: The film contains scenes of violence.

2. About the Movie

1. "After making *Magnolia* (1999) and *Punch Drunk Love* (2002) – skillful but whimsical movies, with many whims that went nowhere – the young writer-director Paul Thomas Anderson has now done work that bears comparison to the greatest achievements of Griffith and Ford. The movie is a loose adaptation of Upton Sinclair's 1927 novel *Oil!*, but Anderson has taken Sinclair's bluff, genial oilman and turned him into a demonic character who bears more than a passing resemblance to Melville's Ahab. Stumping around on that bad leg, which was never properly set, Daniel Plainview – obsessed, brilliant, both warm-hearted and vicious – has Ahab's egotism and command." (David Denby, *The New Yorker*, December 17, 2007)

Daniel is all business – his only interests are oil, his son, and booze. His natural distrust and competiveness eventually lead from a comparison to Ahab to Charles Foster Kane, the title character of *Citizen Kane*. Kane tends to ignore questions, reveal nothing, and master every encounter with either charm or a threat. How would this apply to Plainview?

2. "There can be no debate about Day-Lewis. 'Gargantuan' is a puny word to describe his landmark performance. Try 'electrifying' or 'volcanic' or anything else that sounds dangerous if you get too close. His triumph is in making us see ourselves in Plainview, no matter how much we want to turn away. Day-Lewis and Anderson – a huge talent with an uncompromising gift for language and composition – are out to batter every cliché Hollywood holds dear. *There Will Be Blood* hits with hurricane force. Lovers of formula and sugarcoating will hate it. Screw them. In terms of excitement, imagination and rule-busting experimentation, it's a gusher." (Peter Travers, *Rolling Stone*, January 8, 2008)

Travers obviously has very strong feelings about this film. What examples of "excitement, imagination and rule-busting experimentation" can you find in the film? What are the clichés that the film wants to "batter"?

3. "Numerous reviewers have already made the connection between *There Will Be Blood* and *Citizen Kane*, another story of a great man undone by unresolved family issues. It's a valid comparison. But Charles Foster Kane had memories of his beloved sled Rosebud to cling to. Daniel Plainview, a man whose past is filled with shadows and ghosts, doesn't even have that small consolation. All he can do is watch as his oil geysers gush and his bank accounts fatten, bringing him to that most golden of curses: all the money in the world but nothing of value to buy with it." (Peter Howell, *The Toronto Star*, January 4, 2008)

The film has been described as the American Dream as tragedy that comes from Plainview's indecent rush towards an object of desire while neglecting a fundamental need. What is Plainview's object of desire and what fundamental need is he neglecting? Why does he do this to himself?

3. The Relationship of the Movie to the Theme of the Exercise

1. "Lewis's Daniel Plainview hates other people, and his hatred gives him just enough distance from humanity to be able to use people, shake them down for their money, their patrimony and ultimately their hope. It makes him the perfect capitalist. There's not much in the way of redemption on offer here. Plainview's trajectory through the movie leads ultimately to his alienation from everything that's human." (Michael Swan, *The Catholic Register*, February 10, 2008)

The Exercise tells us that the oppressor is a victim, too. Do you see any hope for redemption in this film? If so, where would you find it? Does anyone reach out to Plainview? How does he react to such offers of help? If redemption is available to all, where is it for Plainview?

2. "Day-Lewis sees the film in more personal terms. He told an interviewer: 'What it takes to get power, as you sacrifice yourself, little by little, in pursuit of the thing you thought you needed, or felt you couldn't live without, and then you only understand too late that you can't retrieve your soul — it's gone, it's torn.'" (Chrisopher Goodwill, *The Sunday Times*, November 25, 2007)

It is difficult not to look at this film as being about America, for it tackles all the big themes about America: blood, oil, religion. Yet it also deals with power and how it impacts the individual. Which theme do you think comes through more strongly? Consider that, while the film reveals, excites, disturbs, provokes, the window it opens is to human consciousness itself.

4. The Relationship of the Movie to One's Self in the Exercise

1. As the Exercise says, when we hurt others we usually have some rationalization for doing so which allows us to live with ourselves. What is Plainview's rationalization for what he does? What rationalization do you use for the time when you feel you hurt someone you care for?

6th Exercise
Jesus Tortured
(Matthew 27:24-31; Mark 15:15-20)

Jesus said to his disciples, "I say to you that listen, Love your enemies, do good to those who hate you, bless those who curse you, pray for those who abuse you. If anyone strikes you on the cheek, offer the other also; and from anyone who takes away your coat, do not withhold even your shirt. Give to everyone who begs from you; and if anyone takes away your goods, do not ask for them again. Do to others as you would have them do to you." (Luke 6:27-31)

How much more worthy of consideration is Christ our Lord, the Eternal King, before whom is assembled the whole world. To all His summons goes forth, and to each one in particular He addresses the words: "It is my will to conquer the whole world and all my enemies, and thus to enter into the glory of my Father. Therefore, those who wish to join me in this enterprise must be willing to labour with me, that by following me in suffering, they may follow me in glory. (Sp. Ex. #95)

This is to ask for what I desire. Here it will be to ask for sorrow, compassion, and shame because the Lord is going to His suffering for my sins. (Sp. Ex. #193)

Denying the Human Bond

After Pilate has declared Jesus innocent, he gives into the demands of the mob, which has been incited by the priests. He orders Jesus to be scourged and crucified, but absolves himself of any responsibility. Scourging so weakens a man that he dies more quickly when crucified. It says something about the horror of the world when its compassion must manifest itself in such brutal ways.

In our world, the free gift of our bodies to another is an act of love. The taking of our unwilling bodies by another is an act of constraint. In the latter case, our liberty is significantly compromised and we become subject to another. Torture goes even further. It radically denies the person any right as a human being or human animal. Its power is in removing those rights in as painful a manner as possible. Torture says to that person, "You are not equal to other human beings; you have no control over your life, your body, or your mind. You are nothing except what the torture creates you to be. You are nothing except in how the torture chooses to humiliate and destroy you." Torture radically denies the bond that connects human to human. For the tortured, isolation focuses their awareness on the violent and brutal pain over which they have no control but which becomes the centre of their identity. They are aware only of their pain.

The Violence of Power

Scourging in Roman times involved stripping the victim naked and lashing the body with a whip made of leather thongs, the tips of which were dipped in lead. Its range covered the whole body. It could remove skin from muscle and muscle from bone, desex the person, smash nerve endings, separate tendons, and even cause toxic shock and death. This was the Roman act of "kindness" to those condemned to be crucified. Jesus received this treatment by the Roman soldiers. Scripture is discreet and succinct on this subject, saying merely that Pilate, "having scourged Jesus, delivered him to be crucified" (Matthew 27:26). When we contemplate this sequence, we are not asked to be voyeurs to this spectacle. Rather, we ask for the grace to be present to Jesus in his agony and to the pain, shame, and confusion we experience as we bear witness to the cruelty of the world and to Christ's love for the world. He loves the world and he endures its testing of that love.

This testing includes the gratuitous humiliations the Roman soldiers inflict upon him after the scourging. The Romans regarded everyone else as inferior, and so many of the soldiers sent to the provinces to guard the borders, to maintain Roman law and peace, and to be the symbol of Roman power and might were arrogant and dismissive of those they subjugated. For them, Jesus was just another nonentity from a treacherous mass of tribal conflicts. After he is scourged, the whole battalion of some 500 men gather. They show him what they think of the Jews and of the one who was said to be the king of the Jews. Instead of an honourable crown of laurel leaves, a wreath of thorns was woven and jammed onto his head; instead of the sceptre of royalty he is given a reed; he is stripped and a scarlet robe, signifying nobility, is draped over him. "And kneeling before him they mocked him, saying, 'Hail, King of the Jews!' And they spat upon him and took the reed and struck him on the head" (Matthew 27:29-30).

Here is someone without power, innocent, woefully accused, and sentenced to death. Now, just after being badly beaten, he is treated as an object of derision and contempt. What are we to make of this act? We may think of the way power abuses the powerless; we may consider how vulnerability brings out the aggression of the insecure; we may even be horrified at humanity's inhumanity to other humans. We could even consider how such things happen today, in foreign places and close to home. We may be filled with a sense of moral disgust and a sense of helplessness. We grieve.

The Mystery of Evil and Suffering

But we are asked to be present to Jesus at a deeper level. He does not curse his tormentors. He does not fall back into a self-enclosed world. He remains open to the mystery as it unfolds – even in the grimmest horror and existential darkness. For him, as for us now, there is the mystery of suffering and evil; the mystery of the Father's presence in that suffering and evil; the mystery of Divine Providence; the mystery of our own path. Finally, there is the mystery of ourselves as we walk that path and ask, Who am I? Why is this happening to me? How can I endure it?

Christ endures it by taking it one moment at a time; we can endure it by being there for him and with him as he journeys to the cross and moves through the darkness to meet his Father.

Questions for Prayer and Reflection

1. How are you doing in these contemplations? Can you stay with Jesus? What temptations take you away from being present to him?

234

2. Where do you find Christ suffering and tortured in the world today? How does that affect you?

3. How are you present to the world of suffering and duplicity that you see in the newspapers and on television?

4. What happens when you become numb to the pain of the world? How does this affect your daily life?

5. How can you be attentive to the world's pain and your own without being destroyed by it?

6. In the above reflection, what points moved you most? What does this say to you? What happens when you go back to those points and remain quietly and prayerfully with them?

7. Where does that prayer carry you?

8. What happens in your conversations with the Father, with Jesus, or with Mary at the end of your prayer? What questions arise? How are they answered? Do any of them ask you any questions? What do you say?

The Movie
WIT

Director: Mike Nichols (2001 – 90 mins)
Starring: Emma Thompson, Christopher Lloyd, Harold Pinter, Eileen Atkins

1. Synopsis

Vivian Bearing is an English professor (a John Donne scholar, in fact) with stage 4 ovarian cancer. Because she is an academic, she approaches her illness as she would approach a research project. Her medical team does the same. Slowly but surely, though, Vivian's humanity and vulnerability bubble to the surface.

The film is based on Margaret Edson's one-act play of the same name.

2. About the Movie

1. "A shrewd and triumphant retooling of Margaret Edson's 1997 Pulitzer Prize-winning play, *Wit* tempers its harrowing tale of an English literary scholar's fierce fight against ovarian cancer with a strong strain of the title trait. While subject matter may be initially off-putting to some, positive word-of-mouth generated by memories of the theatrical experience, Emma Thompson's sensational leading perf and vet Mike Nichols' measured, top-of-his-game direction should put those fears in quick remission. Focused, emotionally draining and ultimately inspiring, *Wit* is nothing less than a cancer comedy with courage and compassion." (Eddie Cockrell, *Variety*, February 15, 2001)

There are many different kinds of comedy. How do you see it as possible to call a film dealing such a topic "comical"? What other films can you think of that have treated death from such an illness as comedy? What about *The Bucket List*?

2. "'Non-abstract Meditation' may sound like a contradiction, but then this film is full of contradictions – like life itself. We are given a look into life and death from the point of view of a poetry scholar who has, in turn, viewed life and death in the abstract through John Donne's poetry. She, in turn, is viewed in the abstract by a renowned doctor who views life and death as a case in a bed and by the scholar's former student who doesn't know how to communicate with patients beyond superficial catch phrases." (Matthew Ignoffo, imdb.com, March 28, 2001)

What are some of the contradictions that are found in this film? How abstract did you find the film?

3. "Perhaps Donne's most famous line is: 'No man is an island.' This would appear to be contradicted by the protagonist of *Wit*, a Donne scholar without family or friends, without a lover, partner, companion of any kind, without even a next-door neighbor to turn out her lights when she must rush herself to the hospital in a taxi for

what will prove to be the last time. All of her passion sublimated into cold, hard intellectualism, she is alone. And in the end, lonely. Yet honest about it. And herein lies the source of her genuine bravery and deep personal integrity as she endures terrible physical pain and faces death with, well, wit." (Dan Jardine, *Cinemania*, January 10, 2010)

We remain fascinated by death. Tragedies are, by definition, awash in death. Operas are full of death. Symphonies have been composed in its honour, while great paintings and profound literature attempt to capture its essence. Ingmar Bergman's *Cries and Whispers* as well as *Ikiru*, probably Akira Kurosawa's most affecting film, are devastating studies of how death affects and disaffects us all. Regardless of the film's scope or overall insight, even the tiniest glimpse can be illuminating. What "glimpse" does this film give us into death and the way one person deals with it?

3. The Relationship of the Movie to the Theme of the Exercise

1. As Elizabeth Kubler-Ross has noted: "People die in character." Through several flashbacks we gain insights into Vivian's life: an encounter with her mentor, E.M. Ashford, who warns her to spend more time with friends; a special moment as a child with her father, who encourages her delight in words and their intricate meanings; and several moments with students in need who were not treated compassionately. How do these moments reflect large reserves of inner courage and willpower that help her endure the suffering?

2. Reflect on Suzie's role in the film. Her humanity is stronger than the inhumanity around her, a light that refuses to be put out by any darkness, a compassion that will not turn aside. Where in Vivian's life do you find such a love? Has anyone been present in such a way for you?

4. The Relationship of the Movie to One's Self in the Exercise

1. The film does not portray Vivian as a person on a spiritual journey. Nonetheless, what spiritual growth do you witness in her, or do you? What does the way you respond to Vivian tell you about where you are on your spiritual journey?

2. We discover the extent of our freedom by being as present as we can to the sufferings of others. How are the medical staff present/not present to Vivian during her suffering and death? What do you see in their responses? In your own?

3. Torture – emotional as well as physical – removes rights as painfully as possible. Has anyone ever removed your rights from you? What were the circumstances? How did this affect you? How did it affect the person who tortured you?

7th Exercise

The Path to the Cross

(Luke 23:26-31; Mark 15:21)

"Do not ask me to abandon or forsake you! For wherever you go I will go, wherever you lodge I will lodge, your people shall be my people, and your God my God. Wherever you die I will die, and there be buried."

(Ruth 1:15-17)

I will beg God our Lord for grace that all my intentions, actions, and operations may be directed purely to the praise and service of His Divine Majesty.

(Sp. Ex. #46)

This is to ask for what I desire. Here it will be to ask for sorrow, compassion, and shame because the Lord is going to His suffering for my sins. (Sp. Ex. #193)

Crushed by Suffering

The distance from where the Roman soldiers mocked and spat upon Jesus to where he would be crucified is a little less than a kilometre. He is too weak from the beatings to walk that distance carrying the crossbeam to which his hands would be nailed. The Roman soldiers force a man from the crowd to carry the wooden post. (Roman law allowed any Roman soldier in the line of duty to conscript a bystander to carry his gear for a mile.) Stumbling to his Calvary, Jesus meets the pious women of Jerusalem who would weep and lament for the prisoners going to their death along this route. He tells them not to grieve for him, but rather for what the Romans will do to them and their children when those same Roman armies destroy Jerusalem in the not too distant future. As Simon of Cyrene, the conscripted bystander, reaches out to help him in his suffering, Jesus reaches out in that same suffering to comfort the grieving women.

It would be comforting for us to see Jesus in this state as a strong, heroic figure, but he is not. He is a man so crushed by suffering that he arouses pity in those who see him. In his dire poverty he accepts help from others, but he still gives something to the women grieving him. There is a bleak simplicity and an abject nakedness in this pilgrim figure stripped of almost all humanity on his way to his death. We can see this figure in the dispossessed of the world: the starving mother crossing the drought plains of Ethiopia, holding a pot-bellied baby too weak to brush the flies from its eyes; the silent stare of a street person in a prosperous Western city, looking in what seems like madness beyond the forms of this world; and, if we are honest, in our own poverty of spirit, the figure of the pilgrim beggar who finds in every act of human outrage its own suffering. But whether we can see this or not, we all journey through a life we cannot control towards a death over which we have no control. We are powerless. We take what we have been given, and we offer what we have. Jesus, on his way to his death, does the same.

238

Transformed by the Encounter with Suffering

Jesus accepts Simon of Cyrene's carrying his cross. Simon, a Jew, had come to Jerusalem to celebrate the Passover and the Feast of the Unleavened Bread, as was required by law for all Judean males. He would have had no desire to carry the cross of a criminal: in doing so he would have become ceremonially unclean and thus unfit to eat the Passover meal. To be drafted to do this by Roman force was not only demeaning for him, but broke the ethical taboos of his religion. Although his act is not one of gratuitous kindness, it has interesting results. Simon's family is mentioned later in the Scriptures as being Christian and helping Paul in his works. The power of his act of humiliation changes the path of his life. It carries him beyond the safe, established confines of his religion to an encounter with a broken man. But instead of being destroyed by that encounter, Simon is transformed. He becomes part of the living force of redemption.

When people go to impoverished countries to help out for awhile, their values are often radically transformed. They encounter the poor in all their misery and ingenuity, and they discover, oddly enough, that that encounter gives their own lives meaning and direction. The same thing happens when we deal with another's poverty and handicap. We might initially experience feelings of distaste and revulsion, but our perceptions change when we discover a common humanity and admit that we do not need to live the life of indifference we had lived before. We may go even further and discover, through another's poverty and suffering, our own poverty and suffering. In touching that intimate and delicate place in ourselves, we become more attuned to the world's pain and suffering, and begin to speak in a language of the heart that is compassion and simple, practical love. If, in our contemplation, we enter into Simon of Cyrene's world and life, we unearth the transformation occurring in ourselves.

Witness as an Act of Resistance

As such, we can reach out to others in our suffering as Christ reaches out to the grieving women on his path that day. In grief, we can be trapped by the pain of our lives. Those women are not there as paid mourners. They are there because, like marginalized women anywhere, they see the cruel fate brutally meted out to their sons and daughters, their husbands and families. Their act of resistance is to witness and to mourn. They line the route and offer what comfort they can. In response, Jesus offers what he can. He tells them the truth of their lives, saying, "Weep for yourselves and for your children .... For if they do this when the wood is green what will happen when the wood is dry?" (Luke 23:28-31). If the living presence of Divine Mercy in the world is treated this way, what will happen after it is killed? Historically, before the century was over, Jerusalem was sacked and the Jews were driven from the city. But Jesus' lament cuts across time and place. He is the fullest manifestation of the Father's love, and the world in its malice and blindness treats him like a despised criminal. How will the world treat those who come after as his representatives? How will the world treat itself and any who fall under its dominion?

We who live in these times know the answer. But in the face of that death, we, like Jesus, can attest with our lives to the love that is beyond death. We live in this world, but we do not have to live by the values of this world. The mystery that calls Jesus beyond death calls us also.

Questions for Prayer and Reflection

1. In the prayer, what moved you most? How? Return to that moment and stay there to see if there is anything else there for you. When you speak to God about this moment, what is revealed to you?

2. In the prayer, what repelled you the most? Where did you feel the driest, or the most alienated, or the least like praying? Why? Return to that moment and stay there for some time to see if there is something there for you. When you speak to God about this moment, what comes to you?

3. Have you ever been compelled to do something for someone else that changed your life for the better? What aspects of your life are like Simon of Cyrene's?

4. In our world today, we are called to witness to violence and to the destruction of innocence without turning away from that destruction. How do we witness to that in ways that maintain our integrity?

5. In your conversations with God, or with Mary, what strikes you?

6. In the contemplations, where do you find yourself – as an onlooker, a participant in the action, or one of the main figures? What does this say to you?

7. Do the prayer or your reflections trigger memories in you? What is the relationship between the prayer and those memories?

The Movie
CRIES AND WHISPERS

Director: Ingmar Bergman (1972 – 95 mins.)
Starring: Harriet Andersson, Kari Sylwan, Ingrid Thulin, Liv Ullmann

1. Synopsis

Agnes, who has cancer, receives a visit from her sisters Karin and Maria. The two sisters seem to feel no empathy for Agnes, and as her condition worsens and the pain increases, they are filled with fear and revulsion. Only the maid, Anna, can comfort the dying Agnes.

Note: If at all possible, watch the subtitled version. Much of an actor's art lies in the use of voice to express emotion, mood, and character. Dubbed movies can never have the full impact of the original. This is particularly important with a Bergman movie.

2. About the Movie

1. "Ingmar Bergman's dark vision of the human condition has focused on individuals incapable of real inter-personal communications except on the most primitive level. Crying for help in a world they can neither cope with nor comprehend, his characters confront a silent universe inhabited by a God whose attitude is at best uncaring, at worst malignant. How the individual adjusts to his plight remains Bergman's central concern, and in *Cries and Whispers* he provides a bravado portrait of four women in this barren emotional landscape." (Variety staff, *Variety*, December 31, 1972)

   How do each of the four women cope with the situation in the film? Which of them shows real compassion for the dying Agnes? How is God represented?

2. "The film's approach is not linear. Through the use of flashbacks, dream sequences, and enactments of journal excerpts, the time line becomes muddled. While the main story focuses upon Agnes' death, the forays into the past concern Anna, Karin, and Maria, giving us greater insight into these three women, showing incidents from their lives that explain why they react as they do when faced with a stricken woman on her deathbed. Anna is the only one capable of comforting Agnes, offering her the consolation of warm, naked flesh as she allows Agnes to pillow her head on her breasts. Karin and Maria are rather horrific individuals who keep their distance. Karin is a pillar of ice; Maria's self-centeredness mutes her ability to care for her sister." (James Berardinelli, *Reelviews*, All-Time Top 100, 2002)

   How do the actions and words of Karin, Maria, and Agnes reveal who they really are?

3. "Even though you won't remember significant dialogue, you are certain to retain those agoniz-

ing visuals that communicate the agony of a tortured soul. Between Bergman's tightly controlled artistry, realized by the visual talents of cinematographer Sven Nykvist, *Cries and Whispers* quietly leaves its existential mark. Those whispers will haunt for a long time after viewing, for aren't we all searching for love, acceptance, and meaning in our lives." (John Nebit, *Old School Reviews*, undated.)

How well do the visuals in this film capture the agony not only of Agnes but also of the other three women? What such scenes particularly caught your attention? How does "showing" this agony rather than talking about it make a stronger impact?

4. "One name often mentioned in conjunction with Bergman is that of director of photography Sven Nyqvist. *Cries and Whispers* represents one of two cinematography Oscars won by Nyqvist (the second one was for another Bergman film, *Fanny and Alexander*). This film has a very specific look which is critical to setting the mood. Crimson abounds. Red is everywhere, from the drapery, walls, and carpeting to the color that suffuses the screen when a transition is made to a flashback. The natural associations one makes with this color, especially in a story like this, are of sin and blood, which is what Bergman intended. In Peter Cowie's liner notes to the DVD, Bergman is quoted as saying, "All my films can be thought of in terms of black and white except for *Cries and Whispers*. In the screenplay, it says that red represents for me the interior of the soul."' (James Berardinelli, *Reelviews*, All-Time Top 100, 2002)

How is Bergman's statement about the use of the colour red observable in the way the film deals with issues of sin and blood?

3. The Relationship of the Movie to the Theme of the Exercise

1. Simon of Cyrene is changed by his encounter with the broken man who is Jesus. He is not destroyed by that encounter; rather, he is transformed and becomes part of the living force of redemption. How are Karin, Maria, and Anna changed by their encounter with the dying Agnes? Or are they changed at all?

2. We are called to live in the world but not live by the world's values. There are many examples of people in the movie who live in the world with the values of the world. There is at least one exception. How would you say that Anna represents someone who lives in the world but does not accept the world's values? How difficult is it for her to do this given her place in the family?

4. The Relationship of the Movie to One's Self in the Exercise

1. The movie contains examples of people whose acts of kindness – unlike Anna's – are not gratuitous. Have you ever been "forced" into an act of kindness? How did it change you? Or did it?

2. Anna alone is able to comfort Agnes in her pain and suffering. Fear and revulsion grip Agnes' sisters, who seem incapable of empathy. How do you react when confronted with the pain and suffering of someone you know? Of someone close to you?

8th Exercise
The Crucifixion of Jesus
(Mark 15:22-40; Matthew 27:33-55; Luke 23:32-49; John 19:17-37)

We know that all of creation groans and is in agony even until now; and not only creation but we ourselves, who have the first fruits of the Spirit, groan inwardly as we await the redemption of our bodies. For in this hope we are saved. But hope is not hope if its object is seen; how is it possible to hope for what one sees? And hoping for what we cannot see means awaiting it with patient endurance. The Spirit too helps us in our weakness for we do not know how to pray as we ought; but the Spirit himself intercedes for us with groanings too deep for words.
(Romans 8:22-26)

We must make ourselves indifferent to all created things, as far as we are allowed free choice and are not under any prohibition. Consequently, as far as we are concerned, we should not prefer health to sickness, riches to poverty, honour to dishonour, a long life to a short life. The same holds for all other things. (Sp. Ex. #23)

This is to ask for what I desire. Here it will be to ask for sorrow, compassion, and shame because the Lord is going to His suffering for my sins. (Sp. Ex. #193)

Witnessing a Death

In a crucifixion, the arms and feet are nailed in such a way that when the body is upright, the shoulders become dislocated. The result is agony, as those limbs are asked to bear the weight of the body. If one relaxes, one suffocates, and so one thrusts against the cross for breath. But this pushes against the nails and that pain becomes unbearable. The gospel writers are aware of the medical effects of such a torture, which was commonplace in their time. Their accounts contain the discretion of the lover who is aware of, but unwilling to depict, the beloved's final anguish. What they hold in their hearts of an experience that goes beyond words, we too can hold in our hearts as we contemplate those final hours of Christ on the day before the Jewish sabbath began.

Yet we are given something in the scriptural descriptions of Christ's dying on the cross. For Mark, the crucifixion plunges us into the profoundest depths of human misery and abandonment. Matthew gives us Jesus as the new Moses, whose suffering allows us to become intimates with the Father without the intermediary of temple religion. Luke presents the Messiah who remains as a healer and reconciler even in the midst of his anguish. John shows us a Christ who, even on the cross, is in full command of his destiny. The central questions for us, though, are these: How are we present to Christ on the cross? What Christ is given to us in our contemplation at this time?

Throughout the Exercises, St. Ignatius presents us with a Christ who enters his poverty to be completely disposed to the Father's will. He witnesses with his life to his trust in the Father's compassionate mercy for all, even in the face of his suffering and death. The Exercises present an encounter with Jesus that is in accordance with the different facets of the crucified Christ of the gospels. We are asked to be present as fully as possible to that Christ.

Those passages leave out many painful things, even though the gospels are written from the perspective of the resurrection. None describe the actual crucifixion and, like the contemplation of the hidden life, we depend on what we need from it to be given in prayer. But we do know that Jesus' scourged and bleeding body was stripped naked and nailed to the cross, which was then lifted and fixed in a hole in the ground. Medical evidence says that a crucified person would slowly drown as the exhausted body slumped and the lungs filled with water. And so the victim dies.

Living Our Own Deaths

But we are here not only to witness to a death, although there is a death. We are here to be present to the way Jesus lives his dying, trusting in a life beyond death. He is stripped and soldiers gamble for his blood-stained clothes. As he hangs there, struggling between the pain of dislocated joints and shattered nerve endings pushing against the nails, trying to breathe, he remains faithful to the Father. This is a level of intimacy that goes beyond emotional bonding. He prays for those who crucified him; he pardons the thief; he gives his mother a home; with his dying breath he hands his spirit over to the Father. All this occurs amidst his growing pain and exhaustion.

It is as not as if he forgets himself. He thirsts, and he acknowledges his sense of abandonment. He is besieged by temptation and cries out, in the words of the psalmist, "My God, my God, why have you for-saken me?" (Psalm 69:21). Even though he feels forsaken by the Father, he dies as he has lived, faithful to that relationship. On the cross, Christ waits on the Father as he has waited on him all his life. In that waiting he is stripped of any felt sense of his relationship with the Father.

We contemplate this dying, knowing how the story continues. We know that at his death there are signs that he does indeed witness to the Father's love for the world. The unbelieving Roman centurion who is stationed at the cross acknowledges, "Truly, this man is the Son of God" (Mark 15:39). Death is overthrown, for as Matthew tells us, "Tombs were opened, and many bodies of the saints who had fallen asleep were raised, and coming out of the tombs after his resurrection they went into the holy city and appeared to many" (Matthew 27:52-3).

But Christ, in his humanity, does not – cannot – live his resurrection before his death. He can only live his death until, at the Father's dispensation, he is raised. He endures the fullness of his death, just as each of us must live out our death; we cannot avoid it. We can know and believe the Father's mercy for each one of us, for we experienced it as we did the Exercises of the First Week. But we do not know, until we experience it, the Father's mercy for us in our dying. Like Christ, we lean into that mercy and that mystery. Doing so allows us to put death in perspective, but it does not allow us to dismiss death. We all must die.

In contemplating Christ's death, we are not asked to die his death, or to take him down from the cross. We are asked only to be as fully present as possible to his dying, and to our own dying, as he was to his. We can do both because his dying reveals to us something that we, even now, find almost impossible to believe: that without cursing or damning us, God

244

manifests his love by enduring a shameful and agonizing death for us, even as we reject him and his
mercy. He does this not to make us feel guilty or
duty-bound to follow him. On the contrary, God
does this to assure us that we are free and that we can
live that freedom in the face of the trials, illusions,
and punishments of this world. When we contemplate the death of Christ, we live the deaths of our
own lives and of our world to the hope of the resurrection.

Questions for Prayer and Reflection

Note: When we contemplate Christ's crucifixion,
anything can happen. We must be careful not to
manipulate ourselves to feel or experience one thing
or another. All we are asked to do is to be present.
Sometimes our emotions go deeper than our feelings,
and we feel nothing. Sometimes we are carried by our
prayer into moments of deep feeling. We need only
to be truthful to what happens in the prayer.

1. How did the prayer go? What stood out for you
   as you entered the scene of the crucifixion?

2. Where were you in the action of the contemplation? Why is this significant?

3. How do you live your life in the face of your own
   oncoming death? How would you like to live
   your life when you face this fact?

4. How does God's mercy shape the way you live
   with yourself and with others?

5. As Christ continually suffers in every act of injustice, every broken relationship, every illusion
   maintained, any beauty despoiled, every act of
   violence, how is the mercy of the Father brought
   to that situation for you?

6. What do you do when the Father does not seem
   to care?

7. How do you pray in the face of pain and suffering?

8. Call to mind times when you were in situations
   that were destructive of the life you needed. How
   did you maintain your integrity at those times?
   How were you rescued?

9. What does the cross of Christ truly mean in your
   life?

10. How is that cross misrepresented and misused in
    this world? How does this trap people?

The Movie
THE MISSION

Director: Roland Joffe (1986 – 126 mins.)
Starring: Robert DeNiro, Jeremy Irons, Ray McAnally
1986. Palm D'Or – best film at the Cannes Film Festival

1. Synopsis

In a 1750 Treaty the Spaniards gave part of Latin America to the Portuguese. As part of the treaty, the Jesuits were ordered to leave the missions which they had founded so that the Portuguese could use the Indians as slaves. Jesuit Fr. Gabriel, who built a mission to convert the Indians, wants the Europeans to learn to live in peace with the Indians. Mendoza, an ex-slaver become Jesuit, organizes the natives to resist the attempted take-over. Watching over all this is Cardinal Altamirano, sent by the Vatican to solve a political dilemma. If the Jesuits remain as defenders of the natives, then the Vatican might be at odds with Spain and Portugal and lose political power.

2. About the Movie

1. "The focus of *The Mission* is the story of the crises of conscience faced by two very different Jesuits when, at last, the Pope's envoy decides against the local priests. Will they take up arms against the crown to protect the Indians, who trust them and to whom they've brought God's love? In addition, will audiences understand the parallels between the 18th century and the late 20th century, when many priests in Latin America have also found themselves at odds with Rome?" (Vincent Canby, *The New York Times*, November 14, 1986) What are the parallels that the critic is speaking about?

2. The striking opening scene of the martydom of the Jesuit is only the first of the many scenes that use water as a symbol. Water has, of course, a religious signficance – the sacrament of Baptism. And the image of water has been used throughout film history. Federico Fellini ended all of his films by bringing his main characters to water to symbolize their rebirth and change. How is water used in *The Mission*? What does it symbolize?

3. "The film hints at many of the contemporary questions Christians face in responding to violent injustice but it does not resolve these dilemmas. We are left only with a sense that, in death, the two Jesuits remained brothers, companions of Jesus." (Mary Jo Leddy, *Catholic New Times*, October 28, 1986) Would you consider the Jesuits who died to be martyrs? What makes a "martyr"?

4. The music composed by Ennio Morricone has become well known on its own, but it was written to provide mood and atmosphere. Here it is

246

much more. What does the music in the movie serve as a symbol for? How is this done?

5. "It is left to the brilliant Irish actor Ray McAnally to find the deepest, most fascinating contradictions in the movie. As the churchman Altamirano, McAnally encompasses a very good man, forced to make a very bad decision. At the end of *The Mission*, Joffe holds on a closeup of Altamirano staring into the camera. There is the guilt and despair of centuries in that look. It sends a cold shudder down the spine." (Ron Base, *The Toronto Star*, November 14, 1986) How did you feel at the end of the movie? With which character did you identify most? Why?

3. The Relationship of the Movie to the Theme of the Exercise

1. Christ was brutally tortured and murdered in a most cruel fashion in the name of politics and religion – evil set out to destroy good. The movie shows the genocide of the Guarani natives by Portuguese soldiers. This bloody spectacle is one of evil obliterating good, all in the name of politics and religion. What other parallels are there between the death of Christ and the death of the Jesuits and the Guarani?

2. The Exercise tell us that Luke presents the Messiah who remains as a healer and reconciler even in the midst of his anguish. In John we have a Christ who, even on the cross, is in full command of his destiny. As Christ-figures, which of these two descriptions do Gabriel and Mendoza most resemble? Why? How is this shown?

3. The crucifixion and death of Christ speaks strongly to us about many things. How does God speak to people through this movie? What does the movie teach us about discipleship in our own time and what it might cost us?

4. The Relationship of the Movie to One's Self in the Exercise

1. Christ died that love might have a place in this world, triumphing over the "might" that would destroy that love. Towards the end of the movie, Father Gabriel, faced with obeying a command that he knows is morally wrong, says: "If might makes right, love has no place in the world; it may be so; I had no strength to live in a world like that." How do you reconcile this in your own life with what we believe Christ died for?

2. The forgiveness scene is one that we can all respond to. At one time or another we have all either forgiven or been forgiven for what we have done. Mendoza reacts in a certain way to this forgiveness. Where in your life do you recall both forgiving and being forgiven? How did you react to this?

3. Mendoza's climb up the waterfall is his own way of the cross – and it is his old self who dies. Any one in search of integrity must begin by also climbing up a metaphorical waterfall. It has been said that such a task is a life project without guarantees. What is your own way of the cross – your own waterfall – that you must face? Will you have the courage to climb up your falls? To face your enemy? To love them – no matter what the cost?

Christ Is Laid in the Tomb

(Matthew 27:55-61; Mark 15:42-47; Luke 23:50-56; John 19:38-42)

Wretch that I am! Who will deliver me from this body under the power of death? All praise to God through Jesus Christ our Lord .... (Rom 7:24-25)

Death no longer has dominion over him. (Rom 6:9)

The more the soul is in solitude and seclusion, the more fit it renders itself to approach and be united with its Creator and Lord; and the more closely it is united with Him, the more it disposes itself to receive graces and gifts from the infinite goodness of its God. (Sp. Ex. #20)

This is to ask for what I desire. Here it will be to ask for sorrow, compassion, and shame because the Lord is going to His suffering for my sins. (Sp. Ex. #193)

The Ruins of a Life

We are told that some of those who followed Jesus witnessed his death. After he died, one of his disciples asked Pilate for the body, and it was taken down. His followers wrapped it with spices and laid it in a nearby tomb. In this contemplation, we are asked to be present to this sequence of events.

When we see someone suffering in agony, it comes as a relief to us when that person dies. We think, well, at least now it is over and we can get to the business of the funeral. This gives us something to do. We get a break from that dreadful burden of waiting and from that painful awareness of our limited abilities to control our own or anyone else's living and dying.

In their waiting by the cross, those who followed Jesus – as family, friend, and disciple – enter into his anguish and grief. Since our lives are all woven together in a common fabric of relationships, the cruelty inflicted on someone who is part of our life traumatizes us. We enter into a sense of disbelief that eats away at what has become familiar, and we are forced to chart a course through the unknown. We may struggle against the strangeness that envelops us, and experience a profound desolation for what is lost. We become strangers to ourselves. As we wait with those waiting by the cross, we mourn the loss of hopes, ideals, and dreams. We had cherished the possibility that God's mercy would touch human hearts, and that the works of the one we followed would bring about that intimate sense of belonging and community where all could find a home.

Instead, we wait for a tortured man to die, a man who has touched our hearts and imaginations and lives. Here hangs someone with whom we were willing to risk our lives. He dies calling out to the Father. In our pain as his lovers, we cannot even begin to imagine the pain of the one who called him "Son" and "Beloved." What can we do now? The big schemes of a transformed world are in ruins. The ache in our hearts, which we finally acknowledged because it seemed something could now be done about it, is again rawly exposed to the absurdity of the world.

An Act of Mercy

That pain, outrage, and despair made Joseph of Arimathea bold. He asked Pilate for the body. Once Pilate had ascertained that the Christ was dead, he gave the body to Joseph. Maybe this is the work of good people in the world, to bury the dead so that they may not be further desecrated. It is a small and manageable good, and may be all that is possible today. The charitable act of burying the dead is a profoundly human concern that echoes through the ages and stories of diverse cultures. We find it in the biblical story of Tobias's father and in the Greek drama *Antigone*, where a young girl follows her heart and attempts to bury her dishonoured brother even though that ritual act has been forbidden on pain of death. Sophocles reveals the capability of the human heart to harbour such malice that even a work of mercy might be regarded as a crime. We find it in stories of indignities suffered by the dead as a show of their persecutor's power, and in the mockery of Christ on the cross. Joseph of Arimathea's action restores some dignity to Christ's body.

To touch the corpse of someone we love is an act of love and relief, though bitterly anguished. It is the body and yet it is not the body. And in the case of Jesus, it is a body transformed: cold, bloody, broken, the smell of terror and human waste. In the gathering dark, his followers can perform only the bare necessities: with no time to prepare the body properly, they bind it with linen cloth and spices, and lay it in the tomb.

Keeping Vigil

In our contemplation, we are asked to keep vigil by that tomb. We are asked to continue to be present as fully as possible. And so we wait. We do not know what will happen or how it will happen for us. We cannot create resurrection for ourselves. It is a gift, and it depends on the dispensation of the Father. We cannot will Christ's resurrection. We can fantasize about what it might be like, and imagine it happening, but such stories come from ourselves. The resurrection, when it happens, comes from beyond ourselves.

As we wait, let us reflect on how we first got to know Jesus in this retreat. Let us reflect on how we became intimates of Jesus. Let us remember our good times and our bad times together. Let us ponder those things that did not make sense at the time.

Even if we run out of things to think about, this does not mean that the prayer is finished. We need to wait in that empty space when first the mind goes blank, and then the heart settles into the silence of the pain and sinks deeper and deeper – past feeling, even past emotion – into that presence that holds us and all things into being.

Questions for Prayer and Reflection

1. What happened to you as you waited for Christ to die?

2. How did you deal with his death?

3. Were you able to be merciful to the body? to the others around you?

4. How did you wait at the tomb in prayer? in silence? just waiting? What came up during those times? What happened when you brought this to your conversation with God, the Christ, or Mary?

5. How do you behave at the funerals of those you have known? How was the prayer the same as, or different from, those times?

6. When has something or someone precious been taken from you? How did you cope? If you re-enter those moments now in your prayer, can you see in them the death of Christ for you? What happens when you do so?

7. What or who are the dead in your life now that you keep watch over? Can you allow yourself reverently to bury them? To offer them back to the mystery Jesus calls "Father"? What happens when you allow yourself to do this?

8. If, in a separate prayer period, you were to go over the events of this Third Week – from the Last Supper to Waiting at the Tomb, as you have experienced them in prayer – what strikes you as most significant? Why? How does this affect you?

9. Is there any unfinished business to this Week, or to your prayer at this time, or to your life as you see it now, that you would like to pray about?

10. Can you speak to the mystery called "Father" about those things? What happens when you do?

The Movie
THE LIVES OF OTHERS

Director: Florian Henckel von Donnersmarck (2006 – 137 mins.)
Starring: Martina Gedeck, Ulrich Muhe, Sebastian Koch

1. Synopsis

The time is 1984. The place East Berlin. The population of East Germany is controlled by the Stasi's 100,000 employees and 200,000 informers, whose goal is to know everything about the lives of others.

Among the most devoted of the Stasi's officers is Capt. Gerd Wiesler, who has no life beyond his work. At a performance of the latest play by Georg Dreyman, he decides to investigate the playwright, whom Wiesler can't believe is as clean as he seems.

Note: Rated R for some sexual content/nudity.

Note: If at all possible, watch the subtitled version. Much of an actor's art lies in the use of voice to express emotion, mood, and character. Dubbed movies can never have the full impact of the original.

2. About the Movie

1. "Goodness, as a subject for art, risks falling prey to piety and wishful thinking, but *The Lives of Others*, one of the nominees for this year's best foreign-language film Oscar, never sacrifices clarity for easy feeling. Posing a stark, difficult question – how does a good man act in circumstances that seem to rule out the very possibility of decent behavior? – it illuminates not only a shadowy period in recent German history, but also the moral no man's land where base impulses and high principles converge." (A.O. Scott, *The New York Times*, February 9, 2007)

What is the answer to the question that Scott proposes about this film: "How does a good man act in circumstances that seem to rule out the very possibility of decent behavior?"

2. "*The Lives of Others* subtly evokes a vindictive society that exists by turning citizens against each other in the interests of national unity and collective security. It serves as a major warning to ourselves and our elected leaders about where overzealousness and a lack of respect for individuals and their liberties can lead." (Philip French, *The Observer*, April 15, 2007)

How might this film be a warning about what could happen in our own society? What examples have you see of such a situation happening in your society?

3. "It is a shock to find the action lasting until 1993 …. Why drag us into the debris of the broken G.D.R.? Against all odds, though, the best is yet to come: an ending of overwhelming simplicity and force, in which the hopes of the film – as opposed to its fears, which have shivered throughout – come gently to rest. What happens is that a character says, 'Es ist für mich' – 'It's for

me.' When you see the film, you will understand why the phrase is like a blessing. To have something bestowed on 'me' – not on a tool of the state, not on a scapegoat or a sneak, but on me – is a sign that individual liberties have risen from the dead…. A movie this strong, however, is never parochial, nor is it period drama. Es ist für uns. It's for us." (Anthony Lane, *The New Yorker*, February 12, 2007)

Why is that phrase – "It's for me" – such a blessing on the character who hears it? Where does it come from? What makes Lane believe that it is a blessing for us today as well?

4. "To achieve their success, both the gifted playwright and his talented but self-doubting star have had to make accommodations to a regime that has blacklisted many of their closest friends and colleagues. Christa-Maria's plight is the most painful: submit to Hempf's sexual advances or find herself banished from the stage. *The Lives of Others* shows, with devastating clarity and intelligence, how the virus of corruption spreads from a political system into the hearts and souls of its citizens, infecting everything it touches. But it also suggests an antidote in the unlikely figure of Wiesler himself, the true believer who begins to see everything in a new light. His enlightenment, however, comes at a steep price." (David Ansen, *Newsweek*, February 12, 2007)

What is the price that Wiesler has to pay for this enlightenment? How does he come to finally appreciate what he has done?

3. The Relationship of the Movie to the Theme of the Exercise

1. As we wait with those waiting by the cross, we mourn the loss of hope, ideals, and dreams. How is this true of Dreyman, especially in the section of the film that takes place two years after the fall of the Berlin Wall?

2. How are viewers led towards identifying with certain characters in this film? How is the viewer invested in the storytelling process? For instance, could we see Wiesler as our surrogate spectator within the film? If not Wiesler, then who?

4. The Relationship of the Movie to One's Self in the Exercise

1. The Exercise tells us that our lives are all woven together in a common fabric of relationships. There are many tangled threads in the relationships in this film. What are your relationships like with the people around you? What holds these relationships together? What tries to tear them apart?

2. In this Exercise we move from suffering with Christ in his death to waiting for what is to come. The experience of death and destruction can be the door which opens us to a life beyond what we previously imagined. In your own life, how have you accepted what Christ's death means to you? How does the film depict our own spiritual state?

10th Exercise

The Descent into Hell – The Interlude Between the Burial and the Resurrection

Now the Lord is the Spirit, and where the Spirit of the Lord is, there is freedom. (2 Corinthians 3:17)

It will be very profitable for the one who is to go through the Exercises to enter upon them with magnanimity and generosity toward his Creator and Lord, and to offer Him his entire will and liberty, that His Divine Majesty may dispose of him and all he possesses according to His most holy will. (Sp. Ex. #5)

This is to ask for what I desire. Here it will be to ask for sorrow, compassion, and shame because the Lord is going to His suffering for my sins. (Sp. Ex. #193)

Intimate Healing

In the next stage on our spiritual journey, we will move onto Christ's resurrection. In the first contemplation to the Fourth Week, which deals with the resurrection and living that resurrection in our daily lives, St. Ignatius makes this interesting observation: "This is the history. Here it is how after Christ expired on the cross his body remained separated from the soul, but always united with the divinity. His soul, likewise united with the divinity, descended into hell. There he sets free the souls of the just" (#219).

The work of the Christ extends through all states of being. In Ignatius's iconography, that work extends to those who, through no fault of their own, are trapped in situations where they cannot express or receive love. What they experience is very similar to what Christ experienced on the cross: a sense of innocence violated and forsaken, of peace frustrated, of goodness tormented, of wholeness broken, of longing unfulfilled, of blessedness misinterpreted. What they experience is their radical helplessness. All they can do is wait, as Christ waited on the cross.

We experience much the same thing today and during our vigil outside Jesus' tomb. But the divine mission of God is not constrained by bodily limitations. That spirit of compassionate love desires to liberate all from whatever limits their freedom to live fully. It enters our places of imprisonment to bring us to a spiritual freedom from oppression. When we are present at the tomb in a state of unknowing, something is happening to us at levels below our bodily consciousness. We are being liberated. This is the continuing work of intimacy. It loves into life what is lost. This is a deep, hidden work. Its effects rise slowly to awareness.

253

Radical Transformation

Just as the Father reaches into death and brings the Son to resurrection, so the Son reaches into the most broken and desolate places of existence to witness with his spirit the depth of the compassionate mercy of his Father. That transformation is one of spirit, of heart, of imagination, of desire, of perception. The spirit is transformed because we experience in the midst of our despair a hope that refuses to give us up. It encourages us to believe that we are redeemable and that, even as we wait by the tombs of our lives and hopes, we are in the process of being redeemed. When we finally dare to allow ourselves to accept that gift, offered freely and simply, we discover our hearts expanding to accept our own suffering and the suffering of others. We find that we can hold the world, without despair or depression, but with a sense of wonder. That wonder transforms our imagination. It realizes that the world and life do not have to be the way they seem depicted, and that we do not have to accept the world in its distortions.

In fact, we discover our heart's desire: that unbroken intimacy with the Father, through Christ, is to re-create the world into a home for all. We can do this because we now perceive the possibilities for life inherent in the situations we live through. We are no longer trapped. We see a path through the gloom. We find the energy to follow it, and we walk that path with hope and commitment, and in union with everyone who lives the same felt relationship with the source of life.

The Liberation of the Most Alienated

Christ's descent into the dead and into hell brings to life what he finds there. What rises from the depths, deeper than original sin, is original grace.

As that grace emerges into our daily lives, it brings with it the deaths it transforms as it passes through them. We discover that we come from God, we return to God, and the path to God *is* God. This is not to say that there is no suffering on the path. In fact, on this journey we constantly leap into the furnaces of affliction, and are transformed there. Thus we do what the Christ did in bringing us to freedom. The creativity of God transforms evil into good, suffering into joy, isolation into community, imprisonment into freedom, death into resurrection.

In death, Jesus waits on the Father for deliverance. He waits in a love that does not deny death and suffering, but accepts it on the path back to the Father. That waiting is active, not passive; in fact, Christ is most creative when he is on the cross. That dying, death, and entombment draw out into the open all the pain and malice of a betrayed creation. There it encounters the constant love of God, who does not shrink from this horror. In that embrace Jesus dies; in that embrace creation is renewed. In the patience of Christ on the cross we discover the patience of the Father, whose gift is time and the open door in every moment of time to the fullness of life. Christ's descent into hell is a manifestation of that gift. The Father's desire is that nothing and no one, in no moment of creation, be lost — not even what seems irredeemable, not even what is trapped in hell.

When we enter into this contemplation and spend time in it, we aid in that redemption and we uncover its effects in our lives.

Questions for Prayer and Reflection

1. What were the most moving moments in this contemplation? Return to them, one at a time,

and wait for their significance to be expanded in your prayer.

2. Is there a pattern to those moments? What does it suggest? How do you find yourself responding as you become aware of that pattern?

3. Can you, in your prayer, bring Christ to those places in your life and in the world where you experience hell? What happens when you do that?

4. When have you been in situations that were sheer hell for you? How were you liberated? How do you account for that liberation? Return to those moments prayerfully and see how the Christ was present at those times. (You might want to ask at the beginning of that prayer for the presence of Christ to identify itself to you.)

5. What was the most desolate moment in this contemplation? Why do you think this moment stands out? Return to that moment in prayer. Stay there and see what happens.

6. How does this prayer, and its repetitions, help you see what has been going on during the Exercises of this Week?

7. In what ways are you creative? In what ways are you now asked to be creative? Pray for the answers to these questions to be revealed to you.

8. How do your conversations about these prayers with the Father, the Christ, or Mary illuminate your life and your path?

255

The Movie
UP IN THE AIR

Director: Jason Reitman (2009 – 108 mins.)
Starring: George Clooney, Vera Farmiga, Anna Kendrick, Jason Bateman

1. Synopsis

Ryan Bingham loves his job. Although his mission is to fire people, he does so with pseudo compassion while enjoying all the perks of travelling first class. When Natalie, a new employee at his company, finds a way for him to do his job by video conference, the life and lifestyle he loves are on the brink of vanishing. To show Natalie that her method can't replace face-to-face interaction, he brings her along on one of his trips. Both Ryan and Natalie start to see their work in a new light as a result.

Note: Rated R for language and some sexual content.

2. About the Movie

1. "The 'interviews' that Ryan does with the folks he fires give you a chill. They're a vision of what's going on in the country today, and *Up in the Air* is the rare film that does justice to economic desperation by expressing it with an honest populist embrace. At the same time, it's a movie about how one man living inside the cocoon of an overly detached culture comes to see the error of his own detachment. *Up in the Air* is light and dark, hilarious and tragic, romantic and real. It's everything that Hollywood has forgotten how to do; we're blessed that Jason Reitman has remembered." (Owen Gleiberman, *Entertainment Weekly*, December 30, 2009)

How is this film "light and dark, hilarious and tragic, romantic and real" – all at the same time? Can you name another recent film that has done the same thing?

2. "This line of work requires a special sort of person, and Ryan was born for the job. To say he has no feelings would be unfair: He does have them, of course. He's just learned to neglect them until they barely exist. *Up in the Air* is the story of a person who has fooled himself into believing that he has no emotional needs – he'd beg to differ with that 'no man is an island' bit – and has invested his energy into more tangible, less complicated goals." (Rene Rodriguez, *Miami Herald*, December 4, 2009

What happens that first helps Ryan see that neglecting his feelings has caused him to lose out on a lot in life? What emotional needs does he have?

3. "Crisply funny and fleetly paced, it's in its quiet way one of the saddest things in the theaters all year. The sadness accrues bit by bit, beginning with an absolute downer of a subject – a corporate terminator-for-hire who wings around the country firing people – and ending, as it must, in

an airport .... But despite a premise that augers loneliness and heartbreak, the film teases us into believing that something rosy might be waiting on arrival." (Amy Biancolli, *San Francisco Chronicle*, December 4, 2009)

Is this film meant to be more than a comedy? More than a satire? Is it mean to sadden and touch each of us? If so, how does it succeed in doing this? Watching the film, did you believe that there might be a happy ending? What gave you that impression?

4. "*Up in the Air* is all about connection – literally, when Ryan rushes to make his flights, and figuratively, when he avoids the emotional version at all costs." (Ann Hornaday, *Washington Post*, December 4, 2009)

Knowing this, it shouldn't come as a surprise that the climax of *Up in the Air* comes as such a shock. Did the climax come as a shock to you? Why? Why not? How involved were you with the main characters of the film? How does that involvement make this film more than just a "good" film?

3. The Relationship of the Movie to the Theme of the Exercise

1. Ryan Bingham is perfectly content with his life and his lack of any meaningful contact with other people. Hell for him occurs when he must interact in a real sense with other people. The world of *Up in the Air* is one of despair and depression. And this is true not only of Ryan and the people who are laid off, but also of almost everyone else in the film. What are some examples of the loss of wonder, of despair, and of depression in the film?

2. The work of Christ extends to all; they have only to accept it. In *Up in the Air*, where do we find examples of

- innocence violated and forsaken,
- wholeness broken,
- longing unfulfilled, and
- blessedness misinterpreted?

4. The Relationship of the Movie to One's Self in the Exercise

1. The Exercise tells us that along our journey we are constantly leaping into the furnaces of affliction. In *Up in the Air*, the characters experience real affliction, yet, for the most part, they are not transformed by it. What are some of the afflictions that you have faced? How have you been transformed by them?

2. As the Exercise says, Christ's descent to the dead and into hell brings to life what he finds when he returns from there. Ryan Bingham never really returns from the hell into which he descends, and so brings nothing back. What is the hell into which you have descended in your life, and what is it that you have brought back from it?

257

11th Exercise
Overview of the Third Week

And he said to me, "You are my servant,
Israel, in whom I will be glorified."
But I said, "I have laboured in vain,
I have spent my strength for nothing and vanity;
yet surely my cause is with the Lord,
and my reward with my God."
And now the Lord says,
who formed me in the womb to be his servant,
to bring Jacob back to him,
and that Israel might be gathered to him,
for I am honoured in the sight of the Lord,
and my God has become my strength —
he says,

"It is too light a thing that you should be my servant
to raise up the tribes of Jacob
and to restore the survivors of Israel;
I will give you as a light to the nations,
that my salvation may reach to the end of the earth."

(Isaiah 49:3-6)

Fifth Point. The fifth, to consider how the Divinity hides Itself, that is, how It could destroy Its enemies and does not do it, and how It leaves the most sacred Humanity to suffer so very cruelly. (Sp. Ex. #196)

To be found in all things by God.

A Transforming Love

The journey through the passion is a journey into intimacy. The lover enters into the despised places of the beloved's world, where the duplicity of the human heart is exposed. There is nothing hidden there that is not revealed. Here one discovers the depths of human depravity. Here one also discovers the dimensions of a human love that can be present to such self-destructiveness in a way that does not deny the integrity of love. This love understands evil as ignorance. It knows those who commit evil do not understand what they do. It sees violence as the frustration of love so thwarted as to become malice.

Love endures the grinding repetition of patterns of sin so ingrained as to distort humanity's nature to be free and joyful. And while this is a journey through the unredeemed places of creation, marked by suffering and hate, death and despair, betrayal and self-recrimination, its journey is also marked by an unwavering passion for life and for the source of all life. Its passage does not take away sin. Such love takes away the power of sin to stop our movement towards the one who calls us to the fullness of life. In that movement, we see the possibilities of transformation that evil cannot see or countenance. Love's very movement is its witness to life.

At every moment of our lives we are on a journey. Every moment is a transition. We leave something behind and we accept something new. Passover

258

is not only a Jewish feast or the roots of the Christian Easter. It is the state of every human's life. We come from God and we ultimately will return to God. Sometimes, like those ancient Israelites, our hardness of hearts causes us to wander in the wastelands until we are purified enough to see the next step home. Christ's life shows us that path home. Our passover happens when we, too, enter into the furnaces of affliction to transform through forgiveness what has been despoiled. We experience and offer such forgiveness when we are not trapped by the past, but offer that past to the future, which embraces us in a hope not seduced by moral disgust. Our passover sees in that past the possibilities of a new creation.

We are still being formed. Sin stops creation and creativity, causing despair. We can be so terrorized by death that we give up living and enter an endless cycle of dehumanizing existence. Then we find life brutal, and in our fallen state we brutalize others. We remain in a state of death.

But passover brings a movement from death to life. We set out on that path to freedom by following Jesus into the darkness where our fears trap us, our blindness causes us to lose the way, our selfishness makes us alone, our greed burdens us, and our self-righteousness condemns us. We discover that we are our own worst enemy in that darkness.

In the passion of Jesus Christ, all of the enemies of our human nature are depicted. Jesus is caught by these, but he is not trapped by them. His passion for the Father, which arises from his intimacy with the one who calls him "Beloved," carries him through death into the arms of the One who loves him.

Our journey along the path of intimacy, which has opened to us in the Exercises of St. Ignatius, roots us in the one who also calls us "Beloved."

The one who has gone before us shows us the way back to the Father. When we pray the Third Week of the Exercises of St. Ignatius, we contemplate that part of Christ's way back to the Father, which leads through his suffering and death. By being present to him there, we discover within ourselves a deeper intimacy with him and with the Father. We discover ourselves to be bonded in the human relationship they have with each other.

In that relationship, we wait at the end of the Third Week for the Father's compassionate love to bring us to resurrection. How or when or what that will be happens in God's time. We wait in the midst of death for that certain love to come to us. In that waiting we are not alone. All of creation cries out to be redeemed. We are a part of that creation. Christ is redeeming creation even here and now. We hold onto him as he does this work of redemption. In the depths of the intimacy we have with him, we are changed. That change rises up in and through us as resurrection.

Questions for Prayer and Reflection

1. In what ways has being with Jesus through his sufferings and death changed you?

2. How do you relate to the Father now?

3. How do you understand intimacy from this new perspective?

4. How does entering into Christ's passion and his relationship to the Father carry you beyond feelings?

259

The Movie
THE GREEN MILE

Director: Frank Darabont (1999 – 189 mins.)
Starring: Tom Hanks, Michael Clarke Duncan, James Cromwell. Graham Greene

1. Synopsis

Based on a serialized Stephen King novel, *The Green Mile* is set on death row in a Southern prison in 1935. The cellblock's head guard, Paul Edgecomb, develops a relationship with convicted murderer John Coffey, a giant of a man who has been accused of the murder of two children, yet is afraid to sleep in a cell without a night light. Coffey is a man who possesses a very special gift that is both mysterious and miraculous.

Note: Rated R for violence, language, and some sex-related material.

2. About the Movie

1. "*The Green Mile* involves assorted acts of cruelty and one lurid, extended electrocution scene that makes the horrors of the death penalty grotesquely clear, but much of it is very gentle. The mystical healing of Edgecomb's bladder trouble brings on some funny moments with Bonnie Hunt, who does a charming turn as his wife. Coffey's peculiar innocence is also given a lot of screen time. The way in which this huge black man, who calls the guards Boss, is given a magical capacity for self-sacrifice has its inadvertently racist overtones as well as its Christlike ones. But as Duncan plays him, Coffey is too flabbergast-

ing a figure to be easily pigeonholed anyhow." (Janet Maslin, *The New York Times*, December 10, 1999)

What do you think of John Coffey? How much of a reach is it to say that his initials – JC – are there to call our attention to the Christ-like symbolism that is found in the film?

2. "This is six-Kleenex Hollywood melodrama of the highest order, a sumptuously appointed fantasy with a core of genuine honesty and sadness. Yes, it's preachy and moralistic, and it uneasily blends childish whimsy on one hand with cruel horror on the other. These have been the qualities of popular storytelling since prehistory, and *The Green Mile* is above all a cracking good yarn that earns its laughter, its wonder and its tears." (Andrew O'Hehir, *Salon*, December 10, 1999)

If the film is "preachy and moralistic," how well does it work for you in presenting "a cracking good yarn"? Or is it more than just a "cracking good yarn"? If so, how is this accomplished?

3. In *The Green Mile*, we see a man's story, where women are mostly victims or helpers; men are often predators, or at least the active characters. Can you describe moments when women are victims? When they are helpers? Can you

describe moments when men are seen to be predators?

4. The seniors in the old age home are mostly white, while the servants are mostly black. These scenes are set in the present time, not 1935. Does this representation of whites and blacks suggest that the social roles of blacks have changed or not changed since 1935? Might this mean that, even in the new century, American blacks are subordinate? (from Neil Andersen, "Study Guide to *The Green Mile* episode on *Scanning the Movies*," December 5, 1999)

5. "Like the best supernatural stories, *The Green Mile* presents us with the darkest questions of human life in outlandish and paradoxical form. For Darabont and King, the Green Mile is a metaphorical vision of the world, where we all wait for our names to be called. It matters how we behave while we're there, but it's hard to say why, since we're all guilty of something and we're all leaving the same way." (Andrew O'Hehir, *Salon*, December 10, 1999)

How does this metaphorical vision of the world compare with your own vision of the world?

3. The Relationship of the Movie to the Theme of the Exercise

1. When Del walks the green mile, John says of him, "He da lucky one." When Bitterbuck and Del are asked if they have any last words, they say, "I'm sorry for what I done." When John Coffey is asked the same question, he says, "I'm sorry for what I am."

What is it that John Coffey was regretting? The fact that he has been convicted of murder?

2. "*The Green Mile* is suffused with Coffey's deep and terrible grief at what he sees around him, and Edgecomb's guilty proximity to this grief. Watching Astaire reminds him that, in the end, he could do nothing or would do nothing for Coffey except arrange for him to watch *Top Hat* in the prison. Coffey watched in rapture, but for Edgecomb, so many years later, it's unbearable – just as a great deal else is unbearable. He's a very old, broken man hoping to die before he has to witness the deaths of more loved ones." (Rob White, *Sight and Sound*, March 2000)

The Exercise talks about loneliness and pain. What is it about his relationship with John Coffey that Edgecomb finds so unbearable? What words were said when John took his leave of Edgecomb? How many films can you name that deal with that kind of grief?

4. The Relationship of the Movie to One's Self in the Exercise

1. In the Third Week we have followed Christ from the Last Supper to his entombment. We prayed for the grace to be as present as possible for this journey. Edgecomb is present for John Coffey's journey, and we have seen how that affects him. What has been the impact on you during this Third Week?

2. Christ's journey was one of pain, loneliness, humiliation, and death. John Coffey's journey was a similar one. How do you react to witnessing such suffering? Did you want to run away? Fall back into yourself? Try to remedy the situation?

Part 4
The Fourth Week – A Transforming Love

1st Exercise
Preparation for the Fourth Week

I am about to create new heavens and a new earth;
The things of the past shall not be remembered
nor come to mind.
Instead there shall always be rejoicing and happiness in
that which I create;
For I create Jerusalem to be a joy
And its people to be a delight;
I will rejoice in Jerusalem and exult in my people.
No longer shall the sound of weeping be heard there,
Nor the sound of crying. (Isaiah 65:17-19)

Consider the divinity, which seemed to hide itself during the passion, now appearing and manifesting itself so miraculously in the most holy Resurrection in its true and most sacred effects. (Sp. Ex. #223)

Here it will be to ask for the grace to be glad and rejoice intensely because of the great joy and the glory of Christ Our Lord. (Sp. Ex. #221)

The True Meaning of Joy

This final set of exercises moves through a sequence that ranges from experiencing the resurrection of Christ to living the spirit of that resurrection in this world. This range brings out yet another dimension of the spiritual intimacy we are invited to share with Jesus and the Father. It brings us to the gift of the Spirit and into the life of the Trinity.

The grace we ask for at the beginning of every prayer period is "To be glad and rejoice intensely because of the great joy and glory of Christ our Lord" (#221). Two things should be noted of this grace. First, the focus is on the great joy and glory of Christ. That joy gives us our own joy – not vice versa. Imagine seeing a young child playing, and feeling happy because that child is having fun. Our first experience of the resurrection is like that. That first state of joy carries us out of ourselves; we pray to be happy because we experience Christ's joy and can enter into that joy.

Ignatius also recommends that we ask for the grace to be intensely glad and to rejoice intensely. Not only do we need to ask for that grace and expect it, we also need to live as if we have received it. At this time, we avoid all those things that may cause us to lose that grace, and we seek those things that contribute to that state of being.

Joy is often equated with loud celebrations. True joy is not like that. Joy is the felt sense of being rooted in God's love. It is calm and focused and deep. The enemy of our human nature does not want us to be joyful, and so lures us away from it. Unless we

262

counteract that temptation, we start moving from being joyful to being happy, from being happy to being excited, and from being excited to being in a state of pleasure. From there it is easy to slip into giddiness and then to desolation. Pleasure is a delight in the things that stimulate the senses. I can take pleasure in a good meal or in an ice-cream cone on a hot day. Excitement is an intensification of that pleasure, to the extent that it blocks out a sense of calm and of control. Happiness occurs when my desires coincide with the energies around me, and I am affirmed in myself. Joy is acknowledging, in a self-conscious manner, my rootedness in a love and a life that is larger than me, and that I know cares for me. In joy, I live out my awareness as the redeemed beloved of the Father; in pleasure, I experience my selfhood solely in a physical way. Joy lies at one end of the continuum of delight; pleasure lies at the other end.

In this Week, as we enter more and more deeply into the resurrection, we want to remain recollected so that we do not lose all the gifts we have been moving towards during our retreat. If we did so, we would be like those people who earn a small fortune working long, hard hours in remote areas, only to lose it in a frenzy of mindless self-indulgence when they return to the world they left behind.

Remaining Recollected

As we remain recollected, we become more united with God. We share the same spirit and the same focus, work, and joy with the Christ as we become his continuing presence in the world. A path leads through this Week of our growing union into the mind and heart of God. We left the previous Week in a state of waiting. That waiting empties us. In that emptiness, we glimpse the risen Christ. As we reflect on these glimpses, learning to believe and accept what we are being given, we enter a state of

quiet, focused awareness of the joy present in every moment and in everything. We celebrate that awareness by sharing with whomever we meet what has been given to us. This work is resurrection in the world. We don't proselytize or graciously condescend from a spiritually superior position. Rather, we live out of the joyful sense that we are related to everything and everyone, realizing that dimensions of that relationship remain oppressed or live with illusion.

As we strive to repair those relationships, we find ourselves back in the world of the First Week, but at a deeper and more comprehensive level. Thus the journey begins again. It is a never-ending journey into the unfathomable depths of God's love. In this we are like Mary, the mother of Jesus. She brings Christ into the world. She shares Christ with the world. She suffers with Christ in the world. She experiences his resurrection, and becomes part of the community that is his resurrected presence in the world.

A Meeting with a Mother

And so we begin with Mary. Ignatius presents Jesus appearing to Mary as the First Contemplation on the Resurrection of Christ. He writes, "He appeared to the Virgin Mary. Though this is not mentioned explicitly in the Scriptures it must be considered as stated when Scripture says that He appeared to many others" (#299). For Ignatius, the relationship between Jesus and his mother is very special. Without her free and generous consent at the Annunciation, his whole mission as a human would have been frustrated. Ignatius has included her in the conversations he invites those making the Exercises to conduct at the end of their prayer periods. Here he suggests that she is the first person Jesus appears to after he is raised from the dead.

He is, after all, flesh of her flesh, for it is through her that he has become incarnate. Beyond the bonds of parent and child, of Jewish mother and son, lies the deeper connection of resurrected body to its closest kin. She is the closest human being to him and so, for Ignatius, it is only in the nature of love that he should appear to her first.

We are invited, as we are at every contemplation, to be present at that meeting in all of its quiet, deeply personal intimacy, when grief and resignation turn to incredulous wonder, mutual concern, and affirmation. What had been told to her before – that he was to suffer, die, and then rise from the dead – and what she had pondered and held in faith, now is seen and felt as fact and truth. In these moments of acceptance between Jesus and his mother, and between them and us in prayer, there is only the simple, open conversation of heart to heart.

We have all heard stories of relationships or people lost, or of a life spent dealing with the emptiness, where what was believed to be gone forever returned forever. Such things happen in real life, too. Soldiers lost in battle are believed dead, mourned, and then turn up again. Families separated by war or other circumstances reunite years later. Reunion is part of the human story.

Here Jesus and Mary experience something similar, except she saw her son tortured and killed. We lived with Mary's grief. Just as her son's life was held as worthless, so too her sacrifices to bring him into the world and to protect him with Joseph had become worthless. Two lives had been wasted. One was devoted to the other, and that other was forsaken and crucified. We must sit with that welling sense of emotion that comes from places too deep to be named, as love comforts love, and claims love. We must sit with Mary's embrace of Jesus and Jesus' embrace of Mary.

We must abide, quietly and passionately, with our embrace of both. We, too, are included in that love.

Questions for Prayer and Reflection

1. Have you ever lost anything and then, against all odds, found it again? Enter into that state of simple joy again. What other memories or incidents does it raise for you? What do you experience as you savour those memories?

2. Where are you in the contemplation when the resurrected Jesus comes to his mother? How did that feel? What were the most moving moments? Why? What did they bring back to life for you? How did they transform the destructiveness of the previous Week?

3. What was your conversation after the prayer with Mary, Jesus, the Father? Where does that conversation lead you next?

4. What do you do to stay in that quiet joy? What must you do to stay there?

5. What are the forces that try to move you away from that quiet, focused rootedness? Can you acknowledge them without being driven by them?

6. As you sit in that quiet joy, what arises as gift for you?

7. What happens as you stay with that gift? As your staying quietly in that simple space opens that gift, you too are being opened by that gift. How does this feel?

8. Do you experience the gift of being able both to give and to receive as gratitude? Do you have a sense of how gratitude can be a way of life?

The Movie
BILLY ELLIOT

Director: Stephen Daldry (2000 – 107 mins.)
Starring: Jamie Bell, Julie Walters, Gary Lewis

1. Synopsis

It is 1984 and, in a northern England mining town, a group of miners are on strike. Billy Elliot, an eleven-year-old whose father and brother are on strike, does not like the boxing lessons he is taking at school but prefers to join the girl's ballet class. Billy's talent is encouraged by the ballet teacher, Mrs. Wilkinson, who manages to obtain an audition for Billy to the Royal Ballet School. Now Billy must face his family.

2. About the Movie

1. *Billy Elliot* begins in a miner's strike "… and as you watch the police beat back the strikers with shield and truncheon, you see the crude ballet of social grievance to which Jamie's answer is a ballet of a far more liberating kind." (Alexander Walker, *The Evening Standard*, September 28, 2000) How do these two types of "dance" illustrate the tragedy that underlies the movie – the narrow mindedness, the resistance to change, the bigotry and violence?

2. "Daldry isn't afraid of going for the emotional jugular, but he deftly sidesteps the mawkish. Yes, *Billy Elliot* follows a well-trod formula, and it hits one or two false notes … But in the face of a movie so artfully made, so deeply charming, so heartfelt, it's not only pointless to resist, it's damn near impossible." (David Ansen, *Newsweek*, October 16, 2000) This is a major point – were you able to resist the movie? Was it indeed so artful, so charming, to heartfelt that you could not help but become involved? Why? Or why not? What does it take to involve you in a movie – make you feel with the characters – to make you possibly even tear up at the end? What is the difference between sentiment and sentimentality?

3. "The achievement here, thanks largely to cinematographer Brian Tufano (*Trainspotting*), is that the film says the obvious through the innocence of a childhood perspective. Yes, unemployment and repression are everywhere here, but joy, the movie suggests, is just about keeping your feet tapping." (Liam Lacey, *The Globe and Mail*, October 13, 2000) What are some of the ways the movie uses the perspective of the child – especially that of Billy? Is the theme of the movie as simple as Lacey suggests? Why? Why not? How would you sum up the theme of the movie in one sentence?

4. "Where this really scores and tugs the emotions, though, is in the dance sequences themselves, set

largely to a medley of '80s hits and comprising unorthodox moves guaranteed to blow away the stereotypes of ballet – with one particularly glorious set-piece guaranteed to have even the most stoic of viewer complaining of something in their eye. Bell is as accomplished a dancer as he is an actor, carrying the movie with astonishing aplomb and turning in the sort of star-making performance that leaves you regretting the fact he won't be playing Harry Potter any time soon." (Caroline Westbrook, *Empire On Line*, Issue 136, October 2000)

Which of the dance pieces in the movie worked best for you? What was it that most caught your attention in the scene? Jamie Bell had never acted before – he was chosen from over 200 who auditioned for the role. He tends to ground the movie with a look or a bit of business. What natural ability does he have that makes him perfect for the part? Think of the opening scene of the movie. How does he take hold of your attention and keep it? What characteristics of Bell's would have either made him a good Harry Potter, or not?

3. The Relationship of the Movie to the Theme of the Exercise

1. After the tumultuous Third Week of the Exercises, we enter into this Fourth Week – a time of joy. We need to experience this joy. Why is this movie possibly one of the best movies for this point in the Exercises?

2. Billy experiences in his dancing a sort of disappearing from himself; he feels a change in his body, as if electricity is coursing through him.

Review the definitions of the following terms in the Exercise:

- pleasure
- being excited
- being happy
- being joyful.

Which best suits Billy at the end of the movie? Why?

3. Billy's father comes to discover, as the Exercise tells us, that we are related to everything and everyone. His eyes are opened to another way of life, which causes hardships in almost every aspect of his life. But it also brings him happiness. How does this change come about in the movie?

4. The Relationship of the Movie to One's Self in the Exercise

1. The grand leap with which Billy propels himself on stage at the end of the movie is an expression of all that he has worked for and the expression of the great gifts he has been given. We hope that he will not lose these gifts as he goes on in his career. You have been moving towards gifts during the Exercises. How will you express these gifts as you move into the Fourth Week? What will you do to try to ensure that you do not waste them as you return to the world after the Exercises?

2. Billy finds his talent and then almost loses the chance to develop it as he misses the first audition. Things change and the lost chance is regained. In your life, where were the lost chances that most affected you? What did you do to

regain them? Or did you just give up and move on? If so, what did you leave behind?

3. Bill's relationship with his mother was a very deep one: recall his visit to her grave and, possibly even more important, the time when he believes he sees her as he is about to drink milk from the bottle. So much is left unsaid but understood in these scenes. Think about the letter Billy shows Mrs. Wilkinson, which his mother wrote him before she died. When Mrs. Wilkinson says that his mother must have been very special. Billy replies, "Na, she was just me mam." For Ignatius, as we read in the Exercise, the relationship between Jesus and his mother is very special and his appearance to her after his resurrection is a time of great joy for them both. What about your relationship with your mother? What times of pleasure and joy can you recall with her?

2nd Exercise

Christise Appears to Mary Magdalene

(John 20:1-18)

Jesus said, "I will not leave you desolate; I will come to you." (John 14:18)

Consider the office of consoler that Christ our Lord exercises and compare it with the way in which friends are wont to console each other. (Sp. Ex. #224)

Here it will be to ask for the grace to be glad and rejoice intensely because of the great joy and the glory of Christ Our Lord. (Sp. Ex. #221)

Waiting in Emptiness

It would be wonderful if we could discern a pattern to the resurrection appearances of Christ, but we cannot. They move beyond the limits of our imagination. When we enter the stories themselves in a contemplative way, we discover that they stretch our imagination by constantly surprising us and by inviting us to deeper and unsuspected intimacies with God.

One such story is the first resurrection account in John's gospel. A woman who had been exorcised by Jesus and had become one of his close followers comes to the tomb. Seeing that the stone has been taken away from the entrance, she runs and tells Peter and John. They go to the tomb, see that what she has said is true, and return home. She, however, stays there weeping and looking into the empty tomb. As she turns from the tomb, she sees someone she mistakes for the gardener, and asks him where

the body has gone. The stranger says her name, "Mary," and she recognizes him as the Christ. She then holds onto him so tightly that he says, "Don't hold onto me so hard, but go to the others and tell them, 'I am ascending to my Father and to your Father, to my God and your God.'" She returns to the disciples, tells them what had happened, and repeats his words to her.

Being Found by What We Lost

In this poignant scene of seeking and finding the beloved, of embrace and mission, we find a sequence of events that transforms our own experience of intimacy with Jesus. He has attracted our attention, he has rescued us, we follow him and become part of his life as he becomes part of our life. Then that relationship is destroyed when he is betrayed and killed. In our sorrow we wait by the tomb, but that in itself does not give life. As we linger there, things come to us – images and feelings of consolation – but we cannot name them properly because we are still caught up in the world of death.

Only when these things strike our sense of identity, which lies deeper than our grief, do we discover what has greeted us. It is the Christ! It is hard to believe – the one we loved and lost returns to us transformed. We fall into the arms of the beloved. But the story does not end there. For that love to be fulfilled, both of us must return to the source of our loving. The path seems to diverge again. Jesus must return to the Father, and we need to create the community that bears his name in its return to the Father. The love we share does not disappear so soon after being found again. There will be a new way of loving – not between individuals and God, but rather in community. The community called Church is the embodied presence of that shared presence of love. As we struggle to understand it, all this might sound like science fiction. But it really isn't. It is simply the nature of love becoming more and more manifest. If we can stay with this state of consolation of being loved, the path to community will unfold. New dimensions of intimacy open to us.

Love does not abandon anyone, and so Jesus in his resurrected state comes back to those he loves. It is significant to note that, in the scripture stories, Jesus does not show himself in his resurrected state to any but those whom he loves and who love him. Those who do not love cannot see love. They always read it as something else. But to those who love and who seek love, love comes. One of the gifts of the resurrection is that it can open us to dimensions of love that we did not think possible. Here, in Mary's loving, we experience someone who had thought she had reached the limits of love. She grieved the end of that love by going to the tomb. To her surprise, she finds it open and empty. On our spiritual journey to love, we come to the stage of emptiness and are asked, as in the final contemplation of the Third Week, to wait in that emptiness. When Mary waits, the Christ comes to her.

Waiting in the emptiness, as Christ experienced on the cross, removes all our preconceptions of how love can present itself. So when the Christ appears to Mary, she does not recognize him. She supposes he is a gardener. Christ does not appear in the drama of worldly power with pomp and circumstance and special effects. He does not seek to impress or to terrorize. He appears in a simple, ordinary way. Resurrection comes in simple, ordinary ways. When we are moving through mourning, we notice signs of new life in our ability to appreciate, perhaps even without knowing it, simple, everyday things. As you journey through the day with this contemplation, try to be conscious of the effect in your life of the little things that give you joy.

Named by God

Jesus goes even further in this manifestation with his friend Mary: he calls her by name. In grief we often lose a sense of who we are; we have entered a new territory where everything is strange and we have even become strangers to ourselves. But when we are found by love, we are brought back to ourselves, and to a new sense of ourselves and of life. This is the gift Jesus gives Mary when he acknowledges her and calls her by name. She responds by recognizing him. This is what the gift of love does – it enables us to recognize others for who they really are. To be called by God in love gives us our identity. To respond to that love changes our perspective and our hearts. We see with the eyes of love, and we see God in the commonplace. What before seemed insignificant now becomes worthy of notice and contemplation. When we enter into that state of contemplation, which is not reserved for prayer periods only, we discover God in all things. Here Mary discovers Jesus and embraces him.

We need to remain in that embrace and to allow that healing touch to transform us. When lovers embrace, they open their spirits to each other in mutual vulnerability. That openness has the effect of giving us courage and a sense of connection that remain even when we are physically separated from the beloved. We see this in little children who are loved. They are not fearful and insecure, but are filled with a sense of wonder and creativity. The same thing happens when people fall in love, and when we are touched by resurrection. We fall in love with God again in a whole new way. Like Mary Magdalene, we are tempted to hold onto that love in ways that are appropriate only to a past life. The new life to which love calls us fills us with a sense of our true identity, of wonder and of creativity. We find ourselves responding to that love as Mary did, by wanting to share it with whomever she encounters. That love does not turn us in on ourselves. It turns us to the world and to those who need to know the good news that love is stronger than death, that the gift of forgiveness is more powerful than any alienation, and that life is more creative than evil. It is this message that Mary carries back to the disciples when she tells them that she has seen and touched the risen Christ.

Always Going Home

Christ's journey, however, is not over. In sharing his resurrected life, he begins his return to the Father when, in him, all things will be restored to the Father. We become his risen body, on our own spiritual journey to the fullness of life. Christ himself returns to the Father. Love responds to love, is attracted to love, and becomes united to love. He goes before us to assure us of where we, too, are going. He does not only show us that death is not the end of life, he also desires us to know that life leads to more and fuller life. Death is just a door that opens to the fullness of life. In this contemplation, we are given not only an experience, but a direction and a gift that opens to broader and deeper dimensions of love and intimacy. We must sit and allow that gift to come to us and open us, so that we may open it.

Questions for Prayer and Reflection

1. What gift was given to you in this contemplation? How do you feel about that gift? How do you receive it? How does it change the way you see yourself, others or the world?

2. How do the prayer periods in this contemplation stretch and liberate your imagination?

3. Have you ever mistaken love for something else? How did you find out what it really was?

4. What happens these days when you find a quiet place and dare to let your deepest longings for love rise in prayer? How are they answered?

5. When you look back over your life, what happens to you when you dare to love?

6. Do you feel that sense of daring now? For what?

7. Where does your creativity come from?

8. What causes you to wonder in delight? Do you think of these as manifestations of resurrection? Do you allow yourself the time to savour these moments? What happens when you do?

9. If you were to examine your life, or even the past few days, looking for those moments of wonder, what do you find? What do those moments tell you?

10. In your conversations after the prayer with the Father, Jesus, or Mary – or all three – what comes across or stays with you?

The Movie
I'VE LOVED YOU SO LONG

Director: Philippe Claudel (2008 – 117 mins.)
Starring: Kristin Scott Thomas, Elsa Zylberstein, Serge Hazanavicius

1. Synopsis

Juliette Fontaine has spent fifteen years behind bars for murder. She is released on probation and goes to live with her sister Léa and her family, whom she hasn't seen since he went to prison. Indeed, she had no visitors at all, and has become bitter and a recluse. Re-establishing relationships with her family does not come easily.

Note: If at all possible, watch the subtitled version. Much of an actor's art lies in the use of voice to express emotion, mood, and character. Dubbed movies can never have the full impact of the original.

2. About the Movie

1. "Redemption shows up reliably in the form of a sensitive single male who has taught in prisons and knows how Juliette feels; a stroke-ridden, yet somehow serene granddad, who provides her with the quiet solitude she craves; and the requisite bad news that will shock her into sharing a secret that neatly slips the burden of guilt off her shoulders." (Ella Taylor, *The Village Voice*, October 22, 2008)

   How do the young man and the grandfather bring redemption to Juliette? And what is the secret that Juliette has to share? Why does the sharing of this secret help her to get rid of her guilt?

2. "For all its moodiness, despair and disconnect, *I've Loved You So Long* is all about acknowledging human error and embracing ties – to family and life – that can't be undone." (Paula Nechak, *Seattle Post-Intelligencer*, November 6, 2008)

   What is it about family and life in this film that make them such powerful ties? And what happens when Juliette does embrace these ties?

3. "Out of either pride or abjection … she refuses to solicit sympathy, or to offer reciprocal, reassuring warmth when it comes her way. But as Juliette makes her way from one day to the next – picking up a stranger for sex, looking for a job, forming tentative bonds with her nieces and with Luc's father, figuring out how to be friends with her needy, nervous sister – it becomes clear that the film is, at bottom, a story of rehabilitation and healing. This kind of narrative is familiar enough, and so are the risks of sentimental talk-show piety associated with it. Luckily, Ms. Scott Thomas's furious honesty rules out easy, unearned redemption, as does the film's tough-minded resistance to the temptations of melodrama." (A.O. Scott, *The New York Times*, October 24, 2008)

What are the various elements in Juliette's journey to rehabilitation and healing? What do each of the major characters in the film contribute to this?

3. The Relationship of the Movie to the Theme of the Exercise

1. The Exercise tells us that it is the nature of love not to abandon anyone. Juliette chooses life as one who in a previous life destroyed all that she loved. The film shows the very human struggle to overcome the self-doubt that is the consequence of such an act. The film reveals Juliette's inability to deal with the suffering of the son she loved. Her life has taught her that it is better not to love. Her return to love, aware of its dangers, and her opening to suffering again in a life beyond her control shape Juliette's road to Emmaus. Who are the people – what are the events – that show Juliette that she has not been abandoned?

2. "Despite the evident tension between the two sisters and between Scott Thomas and Zylberstein's family, *I've Loved You So Long* effectively sublimates the drama until one volcanic eruption towards the end, when everything is laid out on the table. Claudel's restraint gives the scene tremendous power, even while it also raises questions about why Scott Thomas chooses to withhold a secret that might have eased her transition back into the family. Nevertheless, the film deftly sketches a sibling relationship complicated by obligation, guilt, mistrust, and, not least, an abiding love." (Scott Tobias, *The Onion A.V. Club*, October 23, 2008)

How does the love between the two sisters ultimately triumph over all the "obligation, guilt and mistrust"?

4. The Relationship of the Movie to One's Self in the Exercise

1. Love responds to love, is attracted to love and becomes united to love. To whose love does Juliette most respond? Where is there such love in your own life? To whom have you offered love? What has been the result?

2. The Exercise tells us that when lovers embrace they open their spirits to each other in mutual vulnerability. There are many examples of this in the film. How does love in your life make you vulnerable? To what are you vulnerable? What happens as a result of that vulnerability? How does that vulnerability make you feel connected even when you are physically separated from the one you love?

3. To those who love and to those who seek love, love comes. And love is something we all search for in our lives. The main characters in the film are in search of a real love – some desperately, some calmly – and there is a sense that by the end of the movie some of them have found this. In your own life, how often have you sought love? The love of another person? The love of God? Where do you seek such love? And when that love – of another person, of God – does come into your life, what difference does it make to you? As Ignatius would ask: What have you done to seek such love? What are you doing to seek such love? What will you do to seek such love?

272

3rd Exercise

Doubting Thomas

(John 20:19-31)

They said to him, "What must we do, to be doing the works of God?" Jesus answered them, "This is the work of God, that you believe in the one whom he has sent."

(John 6:28-29)

Recall to mind the blessing of creation and redemption, and the special favours I have received. (Sp. Ex. #234)

Here it will be to ask for the grace to be glad and rejoice intensely because of the great joy and the glory of Christ Our Lord. (Sp. Ex. #221)

Fear and Joy

Before the disciples experience the resurrection, they are filled with fear and huddle behind closed doors. In this story, Jesus enters the locked room, wishes them peace, and shows them his pierced hands and side as proof of who he was. Their fear is transformed into joy. In this joy, he breathes the Holy Spirit onto them and missions them to forgive sins. One of the disciples, Thomas, is not there when this happens, and refuses to believe it took place. Eight days later, as they are all gathered again, Jesus reappears. He shows his hands and his side to Thomas, exhorting him to believe. Thomas, transformed by that empirical evidence, believes.

This story opens with Jesus repeating in dramatic fashion the mystery of the Incarnation. In both mysteries, he enters our human world, which is self-enclosed out of fear, and his presence transforms that world. In this resurrection narrative, the disciples are afraid they will be treated as Jesus was by the authorities and the mob. The resurrected Christ does not abandon them in their fear, but enters their little world and wishes them peace. Inasmuch as we become manifestations of the resurrected Christ, we, too, are asked to enter the worlds of fear and self-enclosure and bring a peace that comes from rootedness in the Father's love. That relationship casts out fear. Interestingly, when we do this, we are tested as Christ was tested. We need to show signs that we live out of our relationship with the Father before others will believe us. The most effective sign of this is when, in our suffering, we remain faithful and loving.

When the disciples see the risen Christ, he shows them signs that it is truly he. In our prayer these days, when we might have difficulty believing the resurrection can be present in our lives, we need to ask for that grace of having the risen Christ identify himself to us in ways we can believe. In our ill-conceived pride we might wish that we do not need this, but in our experienced poverty, we know that we do. This shameless petition of the beloved is our prayer for a particular grace. As in any love relationship, we cannot demand that the one we love does what we seek, but we can ask and we can dispose ourselves to receive what we request. The same is true of God. He does not demand that we behave as he wishes, but he asks and disposes himself to receive what we are willing to offer in love.

The Gift of the Spirit

Christ asks that, when we accept the proof that he has risen from the dead, we live as he lived and love as he loved. As he says, "As the Father has sent me, even so do I send you" (John 20:21). But to do this we need the same spirit as the Christ: a spirit of loving reverence for all, of courage and creativity, of joy and compassion. The spirit embodies Christ's relationship with the Father. Christ gave the disciples that relationship and that spirit when "he breathed on them and said to them, 'Receive the Holy Spirit'" (John 20:22).

This action echoes the creation of humans in the book of Genesis. There "the Lord God formed man of dust from the ground and breathed in to his nostrils the breath of life; and man became a living being" (Genesis 2:7). In the scriptures, a human is not body and soul – this is a Greek distinction – but dust animated by the Lord God's breath or spirit. This makes humans living beings. When Christ breathes on the disciples, he creates a new being out of the chaos of their creation. When we enter this contemplation, we dispose ourselves for God to breathe on us and make a us a new creation. We become transformed. We move from fear to love, from self-doubt to self-acceptance, from confusion to creativity. This new creation makes us more like Christ. We find ourselves filled with his spirit, doing what he has been doing in the world: forgiving sins. In the passage from John that we are contemplating, Jesus says, "Receive the Holy Spirit. If you forgive the sins of any they are forgiven; if you retain the sins of any they are retained" (John 20:22-23).

Forgiving Sin

But what does it mean to forgive sins? Maybe it would help if we looked at what sin does. It causes division by setting people against each other and even against themselves. It promotes self-hate and spreads illusions that deceive us about our true nature. It is destructive and does not delight in joy or in celebrating life. It oppresses. To forgive sins, therefore, is to create community and self-acceptance. To forgive is to seek the truth and maintain it. To forgive is to cherish creativity and to celebrate life wherever it may be found. Forgiveness transforms chaos into relationships that foster healing and peace. It liberates the imagination and the spirit. Forgiving grounds us in that constant and compassionate presence of the mystery we call Father. We see that this is what Christ's coming into our world has done for us: when we experience resurrection, we find our new and transformed selves doing the same thing for the world.

Until we experience the risen Christ in our lives, we cannot see how this is possible: all we have to inspire us are the exhausted, pragmatic politics of the world and the tragedies that result. We consider it escapist fantasy to believe otherwise, and we think spiritual maturity means accepting the world as it is and accommodating it. We refuse to believe that we can experience the risen Christ in our prayer. Lest we be hurt or disappointed, we refuse to open ourselves to believe that the Christ desires to come to those who, in their own small ways, love God.

Personal Proof Beyond Disbelief

This is Thomas's problem. He was not with the original eleven when Christ appeared to them in the closed room. He does not think that what they have told him is possible. Yet, in his mercy, Christ appears to Thomas and to the others once again that very next week, in that very same place. He tells Thomas, "Put your finger here, and see my hands; put out your hand and place it in my side; do not be so faithless, but believe" (John 20:21). Jesus does not say, Well, if Thomas does not believe, that is his problem. The Thomas he knows and loves is the Thomas he chose to be his companion. It is this same Thomas who said, when the plots were strong against Jesus, "Let us go up to Jerusalem and die with him." Jesus knows Thomas loves him in his own way. He also knows that Thomas really cannot believe that the Father's love can raise Jesus from the dead, or that Jesus, after all he had been through, including being abandoned by his disciples, would care to return to them if he had indeed been raised from the dead. But Jesus did both things, and here he does one extra thing. He comes back just for Thomas. He gives Thomas the proof he needs to commit himself to that love Jesus offers. And Thomas, in a passionate response, commits himself, crying out, "My Lord and my God!" (John 20:28).

Thomas is like us. When we have been loved beyond our disbelief, we can acknowledge personally and intimately what love is. In this contemplation, we ask for that grace to experience this personal love that God has for each of us in ways that move us beyond our disbelief into a new way of seeing and being that makes us creative, compassionate, and joyful.

Questions for Prayer and Reflection

1. When you entered this contemplation, what were the elements of personal surprise? How did they manifest themselves? How did you respond?

2. How did you experience the risen Christ in this contemplation?

3. What is the relationship between your fear and your lack of belief? Can you see in your history where that fear shaped the way you believe?

4. Where did that fear come from? Can you invite the risen Christ to enter into that fear, or those areas and sources of fear? What happens when you do this in prayer?

5. How do you respond to the experience of the risen Christ in your prayer?

6. What difficulties do you have in forgiving yourself, others and the world?

7. What happens when you ask that the breath of Christ be blown on those areas? How do you experience that breath?

8. In what ways are you like Thomas? What happens when you contemplate the Thomas incident in these prayer periods? What happens to the Thomas aspects of yourself?

9. In your conversations with God, Jesus, or Mary – or all three – after the prayer, what surfaces that is significant?

10. What is the next step in your growth to spiritual freedom after these prayer periods? What will you do, concretely and practically, to facilitate that next step?

The Movie
ONCE

Director: John Carney (2006 – 85 mins.)
Starring: Glen Hansard, Marketa Irglova, Hugh Walsh

1. Synopsis

A Dublin guitarist/singer-songwriter makes a living by fixing vacuum cleaners in his dad's Hoover repair shop by day, and singing and playing for money on the Dublin streets by night. A Czech pianist does odd jobs by day and takes care of her mom and her daughter by night. The two musicians get to know each other when she helps him make a demo to take to London, where he hopes to get a record deal. As they work, they reveal their love for each other through music.

2. About the Movie

1. "Just about everyone with a heartbeat has had this tingly experience. You're at a movie, and a song, as if by magic, breaks through the surface of the drama. Suddenly, you're no longer sitting and watching – you're soaring. That's the feeling you get at the 1954 *A Star Is Born*, or at *Moulin Rouge*, and you can get it, as well, from naturalistic movies that are built like musicals, such as *Nashville*, *Saturday Night Fever*, or *Sid & Nancy*. But until *Once*, which was written and directed by John Carney, I'm not sure that I'd ever seen a small-scale, nonstylized, kitchen-sink drama in which the songs take on the majesty and devotion of a musical dream" (Owen Gleiberman, *Entertainment Weekly*, May 16, 2007)

Which movie musical has made you "soar"? What does "soaring" entail for you? The musicals to which he refers are mainly big scale films; this film is not. What is meant by "kitchen-sink" drama films? How does this apply here?

2. "John Carney's sadly beautiful *Once* is a musical for people who only think they hate musicals, and not just because it boasts virtues seldom associated with the genre, such as realism, intimacy, and low-key verisimilitude. Musical-bashers often complain about the suspension of disbelief required for spectacles in which characters spontaneously break out into song-and-dance routines, but *Once's* songs are integrated into the story so organically that it'd be unrealistic if the characters weren't largely immersed in them. They are musicians, after all, and the songs they sing say more about their characters than any monologue possibly could." (Nathan Rabin, *The Onion A.V. Club*, May 17, 2007)

Choose any two songs from this film and talk about what they say about the characters. If their feelings were to be expressed in a monologue, how different would your emotional reaction be? Why do most musicals have difficulties being real, being intimate, and not needing to rely a "suspension of disbelief"?

3. "While all of this may sound forced on paper, it does not play that way on screen for a pair of interlocking reasons. For one thing, *Once's* inevitably romantic plot is modern enough to shrewdly avoid ever playing out the way audiences will anticipate. For another, the music is so rich and completely satisfying and the characters so appealing 'Once' makes us believe that this is all happening right in front of our eyes. We fall for each of these young people at the precise moment they are falling for each other, and what could be better than that?" (Kenneth Turan, *Los Angeles Times*, May 16, 2007)

How did you anticipate that the film would end? How appealing did you find the two young lovers? Did you "fall" for them as they did for each other? Why? Why not?

3. The Relationship of the Movie to the Theme of the Exercise

1. Sin fragments and causes division by setting people against each other and even against themselves – so the Exercise tells us. How is this seen in this movie? What is the "sin" here?

2. The sin in the world is destructive and does not delight in joy or in celebrating life. It oppresses. It oppresses in every aspect of our lives. How does sin oppress the two young lovers in this film?

3. As the Exercise says, to forgive sin is to create community and self-acceptance. How is this evident at the end of this movie? For the boy? For the girl?

4. The Relationship of the Movie to One's Self in the Exercise

1. Sin promotes self-hate and spreads illusions that deceive us about out true nature. It is clear how this works in the lives of the two young people in this film. Where does this take place in your life? What can you do to change this – to become what God calls you to be?

2. Why is the title *Once* important to understanding the film? What is the role of music in the film? What do we find in our present moment that gives life and hope? Do we see life out of our hurts, or out of our hopes? Or out of both? How do they affect each other and our general perspective? Which one usually wins out? What are our false expectations of resurrection that are not borne out in the gospels, in the lives of those who live in intimacy with the risen Christ, and in our own resurrection experiences? How do our encounters with love help us to accept our brokenness and to live creatively in it?

3. As we enter this Exercise, we enter the process of being transformed. We have seen in the film how the main characters move from fear to love; from self-doubt to self-acceptance; from confusion to creativity. How is this taking place in your life at this point in the Exercises?

4th Exercise
The Road to Emmaus
(Luke 24)

Make me know your ways, O Lord;
Teach me your paths.
Lead me in your truth and teach me,
For you are the God of my salvation;
For you I wait all day long.
Be mindful of your mercy, O Lord, and of your steadfast love,
For they have been of old.
According to your steadfast love remember me,
For your goodness' sake, O Lord. (Psalm 24:4-7)

This is a cry of wonder accompanied by surging emotion as I pass in review all creatures. How is it that they have permitted me to live and have sustained me in life!
(Sp. Ex. #60)

Here it will be to ask for the grace to be glad and rejoice intensely because of the great joy and the glory of Christ Our Lord. (Sp. Ex. #221)

Moving Beyond Our Fantasies

As we continue to contemplate the resurrection, we find that our joy becomes more integrated into our sense of self. That transformation allows us to become even more open to the mystery that is the journey of our life. We tend to understand this mystery by the story we tell ourselves about our life. Resurrection changes this story. We cannot change it ourselves. In fact, when we try to, we end up with fantasy. There are many kinds of fantasy: simple escapist fantasy, untouched by existential reality, where we can daydream about perpetual youth and riches, or about utopian societies where all are politically equal; modified forms of fantasy, such as a perfect, anxiety-free existence fuelled by the narcotics of drugs, ambition, or social conditioning; and ideological and religious fantasies. In fact, we feed on fantasy. Sometimes we think we are converted, but all we have done is substitute one fantasy for another.

There comes a time when we discover that the fantasies we have lived out of are unable to bear the burden of brute reality. The large systems in which we might have trusted and even may have devoted our lives to maintaining break down. We find ourselves slipping between the gaps of their supposedly impermeable surfaces. We are hurled back into chaos and uncertainty. We suffer from anxiety and a sense of meaninglessness. We hold on to lesser things, knowing their inadequacy, just for the sake of holding on to something. We sometimes guard those things — hobbies, jobs, political affiliations, ethnic partisanship — fiercely and blindly, knowing that without them we would be lost. We even claim that such commitment gives us access to God. One of the fantasies we have is about God and how God operates and is present in the world. When bad things happen, we ask, "How can God allow this?" Unless we find a suitable answer to that question, we abandon God. That is not a bad thing, surprisingly, because what we are abandoning is not God, but a fantasy of God. Our spiritual drive to seek the true God – our deepest desire – takes over and we begin a spiritual journey that moves beyond our fantasies. We encounter the God who is always coming towards us and walking with us in our pain.

After the celebration of Passover and the Sabbath, two disciples of Jesus are walking to Emmaus, about 20 kilometres outside Jerusalem. They discuss similar fantasies about Jesus. "We had hoped he was the one to redeem Israel" (Luke 24:21). Instead of the political hero they wanted, they got a crucified prophet. In their disillusionment, even when they heard the reports of Jesus' resurrection, they could not grasp its import. For them, it was just anecdotal data. It made no sense in the way they viewed the world.

But something happens to them. On their way back to Emmaus, they encounter the risen Jesus but do not recognize him, because they see through the eyes of their fantasy. Jesus unravels the material of their fantasy – in their case, the Scriptures – and reinterprets it in light of his relationship to the Father. This allows him to show the path of the Messiah as depicted in their sacred writings. He explains that the Christ was destined to suffer and then enter into his glory. When they hear these things, their deepest desire is felt and held, given expression and answered. They move from being despondent to being inflamed in the spirit. They reflect, "Did not our hearts burn within us while he talked to us on the road, while he opened to us the scriptures?" (Luke 24:32).

Reimagining God

Even though we live in a resurrection context, we, too, need to look at our mistaken expectations of how God should behave. Such expectations cause us to miss the resurrection experience that is present to us even at this moment; we need to ask to have the scriptures of our lives and of our religion opened to us so we may see who Christ is for us here and now. To help us in this process we might, in this prayerful contemplation, imagine walking with Jesus on the road to Emmaus, and bring to him all the areas in the world and in our lives where we do not see the merciful presence of God. We need him to open our hearts, our minds, and our eyes to him.

Journeying with God

In the Emmaus story, this is exactly what Christ does. The two disciples so share his spirit that when they arrive at their little town as evening falls, and he appears to be going further on, they ask him to spend the night with them. As he blesses and breaks the bread at supper, they recognize him, and he disappears from their midst. The journey they have made with him changes them; they now share his same spirit. They have become community, which is manifest in their desire to share their home and their meal with him. Through this sharing, they recognize him in the breaking of the bread – the same act of community that he had enacted at the Last Supper – saying that what they shared then was his body. In their new story, the two disciples become the continuing body of Christ on earth.

In their transformation, they do exactly what Christ has done to them. Even though it is night and they are tired, they set out at once for Jerusalem to tell the others what has happened. While they are gathered as community, Christ appears to all of them, "and while they still disbelieved for joy, and wondered, he said to them, 'Have you anything here to eat?' They gave him a piece of broiled fish and he took it and ate before them" (Luke 24:41-43).

The joy the two disciples felt on the road to Emmaus increases as they share their experiences, and in that community Christ comes. His reappearance increases their joy so much, they cannot believe such a thing is possible. To prove he is not a ghost, the Christ eats a piece of fish. When they accept that it is truly him, he missions them to continue his work of reconciling all to each other in the building up of community.

The Path of Joy

As we enter more and more deeply into this contemplation, we discover that the joy we experience opens up to more and deeper joy, and that this deepening joy comes about by the creation of community. In the gospel story, the two disciples encounter the risen Christ and become joyful. To share this joy, they return to the other disciples with the good news. The larger community is missioned to share this joy. That path of joy extends from those two to the rest of the apostles and through these, in mission, to the whole world. That path becomes possible when the disciples accept the reality of a Christ who, through journeying into suffering and death, has risen. He witnesses, with his very life, to the reality of a love that is not fantasy. The compassionate mercy of God that embraces each and every one of us creates an almost unbearable intimacy. If we undertake that journey to Emmaus with our own broken illusions, we experience the growing joy that transforms us, and, through us, transforms the whole world.

Questions for Prayer and Reflection

1. What fantasies did you have about God?

2. What were the most significant moments for you in this contemplation? Why?

3. As you walked with the risen Christ through the path of your life, what was explained to you that is helpful for you now?

4. Think of the community of people who are important to you. How do you share life with them? In what way is this a manifestation of the risen Christ?

5. How does this contemplation address the suffering in your life?

6. The contemplations of the Fourth Week invite you to enter into a relationship with the risen Christ and to experience how that intimacy opens up your life. As you reflect on these contemplations, how is your life being opened up?

7. How can you distinguish between fantasy and experiences of the resurrected Christ? How do suffering, forgiveness, community, and an ongoing relationship with the compassionate mystery of the Father help you learn to make that distinction? What happens when you ask the Christ to help you make the distinction? What response do you get?

8. What arose from the conversation you had at the end of the prayer with the Father, Jesus, or Mary?

The Movie
THE DIVING BELL AND THE BUTTERFLY

Director: Julian Schnabel (2007 – 112 mins.)
Starring: Mathieu Amalric, Emmanuelle Seigner

1. Synopsis

This is the true story of *Elle* editor Jean-Dominique Bauby. In 1995, when he was just 43, he had a major stroke. The only part of his body he could move was his left eye. Amazingly, he used that one eye to dictate his memoir through blinking. He eloquently described his inner world and how it felt to be a prisoner of his own body, as well as telling stories about places he had never been to except in his imagination.

Note: If at all possible, watch the subtitled version. Much of an actor's art lies in the use of voice to express emotion, mood, and character. Dubbed movies can never have the full impact of the original.

2. About the Movie

1. "The picture is so imaginatively made, so attuned to sensual pleasure, so keyed in to the indescribable something that makes life life, that it speaks of something far more elemental than mere filmmaking skill: This is what movies, at their best, can be." (Stephanie Zacharek, *Salon*, November 30, 2007)

What do you think Zacharek is speaking about when she says this film is keyed in "to the indescribable something that makes life, life"? And how do you see this exemplified in this film?

2. "The adjective 'inspirational' doesn't do justice to the quality of Schnabel's film. *The Diving Bell and the Butterfly* isn't about feeling better about terrible things, but about cherishing imagination as the force that sustains life." (Liam Lacey, *The Globe and Mail*, December 23, 2007)

What adjective would you choose to "do justice to the quality of Schnabel's film"? What elements of this film led you to choose that particular adjective?

3. "Bauby invented his own metaphor for the reality of his body held prisoner. 'My diving bell becomes less oppressive, and my mind takes flight like a butterfly,' he wrote. 'There is so much to do.' This movie does what Bauby wanted to, with appropriate panache." (Lisa Schwarzbaum, *Entertainment Weekly*, November 28, 2007)

What is that that Bauby wants to do? How does the medium of film allow the director to show us what Bauby can only describe in his book? How successfully does director Schnabel capture the "much to do" of Bauby?

3. The Relationship of the Movie to the Theme of the Exercise

1. The Exercise tells us that we understand the mystery that is the journey of our life by the story we tell ourselves about our life. Resurrection changes that story. When we try to change that story ourselves, we end up in one of the following fantasies:

   • a simple escapist fantasy where we can dream of perpetual youth and riches or of an utopian society;

   • modified forms of fantasy where there is an anxiety-free existence fuelled by drugs, ambition, or social conditioning;

   • ideological and religious fantasies.

   Does Bauby's life after the accident fit into any of these fantasies? Why? Why not? Is his fantasy his reality? Or is his reality his fantasy?

2. It would be wonderful if we could discern a pattern to the resurrection appearances of Christ. We cannot. They move beyond the limits of our imagination. When we enter the stories in a contemplative way, we discover that they stretch our imagination by constantly surprising us and by inviting us to deeper and unsuspected intimacies with God. Something similar happens to Bauby. Bauby's imagination and memory are far from paralyzed. With his mind, Bauby discovers he can go anywhere, do anything, be with anyone. His fantasies begin with whimsical relish but quickly become trips into esoteric splendor and sublime tranquility. Recall some scenes that show these changes taking place in Bauby. When does his breakthrough come?

4. The Relationship of the Movie to One's Self in the Exercise

1. The Exercise reminds us that sometimes we think we are converted, but what we have done is substituted one fantasy for another. Towards the end of the movie, it is clear that this has happened to Roy in a very stunning way. Where have you either been tempted to do this or actually done it in your own life?

2. In his journey, Bauby finds that Claude becomes an anchor to him. Her patience helps him open new paths into life, helps him overcome the demons that haunted him. Who is the "Claude" in your life helping you on your spiritual journey to God? What has "Claude" done to help you along in this journey? Have you always been open to "Claude"? If not, what stopped you?

3. At the end of the movie, Bauby has abandoned at last his fantasies, and finds peace and serenity precisely at the moment of his greatest imprisonment. While this is – explicitly – not expressed as being God, it is a place where he can find peace of mind. What fantasy do you have to abandon before you can reach your deepest desire – God?

5th Exercise

Feed My Sheep

(John 21)

For God alone my soul waits in silence;
For my hope is from him.
He only is my rock and my salvation,
My fortress; I shall not be shaken.
On God rests my deliverance and my honour;
My mighty rock, my refuge is God.   (Psalm 62:5-7)

I will ponder with great affection how much God our
Lord has done for me, and how much He has given me of
what He possesses.   (Sp. Ex. #234)

Here it will be to ask for the grace to be glad and rejoice
intensely because of the great joy and the glory of Christ
Our Lord.   (Sp. Ex. #221)

The Mission

Even though Jesus' companions now know that he is risen and is present to them, they do not know when and how he will appear to them. This seemingly haphazard way of relating disconcerts them. In retrospect, we see that he has breathed on them and given them his mission and spirit: now they need to learn to live out of that mission and spirit. If he remains with them, they will depend on him and not on the spirit, which is his intimate relationship with the Father.

In the last chapter of John's gospel, Peter and the others wait for Jesus. He does not appear. During the night, Peter decides to go fishing, and the rest go along. When morning breaks, they see someone on the shore. He asks them affectionately if they have caught anything; they say no. He suggests casting the net on the other side of the boat: when they do so, they catch an incredible number of fish. Realizing it is the Lord on the shore, John tells Peter, who jumps overboard and swims to the beach. When the rest arrive, they find that Jesus has prepared fish and bread for them on a charcoal fire.

Like the disciples, we cannot predict how and when the risen Christ will appear to us. We realize that Jesus has risen from the dead and that, in some profound way, he is with us, even though we do not experience him all the time. We cannot compel him to remain with us. Like Mary Magdalene, we want to cling to him, but he says, "Do not cling to me." We feel we are not yet ready to strike out on our own, to trust ourselves as he obviously trusts us. But we know we can't just mope. Life must go on. We pick up our lives and our jobs and continue. When we do that, conscious of how inadequate it all is, he comes and offers, within our daily lives, even more than we can imagine. With this we are fed for the next step.

Beyond Friendship to Love

In that next step, Peter and Jesus go walking. Jesus asks Peter, "Do you love me?" He uses the Greek word *agape* (a-ga-pay), which means a self-sacrificing love that gives all of life meaning. Peter replies, "Yes, Lord, you know I love you." But the word John uses for Peter's answer is *philia*, meaning friendship. Jesus responds, "Feed my lambs." Again Jesus asks Peter the same question using the same words, and again Peter replies using the same words. Jesus says, "Tend my sheep." The third time Jesus asks the question, "Do you love me?" he uses the word Peter uses: *philia*. It is as if he is saying, "Are we really friends, then, if not intimates?" Peter cries because he knows what he is capable of and what he is not capable of. He replies that they are indeed friends, and Jesus says, "Feed my sheep." There is a movement in Jesus' questions in terms of Peter's capabilities. The difference between feeding lambs and tending sheep is that lambs are born in enclosures that protect them; sheep are left out in the open. Easily excitable and somewhat stupid, these animals can forage for themselves, but need to be protected from thieves and beasts of prey. That third mission Jesus gives Peter is to not only shepherd but also to nourish Jesus' flock. In accepting and living out this mission, Peter moves from fisherman to shepherd, from being Jesus' friend to sharing his spirit, from *philia* to *agape*. This is his baptism, and it changes his life. In that journey to intimacy, he discovers a love that carries him to a death similar to the Christ's.

In our journey through the resurrection, we are also called to move from being friends of Christ to sharers in his spirit and mission. We discover what it means to die to ourselves, to take up our cross daily and to follow Jesus' path. Opening the gift of the resurrection does not necessarily make our lives easier, and we may be tempted to stop at any part of the journey. But if we walk that journey, even as we grow in freedom, we find that our liberty is constrained. We become committed to a way of life that demands a practical and spiritual asceticism. We ask ourselves if our daily lives bring us closer to God. This examination calls us to adopt what brings life and to avoid what leads to despair. We realize that we are not at liberty to do and act as we please: even though our lives are more our own, they are at the same time less and less so.

Sinking into Selflessness

This rootedness that allows self-transcendence is common in the traditions of the spiritual path we walk. In Buddhism, for instance, Dogen writes, "To study the Way is to study the self, to study the self is to forget the self, to forget the self is to awaken into the ten thousand things." The asceticism of living the resurrection calls for a deep entry into ourselves, to the point where we realize our basic emptiness. Through that emptiness, at their own time, the energies of the resurrection arise. Their rising carries us beyond ourselves into the work of redeeming creation. That work also requires asceticism – the asceticism of self-forgetfulness that promotes joy and community. As the medieval Christian mystic Meister Eckhart points out, "The more deeply we are our true selves, the less self is in us." This is what Jesus tells Peter on their morning walk after Peter commits himself and receives his mission: "Truly, truly, I say to you, when you were young you girded yourself and walked where you would; but when you are old, you will stretch out your hands and another will gird you and carry you where you do not wish to go" (John 21:18). Accepting and opening the gift of the risen Christ carries us beyond ourselves into an afflicted world that cries out to be saved. The cost is no less than everything – even our very lives, as we may imagine them.

Why do it, then? Because heaven is sharing the vision and the work and the ministry of the Father. It is a way of seeing and labouring and being here in the world that unites us through space and time with all those forces that unceasingly build up a new creation.

In this new creation, God is all in all, and everything and everyone has been healed and transformed by love, celebrating that love in every moment of their lives. Yes, this is hard work, and we experience the suffering of a creation being transformed, but we also know the profound and abiding delight that comes from being rooted in love and being creative through that loving.

If we are honest with ourselves, we can see how much we are like Peter in our relationship with Jesus. We would love to be better companions of Christ, but we are aware of our weakness in the face of suffering. We can offer only friendship. Still, Christ sees what we need, and he knows what we can do when we are given what we need. He knows we need the Spirit; when we are given that Spirit, we become his continuing resurrected presence on earth. For now, that is enough.

Questions for Prayer and Reflection

1. How are you living these days with your prayer experiences?

2. How do they shape each other?

3. This contemplation has three parts: the frustrating evening of fishing; the breakfast with Jesus; the missioning of Peter. Which part engaged your attention most? What does that suggest to you? Return to that moment and let it engage you again. What happens?

4. How does this contemplation adjust the way you might have thought about living the resurrection? What questions does it raise for you? How will you deal with those questions?

5. In what ways is the resurrection changing your life? What do you need in order to live those changes in wholesome ways?

6. How do you experience the difference between being a friend of Jesus and a lover of Jesus? What do you need to ask him to do to help you be one with his spirit?

7. The gospel story contains other elements not touched upon here. Do any of them lead you to a closer understanding of yourself and a closer identification with the risen Christ? What does that tell you about yourself and about the way God sees you?

8. Do you think Peter feels guilty during his conversation with Jesus? Do you think Jesus is trying to make him feel guilty? Why is guilt not helpful in loving someone? In what ways does your perception of God make you feel guilty? Do you use guilt to distance yourself from God? How does God respond to you when you are in that state?

9. How does God ask you to feed his lambs and his sheep?

10. How do you feel about being asked to share God's creativity and love?

11. In your conversations at the end of the prayer with the Father, Jesus, or Mary, what do you discuss? What do you hear?

12. Can you stay in the moments of gratitude that this contemplation and its repetitions create in you? How?

The Movie
WATER

Director: Deepa Mehta (2005 – 117 mins.)
Starring: Lisa Ray, Sarala, Seema Biswas, Ronica Sajnani

1. Synopsis

In 1938, Gandhi's party is making inroads for women's rights. Chuyia, a child already married but living with her parents, becomes a widow. By tradition, she is unceremoniously left at a bare and impoverished widows' ashram beside the Ganges during monsoon season. The ashram's leader pimps out Kalyani, a young and beautiful widow, for household funds. Narayan, a follower of Gandhi, falls in love with her. The ashram's moral centre is Shakuntala, deeply religious but conflicted about her fate.

Note: If at all possible, watch the subtitled version. Much of an actor's art lies in the use of voice to express emotion, mood, and character. Dubbed movies can never have the full impact of the original.

2. About the Movie

1. "Mehta never preaches but instead tells a story of intertwining strands in a wholly compelling manner. *Water*, set in the British colonial India of 1938, is as beautiful as it is harrowing, its idyllic setting beside the sacred Ganges River contrasting with the widows' oppressive existence as outcasts. The film seethes with anger over their plight yet never judges, and possesses a lyrical, poetical quality. Just like the Ganges, life goes on flowing, no matter what. Mehta sees her people in the round, entrapped and blinded by a cruel and outmoded custom dictated by ancient religious texts but sustained more often by a family's desire to relieve itself of the economic burden of supporting widows. As a result, she is able to inject considerable humor in her stunningly perceptive and beautifully structured narrative. *Water* emerges as a film of extraordinary richness and complexity." (Kevin Thomas, *Los Angeles Times*, April 28, 2008)

    What are some examples of the ways in which Mehta presents the plight of the widows without preaching and with the use of humour?

2. Deepa Mehta said that she removed much dialogue when she revised the script for *Water* because she wanted the story to be told in images and actions rather than words.

    Which scenes most effectively tell the story in images and actions?

3. In film as in literature and the other arts, the use of water imagery signals many things. There is a contemplative aspect to water – it seems to connect us back to ourselves somehow – and so it is a time and a place where characters go when they want peace. Water might also be used to symbolize a cleansing. All of Fellini's films ended at a body of water and we came to understand that

this meant a change in one of his main characters.

What does water symbolize for the various characters in this film – for Kalyani, Narayan, Chuyia, Shakuntula, Gulabi?

3. The Relationship of the Movie to the Theme of the Exercise

1. The Exercise points out two different types of love:

   • *Agape* = a self-sacrificing love that gives all of life meaning.

   • *Philia* = friendship

   What kind of love does Shakuntala express towards Chuyia? Do Narayan and Kalyani express for each other?

2. In an interview, Deepa Mehta said, "The main protagonist of *Water* has always been Shakuntala. She accepts her lot in life and she's comfortable with herself. It's the core of her faith which she has questions about, and those questions become really big questions, and that's the journey …. You know that conversation between the priest and Shakuntala towards the end of the film where the priest says that Gandhi's one of the few men in the world who acts on his conscience? Shakuntala asks him, 'What if our conscience conflicts with our faith?' That for me is the crux of the whole film, what *Water* is about. It's about the conflict of conscience and faith." (interviewed by John Pungente for *Scanning the Movies*, June 2005)

   How does Mehta present this conflict in this film?

3. When Shakuntala takes Chuyia to the train station, Gandhi says, "My dear brothers and sisters, for a long time I thought that God is truth. But today I know that truth is God. The pursuit of truth is invaluable for me. I trust it will be the same for you."

   How are these statements different from the other religious explanations she has heard? How do they help her make sense of her life? How do they influence her handing Chuyia to Narayan?

4. The Relationship of the Movie to One's Self in the Exercise

1. The Exercise speaks of sinking into selflessness. The film has many examples of this: consider the actions of Shakuntala and those of Kalyani.

   Where in your own life are you sinking into selflessness? If the answer is "nowhere," then why not? What can you or will you do to change that?

2. In the Exercises we learn that, even though our lives are more our own, they are also less and less so. We see examples of this in the Widow House. How is this true at this point in your life?

3. The films offers us many examples of people called to be friends only. Christ calls you to share in his spirit and in his mission. How does he call you to share in his spirit? In his mission? And what is your response?

6th Exercise

The Ascension
(Luke 24:44-52; Acts 1:1-11)

Jesus: "I do not pray for these only, but also for those who believe in me through their word, that they may all be one; even as you, Father, are in me, and I in you, that they may also be in us." (John 17:20-1)

Reflect how God dwells in creatures. (Sp. Ex. #235)

Here it will be to ask for the grace to be glad and rejoice intensely because of the great joy and the glory of Christ Our Lord. (Sp. Ex. #221)

Our Mystical Life

We come from God and we return to God. We know this is true, but we do not know exactly how it happens. We live day by day, we have projects and long-term plans, we have a general direction to our lives. Depending on the decisions we make, we can either aid or hinder the community of God's people. Underneath this sense of identity are the larger dynamics of our clan, our society, our culture. These also have projects and orientations, and play themselves out more or less unconsciously in our lives. But pervading all these, rooting and transcending them, are the creating energies of God, present in and working in everything and everyone to bring us to ever fuller and more joyful dimensions of being with God. This will not cease until all becomes all in God.

We start this journey even before we are born, and we continue it even after our bodies have died. In this journey, we imitate the one made by Christ, the Second Person of the Trinity, who became human, died, rose from the dead, and returned to the Father. When we contemplate Christ's return to his Father as we pray on the Ascension, we enter into the dynamics of a mutual love relationship that reaches through death to achieve a union of intimacy and creativity big enough to encompass the whole of creation. This is our entry into a life of mysticism that is our true nature. But how do we enter into that mysticism and experience it in our own prayer? First, we participate in the story of the Ascension.

In the story in Acts, Jesus led his disciples to Mount Olivet after proving that he had risen in his body from death and after promising to send them the Holy Spirit. On this mountain he was lifted from their sight. As they gazed into the sky, they noticed two men in white, who informed them that the Christ would return the same way he left – in glory.

Claiming Our Deepest Desire

Entering the contemplation, we can experience the joy of the resurrected Christ's return to the Father and the joy of the Father's reception of his Son. This is the moment when Jesus' deepest desire is answered. Resurrection allows us to admit our deepest desire in all of its raw urgency, because we see in the Father's raising Christ from the dead that that desire is answered. We experience the joy of the resurrection

288

when we let ourselves admit that our deepest desire can and will be answered. What does that desire look like? We desire life – life in all its fullness. We desire that all our hurts be healed and all our joys celebrated in ways that even now we cannot imagine. We desire that the terrors of the world be transformed into ecstasy. We desire that broken relationships be healed, that whatever is oppressed be liberated, and that all see and know and love themselves and all others the way the Father sees and knows and loves all. We desire that we become like God, for we are made in God's image and likeness.

In the contemplation of the Ascension, we experience in prayer Jesus' deepest desire being answered, and we enter into the intimacy of that answering. Here the totality of human love embraces and is embraced by divine love. That totality of human love includes our deepest nature, as well as all the manifestations of love that we have been offered or have desired. As we enter into this contemplation, we can allow ourselves to experience the love we need to be fulfilled. We can allow ourselves to be immersed and embraced by its delight and its joy of finding its beloved. We can experience something of what the Father and the Son experience at that moment.

Leaning into Love

We can also experience, as in any human parting, the sadness that Jesus' companions felt when they saw him leave. This is not the sadness of a broken relationship; their desire is held by the promise of that further gift of the Spirit that Jesus shares with the Father, and by the promise of Jesus' eventual return. We, too, can experience the gift of desire and of anticipation. This is rather like the feelings of a child on Christmas Eve who waits to celebrate Christmas, to receive presents, and to enjoy the gathering of family and friends at Christmas dinner. We can sit with the sense of Jesus' promise, knowing that, even as we have already received more than we expected, what is to be given is more than we can imagine. In that spirit of passionate waiting, we lean into a love that transforms us – body, spirit, and soul. Our bodies in resurrection become as Christ's body did, and so the divine love that embraces us not only liberates our spirit and purifies and redeems our soul, it also reveals to us that our bodies likewise will be glorified, not subject to illness, time, decay and the laws of nature as we now understand them. The energies of the Ascension show us that the body is not left out of our relationship with the Father. What happens to our body is a symbol of the commitment of that love. The love of the Father that calls Christ back to him in his body also calls us back in our body to the same glory that Christ shows.

In our contemplation here, we can experience in our body something of that glory. We know that matter is compressed energy. In resurrection, the matter of the body becomes liberated. In the Ascension, that liberated energy becomes a manifestation of love. As we pray this contemplation on the Ascension, we can pray to experience our bodies as energized into a love liberated for intimacy with the Father and for creative service in the world.

Questions for Prayer and Reflection

1. What were the significant moments of this contemplation for you? How did you experience them? Why were they significant?

2. What does this contemplation reveal to you about the Father's love for you?

3. How does it reveal you to yourself?

4. What does it reveal to you about what your body is capable of being? How does this change your self-image?

5. How do you find yourself leaning into the love that desires you?

6. When you reflect on the journey that is your life, what can you chart as the significant moments that made you more aware that you are loved and capable of loving?

7. What stops you from loving?

8. What do you need to transform those blocks into creativity? What happens when you pray out of that need?

9. In your conversations at the end of the prayer with the Father and with Jesus, what has been given to you?

The Movie
RATATOUILLE

Director: Brad Bird and Jan Pinkava (2007 – 111 mins.)
Starring: Patton Oswalt, Ian Holm, Brian Dennehy, Peter O'Toole

1. Synopsis

Rémy is a young rat in the French countryside who refuses to live by the common definition of how a rat is supposed to see himself and to act. Rather than rooting around in garbage, he desires to live out of his gifts and to be a gourmet chef. Driven from his country life, he is symbolically swept through the sewers and ends up in the Paris of his desires.

2. About the Movie

1. "It's an archetypal story: a young person – rodent – who insists on going his own way in the face of a disapproving dad and a society that can see him in only one role. What makes the tale seem less sentimental, less wearyingly familiar, is the fundamental visceral disconnect of its happiest images: rat in kitchen … rat on stovetop … rat in walk-in fridge with pink nose sniffing food … ewwwww … Brad Bird wrote and directed *Ratatouille* and tops his previous work. Since his work includes *The Iron Giant* and *The Incredibles*, this puts him somewhere between Chuck Jones and Michelangelo." (David Edlesstein, *New York Magazine*, July 2, 2007)

   How does the film offer us all the ingredients for an archetypal story? How is it possible to make a rat lovable? Or could you get past the fact of a rat in a kitchen?

2. "The moral of *Ratatouille* is delivered by a critic: a gaunt, unsmiling fellow named Anton Ego who composes his acidic notices in a coffin-shaped room and who speaks in the parched baritone of Peter O'Toole. 'Not everyone can be a great artist,' Mr. Ego muses. 'But a great artist can come from anywhere.' Quite so … *Ratatouille* is a nearly flawless piece of popular art, as well as one of the most persuasive portraits of an artist ever committed to film. It provides the kind of deep, transporting pleasure, at once simple and sophisticated, that movies at their best have always promised. … Its sensibility, implicit in Mr. Ego's aphorism, is both exuberantly democratic and unabashedly elitist, defending good taste and aesthetic accomplishment not as snobbish entitlements but as universal ideals." (A.O. Scott, *The New York Times*, June 29, 2007)

   How does *Ratatouille* celebrate the passionate, sometimes aggressive pursuit of excellence, an impulse it also exemplifies?

3. "Bird has turned disgust into a celebration of efficiency, and, on the fly, he offers the most detailed cooking lore and the most ardent celebration of the chef as artist since *Babette's Feast*. Toques off to

Mr. Bird. At a time when many Americans have so misunderstood the ethos of democracy that they hate being outclassed by anyone, when science is disdained as dangerous and expertise as élitism, this animation artist, working in a family medium, has made two brilliant movies that unequivocally champion excellence. *Ratatouille* suggests that some omnivores are better than others. There's nothing to do but get over it." (David Denby, *The New Yorker*, July 23, 2007)

How exactly does Bird "champion excellence"? Give some examples of where this appears in the film: consider the meal at the end cooked for the critic.

4. Brad Bird "is also, at least implicitly, a severe critic of the laziness and mediocrity that characterize so much popular culture. He criticizes partly by example, by avoiding the usual kid-movie clichés and demonstrating that a clear, accessible story can also be thoughtful and unpredictable. *Ratatouille* features no annoying sidekick and no obtrusive celebrity voice-work, and while Remy is cute, he can also be prickly, demanding and insecure." (A.O. Scott, *The New York Times*, June 29, 2007)

Given all of the above, how is Remy's basic moral conflict – between family obligation and individual ambition – handled? Is there unusual subtlety and complexity in dealing with this conflict? Do you feel that the reassurances and resolutions of the movie's end feel earned rather than predetermined? Why? Why not?

3. The Relationship of the Movie to the Theme of the Exercise

1. The Exercise tells us that our decisions can aid or hinder the building up of the community of God's people. Underlying our own identity is, among others, the culture to which we belong. Remy not only belongs to a different culture, but to a different species. How is it possible for Remy to move from living with one species to another? What does it do to build up the community of God's people? What drives Remy that his family does not have, that makes them content to remain what and where they are?

2. Pervading all that we do are the creative energies of God present in everything and working in everything and everyone. How are these "creative energies" shown to be present in the various characters in the film?

4. The Relationship of the Movie to One's Self in the Exercise

1. In his passion for cooking, Remy could be said to find what this Exercise calls the love he needs to be fulfilled. This is a symbol of the love of God that we need so that we might be fulfilled. Where in your life – as you strive to accept God's love – have you found a love that helps you on your journey?

2. The film has much to say about both the positive and the negative aspects of community. Remy's journey for acceptance and understanding of his gifts can be read as a parable of spiritual values – the stone rejected by the builders becomes the cornerstone of new life. What are your gifts? What gifts have you explored and celebrated in your life? What gifts remain at the level of unfulfilled desire?

7th Exercise
The Gift of the Spirit
(Acts 2)

The fruit of the Spirit is love, joy, peace, patience, kindness, goodness, faithfulness, gentleness, self-control.

(Galatians 5:22-23)

We call Spiritual Exercises every way of preparing and disposing the soul to rid itself of all inordinate attachments, and, after their removal, of seeking and finding the will of God in the disposition of our life for the salvation of our soul. (Sp. Ex. #1)

Here it will be to ask for the grace to be glad and rejoice intensely because of the great joy and the glory of Christ Our Lord. (Sp. Ex. #221)

Finding Who We Are

Living fully and willingly in the world, without being seduced by its illusions, carries us farther along our spiritual journey to intimacy. We are not invited to flee from that world because of its brokenness. We do not deny this life and this path in favour of some other-worldly paradise, nor stoically defy death by pursuing pleasure. Rather, we are to live fully, with all our pains and problems, and within the continuing wretched situation of the world. This is possible when we live rooted in our relationship with the Father, and share the gift of the intimacy between Father and Son.

That intimacy reaches another stage of its fulfillment in the Ascension of the risen Jesus back to his Father. Then there is an explosion of love – a "Big Bang" of spiritual intimacy – that results in the second manifestation of the new creation. The fruit of that coming together for us is Pentecost. That intimate union of the risen human Christ with the Father results in their united Spirit that is given to us. We may think of this as a wedding in which we are invited guests sharing in the joy of the union. In sharing this joy, we become part of that union while living in this world. This joy transforms the world and gives us the energy, courage, vision, and love to be personal embodiments of God's Spirit in the world. This is what happened to the disciples in the upper room in Jerusalem after the Ascension.

They were gathered together there when "suddenly a sound came from heaven like the rush of a mighty wind and it filled all the house where they were sitting. And there appeared to them tongues as of fire, distributed and resting on each one of them. And they were all filled with the Holy Spirit and began to speak in other tongues as the Spirit gave utterance" (Acts 2:3-4).

We need to know that the word for "wind" and the word for "spirit" are the same in Hebrew. We also need to see that the giving of the Spirit in tongues "as of fire" manifests itself in the speaking in "tongues," which enflames the spirits of those who hear them and leads them to become disciples (Acts 2:41-42). At Pentecost, that first year in Jerusalem, God's very own Spirit is given to Jesus' companions, who share it with the world. It is the nature of love not to be withheld. In that sharing of intimacy, love becomes more and more present in the world and community is created.

Receiving the Gift

When we enter this contemplation, we ask to be given God's Spirit. We enter the scene as one of Christ's chosen gathered in prayer, and we open ourselves to receiving that Spirit. We allow that gift to descend through our bodies, feeling the Spirit's descent into every aspect of ourselves so that we are intimately connected to both heaven and earth. We feel the rootedness that grounds us, body and soul, arise until, in that descent and arising, we know we are the presence of love in the world. We remain in this state of consolation, calmly breathing in love to our depths and breathing out love to the world. We stay in this state as long as possible, and return to it during all the repetitions of this contemplation.

What we are given in this state of intimacy allows our vocation, whatever it is, to become manifest in the world. The word "vocation" and the word "voice" have the same Indo-European root – *uek(s)*, "to speak." When we find our vocation, we find our voice. Finding our vocation means expressing our deepest desire in our life and with our life. The "tongue of flame," given to each of those in the upper room in Jerusalem after Jesus' ascension, is given to us. Our daily lives manifest a life that is the Spirit in the world. A vocation is an expression of life that gives life, shares life, and celebrates life. A vocation to priesthood or religious life is only one of countless forms of vocation. What the disciples received at Pentecost was such a vocation. Through it they finally found their voice. Their lives, difficult though they would be, become a celebration of intimacy.

Sharing the Gift

After the gift of the Spirit in tongues of fire, the disciples spoke in tongues so that all who heard them, even though they were of different nationalities and spoke different languages, understood. This gift allowed them to enter into other people's worlds, to touch their lives and transform them. We have contemplated this pattern of God's mercy before. In the Incarnation, God became a vulnerable human and was born a baby in Bethlehem. In the passion and death of Christ, that same God entered into the world's pain and suffering. Through his death, he entered the hellish confines of human existence where whatever is good, but alienated from the larger community of the good, is offered freedom and life-giving relationships.

Now, at Pentecost, we see that mercy fearlessly and compassionately entering the lives of those who had not experienced God's compassion. We experienced this in the first three Weeks of the Exercises. In the First Week, we encountered that love coming to us to heal and liberate us from sin. In the Second Week, we walked intimately with Christ into our own poverty and the world's to bring that mercy to others. In the Third Week, as companions of Christ, we journeyed with him into the depths of evil as he reveals in that evil a path to the transforming mercy of the Father. Now, in the Fourth Week, we are offered the same Spirit that was given at Pentecost, so that we can live in the world creatively, joyfully, and fully alive. Because of the gift of intimacy we have received, we, too, can find a path through the evils of our day to the ever-present mercy of God. Our lives become a witness to that gift and to that path.

The creativity and joy we pray to receive in this contemplation is not just for ourselves but for others. This joy desires to be shared with anyone who has experienced that profound and ceaseless yearning, common to all, for life, love, freedom, joy, and for a community where we feel always and deeply at home. There everyone speaks and understands the language of the heart.

Questions for Prayer and Reflection

1. What happened of significance when you prayed for the gift of the Spirit? How did you feel? In what ways were you energized?

2. What struck you most deeply as you entered the contemplation as one of Christ's disciples?

3. Where else in your life do you feel creative and alive? How do you express this?

4. Where do you see the need for creativity and a fuller sense of life? Is there a link between your creativity and the areas of need in the world?

5. Do you have, or feel connected to, a community of creative people? How do you celebrate life together?

6. Who has helped you on your journey to being creative, free, and loving?

7. Whom are you helping to live life more joyfully, creatively, simply, hopefully? What is your relationship with that person or group?

8. What happens when you explore your spirit links with significant people in your life – living or dead, near or far, throughout the ages or in different religious traditions? How have these people made you who you are? How do they encourage you or confirm you in your spiritual journey?

9. Where is the Spirit leading you now?

10. In your conversation at the end of the prayer with the Father, with Jesus, or with one of your spiritual mentors, what comes to you that is significant?

11. When you prayed through the above reflection, what aspects struck you the most? What happened when you used those as an entry into prayer?

The Movie
INVICTUS

Director: Clint Eastwood (2009 – 134 mins.)
Starring: Morgan Freeman, Matt Damon

1. Synopsis

The film tells the true story of how Nelson Mandela, the newly elected president of South Africa, and the captain of the South African rugby team collaborate to bring their country together through a common love for sport. Apartheid is over, but its after-effects are all too real. Mandela rallies the national rugby team as it makes its way to the 1995 Rugby World Cup Championship match.

2. About the Movie

1. In 1985, Nelson Mandela, then in prison for twenty-three years, set about winning over the fiercest proponents of apartheid, from his jailers to the head of South Africa's military. In 1990 he earned his freedom and in 1994 he won the presidency in the nation's first free elections.

   What kind of person was Nelson Mandela? How do the following lines, spoken by Mandela in the film, help us see his character as it is presented in the film?

   • "Forgiveness removes fear."

   • "You have to know the enemy in order to prevail."

   • "You have to surprise them with compassion and restraint."

   • "In order to build a nation, we must all exceed our own expectations."

   • "This country is hungry for greatness."

   • "Sport has the ability to change the world. It has the power to inspire, the power to unite people that little else has … It is more powerful than governments in breaking down racial barriers."

2. When the Springboks took the field that June day for the championship match against New Zealand's heavily favoured squad, Mandela sat in his presidential box wearing a Springbok jersey, while 62,000 fans chanted "Nel-son!" "Nel-son!" Millions more around South Africa watched the Springboks defy the oddsmakers and cap Mandela's miraculous ten-year-long effort to bring 42 million South Africans together.

   That is how history sees that moment. How does the film portray it? To make it work – to make us appreciate the magnitude of this moment – the film must make us feel its importance. There must be a palpable excitement on the screen that reflects the South Africans excitement. We must feel that all that has happened during the movie leads to this triumphant moment – one that was both athletic and political. How well does the movie succeed in doing this?

3. "But if *Invictus* is predominantly an absorbing character study of one of the most extraordinary characters of our time, it is also fleshed out with well-sketched minor players and subplots that illuminate the progress of racial rapprochement in its comic human dimension. The black body-guards and their white colleagues proceed from hostility to wary tolerance to guarded warmth in a way that is pointed without being overstated. And that, for the most part, characterizes Mr. Eastwood's direction, which is always unassuming, unhurried and efficient. In this film he tells a big story through a series of small, well-observed moments, and tells it in his usual blunt, matter-of-fact way, letting the nuances take care of themselves." (A.O. Scott, *The New York Times*, December 11, 2009)

What are some of these "small, well-observed moments" that you noticed? What do they add to the film?

3. The Relationship of the Movie to the Theme of the Exercise

1. When we accept the Spirit, we feel intimately connected to both heaven and earth. At what point in the movie does Mandela reach this moment of intimacy? What are the steps he must undergo to reach this point? How does the Spirit guide him?

2. *Invictus* is based on the book *Playing the Enemy: Nelson Mandela and the Game That Changed a Nation*. The title of the book clearly indicates what the book is about. "Playing the Enemy" is also ambig-uous, and might mean that Mandela was playing a game, with his enemies as the other team, or that he was playing apartheid-loving South Africans into willingly supporting the new nation.

Which of the titles do you find more interesting? Why? How does changing the title from a focus on Nelson Mandela (*Playing the Enemy: Nelson Mandela and the Game That Changed a Nation*) to a focus on self-determination (*Invictus*) change the way that people might understand the story?

4. The Relationship of the Movie to One's Self in the Exercise

1. There is within all of us, as the Exercise notes, a profound and ceaseless yearning, common to all, for life, love, freedom, joy and a community where one feels always and deeply at home. With his release from prison, Mandela knows that he must begin a journey to bring such a community to the people of South Africa. Where in your own life have you reached a point where you realized that you have not fulfilled your own yearnings? What did you do about it?

2. In the film, different stories overlap: the political, the social, the emotional, the familial, the personal. For us also, the different stories we narrate to make sense of our lives overlap. How do we deal with the different demands of the different stories we live out of? How do we discern? How do we distinguish between our wishes and our deepest desires?

8th Exercise
Contemplation to Advance in Love (1)

Therefore I tell you, do not be anxious about your life, what you shall eat or what you shall drink, nor about your body, what you shall put on. Is not life more than food, and the body more than clothing? Look at the birds of the air; they neither sow nor reap nor gather into barns, and yet your heavenly Father feeds them. Are you not of more value than they? (Matthew 6:25-27)

Consider all gifts and blessings as descending from above. (Sp. Ex. #237)

This is to ask for what I desire. Here it will be to ask for an intimate knowledge of the many blessings received, that filled with gratitude for all, I may in all things love and serve the Divine Majesty. (Sp. Ex. #233)

The Spiritual Journey

Our spiritual journey is like a spiral: we seem to return to the places, situations, or projects we left behind. We re-enter that world not as prisoners trapped by its seductions, its illusions, and its temporary stays of relief, but as freed spirits. We see it in all its incompleteness and brokenness. In joy we realize that we are invited to work towards bringing it to a right relationship with God, so that it is part of the community of all creation and an ongoing manifestation of God's endless creativity.

And so we are inspired – by the love that calls us to life and then to more life – to share that life with those who reach out for love. We also gratefully accept the love that is offered to us by those who travel on the same path to the fullness of life. We give and we receive in love. In this contemplation, St. Ignatius offers some insightful observations about the nature of love, knowing full well that it is one of the most misused and misunderstood words in any language. He says first that "love ought to manifest itself in deeds rather than in words" (#230). What we do reveals who we are. Who we are is revealed by what we value. We experienced this when we contemplated God's relationship to creation. God values us. We are the beloved. That love is shown in a mercy that forgives us our alienations and offers us an almost unimaginable intimacy with the Trinity and with all of creation. This is not theological theory or romantic piety. It is what God does, because, for us, that is who God is. In these contemplations, we experience a God totally involved in creation. God never stops producing, maintaining, and transforming it and us.

Here we encounter a God who enters a self-distorting creation to heal and redeem it from the perversions evil has inflicted on it. We encounter a God willing to transform evil into good by embracing the alienating forces of evil and death. That embrace allows the compassionate mercy of the Father to bring those forces into community. This is resurrection. We have met in our prayer a God who became human as we are human, who walked the path of being human in all of its joy and its terror, and who shows us the path that leads back to the one he calls, intimately and simply, "Abba." This is a God whose word is incarnate, whose relationship with us is found in what he has done for us. When we enter that relationship – as we have done in the contemplations in the Exercises – we discover a God who works with us and for us. This is a God who invites us to work with him, and with all those forces of creation who have committed themselves in him to love.

Creating Community

Such a love is communal and mutual. We do not love alone or in a vacuum. Always – before us and behind us, above us and below us, surrounding us and embracing us – is the love of the Father and the Son. We experienced that love in the outpouring of the Spirit on us at Pentecost. That outpouring never ceases. In it we live and move and have our being. In prayer we come to deeper and more conscious realizations of that abiding presence, which is a pure, simple, unconditional gift. In setting up this contemplation, St. Ignatius says that love consists in the mutual sharing of what is good. "For example, the lover gives and shares with the beloved what he possesses, or something of that which he has or is able to give; and vice versa, the beloved shares with the lover" (#231). God shares Himself with us. In love, we are invited to offer ourselves to God. We receive and give in intimacy. The giving and receiving is love.

Narcissism is the opposite of love. Narcissists demand love and see themselves as the sole object of love. Narcissists cannot return love. What they claim to offer as love usually benefits only themselves. Narcissism destroys community. Love, on the other hand, works to create community. Such a community is manifest in a mutual giving and receiving. It roots itself in the free generosity of God that extends itself everywhere and to everyone. Narcissism is closed by a selfishness that can be personal or ghetto-like, ethnic or racial, social or national.

Community is different. Community is the celebration of the gift of the other as other. Our intimacy with God does not make us God. Intimacy makes us most truly ourselves, and makes us see God as always the Other, always open to us without devouring us. As creatures journeying into intimacy with God, we will never come to the end of that journey.

Community as relationship is open to this depth of intimacy. Integration into community does not mean being subsumed under a common ideology. It means maintaining the integrity of other-ness. At Pentecost, those hearing the apostles heard their own tongue. They did not hear an imposed national or ecclesial language. The gift of the Spirit creates intimacy. In intimacy we discover our identity.

The identity that community offers is realized in the personal, the social, the national, and the cultural. These different levels of being human have common bonds. These in themselves cannot bring us all to the fullness of life. This is found only in the mystery we call God. In themselves, these are incomplete and transitory manifestations of the divine creativity in time. They are not ends in themselves. Who we are changes. Our societies are in flux. Our national identity is constantly being reinterpreted. Our culture evolves. They point beyond themselves to that creativity and to the fuller dimensions of community. We are always in transition. Even tradition is transitional. Evil emerges when these incomplete manifestations of creation hold themselves as fixed and whole and complete in themselves. Then they are not open to the continuing creativity of God.

The work of loving is, first, to see everything and everyone as incomplete, and, second, to realize that incompleteness is not a curse but a blessing that allows us to reach out, without illusions, for that fullness of life offered to us and to all by the beloved, who is divine.

In that reaching out we share what has been given to us.

An All-Embracing Love

To experience this grace more fully, as we begin this prayer we bring to our awareness that we are always in the presence of God and the saints. We are always surrounded by the love of those who love us and by the forces of all that is good in creation. We acknowledge that all of these work for our good by protecting, interceding, encouraging, and celebrating our lives and our paths. The prayer reminds us that we are never alone, and that the energies of our lives are woven together in a community of love that extends through time and space. This community works to heal our disorders, enlighten our ignorance, transform our alienations and unblock our creativity. As we become aware of this community, which is always present to us, even here and now, we can see it at work in our lives and in our prayer, which participates in this unceasing activity. Prayer and work, sleep and play, eating and voiding – all of these activities operate from the same stance of being one with God's spirit and God's energies in the world.

In this and the following contemplations, all of which are designed to make us more and more aware of this all-embracing love, St. Ignatius suggests that we ask for what we desire. "Here it will be to ask for an intimate knowledge of the many blessings received, that filled with gratitude for all, I may in all things love and serve the Divine Majesty" (#233). It is a grace to see our lives as they are. It is a great grace to see in all the aspects of our lives the abiding presence of love holding and transforming us even in the dark

times. We will know we have received this grace when we discover that our prayer is filled with gratitude, and, when out of that gratitude and that gratitude only, we are moved to enter into the work of building up the community of love that offers life to all.

Questions for Prayer and Reflection

1. In this contemplation, what moves you the most? Why?

2. How does this contemplation put your life in context?

3. What things in your life are, or have been, a blessing for you? What happens when you take time out to be grateful for them? How does that gratitude shape the way your feel about your life now?

4. How do you feel called to live a loving life now?

5. What areas in your world do you feel need transforming? What part can you play in transforming the world?

6. Make a list of the people, past and present, who form your community of love. What happens when you have a prayerful conversation with them as part of this contemplation?

7. In the course of these exercises, what has been given to you as pure gift?

8. What, in your loving, do you offer to your beloved? What do you offer to God?

9. How does your life reveal to you and to others what you really value?

10. In your conversations with the Father or with Jesus, what is given to you that is significant for your life?

300

The Movie
PRIDE AND PREJUDICE

Director: Joe Wight (2005 – 129 mins.)
Starring: Keira Knightley, Donald Sutherland, Matthew Macfadyen, Judi Dench, Brenda Blethyn

1. Synopsis

This tale of love and values unfolds in the class-conscious England of the late eighteenth century, when the family's future happiness and security is dependent on the daughters making good marriages. Life is uneventful until the arrival in the neighbourhood of the rich gentleman Mr. Bingley, who rents a large house so he can spend the summer in the country. Mr. Bingley brings with him his sister and the handsome, rich, and proud Mr. Darcy. Love is soon in the air.

2. About the Movie

1. "It is a truth universally acknowledged, that a single man in possession of a good fortune, must be in want of a wife. However little known the feelings or views of such a man may be on his first entering a neighbourhood, this truth is so well fixed in the minds of the surrounding families, that he is considered the rightful property of some one or other of their daughters." (Jane Austen, *Pride and Prejudice*)

   How do these words, which open the novel, set the tone for this film? Is this film meant to be "romance" or is there a twinge of satire on the part of the director, such as is found in Jane Austen's novel?

2. This film "gathers you up on its white horse and gallops off into the sunset. Along the way, it serves a continuing banquet of high-end comfort food perfectly cooked and seasoned to Anglophilic tastes. In its final minutes, it makes you believe in true love, the union of soul mates, happily-ever-after and all the other stuff a romantic comedy promises but so seldom delivers. For one misty-eyed moment, order reigns in the universe …. In the film's most intoxicating scenes, the camera plunges into the thick of the crowded balls attended with delirious anticipation by the Bennet sisters and moves with the dancers as they carry on breathless, broken conversations while whirling past one another. That mood of voluptuous excitement, barely contained, is augmented by Dario Marianelli's score, which takes the sound and style of late 18th- and early 19th-century piano music in increasingly romantic direction." (Stephen Holden, *The New York Times*, November 11, 2005)

   What makes this British "romantic comedy" so different from the many romantic comedies that Hollywood churns out year after year? How does the film make you believe in "true love, the union of soul mates"? Consider the actors, especially Keira Knightley, whose radiance lights up the screen and wins our hearts. Consider the camera work, particularly the ballroom scene Holden describes. And consider one major element we might overlook: the music of Dario Marianelli. What mood does his music evoke? Consider the opening of the film and gentle rising volume and lyricism of the music. What tone does this set for this film?

3. *"Pride and Prejudice* moves fast – it doesn't unfold languorously, the way many adaptations do, as if they were desperately trying to mimic the experience of reading. But everything in it feels essential, and in that way, watching it is like reading. As historically authentic-looking as *Pride and Prejudice* is, it has far more invested in emotional authenticity – you feel engaged every moment." (Stephanie Zacharek, *Salon*, November 11, 2005)

The novel is one of the most famous of all novels. Novels are to be read and enjoyed for the places, characters, feelings, moods, etc. that are conveyed to the reader through language. Novels come to life in the reader's imagination. This is the joy that reading offers. Film does not have the luxury to move at that same pace. But film can involve us just the same. How does this film retain all the characteristics of Austen's novel and at the same time bring out the emotional intensity that Zacharek talks about?

3. The Relationship of the Movie to the Theme of the Exercise

1. Ignatius tells us that love is shown in deeds rather than in words. The Exercise expands on this when it says that it is what we do that reveals who we are, and it is what we do with who we are that reveals what we value. How does apply to Mr. Bennet? To Darcy? To Elizabeth?

2. At this point in the Exercises, we realize that we are called to share the love and life we have been given with those who reach out for love and, at the same time, to accept love from others. How does Elizabeth try to reach out to the people around her – especially her family – to give them love? From whom does Elizabeth come to accept love?

4. The Relationship of the Movie to One's Self in the Exercise

1. The love that we have been given by God allows us to reach out – to share what has been given us. In the film, we see how love grows and is shared. What is the love that you have been given? How are you going to share this with the community in which you live and work?

2. The role of music in this film is most important to set mood and to add to moments of great emotion. Consider the music under the opening scenes of the film and how it moves us from the dawn of an English countryside to the bustle of the Bennet home. This use of music is an example of the new way of seeing, of being creative, of being compassionate and joyful that the Exercise describes. Where in your life has music played such a role?

Contemplation to Advance in Love (2)

Blessed be the God and Father of Our Lord Jesus Christ, who has blessed us in Christ with every spiritual blessing in the heavenly places, even as he chose us in him before the foundation of the world, that we should be holy and blameless before him. He destined us in love to be his own through Jesus Christ. (Ephesians 1:3-5)

I must be convinced that in Christ our Lord, the bridegroom, and in His spouse the Church, only one Spirit holds sway, which governs and rules for the salvation of souls. (Sp. Ex. #365)

This is to ask for what I desire. Here it will be to ask for an intimate knowledge of the many blessings received, that filled with gratitude for all, I may in all things love and serve the Divine Majesty. (Sp. Ex. #233)

All Creation Is Charged with God's Energies

What have we received from God? Rather than thinking about it, let us allow the love that shapes us to reveal it. We are creatures, a part of God's constant creativity. We do not have the power of our existence within ourselves; in fact, should God remove his loving attention from us, we will simply cease to exist. The very basis of our existence is radical dependence upon God.

At our most material level, the elements that make up physical existence were formed at that first physical moment of creation. The very matter that was formed in the Big Bang billions of years ago when energy became physical and exploded outwards – in the creation of universes and galaxies and solar systems that are still expanding into nebulae, burning up into supernova, and imploding into black holes – is the same matter that makes up our bodies. Our physical bodies contain the memory of the cosmos from its very beginning, and each of our bodies is a symbol of that cosmos. Our relationship to that cosmos is basic and eternal. We do not know all the properties of the matter of which we are made, but we do know that it makes us one with all of creation. Let us stay for a while in the mystery of our oneness with the elements of creation. In them and in us is the gift of God's indwelling.

Creation is made up of levels of existence. Biological life emerges from the swirl of proteins and carbon; we share that higher level of existence with the myriad plant forms that grace our planet. Grasses and seaweeds, giant trees and orchids, wheat and lichen are all related to our biological bodies. If we open our awareness to our ecological interconnectedness, we discover a mutuality in which we shape, and are shaped by, our relationships to plant life. We cultivate certain crops and modify the DNA of others. We depend on the pharmaceutical properties of some of these to maintain our lives or enhance our awareness of the mysteries that surround us. The mystery of God's indwelling is in them and in us. Let us ask for the grace to experience the wonder of that unity we share with the biosphere, and to experience God's indwelling there.

Beyond that level is our animal existence. We have heightened sensation and possess innate skills to gather food, reproduce, care for our young, create a clan structure, and explore our environment. Within our symbiotic relationship to the animal world are the totemic forces of our spiritual nature that are given animal energies, characteristics and structures. Our human body is more than an animal body, to be sure, but our bodies belong firmly and irreducibly to the animal kingdom. In this prayer of thanksgiving, let us be aware of the gift of the body, the delight of the senses, our rootedness in the physical, which allow us to connect and communicate with others to form community and express intimacy. Let us allow ourselves to be open to the mystery and to the delight of God's indwelling in our bodies.

Sacred Spaces

Encompassing all of these is Christ incarnate. In becoming human, Christ takes up into himself what makes us human – the material, the biological, the animal, the social. The humanity of Jesus finds its deepest expression as intimacy with the Father. The incarnate God shares with us the gifts of memory, understanding, will, imagination, creativity, and the freedom to choose and celebrate life. He shares with us as a member of the human family. He offers us the gifts that the Father has given to him: the gift of resurrection and the gift of union with the Father in the life of the Trinity. That gift allows us, even in our earthly pilgrimage, to become sacred spaces wherein the divine may dwell and embody the divine compassion on earth. When we open ourselves to that gift and experience it, we become the image and likeness of God on earth. Let us open ourselves to celebrating that gift of the fullness of life offered to us freely and joyfully now.

All of this enormous sweep of God's love – from the beginning of time through the cosmos, through evolutionary history and through the community of human history – leads up to the Incarnation and the resurrection of the Father's Son. It continues through the traditions of love that he offers to all. It comes, at this very moment, to our own life and loving. Let us take some time to enter into this history contemplatively. Let us allow the love that creates us and redeems us and loves us into journeying back to the Father to carry us to that intimacy of passionate union with him. There we may savour with our senses, physical and spiritual, the delight he has in us.

We have been given our own path, with our own blessed history, and our own personal encounter with salvation. We all have our own personal entry into God's particular love for us, and our own intimate sense of being the beloved of Jesus and of the Father. Let us enter into that blessed history revealed to us in this journey. Let us open and savour the gift that allows us to know deeply, intimately, and truly that we are the beloved and intimate of God.

In order to appreciate what we have been given, St. Ignatius, in the Exercises here, offers a prayer we can pray out of the deep affection we feel for God. *Take, Lord, and receive all my liberty, my memory, my understanding, and my entire will, all I have and possess. You have given all to me. To you, O Lord, I return it. All is yours, dispose of it wholly according to your will. Give me Your love and Your grace, for this is sufficient for me.* (#234)

In this context of love, the lover has given his life for the beloved. It is because of Christ's love for us that we have the path of intimacy, which leads to the fullness of love we desire. Here we offer our very identity to Christ, the lover. All we ask for is Christ's love and the gift of the spirit. It is enough, for this love creates, sustains, protects, and transforms us. This love lives out of the intimate knowledge that all is gift.

Questions for Prayer and Reflection

1. How do you relate to the community that is creation? How do you live out of those deep connections that extend through time and space and all of human history?

2. What are you grateful for? How do you show this gratitude?

3. What do you take for granted? How do you deal with those things?

4. How do you experience your rootedness in God and in creation? How does this manifest itself in your prayer and in your daily life?

5. What in this prayer moved you? What moved you the most?

6. How does this prayer shape your relationship with God?

7. If you were to write the "Take, Lord, receive" prayer of St. Ignatius in your own words, what would it look like?

8. What offering can you make out of love to the source of all loving? What occurs to you as you pray this question?

9. Where is the place of evil and human suffering in this dynamic of loving?

10. Where do you fit into it?

The Movie
TRIPLETS OF BELLEVILLE

Director: Sylvain Chomet (2003 – 80 mins.)
Starring: Beatrice Bonifassi, Lina Boudreau, Jean-Claude Donda

1. Synopsis

Madame Souza is on a mission: to save her grandson, Champion, who is kidnapped during the Tour de France. With the help of her dog, Bruno, and a trio of sisters who used to sing and dance during the glory days of Fred Astaire and Ginger Rogers, Madame Souza sets out to rescue Champion.

Note: If at all possible, watch the subtitled version. Much of an actor's art lies in the use of voice to express emotion, mood, and character. Dubbed movies can never have the full impact of the original.

2. About the Movie

1. "The movie isn't aimed at kids, but they will find plenty to beguile them. And don't worry that the film is French; it has hardly any dialogue. Doesn't need it. The gnarly imagery and the movie's understanding of the human impulse not just to survive but also to save others are eloquent enough." (Richard Corliss, *Time*, November 9, 2003)

    How does the director convey this notion of our need not only to survive but also to save others? How well do you think he accomplishes this?

2. "There are some works of animation that are notable for their realism, for conjuring imaginary worlds whose inhabitants – the sea creatures in *Finding Nemo*, the witches and princesses in classic Disney fairy tales, the wide-eyed heroines of Japanese anime – move in more or less plausible ways through fantastical settings. Others – the cartoons of Tex Avery and Chuck Jones come to mind – rewrite the laws of physics and the conventions of physiology to suit their own fanciful requirements. *The Triplets of Belleville*, the first feature film by Sylvan Chomet, surely belongs in the second category. Mr. Chomet's is a universe of sheer impossibility, where size, proportion and balance are ruled by the whims of his perverse pen and peculiar imagination." (A.O. Scott, *The New York Times*, November 26, 2003)

    In what ways do Chomet and his animators "rewrite the laws of physics and the conventions of physiology to suit their own fanciful requirements"?

3. "Its main audience is adults, though. And not just any adults, but those in the mood for venturesome fare that's both surreal and hilarious …. It's downright daft at times. But it's ingeniously crafted, marvelously drawn, and utterly unpredictable. It's also the modern equivalent of a silent movie, with music and sound effects but hardly a speck of dialogue. Take a chance on it.

Whether you love it or not, you'll have to admit it's unlike anything you've seen before." (David Sherritt, *Christian Science Monitor*, November 21, 2003)

Which are the most "surreal and hilarious" characters in this film and how does Chomet make them that way?

4. "*The Triplets* may be the oddest movie of the year, by turns sweet and sinister, insouciant and grotesque, invitingly funny and forbiddingly dark. It may also be one of the best, a tour de force of ink-washed, crosshatched mischief and unlikely sublimity …. The twisting of cultural stereotypes has long been part of the cartoon heritage; think of the amorous Pepe le Peu, for example. In any case the tether that connects Mr. Chomet's imagined world with the real one is long and loose. He is a master of surprise, terror, silliness and sheer eccentricity, and this compact movie is stuffed nearly to bursting with astounding sequences." (A.O. Scott, *The New York Times*, November 26, 2003)

What are some of the sequences in this movie that show that Chomet "… is a master of surprise, terror, silliness and sheer eccentricity"? Consider Madame Souza setting out in the moonlight, by pedal boat, in the wake of a giant ocean liner; her dog, Bruno, dreaming in black and white; one of the triplets hunting frogs with a hand grenade. What are some of the other similar sequences?

3. The Relationship of the Movie to the Theme of the Exercise

1. This Exercise is about love – about a love that will never end. What examples of various kinds of love do you find in this film?

2. As we give thanks for the gift of the body and how it allows us connection and communication with others to form community, consider how this is shown to us throughout the film. What is one scene in the film where you see this clearly exemplified?

3. The Exercise talks of the use of the imagination and the awareness of the delight of the senses that we need to find. Think of the use of music and of pop culture references in the movie. How are these used to express the imagination and the delight of the senses?

4. The Relationship of the Movie to One's Self in the Exercise

1. The Exercise asks us to consider what we have been given, and reminds us that we have been given our own path, our own blessed history, our own personal encounter with salvation, our own knowledge of being loved by God. The film shows us how the Belleville sisters were also given much and what they gave in return. What about you? What gifts have you been given that the Exercises have made clear to you? How different might they be from the gifts you thought you had before making the Exercises?

2. We know what return the Belleville sisters made for what they had been given. At this point in the Exercises you need to ask what return you can make for what you have been given. It has been said that "The greatest thing you'll ever learn is to love and be loved in return." How will you take the prayer of Ignatius found in this Exercise and make it into something real in your own life?

307

10th Exercise
Contemplation to Advance in Love (3)

I give thanks to God always for you because of the grace of God which was given you in Christ Jesus, that in every way you were enriched in him with all speech and all knowledge — even as the testimony to Christ was confirmed among you — so that you are not lacking in any spiritual gift, as you wait for the revealing of our Lord Jesus Christ, who will sustain you to the end, guiltless in the day of our Lord Jesus Christ. God is faithful, by whom you were called into the fellowship of his Son, Jesus Christ our Lord. (1 Corinthians 1:4-9)

Soul of Christ, sanctify me
Body of Christ, save me
Blood of Christ, inebriate me
Water from the side of Christ, wash me
Passion of Christ, strengthen me
O Good Jesus, hear me
Within your wounds, hide me
Permit me not to be separated from You
From the wicked foe defend me
At the hour of my death call me
And bid me come to you
That with Your saints I may praise You
For ever and ever. Amen. (Prayer of St. Ignatius)

This is to ask for what I desire. Here it will be to ask for an intimate knowledge of the many blessings received, that filled with gratitude for all, I may in all things love and serve the Divine Majesty. (Sp. Ex. #233)

The Gift of Life

There are levels to revealing a gift. First the gift must be offered; then it must be received and accepted. Next it must be opened and used. Finally, it must be shared. Sharing celebrates not only the gift, but the giver, the receiver, and the community that gift creates.

No matter who we are or what state we are in, we have all been given a gift: life. That gift goes beyond mere survival as wounded individuals. That gift of life asks us to see, know, and love ourselves the way God sees, knows, and loves us. Often our own pain, or the lies of the world, prevent us from seeing that gift. Instead, we see life as harsh, nasty, and brutal, a vicious struggle for survival. And so the very idea of life as a gift of love for love seems, at best, naive and sentimental and simply untrue. Many of us refuse to receive the gift. We see the gift-giver as demanding and judgmental, powerful and capricious, cruel and terrifying. We might say that since we did not ask to be born, we are condemned to live. Even if the gift has been thrust upon us, we do not accept it.

But we all have a dreadful hunger for love and truth, justice and community, beauty and joy, security and acceptance. Even if we do not accept the gift of life, the longing for such life never leaves us. It haunts our every waking moment and all we say and do. It haunts our dreams and all our fumbling attempts at relationships.

308

Imagine one day saying to ourselves, "There must be more to life than what I have been enduring." We set out in our own quiet and secret way to see what that "more" could be. As we do, we start opening the gift of life. This is a difficult and a lifelong task, for we must become aware of the lies in our life. They present the false image of ourselves as unlovable and unloving. They deceive us that we are alone and that God is a tyrant. Moreover, our lives are multi-layered. At every layer, lies and deceptions must be unmasked and the work of restoration begun. As we enter this work, we continually discover the joy of living, and we discover the God who labours constantly to bring us to that joy.

Sharing Life

Indeed, in this contemplation to experience love, St. Ignatius asks us to "consider how God works and labours for me" (#236). As we labour to bring a fuller life into our world, we labour with a God who delights in bringing that life into our world. In that labouring, we discover a God who has invited us to be co-creators of the community of love extending through time and space. We also discover our bonds with those others who also work at this one project of community. At this level we find out how interrelated we are with the saints and martyrs and mystics, the holy ones of every spiritual path and tradition. We learn that their works of love, as diverse as their identities, all share the one work of love – the work of a God whose compassionate care and mercy manifest themselves in that unceasing activity of creating.

When we join in this creating, we see and love the world as God does. We see its beauty and its bro-kenness, and join with the holy ones of all time in the sacred work of redemption. Then every simple act of kindness, every moment of humble service, every work of unnoticed devotion, every silent prayer, every quiet gesture of forgiveness, every act of celebration, is an expression of that sacred work. That shared life is the opening of the gift and the celebration of the gift.

Celebrating Life

All of this comes from deep within us and pours itself out in our daily lives. What we offer to all has first been offered to us. It is the gift of life. We humbly share it, knowing that when we act as the face and hands and heart of God in the world, we do so in lives that we have handed back to God. We do so knowing that what passes through us into the world, though shaped and coloured by our unique personalities and times, is that unending, compassionate mercy of divine love. The sole delight of that love is that everyone and all things come to the fullness of life. There all evil will be transformed into creativity, all suffering will be healed into joy, all oppression will be rewoven into community, all death will be lifted up to resurrection. This is the journey to the fullness of life. It is reached through the gift of intimacy. It is a journey that never ends. We have before us the delight of celebrating life in ways beyond our present imaginings. Each moment opens to that delight. We enter it and are transformed. The furnaces of affliction become the flames of divine love.

When we enter the world with a heart transformed, the world is transformed no matter what we do.

Questions for Prayer and Reflection

1. Where are you on your journey of life as a gift?

2. What obstacles are you facing on that journey? How do you live with them?

3. What started you off on your journey? How has your life changed since you began it?

4. What image do you have of yourself? How does this shape what you do and how you do it?

5. What image do you have of God? How does this shape your relationship with him/her/the Trinity?

6. What sense do you have of the world and of your being in the world?

7. Where do you find others who openly share your values and your deepest desires? How do you support and encourage each other?

8. How do you celebrate life?

9. What is the next step on your journey?

10. What happens when you ask God and the community of God that question in prayer?

11. In this contemplation, and in your repetitions of it, what moves your spirit most to a deeper intimacy with God?

12. In your conversation with God or the community of the holy, at the end of your prayer, what emerges as important for you now?

The Movie
THE STRAIGHT STORY

Director: David Lynch (1999 – 112 mins.)
Starring: Sissy Spacek, Richard Farnsworth, Joseph A. Carpenter

1. Synopsis

Alvin Straight was 73 when he got the call about his brother. Alvin couldn't see well enough to hold a driver's license. He walked only with the support of two canes. He didn't much care for anybody else helping him out. But when he got the call that his brother Lyle – separated from him by hundreds of miles and a decade a proud silence – had suffered a stroke, Alvin knew he had to reach him. With little money, he begins a one journey across America's Heartland. Filmed along the 260-mile route that the real-life Alvin Straight traversed in 1994 from Laurens, Iowa, to Mt. Zion, Wisconsin, the film chronicles Alvin's patient odyssey. When not rolling around at five miles an hour aboard his '66 John Deere, Alvin encounters a number of strangers, from a teenage runaway to a fellow World War II veteran. By sharing his life's earned wisdom with simple stories, Alvin has a profound impact on the characters that colour his pilgrimage.

2. About the Movie

1. "For a notion of just how far removed most American movies are from actual experience, consider the startling effect that Farnsworth has on screen. This actor, rancher and former stunt man, enough of a film veteran to have driven a chariot in *The Ten·Commandments*, cuts a startling figure as an unabashedly old man. Unshaven, infirm, scraggly-haired and without makeup, he automatically frees the film from any sense of artifice and delivers an amazingly stalwart performance that will not soon be forgotten." (Janet Maslen, *The New York Times*, October 15, 1999)

This is one of those cases, like Henry Fonda in *The Grapes of Wrath* or Gregory Peck in *To Kill a Mockingbird*, when an actor is so perfectly matched to his part that his humanity can't help but shine through. What is it about his character that puts us at ease. Look at the scenes where he encounters a variety of strangers (a pregnant hitchhiker, a team of cyclists, a priest and a fellow war veteran). What is it about his voice and his wisdom that cause people to be taken in by him?

2. "Through Farnsworth, we see that Straight's journey was more than a quirky gesture of cussed independence. Going to Wisconsin was a spiritual pilgrimage for him: a chance to heal a 10-year-old rift with his brother and a way to reconnect, maybe for the last time, with the world outside of Laurens, Iowa." (Edward Guthman, *San Francisco Chronicle*, October 22, 1999)

Why do you think that the critic call Straight's journey a "spiritual pilgrimage"? Do you agree with this notion? Why? Why not?

3. "David Lynch starts with clichés – a picture-postcard view of a small American downtown, conversations conducted in 'Gee whiz!' or 'Well, whaddya know about that!' exclamations – and comes up with the unarticulated longings, joys and sorrows those clichés struggle to contain …. David Lynch makes movies about the moments when the familiar becomes as thrilling and strange as orbiting the Earth. It's no accident that in the first image of *The Straight Story*, we're staring at a nighttime sky impossibly heavy with twinkling stars, while listening to the reassuring chirp of crickets. The image sums up the dual pull of Lynch's work: the simultaneous desire for the comfort of the familiar and the compulsion to find out what else is out there." (Charles Taylor, *Salon*, October 15, 1999)

How is this "dual pull of Lynch's work" seen in this film? Give some examples that perhaps start as clichés and end up as so much more. Consider the scene where Straight talks with a fellow soldier from World War II.

4. "Alvin's journey isn't much about a destination. Lynch, working from a lovely and succinct screenplay by John Roach and Mary Sweeney, invests each phase of the trip with resonance about Alvin's life and the lives of those he meets, so that each encounter takes on an unforced larger significance." (Janet Maslen, *The New York Times*, October 15, 1999)

What is the larger significance in two of the encounters Straight has on his trip? How does the director do this without forcing the significance on us?

3. The Relationship of the Movie to the Theme of the Exercise

1. There is in each one of us a dreadful hunger for love and truth, justice and community, for beauty and joy, for security and acceptance. We see this not only in Alvin but in the people he encounters as he journeys to meet his brother. How does this hunger drive each of them?

2. The Exercise tells us that there are layers in our lives and at every layer the lies and deceptions must be unmasked and the work of restoration begun. In the film, how does this apply to Alvin and to the people he meets along the way?

4. The Relationship of the Movie to One's Self in the Exercise

1. This final Exercise reminds us that the lies of the world stop us from seeing the gift of life given to us by God. Alvin finds out that by letting go of the things that caused the rift with his brother he will come to possess what is real. What have the Exercises showed you that you must let go? And what is the "real" which you hope to possess?

2. At the close of the Exercises, we read that when we enter the world with a heart transformed, the world is transformed no matter what we do. Alvin's journey transformed himself and his world. Consider what have you done to transform your world? What are you doing to transform the world? And what will you do to transform your world?

312

11th Exercise
Overview of The Fourth Week

Each of us is on a spiritual journey. Most of us are not aware of it. The Spiritual Exercises of St. Ignatius is one way in which we can become aware of living our desire for the fullness of life and of encountering a God who desires to offer us that fullness of life. The path to that intimacy with God lies first in becoming aware of what traps us and separates us from that gift. We cannot find this out for ourselves, since most of us have become so habituated to our disorders that we have come to accept them as normal; we think the way we see life is exactly how life is. But the truth is that most of us live our lives out of our hurts. Our sense of the world, of the way others operate, is shaped by the way life has treated us, and, as the Buddha's First Noble Truth tells us, everyone suffers. We are born into a history of human disaster. Our families are dysfunctional. We ourselves have not only suffered the slings and arrows of outrageous fortune, but have become complicit in the disorder in which we find ourselves.

But it is the nature of God not to let us become so overwhelmed by those forces of destruction that we end up living lives that are not our own. God desires that we discover our integrity: that we are loved; we are lovable; and we can love. But how is this discovery to occur? We start off by looking at the reality of our lives held in the loving embrace of God. We discover that, in spite of the enormous forces of destruction bearing in on us since the beginnings of human history, we are not destroyed. There are stron-

ger forces at work. These are the forces that are aligned to God and who, with God, hold and maintain creation as God desires it, working to transform its disordered elements to bring new life to us all. As we are held in love we discover not only how we have been trapped, but, more significantly, we discover how we are constantly loved into being.

Being loved encourages us to love. We learn to love, and part of that learning is to be able to discern what forces in our lives lead us to become more and more human and what forces are the enemy of our human nature. In each of our lives these two forces operate; learning to love calls for discernment so that we might follow what is good and be able to avoid what is destructive. We reach a stage of self-awareness when we can consciously commit ourselves to doing good. But walking such a path in this world often brings us into conflict with those other forces that seek to destroy the good to which we have committed ourselves. We can find ourselves in situations when our lives are on the line. We can, like the Christ, even lose all that we have. But, like the Christ, we do not lose who we are. We are the beloved of the Father, and our path through this world, and even through death, carries us to the One who loves us and who comes looking for us.

That coming together is experienced as resurrection. God rescues us by giving us new life that is not a return to the old life. This new life does not remove us from the world, but it allows us to deal with the world differently. We become witnesses to the joy of being rescued, and we become part of the joy of the One who has rescued us. In that spirit of shared joy, we desire to love as we have been loved. We live in the world not as victims but as ones desiring to liberate others who are victims. Our path through this world is to love others into being as we have been loved.

This, in brief, is the journey through the Spiritual Exercises of St. Ignatius. We can appropriate this journey by becoming attentive to what moves us, either positively or negatively. What moves us – that is, touches us deeply – does so because it touches not only what we most value but where we are most vulnerable. A true spiritual journey starts when we can acknowledge our vulnerability and our values.

It is there that we are most intimate – on one hand, capable of love, and on the other hand, capable of defending ourselves against that openness by closing in on ourselves.

When we look at what has happened to us, can we identify our brokenness? Can we acknowledge what loves we have in our lives? Can we bring that brokenness to that love?

A spiritual path begins when we allow brokenness and love to come together. Reflect on where you are on your spiritual path. Try to see the pattern in the good experiences that you have had. Try to see the pattern in your negative experiences. Think of the ways your bad experiences turned out to be good.

When you do this, you can see how you are trapped and how you get trapped; how you are loved and how you respond; how you are freed and how you get free. This reflection asks how that freedom you were given develops in your life and how the freedom you now experience brings others to freedom.

There are stages in accepting the gifts of the resurrection and of sharing them with others. The first is accepting the gift. For this we need to look at those covenant moments in our life when we have been rescued by others from situations that seemed impossible to change. Then we need to see how those transformations have changed us for the better. Here we look at the ways in which we have used the gift we were given. Then we look at the ways in which our changed lives have touched others' lives and affirmed their humanity. Here, we are sharing the gift we have been given. Finally we celebrate the gift we have been given by acknowledging the joy in our lives and in the lives of others. This sense of joy creates community. We can reflect on how we celebrate life and how that celebration causes others to be grateful for the path to life that they walk.

The Fourth Week of the Exercises becomes the fulfillment and the context for the previous weeks. In love we have been created; through love we have been rescued (Week One); from love we learn to love (Week Two) ; with love we return to the Father (Week Three); and, by love we help transform the world (Week Four). We share what we have been given. The spiritual journey returns us to the world and to the Father. By loving we become intimates with the Father; by loving we embrace the world to make it a community of love.

The Movie
UP

Director: Peter Docter, Bob Peterson (2009 – 96 mins.)
Starring: Edward Asner, Christopher Plummer, Jordan Nagai

1. Synopsis

After his wife dies, 78-year-old Carl Fredricksen sets out to fulfill a promise he made to her – that they would see the wilds of South America. He ties thousands of balloons to his house and sets off, only to realize that he has a stowaway: Russell, an eight-year-old who is hoping to earn a badge for helping an elderly person. An unforgettable adventure with a wide-ranging cast of characters ensues.

2. About the Movie

1. "*Up* sees the world as real, full of life and pain. Some theaters are showing Up in 3-D, which dims the color a bit, but the dimensions that count are in the movie's mind and heart. The opening sequence is touched by genius. A young Depression-era boy named Carl goes to the movies and watches a newsreel about Charles Muntz (a complex portrait in voice by the great Christopher Plummer), an explorer who takes off for South America in a dirigible to track a giant bird at Paradise Falls. Quiet Carl wants to explore as well. He meets an exciting, motor-mouthed girl, Ellie, who shares his feelings. They grow up, marry and grow old without fulfilling their dreams of children or adventure." (Peter Travers, *Rolling Stone*, May 28, 2009)

The story of Carl and Ellie is told almost as a silent film. What would the impact be if this section was filled with dialogue and lengthened considerably? Would this be a good thing or a bad thing? Why? Why not?

2. "*Up* is unapologetically life-affirming, for those who like to have life affirmed. And from a technical standpoint it certainly is beautifully executed. But save for a few inspired canine gags and a handful of very pretty visual details, *Up* left me cold. Its charms appear to have been applied with surgical precision; by the end, I felt expertly sutured, but not much else." (Stephanie Zacharek, *Salon*, May 29, 2009)

It may have come as a shock to Zacharek to find that most critics and audiences alike loved what they saw in this film. Why does she see the film as "life-affirming" but only for those viewers who want life affirmed? And is there anything wrong with affirming life?

3. "The treatment and imagery is even more bizarre. It's a character study of a cantankerous old git. It's a buddy movie where the buddies are separated by 70 years. It's a love story where the love transcends death. ... *Up* shares trace elements with *Chaplin*, *The Station Agent*, *The Wizard of Oz*, *It's a Wonderful Life*, *About Schmidt*, *Gran Torino* and

Hitchcock .... For all its fantastical leanings, *Up* is that rare animated film that sees the world as real. Its pains feel real and its joys feel earned. That may be an obvious thing, but it lifts *Up* into a class by its beautiful self." (Ian Freer, *Empire*, October 5, 2009)

How is love shown to transcend death? How much does this have to do with the way this film sees "the world as real"? What are some of the pains that feel real and the joys that feel earned?

3. The Relationship of the Movie to the Theme of the Exercise

1. The final set of Exercises moves from experiencing the resurrection of Christ to living the spirit of that resurrection in the world. We are to live as though we have received the grace we ask for – the grace to be intensely glad and to rejoice intensely. How does Carl come to accept this grace in his own journey?

2. During the Fourth Week, we are invited to advance in love through contemplation. This film is deeply rooted in the story of one true love. Why have the opening twelve minutes been called the most heartfelt – the most sincere – love story in recent memory? Consider the various loves shown in those opening minutes: the love between a boy and a girl, who become a man and a woman, who become a husband and a wife, who become a widower and a memory that haunts the rest of what follows.

3. One of the themes of the Fourth Week is transformation. How might you see the film as a contemporary parable on transformation? Consider how the film moves from life through death to a new life. What are the deaths that Carl must walk through and how does he eventually celebrate new life?

4. The Relationship of the Movie to One's Self in the Exercise

1. In the Fourth Week, the Exercises tell us to remain recollected so that we do not lose all the gifts we have been moving towards during our retreat. Carl remains focused on the gift of love he shared with Ellie. What gifts have been offered to you during this Fourth Week? What has distracted your own recollection of these gifts?

2. Throughout the exercises of this Week, the notion of community plays an important role. Carl comes to see the importance of community. How is community created in your own life? How do you distinguish between community and, say, sharing an address, or being in the same context? What are the difficulties you face in creating community? What means will you take to overcome those difficulties?

3. During the Fourth Week we have been offered many gifts from God that will change our lives. Through humour, this film shows how Carl finds the humility to accept the gifts he is offered. Gifts need to be received, accepted, opened, used, shared, and celebrated. Think of the gifts that have been offered to you. How have they been shared and celebrated? Where will be the humility and the humour in doing this?

Conclusion
The Gift of Spiritual Intimacy

The Journey Begun

Through the Exercises of St. Ignatius, you have gone on a journey where you have allowed yourself to be found by God. You have entered into a union with God that manifests itself in our mutual labouring to transform creation into community.

The Exercises offer us a way of looking critically and lovingly at ourselves, and offer us choices of how we wish to be present to our world. The illusions we accept to be ourselves are taken away in the First Week. We find our true life in the Second Week. In the Third Week, this life stands the test of death. In the Fourth Week, we are liberated from the power of death for the service of the Divine Mystery. Our journey calls us always to move beyond ourselves and ever deeper into the love of God. To do this, we are constantly drawn from the worlds we have imagined and into the world as imagined by the mystery of the God we describe as Compassionate Mercy. This journey never ends. As we journey through the Fourth Week, we discover that we are not carried to a mythic paradise. We find ourselves once again in the First Week, when we must discover even more deeply how we are loved. There is no end to God's love, and no end to our journeying ever deeper into that love and the community created by that love.

The Importance of Reflection

For St. Ignatius, the most important thing in a person's life is to find God. Everything else is secondary. Finding God means more than having encounters with God. It is about more than recognizing that we have had those encounters. It involves discovering what those experiences mean and what direction they have given to our lives. That direction shows itself in what we do with our lives, in the friends we choose, and in the values we hold. For Ignatius, then, reflecting on our actions is essential; it is the only way of keeping hold of the gift of our lives.

In spiritual direction there is some confusion about this way of proceeding. Some people want the reflection to have the same sense of drama and involvement as the prayer. When this does not happen, they overlook or dismiss the reflection process.

Ignatian prayer consists of three parts. First is the preparation. Here we choose a suitable place and time for the prayer. We read over or consider what we will pray about. We ask for the grace we are seeking, and ask the Spirit to enable our prayer. This disposes us to the state of praying. The second stage is the experience of the encounter with God. Anything can happen here. The third stage is the reflection on the experience. Did we receive the grace for which we prayed? How was it given? What were the moments of consolation and desolation in this experience? Why are those moments significant?

This book divides each exercise in this way. The first part disposes us to the prayer. The second part gives us the material of the prayer, while the third part presents a series of questions to help appropriate the prayer. These three stages are all part of Ignatian prayer, but each has its own style and mode of operating. Each builds on the previous stage, and the final stage completes the prayer experience. Avoiding that stage causes God's communication with us to be incomplete.

In this concluding chapter, we get an overview of the communication that God has been having with us through these Spiritual Exercises. It deliberately uses a style and voice different from the rest of the book in order to create the necessary distance that will allow you to see where you have gone and where you are going. We will pan back and out from the close-ups of the individual exercises and from the medium shots of the reviews of individual Weeks, arriving at an overview of what you have experienced since the moment you committed yourself to the journey of engaging with this book. This overview is a necessary part of the prayer experience, your encounter and communication with God.

If you abandon this stage or try to make it similar to the contemplative moment of prayer, you lose the fruit of that contemplative moment. As a result, you will not know what the prayer means, or where God is in your life, or what direction your life is taking. You fall back into uncertainty and sometimes even question the validity of what you experienced, especially when you encounter hard or painful passages.

We are not doomed to live our lives in uncertainty. Our journey shows us that we are rooted in love and are loved even when we doubt ourselves or others or the path we walk. That love is present and communicates with us in our daily lives. When we reflect on what we have been and are given, we discover how God communicates with us. This is individual, personal, and intimate. No one else can teach us that language. It is the language of lovers.

It is one thing to love, but something else to know we are loved, and how we are loved. For some, that is more than enough. Still, there is always that excess, which is love's nature, to give more and still more of itself. Now it invites us to examine how we have journeyed into that love, and how we experienced each stage of that love in our lives. The Ignatian tradition breaks this down into the experience of each Week. It seeks to show how that gift of intimacy was able to develop through the overall structure of the Exercises.

We look back to discover what happened to us and how God speaks to us now, taking unto ourselves more passionately and intimately the experience of the Exercises. Sometimes it is only years later that we come to understand what happened to us in a particular prayer period. It is only in the process of living and reflecting that we come to some understanding of what has been given.

Basic to the Exercises is the compassionate mercy of God. It runs through every Week, and every Week develops a deeper and more comprehensive awareness of how intimately that compassionate mercy is woven into our very lives on a unique and personal level. That mercy comes to us in the First Week to liberate us when we are trapped in sin. That mercy, in human form, invites us to walk a very human journey with him in the Second Week as we both return to the mystery he calls "Abba." That mercy enters into death to conquer the forces of death in the Third Week, and we are asked to endure with him. Finally, that mercy shares with us the Spirit of the resurrection and union in the Father in the Fourth Week.

Our Personal Worlds

This mercy not only enters our human world, it enters each of our unique and personal worlds. We each live in a world that is shaped by our personal experiences. No two persons' experiences are alike. This is not to say that each of us is trapped in our own little world, though sometimes it may feel that way. We can communicate with one another, in spite of the many differences of culture, gender, race, age, and temperament, because we share at a most basic level the same human spirit. But the world that each of us is intimate with is a unique world of feeling and value. That world, personal and real for us, is a construct of our imagination. We live in imagined worlds, and the imagined is real. We may share a communal imagination, but each of us has a private imagination that is a unique composite of the diverse elements of the communal world. The way that composite is structured and maintained is individual. From this unique perspective we read ourselves, others, what passes for the world, and God.

To say that we live in these imagined worlds is not to say that we live in imaginary worlds. It is just that the imagined is the real. What we imagine is maintained by the stories we live out of. The imagined is a constructed world of texts. These are narratives that range from the genetic codes that name us, through individual and family stories, to the cultural histories that situate us in the bigger world. Our understandings of ourselves are encoded by these texts. When we engage in an Ignatian retreat, the conversions we experience move us from one way of reading ourselves, others, God, and the world, to another way. This occurs through yet another text that we call the Spiritual Exercises. The Exercises enable us to examine the stories we tell ourselves and others in order to hold onto our imagined worlds, but they also help us see the lies and deceptions these stories embody. This does not leave us without any stories. We need stories to live. We are never without stories, or ever outside of a story. The Exercises offer us a way of restoring our lives in such a way that the new story we find frees us and our imaginations. That new story is one told by the Father through the Word

made flesh. It is a story still being written. But we are not merely puppets in this drama. Good authors tell us that when they are writing, the characters come alive and take on a life of their own. They also shape the text. It is the same with us and God. Our lives are co-creations. They are constructed out of the found materials of our experience.

These constructed worlds we live in are real to us. They affect how our energies are manifested or repressed, are known or unknown. We accept as normal, first, the ways our families have formed us and, next, the ways of life our societies and cultures offer us. The way we understand our very being has been informed by these stories, and while these texts allow some expression of who we are, they repress or ignore, subvert or displace those other expressions that could contribute to how we see ourselves. When this happens, the "I" that I feel myself to be, the "I" that I act out of, is not really my identity. Who I think and feel and say I am is not who I really am. In fact, we do not know ourselves. Other people know us. God knows us. It is these who inform us about ourselves. The Exercises offer us a way of seeing, knowing, and loving ourselves the way God sees, knows, and loves us, a way of understanding ourselves that we rarely experience.

So how we read ourselves, the world, and others, including God, is a constructed text that, being distorted, distorts our reading. We might consider that text to be real, but "realism" is not "reality." Furthermore, this "realism" contains theologies. We create a God and believe it to be truly God. Often these theologies are not written from a rootedness in God. Rather, they emerge from an unredeemed world. Then how we see God and ourselves is quite different from the way God sees God's own self and us. God sees us as lovable and capable of even the most self-sacrificing love. This is the story given to us in the sacred texts of human history. The sacred text Ignatius uses is the Bible.

In the Spiritual Exercises, these two stories meet. The story changes as we journey through the Weeks. The lies that we have accepted as real and that have shaped our lives are uncovered, and their abusive power is broken. Now we can enter a new story in which we journey with Christ through his birth, life, death, resurrection, and return to the Father. In that journey we discover that our story is a contemporary manifestation of the gospel. Our personal story becomes symbolic of the larger story of salvation. To appreciate fully that almost unbelievable gift of salvation, we must see what has happened to us in our spiritual journey. We will do this by looking at the experience, the dynamics, and the way the graces we prayed for came to us during the Four Weeks

The First Week: Discovering God

Understanding Ourselves

Ignatius asks us in the First Exercise of the First Week to meditate on a particular telling of creation history. We may not approve of the way the myth depicts creation history, but it does contain valuable insights into our self-understanding. The myth Ignatius uses moves from the first sin – that of the angels – to that of Adam and Eve "and the enormous corruption it brought to the human race" and, finally, to the effects of one radically significant sin in the life of someone just like us. The first insight this myth contains is that the stories that shape our particular being participate in that history of corruption, however it may be understood. The stories of our selves extend through time and space and spirit. Whether we like it or not, we are part of that larger story.

It is the nature of the ego to deny or ignore that larger history, of which we are just a tiny part, and to seek to establish itself as the centre of the cosmos. In the first exercise, the presentation of that history, in mythic form, casts our usual view of ourselves into a more realistic mode. Even before we were born, the creation we will enter has been corrupted, and to such an extent that often and unwittingly we participate in that corruption. In the Exercises, the question arises whether it is "useful" to give this meditation in its literal state. Some claim that the language of the "sin of the angels" and of "Adam and Eve" is not relevant to contemporary culture. However pertinent that may be, a deeper resistance must be overcome in seeing that our very selves, and our very self-understanding, is caught up in the denial of that larger context. The quest for relevance often subverts the more difficult question of transcendence.

Exploring Our Blindness

Only when we see how we are trapped by forces larger than ourselves and beyond our control can we begin to realize why we have not been destroyed by those malignant agencies in creation. We have been protected by a love even larger than cosmic and human evil. The larger context of disorder is contained within the absolute context of the "Infinite Goodness" of God. When we ignore either of these contexts, or both, we operate out of a false notion of our selves. This false perspective distorts everything we see and do. Even our understanding of God then becomes falsified, and our theology becomes a form of self-justifying ideology. We misread everything, not only from our own personal bias, but also from the deeper social and cultic narratives that give us the communal systems of understanding ourselves. The first exercise exposes our blindness. First it presents the reality of our lives in a mythic form; and second it presents in prayer our lived reality held in the love of God. That love allows us to see our lives as they are. It is the first stage in the path of intimacy.

The knowledge we gain from the first exercise helps us see our own sins. This happens in the second exercise. There we look at the ways in which we have personally been seduced and trapped by evil, and have even participated in doing evil. We cannot simply blame heredity or the social context for our sinning. We ourselves are also culpable.

Against this growing self-awareness comes the deeper awareness that we are held by God. Ignatius facilitates the journey from the first to the second through questioning (#53) and comparison. "What am I compared with all of humanity? ... What are they when compared with all the angels and saints in paradise? ... What is all of creation when compared to God?" (#58). The movement in those questions is from the self to God. In this intense, prayerful questioning, our image of ourselves as the centre of our universe breaks down. This does not happen in a vacuum, but within the mercy of a God who desires that we know ourselves truly as being loved even though we are sinners. Ignatius asks those making the Exercises to have a conversation with Christ on the cross, before whom they place themselves (#53).

For Ignatius, Christ on the cross represents a God who is willing to endure even a painful and humiliating death so that nothing and no one will be lost. It is a manifestation of love that goes beyond the limits of the human imagination. In our prayer we dispose ourselves to being loved in an intimacy that reveals our sin without destroying us. What is destroyed are the illusions that constitute a false self. In this encounter with such a love, the bonds that limit the human imagination are broken. Energies of the self are liberated, integrated, or renewed. But this is not easy for those on this path. They endure the struggle of the false self to hold onto fixed and cherished ways

of seeing and behaving that are second nature. Fear traps them. But intimacy overcomes fear. When this happens, they experience a liberation of energy and a sense of wonder. They are amazed as they discover that such a love exists and that such a love cares for each one of us so intimately and personally.

The energies that make up our spirit are not just an amorphous collection of power. That power has been trained to express and understand itself in ways that have been shaped by society and the significant units of society, such as family, education, and religion. Even our basic desires have been socialized. What we feel we truly desire is not what we really need. One of the gifts of the First Week is to discover what we truly need.

When we do accept it, we discover who we truly are. This discovery energizes us in much the same way prisoners or addicts might feel when they are set free from what holds them captive. Here, the liberation from the distortions we have accepted as ourselves is not anarchy but rather the response to being loved as we are. The wonder and surging emotion we experience in the First Week comes because our lives have changed. We understand them differently.

Rather than dwelling in the obsessive enclosures of narcissism, we discover that we are invited to live out of the open myth that incarnates God's mercy. We do not have to be trapped by a single and reductive understanding of ourselves. The liberation allows us to hold simultaneously the many different and diverse stories that make up each of our lives. We can admit that we are blind, and that we sin in our blindness, but we also discover that we are cared for even as we sin and live in sinful situations. The tunnel vision that has dominated our lives and our understanding of them opens up into a fuller context of accepting God's mercy. As a result, we open to wonder and to the surging emotion of other possibilities for our lives. In our new stories, we discover ourselves as loved and as sinners.

Love Offered and Accepted

The dynamics of the First Week deconstruct the story of self and the illusions of that false self. Those illusions consist of the way we see ourselves, others, the world, creation, and God. The deconstructions work by bringing to light what has previously been ignored or taken for granted in the false story. They bring to light the larger story of God's love. It shows us a love that has always been present in creation's time and in our own personal histories.

The larger story of a fallen creation is shown to affect the narrow world of immediate needs out of which we often live. In the Ignatian Exercises, that larger story moves from the fall of angels, through Adam and Eve — one radically destructive act — to our own sins, and then to hell. Additional exercises may include "death and other punishments of sin, on judgement" (#71). We are enclosed in a reality that goes beyond the immediate borders of our everyday concerns. We find ourselves in a "controlled" setting in which God's creativity is not apparent. The effect is a sense of entrapment beyond our power to escape. The "escape" provided comes neither from the world, nor from creation, nor from the sense of self we seek to maintain. It comes from Christ on the cross — a figure of the wholly absurd to the worldly self. That manifestation of God's love makes no sense to any form of selfishness. To be prayerfully present to that self-sacrificing love draws out all the poisons that prevent us from recognizing our truest selves. What emerges from this encounter is a history of sin and of our involvement in sin.

This does not foster a complacency with the self and its constructed self-serving stories. The ego's self-assurance is undermined. Moreover, the graces of shame and confusion (#48), sorrow (#55), and abhorrence (#63) that we pray for in the First Week erode the pride of the false self. I feel "shame" when "I" admit "I" am accountable for my sinful actions, and I experience confusion when the "order" of the ego is experienced as disorder. Sorrow emerges from an awareness that we have created chaos when we thought we were doing only good. We experience ourselves embroiled in a lack of order from which we cannot extract ourselves despite our best efforts.

Then we abhor the evil we have done and we abhor the nature of our world. This debases our humanity by encouraging and promoting those forms of disorder that trap us, sometimes using even our most noble desires.

But with the deflation of the ego in the First Week, we discover that we are not destroyed. Instead, we discover a God working to find us through creation and to sustain our humanity even as we sin. We discover a God who is there for us in our helplessness and deceptions. The focus of the First Week is not to humiliate or destroy us. The grace we are given is that we are loved with a love that seeks and knows us as we really are. That love does not turn aside from loving us even when we turn aside from whom we really are. That awareness of being so loved opens us up and directs us to desire lives of greater integrity. The intimacy we experience in the First Week liberates our desire. It moves us to the path of the Second Week. There we desire to restore the world: the human contexts we live out of; our histories; our relationship with God; our story of who God is. But we know that even though we are loved, the dynamics of disorder still run through our lives. How are we to live and share the intimacy given us in the First Week in ways that are creative and genuine?

The love we have been offered and have accepted in the First Week of St. Ignatius's Spiritual Exercises is just the beginning of the journey to unpack the gift of intimacy. To live it, share it, and celebrate it in our daily lives carries us to the rest of the Exercises. By the end of the First Week, we have been given an entry into reality. We now need to learn how to live that reality without falling back into selfishness. We need to learn to love ourselves properly: to express our deepest desire, to incarnate what we truly value, and to manifest our true relationship with God.

The Second Week: Discovering Ourselves

Looking at the World God's Way

In the First Week, God enters our story. In the Second Week, we enter into God's story and God's way of telling stories, which is always through humans. God tells his story through our stories. This interweaving of our story and God's is done through contemplation on gospel texts. When we contemplate, we bring our life energies into dialogue with the life energies of God, as expressed in the incidents of scripture. In this weaving together of our energies and the divine energies, we become gospel: living texts of God. Then there occurs an incarnation that is personal and unique to each one of us.

In the First Week, we operated out of a limited context of fallen creation. But, in the Second Week, the story broadens. The movement is from the world perceived in worldly terms to that same world perceived from the perspective of God. The liberation that is achieved at the end of the First Week allows us to see human affairs from God's point of view. The work of the Second Week is to shift us from the nar-

cissistic projections of the ego to the humble service of one called to be an intimate companion of Christ.

In the Second Week, we are invited to look at the world with the eyes and heart of God. We enter our first contemplation from the perspective of the Trinity, above time looking into time. With this contemplation on the Incarnation, our imaginations enter the space and the concerns of the three Persons of God. If today's secular postmodernism, with its emphasis on image and sign, holds that we become what we perceive, the Exercises offer us a spiritual postmodernism that carries us to become what we imagine, energized by God's love.

The Second Week dares us to imagine. It dares us to imagine that we can make the world a more human place. Our imaginations can do this because First Week graces erase the repressive structures and dynamics of an imagination distorted by sin. It allows for something new to emerge – a personal dialogue with God that transforms the world. Here we can co-operate in the ongoing formation of a new creation. It is hard to imagine, given the violence of the present world, how this is possible.

Following God More Closely

Yet, despite the present climate of atrocity, the unimaginable is at work. God cares. God cares enough to find a way to save us. Even harder to imagine is that we can become God-like in our caring and in our doing. That is the grace of the Second Week: "To follow and imitate more closely our Lord who has just become man for me" (#109).

The Ignation text defines for us – in story form – how God operates in the world. This is a God of humility, born "in extreme poverty, and … after many labours, after hunger, thirst, heat and cold, after insults and outrages, [that] He might die on the cross, and all this for me" (#116). When we enter God's story through Ignatian contemplation, we imitate God's way of being in the world. We start to become the continuing presence of Christ in the world. We give up the self-aggrandizement of our ego for a path of humble service, desiring only what God desires.

We do this because we desire to be one with the love that has liberated us, a love that manifests itself in the emptying out described in Philippians 2:1-11. Thus, in the Nativity contemplation, which follows the Exercise on the Incarnation, the Ignatian text suggests to the one making the Exercises, "I will make myself a poor, little, unworthy slave ... and serve ... with all possible homage and reverence (#114) Joseph and Mary in their time of need." Here the abstraction of the first line of the Principle and Foundation – "Humans are created to praise, reverence, and serve God" (#23) – is picked up and made human. We serve God in whatever way is helpful.

Those who engage in the Ignatian Exercises find themselves in an intimacy with Christ. It overflows in a service of contemplative love where they are united with the beloved. They embody the creativity of a God labouring in the world. This human labouring is modelled by the scriptural life of Christ.

Choosing a Standard

In the Exercises, the scriptural contemplations on the infancy narratives and the private life of Jesus act as prefaces to the contemplations on the public life of Christ. The significant meditation on "Two Standards" links the two, showing how Satan and Christ operate in the world. But the focus of the Exercise is to discover how the dynamics of Satan and of Christ operate in the very lives of those engaged in the Exercises. Here it is not a matter of choosing between the two, but of refining the ways we examine our lives so that we may better understand how we can be trapped, and how we may better follow Jesus. The exercise helps us to identify with Christ and with his way of living in our world today, and to become aware of the wiles and strategies of that enemy who seeks to stop us from living like Christ in our world. It raises the question of how we discern when we seek to live out in our daily lives our deepest desire: union with the divine. In this meditation, we learn how we are tempted and how we are called by God.

When we enter areas of personal vulnerability, we find ourselves swayed by conflicting feelings. Ignatius describes these as the Standard of Satan and the Standard of Christ. The Standard of Satan is to covet riches – by using our supposed strengths to overcome that vulnerable situation – so we may more easily attain the empty honours of this world, [and so] come to overweening pride (#142). This approach reinforces our narcissism. Then we use our gifts not for some greater good, but to enhance our self-esteem in the eyes of the world. The Standard of Christ, on the other hand, invites us to accept our poverty in the face of that vulnerability, knowing that such a position means rejecting – and being rejected by – the corrupt values of this world. From this approach springs humility (#146).

Here the Ignatian Exercises present us with a certain reading of the Christ story and a certain way of inserting ourselves into that story. Christ's story is one of evangelical service to the Father through humility. The mission of Christ is to offer to the world the compassionate mercy of the one he calls "Father." He does the Father's will in all things. This is the basis of the Ignatian dictum of "finding God in all things." When we do the Exercises, we are disposed to find God in all things, as Christ did.

The process of intimacy and identification with Christ continues with a contemplation of specific incidents in Christ's life. Indeed, the rest of the Second Week outlines this call to service. The previ-

324

ous contemplations, from Jesus' Nativity to his setting out to the Jordan, show a Christ who manifests a radical dependence on God and on God's existential mercy. In that growing relationship with the Father, he waits on God to reveal most clearly what he must do. Jesus waits – from his boyhood experience in the Temple to his baptism at age 30 – for the Father to show him what to do next. In this hidden life, Christ is not inactive. He learns to be patient and to be attentive. He learns to wait. He disposes himself to the Father's time and to the Father's will. That gift is given to him at his baptism in the river Jordan. That radical and focused attentiveness is named in the baptism by the Father as "my beloved Son." As we enter these contemplations, we also wait to be named, in our attentiveness, the Beloved of God.

The sequence of contemplations on Christ's earthly ministry given in the Exercises promotes the growing intimacy with the Father through union with Christ. This culminates in the last contemplation of this Week. It is Christ's entry into Jerusalem as king, which Christians celebrate on Palm (Passion) Sunday. From this sequence we learn what it means to be God in the world – not triumphalism or the despotism of an ego demanding worship, but focused, humble service in bringing the compassionate mercy of God to the concrete situations of daily life.

The kingdom meditation that introduces the Second Week reappropriated in Palm Sunday, where Christ the King enters Jerusalem: not as conqueror, but as one whose life is so focused on his love for God that he is willing to face the seeming failure of his earthly mission and a painful death on the cross. At this stage, those doing the Exercises are likewise disposed to a similar passionate love for God. Ignatius's choice of scripture texts promoting this identification are those of evangelical service. They are not texts of healings, exorcisms, or power, though one may expe-

rience any of these in a contemplation. They are texts that witness in a specific, incarnate way to the mercy of God present in the world.

We should also note the peculiar absence of Mark's gospel in the pre-passion contemplations of the Exercises. Ignatius's Christ is not the existential mystery of Mark. Rather, he manifests the identity of a humble servant intimate with, and waiting on, the Father. Those of us doing these Exercises are invited to walk a similar path. We are not mysteries. We are to be known as ones who become intimate with the Father by what we do in the world.

The Three Classes

This witness is reinforced by a self-awareness that emerges from the Two Standards, and is intensified by a reflection on the Three Classes of People and the Three Degrees of Humility. The latter two Exercises, which immediately follow the Exercise on the Two Standards, develop the stance of resisting selfish desires. They promote a desire for poverty because Christ was poor, and, from that identification with Christ, a desire for a similar humble evangelical service in the world.

Ignatius sees those in the Second Week of the Exercises as being in the company of the creator and the redeemed aspects of creation. For example, in the Three Classes of Persons, the setting of the meditation is "to imagine me in the presence of God and all his saints" (#151). This is not a privileged moment. We live in that state every second of our lives, even though most of the time we are not aware of it. There we are invited to labour to redeem a fallen world. How can we respond to this invitation? This meditation shows the three possibilities open to us. We can live heedless of God or of ourselves. We can live in the hope that God will approve of all that we choose to do. Or, we can live simply for God.

Ignatius places this Exercise before any contemplations of Christ's public life. Christ serves the Father. Ignatius expects us to make similar choices in the way we live. The pattern of Christ's life is one of waiting on the Father. He waits eighteen years after telling his parents that he must be about his Father's business. He waits after his baptism in the Jordan. He waits in the temptations in the desert to do his Father's will in how he uses his gifts, fulfills his mission, manifests his identity. He waits for that moment when the Father enlightens Peter, who then sees Jesus as the Father sees Jesus. For them both, Jesus is the Messiah. Jesus waits on the Father to tell him when to go to Lazarus, whom he knows is sick, then dying, then dead, then buried. He could have healed him at any time and from any distance. But he goes only when it is for the glory of the Father. He waits on the Father in his agony in the garden. He waits on the Father on the cross. He dies waiting on the Father. He waits on the Father to resurrect him. As we grow in intimacy with Christ, we also wait on the Father. It is the Ignatian stance in the world.

Our own growing resonance with the Father makes us contemporary words of God. Our growing closeness to Christ allows our own entry into his passion. We follow him wherever he is. In placing ourselves this way, we declare ourselves for God even in the face of death. We discover that we are willing to become "fools for the sake of Christ" (#167) as he is willing to become a fool for the sake of the Father.

If a person enters into the Spiritual Exercises with the desire to make a concrete decision about something, that decision is made during this Second Week. The grace of the Second Week is a bonded intimacy with Christ that leads us to desire to be with him, whatever he does, and to share with him whatever the Father decrees. Any correct decision resonates with Christ's own stance of waiting on the Father. Both witness to a dependence on the Father in works of evangelical service. His and our active entry into that servant poverty happens for us in the Third Week.

The Third Week: A Passionate Love

The Ignatian Magis

In the Third Week we contemplate the torture and death of the physical body of Christ as written in the gospels. Those texts, presented from the perspective of the resurrection, depict his passion and death by the powers of the world as his total abandonment of his self-identity to the mystery of his Father, for whom he is the Beloved. Inasmuch as we have identified with Christ in the Second Week in our contemplations on his sufferings, we now share, on a spiritual and imaginative level, his fate.

The imagined world we constructed with the Christ during the Second Week, the decisions we have made, and the sense of intimacy we sought and found with him are all offered up to the all-consuming mystery of the Father in the Third Week. Then we become vulnerable. Our world, our decision, and our relationship to Jesus and to the Father are attacked by the powers of evil, to which we are still prey. That evil moves to render meaningless the things and relationships we hold dear. We experience this abandonment in our prayer. Our prayer moves through the levels of grief and anguish to a sense of numbness and then to a felt sense of nothingness. Here we experience no more than Christ did, and no more than his disciples did when he died. We sink beyond the narrative structures that inform our life. We sink even beyond the feelings that spontaneously tell us what we value.

Inasmuch as we can enter into the action of the Third Week, our world – the imaginative system we live out of – is exposed to the same dynamics that Christ and his companions encountered. This is different from the destruction that is a necessary part of the liberating process of the First Week. There the systems of illusion and deception were unmasked and devalued. In the Third Week, the Word made Flesh, the highest possible good on the human level, is undone. In the Ignatian magis, the human best is displaced by the divine better. Thus scripture quotes Jesus in his agony saying to his Author, "Not my will but yours be done."

Our commitment to the Ignatian magis permits the transformation of human effort into modes of resurrection. Then, like Christ in his passion, we "surrender" self-love and personal will and interests to that of the Divine Creativity. Out of that death comes resurrection. But, because we are human, our egos never disappear. However, death radically questions the ego's meaning and its activities. Hence the question Ignatius offers to the person contemplating Christ's passion in the presence of the creative mystery of God's love: "What ought I to do?" (#197).

What are we to do? How are we to describe the response of those in the Third Week? Think of what happens to you when you accompany a loved one who is dying. After a while there are no words, no story, even no feeling. Emotion does not necessarily express itself in feeling. Instead, we experience numbness, blankness, a growing sense of the meaninglessness of what might be considered socially appropriate at that time. All forms of human comfort and connection are erased. We simply wait in mystery. What remains is a radical simplicity oriented to the one Jesus calls "Abba."

This simplicity is also manifest in the Ignatian texts of that Third Week. It is the only Week in which there are no meditations or contemplations constructed by Ignatius. For those praying through that Week, Ignatius provides the simple division of the passion into sections, if those divisions are helpful, and some limited instruction. The self-understanding created by the constructs and dynamics of the self, as depicted in the Exercises and mediated by personal history, is reduced to its basic orientation: towards God. If the person made and offered up a decision for discernment, here it is tested. Can it be maintained without the support of that person's giftedness, or society's approval, or the impetus of narcissistic behaviour? Is it still viable without "riches," "honour," or "pride"? If the decision is a manifestation of these latter three, its impetus is destroyed in the entry into Christ's passion. The person holding that decision is unable to be with Christ in his passion.

In the Third Week, we enter into some experience of the mystery that we are to ourselves. This mystery connects intimately with the mystery we call "Father." The correctness of any decision made is based on whether it facilitates or hinders the intimacy between these two mysteries.

The texts of scripture and the text of Ignatius mediate between these two mysteries. The scriptural texts contain a minimal narrative of what is happening inside Jesus and very little information of what is happening outside of him and around him. Similarly, the Ignatian text lacks much instruction or reflection. Both texts tend towards "emptiness." Both are characterized by huge gaps. For example, in Matthew's gospel (ch. 27, between verses 35 and 36), the act of crucifixion is not described. Moreover, in that paragraph (verses 32-44), five of its nine sentences begin with the metonymic conjunction "and." Metonomy indicates the fragmentation of perspective where moments are not joined by the unifying context of metaphor. People in trauma are not coherent. They babble. They do not priorize or evaluate in an integrated manner what they have experienced. Every fragment of their experience – from the most essential to the most unrelated – is given equal value. The scripture passage, though written years later, still reveals the rhetoric of trauma. What has happened goes beyond the limits of the human imagination. We are left with a set of fragments of differing spiritual value linked together by "and." What holds each of the texts of the Scriptures, of the Exercises, and of the retreatant together is beyond earthly powers. This is not faith as intellectual accent but faith as relationship. It is the entry into a passionately lived intimacy with God that goes beyond the sensible. It establishes a rootedness in the Father that is the mission of Christ. Yet, it feels like "nothing" (Isaiah 49:4).

Shame and Confusion

A similar erasure of human meaning occurs through the graces to be prayed for at this time. Those involved in the Third Week are instructed to beg for "shame and confusion," which we experience when the self dissolves into mystery. This is not the shame and confusion that come in the First Week with a true awareness of ourselves as sinners. This shame and confusion comes when we move to a felt sense of loss of the self and the meaning we found in the Second Week. A sense of identity that fills us with life and purpose has been taken away. What was taken away from Jesus in his human suffering is taken away from us as we remain with him.

How, then, are we to understand this shame and confusion that is the grace of that Third Week? It emerges from the sense of horror and the abjection of self we experience in the presence of the sublime. It is the sense of defilement (as when Moses takes off his shoes in the presence of the burning bush, because the place is holy) that we experience when we "intrude" on a sacred space and moment. The shame and confusion occur because we are breaking taboo.

When Christ broke taboos, the social texts of belonging – by not washing, by desecrating the Sabbath, by consorting with the impure, by calling himself the Son of God, by cleansing the Temple – he did so in response to the higher value of his calling as the Beloved of the Father. But while this higher value radically relativizes the norms of the social and religious order, and displaces their claim to legislate the Absolute, the "lower" powers assert their authority in destroying him physically.

Similarly, when we break taboos within our own socialized ways of acceptable behaviour, both patriarchal and matriarchal, we, too, are destroyed. When we have interiorized these ways of being, we experience that destruction as emptiness. This is the experience of the "nothingness" we encounter in the Third Week. But when we break these taboos within lived awareness of God's mercy, we also open ourselves to being resurrected.

From Death to Life

The Third Week, then, is the passage through the death of self. In that passage, the worldly understanding of death is inverted. The implicit order of the divine plan becomes explicit. Death is revealed not as the end of life, but as a transition to that mystery beyond sin's power, absorbing and transforming the meaning of death. The meaning of sacrifice we encounter here is both "to kill by offering up" and "to make holy" at the same time. What is confusion n the secular context is mystery in the faith context. Sacrifice changes the fragmentation by death of the closed and broken myths of life to the open myth of resurrection.

In sacrifice, what constructs and maintains the social world, the symbolic order of laws, institutions, customs, traditions, is torn apart. In Matthew's gospel, this is shown at Christ's death when the temple

328

veil is split, and the dead rise and roam about the streets. The division between the two worlds – the secular and the sacred, the worldly and the other-wordly – is overcome. Worldly values are overturned or inverted. To the Jewish sensibility of Jesus' time, crucifixion was an abomination. It was the manifestation of a radical impurity incompatible with temple order and ritual. Their symbolic order could not countenance the order of "Abba" where a shameful death introduces the unimaginable Other into the world. But that is what happened. As Peter points out to the rulers of that symbolic order after the resurrection, "This is the stone which was rejected by you builders but which has become the cornerstone" (Acts 4:11). For the believer, the crucifixion is not an abomination but the highest manifestation of self-sacrificing love.

In God's merciful love for all of humanity, what has been laid waste by the powers of the world still continues transformed in that world, but beyond the imagination of that world. The wasted becomes the resurrected body, the food of life, the Body of Christ for the Christian community. The same mystery that feeds those enduring the annihilations present in the Third Week is the very same mystery to whom Christ turns in his first temptation in the desert. It is not food, but rather the relationship with God, which gives life. It is significant that Ignatius puts the "Rules with Regard to Eating" within the Third Week exercises. There he emphasizes the control of the appetite and the disordered appetite by focusing on more spiritual things (#214, 215). Those spiritual things give value to the appetite. The physical finds its full meaning only in the spiritual.

In the Third Week, and at those times when social norms and constructs lose their authority, it is very easy to fall into the more primitive mode of basic gratifications. Ignatius prevents this return to those First Week temptations and to the sensual body as the basis of satisfactions by asking us to share, or at least bear witness to, what "Christ Our Lord suffers in his human nature" (#195). The Third Week asks, "What ought I to do and suffer for Him?" (#197). Within the mysterious freedom of God's mercy, for whom anything is possible, the Third Week indicates a process of salvation in which love is not a cure or a return to some stable and established mode of existence, but rather a radical irruption of the divine into human suffering, carrying it to resurrection.

In that human passion we enter a love that risks death. The Son enters death in a passionate love for the mystery he calls Father. The Father, in his passionate love for his Son, the "Beloved," reaches into death and brings the Christ to resurrection. Resurrection belongs to a significantly different order of existence than rebirth, the cycle of nature, or a return from the dead, as happened to Lazarus and to Jairus's daughter. Resurrection creates an openness to the miraculous, to what is possible but beyond the powers of creation. It comes as pure gift from God. It is offered to us as a manifestation of the intimacy that those who follow Christ have with the Father.

The Fourth Week: Celebrating Life

A New Way of Being

We cannot journey to resurrection. It comes to us. We can choose the way we live, and thus create the way we approach death, but death defines the limits of human endeavour. Only the power of God transforms the meaning of death for us, and only the power of God controls what happens after death. So resurrection remains a mystery. All we can do is reflect prayerfully on the stories of resurrection given to us. In doing so, we open ourselves to the power those stories point to and describe. That power breaks into our world to transform the way we imagine ourselves, others, and God.

This new way of being is one of openness. In that space we submit to being re-created by the Father. It is he, not history, who defines us. This is apparent in the First Contemplation (#218) in the Fourth Week of Ignatius's Exercises, when Our Lord appears to Our Lady. This encounter is not mentioned in scripture, but as Ignatius says, "It must be considered as stated when Scripture says that He appeared to many others" (#299). When we are gifted with the graces of the Fourth Week, we become an open text, sacred scripture, written by the Father. Our brokenness does not disappear; it is given new meanings. We are still broken people in ways the world sees and understands, but that brokenness becomes the script with which God writes a new story. As St. Paul says in his understanding of this gift, "I will boast all the more gladly of my weakness, so that the power of Christ may dwell in me. Therefore I am content with weakness, insults, hardships, persecutions and calamities for the sake of Christ; for whenever I am weak, then I am strong" (2 Cor 12:9-10).

Sin, the powers of the world, and our personal bias all tend to limit the meaning of things. Sin tells us that we are unlovable and incapable of loving. The world defines who we are in terms of nationality, ethnicity, and gender. We choose how we will present ourselves to others, and control who we think we are. Resurrection breaks down the power of these limitations. We discover that we are loved radically and unconditionally. We discover the gift of intimacy. We discover that we can love others in a self-sacrificing way for their good. We discover that we can be human in ways that are not conscripted by borders. We start seeing ourselves as mystery, participating in the Mystery we so inadequately call "God." We are possessed by a sense of wonder and creativity as we behold our world.

Then we start to see in our own lives the dynamics of salvation history. We come from God; the path we walk is of God; and we return to God. The pattern, described in scripture as being found, getting lost, and being found again, echoes not only our individual journeys, but the journey of the human race and all of creation. What has happened in our lives is first the intimate entry of the Incarnation in our own personal, self-enclosed worlds of closed and broken myths. When we are opened out because of that love, we are invited to a deeper intimacy of journeying with the one who loves us. In that journey, Jesus brings us to the Father, and there we become companions of the Christ. We share intimately Christ's passion, where he disposes himself totally to the very human desire in him that seeks to be reunited to the Father. That journey home to the source of his life continues in the resurrection and ascension. That union of the resurrected humanity with the divinity of the Father results in an explosion of love we experience as Pentecost. In this gift of the Spirit, we become intimately connected to the life of the Trinity and to the work they do in creation to transform all that is, was, and ever will be into a community of love. We share the life and the work of the Trinity in whatever we do. We see ourselves as committed to a loving relationship with all of creation. We see our lives as symbols of that commitment.

This awareness of mutuality is present even in the texts of the Exercises themselves. Thus, the riches and honour that Satan uses to tempt humans (#142) in the Second Week are now gifts shared between lover and beloved (#231) in the Fourth Week. Similarly, creation is not seen as going to hell (#106), but, from this new perspective, is an instrument of the sanctifying process (#236) of a God who works and labours in all things for our salvation. This is a God who gave us the Christ. When we bond with that Christ in the Exercises, we journey with him back to the Father and receive the gift of their mutual Spirit. We become signs of the continuing presence of the resurrected Christ on earth. Here we witness for others to Jesus' resurrection, which creates the open access all now have to the Father. As resurrection symbols, we live beyond ourselves into the self that we will become. Hence, in the Fourth Week, we were invited to "ask for the grace to be glad and rejoice intensely because of the great joy and glory of Christ our Lord" (#221). That joy and glory are not our own. They occur because of what has happened to Christ and has been manifested through his body. That resurrected body shows what is possible for every body, manifesting the gift of the Father offered to each of us.

For those living in the graces of the Fourth Week, that commitment is manifest in what we do. Ignatius points out that "love ought to manifest itself in deeds rather than words" (#230). Christ's resurrected body does different things than he did before his death. The risen Christ performs no healing; he does not fight worldly or religious authority, but the disciples do so after they receive his risen Spirit. As he promises them, with the Spirit, they do more than he did. Still, his appearing transforms the way those close to him see and act. Resurrection becomes a site of new meaning. Thus, for Mary Magdalene, the "gardener" becomes "Christ" (John 20:15); for the disciples in the upper room before Pentecost "fear" becomes "gladness" (John 20:19-21); for the disciples who are catching no fish one early morning, a lack becomes abundance (John 21:3, 11). Jesus' scarred body manifests the divine love.

Renewing Creation

As we participate in the gifts of the Fourth Week by accepting the gift Christ shares with us, we become resurrection sites for others. We experience the power of God moving through our brokenness to create Incarnation in our lived world. This emptiness is the necessary condition for the power of resurrection to become manifest through us. Awareness of our emptiness never goes away. It shows us that the grace of the Fourth Week is a pure gift. It is a manifestation of God's mercy, not our intrinsic right. We remain broken, even in our joy, just as the Christ, in his resurrection, still bears the scars of his passion. Through our emptiness, God's mercy enters the world, and draws up and out the pain and misery of fallen creation. In that emptiness, the world's misery meets the Father's mercy. The Buddhist concept of *shunyata* depicts this. In human consciousness there is "emptiness/the fullness of being" at the same time. In resurrection we experience *shunyata*: simultaneous emptiness and the fullness of Being.

We do not disappear in that emptiness. Our identity is not found in ourselves but in the relationship God has with us. Now we understand "self"-as-emptied to embody mystery. As such, it is not, in its freedom, limited by worldly norms of acting and self-understanding and presentation. It is flexible – it is all things to all people (1 Cor 9:22) – and it is indifferent, which allows it to be so passionate for the Father as to allow us to become "fools for Christ" (#167). Here we become signs of contradiction in the world and displace closed myths with mystery.

The destruction of the power of closed myths, especially death, produces the creative and joyful quality of the Fourth Week. Particular ideologies with single and restrictive readings of reality are devalued, and the diversity of what is given through God's abundance is celebrated:

> All things counter, original, spare, strange;
> Whatever is fickle, freckled (who knows how?)
> With swift, slow; sweet, sour; adazzle, dim;
> He fathers-forth whose beauty is past change.
>
> (Gerard Manley Hopkins, "Pied Beauty")

In the same way, we are accessible multiple readings, so that we become, like St. Paul, "all things to all people" (1 Cor 9:22). This delight in difference is the manifestation of joy, which is a grace of the Fourth Week. As a eucharistic preface for Easter tells us, it is "the joy of the resurrection [that] renews the whole world."

The entry into joy is not for spiritual self-gratification but for the renewal of creation, where we labour with the Beloved, as together we do the Father's will. Ignatius does not impose what we must do. He leaves it up to each of us to discern what we can do lovingly. He merely points out in the contemplation "Leaning into Love" that, after considering what God does for each of us, and shares with each of us, "I will reflect upon myself, and consider … what I ought to offer the Divine Majesty, that is, all I possess and myself with it" (#234). How we do this depends on our situation and abilities. As we share in the life and the gifts of the divine, we also share in a care for creation. All this arises from our loving response to God's mercy. As we take up this care, we discover that we are interconnected with all levels of creation and connected with the Creator. We live our lives only in the context of this connectedness, and not from some intrinsic nature, since at this level of commitment, the self is "empty," or at best a trace, or gesture of the Divine Mercy to the world.

This work that we do in the spirit of gratitude and joyful service and our dialogue with the world become possible from this perspective. As the Spiritual Exercises of St. Ignatius show, when we accept and live out the orientation to love – our basic desire – this creates open spaces, possibilities, and transformations through which the Word becomes flesh in our time and in our bodies.

The path of intimacy that we followed here has brought us from alienation to community. We discovered the spiritual intimacy of a God who enters into the unloved areas of our life and shows us that they can be converted when we accept them to be held by God. The path of intimacy allows us to touch and be touched by all of creation held in the love of the constantly creating Trinity. We journey into that love, of which there is no end. We acknowledge all in delight and gratitude as companions on that journey. Blessings always.

332

The Movie
SEABISCUIT

Director: Gary Ross (2003 – 141 mins.)
Starring: Jeff Bridges, Chris Cooper, Tobey Maguire

1. Synopsis

It was the Dirty Thirties, a time of want and desperation all over the world. Americans needed a hero to help them rise above their problems, and a racehorse named Seabiscuit filled the bill. This is a poignant story of love and friendship that brings healing to the lives of all concerned in Seabiscuit's race for glory.

2. About the Movie

1. "Although horse-racing is its ostensible subject and the races are dynamically shot and edited, *Seabiscuit* is a populist epic about the hopes and fears, collapse and recovery of the United States in the first 40 years of the twentieth century with the horse as a symbol of America itself. The film's first 50 minutes of this rich hunk of Americana are devoted to establishing the backgrounds over some 25 years, from 1910 until the mid-Thirties, of the three men from different backgrounds who will be brought together as owner, trainer and jockey of Seabiscuit." (Philip French, *The Observer*, November 2, 2003)

   Did you see this film as just the story of three men and a horse? Or did you see it as being all that French talks about in his review quoted above? Would it make the film any less enjoyable if you saw it as merely the story of three men and a horse?

2. "It's rare – these days damn near impossible – to see a big-bucks, big-studio production take the kind of chances Ross unselfconsciously takes here. What eventually steals over you as *Seabiscuit* unfolds is that its New Deal America is a lot better than the one we inhabit – more generous and shyly exuberant, less noxiously self-centered and confident. Maybe that's just a movie illusion. But it wouldn't hurt us – politically, socially, humanly – if we began believing we could re-create that sweet, sustaining dream." (Richard Schickel, *Time*, July 27, 2003)

   How does director Ross convey the notions that Schickel mentions here? Again, is this reading more into the film than is actually there? One of the key concepts of media literacy reminds us that the most important elements that we bring when we view any media text are ourselves and all that makes us who we are. How would that concept apply here?

3. Seabiscuit, the horse, is a product – some would say – of three men. The affable owner Charles Howard (Jeff Bridges), taciturn trainer Tom Smith (Chris Cooper), and tormented jockey Red

Pollard (Tobey Maguire). What we can call the first act of the movie – keyed to the Great Depression – shows each man suffering a terrible loss. Self-made industrialist Howard loses his son; cowboy Smith is cast adrift by the closed frontier; and Red is deserted by his newly destitute parents.

What happens to each of the three in the rest of the movie? What role does the horse play in the "redemption" of each of these three men?

4. "Is *Seabiscuit* sappy? Yeah, kind of. But who cares! It's kind of cool when the big dude next to you is tearing up in a movie. But *Seabiscuit* is more than *Rocky* on a horse track. It's a moving story about people and how their lives intersect at just the right time. It's also a simple story about second chances." (Don Lewis, *Film Threat*, July 29, 2003)

Do you consider *Seabiscuit* to be "sappy"? How do you define "sappy"? Why is it all right if there is a "sappy" element to a film? Don't we all need some of that in our lives? Can you name another film that – though "sappy" – really works?

3. The Relationship of the Movie to the Theme of the Exercise

1. How would the characters in this film represent the various themes of the four weeks of the Exercises?

2. How do the themes of the film coincide with the themes and graces of the four weeks of the Exercises?

4. The Relationship of the Movie to One's Self in the Exercise

1. In each of our lives there are moments or patterns that still cause us grief, pain, or distress. In spirituality these are called our unredeemed history. When we live out of the hurts of our unredeemed history we become alienated and destructive. Then we see ourselves, others, the world, even God, as less than who these really are. In the film we have moments where characters live out of their unredeemed history. How do we relate to those moments? How do these evoke our own unredeemed moments? How do we live out of those moments?

2. Most significantly in the film and in our lives are those moments when our unredeemed moments are transformed into redeemed moments. The film is about such a transformation. How do we respond to such events? Do those moments evoke any such moments in our own lives? Do those moments evoke in us the desire to have such moments in our lives? What is it that we desire to have transformed? How do we live with that desire?

3. This Exercise serves as a summary of the four weeks of the Exercises. Which film from each week best helped you to understand and experience the grace of that week? Why did you find that particular film so helpful?

- 1st Week: The Mercy of God
- 2nd Week: Walking with God
- 3rd Week: A Passionate Love
- 4th Week: A Transforming Life

Appendix

Adapting the Exercises for Shorter Periods of Time

The path to intimacy is walked one step at a time. While this book presents a way of walking that path over an extended period of time, some readers may wish to use some of the material in a shorter period of time. There are many ways to do so. One way is to review the table of contents and see what appeals at the moment. This is not just a matter of chance. The Spirit speaks through our desires. Another way is to follow the suggestions given below. Some are offered as a retreat format, while others are listed by theme.

1. A Day of Recollection –
Becoming Aware that We Are Loved

The Second Week: 18th Exercise – A SERIOUS MAN
The Fourth Week: 1st Exercise – BILLY ELLIOT ✓

2. A Weekend Retreat

The First Week: 2nd Exercise – NO COUNTRY FOR OLD MEN
The First Week: 8th Exercise – THE LOVELY BONES
The First Week: 6th Exercise – PRECIOUS

3. A Five-day Retreat

The Fourth Week: 6th Exercise – RATATOUILLE
The First Week: 3rd Exercise – MAGNOLIA
The Second Week: 9th Exercise – ATONEMENT ✓
The Second Week: 5th Exercise – THE YOUNG VICTORIA
The Fourth Week: 7th Exercise – INVICTUS ✓

4. An Eight-day Retreat

The First Week: 1st Exercise: 2nd part – PARADISE ✓ NOW
The First Week: 9th Exercise – BLUE ✓
The Second Week: 7th Exercise – THE INFORMANT! ✓
The Second Week: 14th Exercise – TOY STORY 3 ✓
The Third Week: 2nd Exercise – WHERE THE WILD ✓ THINGS ARE
The Third Week: 9th Exercise – LIVES OF OTHERS ✓
The Fourth Week: 8th Exercise – PRIDE AND ✓ PREJUDICE
The Fourth Week: 10th Exercise – THE STRAIGHT ✓ STORY

5. A Healing Retreat

The First Week: 3rd Exercise – MAGNOLIA
The Second Week: 8th Exercise – BROKEBACK MOUNTAIN
The Third Week: 4th Exercise – THE DARK KNIGHT
The Fourth Week: 3rd Exercise – ONCE

6. Affirming Our True Self

The First Week: 1st Exercise - INCEPTION

The Second Week: 1st Exercise - HARRY POTTER AND THE DEATHLY HALLOWS

The Second Week: 13th Exercise - JULIE & JULIA

The Third Week: 1st Exercise - DANCER IN THE DARK ✓

The Fourth Week: 4th Exercise - THE DIVING BELL AND THE BUTTERFLY ✓

7. Making a Discernment

The First Week: 9th Exercise - BLUE ✓

The Second Week: 3rd Exercise - CHILDREN OF MEN ✓

The Second Week: 12th Exercise - CORALINE

The Third Week: 8th Exercise - THE MISSION

The Fourth Week: 6th Exercise - RATATOUILLE

8. The Passion of the World

The First Week: 1st Exercise - INCEPTION

The Second Week: 10th Exercise - MOTORCYCLE DIARIES

The Third Week: 5th Exercise - THERE WILL BE BLOOD

The Third Week: 3rd Exercise - SOLITARY MAN

The Third Week: 10th Exercise - UP IN THE AIR

The Fourth Week: 2nd Exercise - I'VE LOVED YOU SO LONG

9. A Light in the Darkness – Living Through Hard Times

The Second Week: 6th Exercise - LET THE RIGHT ONE IN

The Second Week: 15th Exercise - SLUMDOG MILLIONAIRE

The Third Week: 4th Exercise - THE DARK KNIGHT

The Third Week: 7th Exercise - CRIES AND WHISPERS

The Fourth Week: 5th Exercise - WATER

10. The Beatitudes – Becoming One with God

The First Week: 3rd Exercise - MAGNOLIA